An Introduction to
Behavioural Geography

An Introduction to Behavioural Geography

JOHN R. GOLD
Senior Lecturer in Human Geography
Oxford Polytechnic

OXFORD UNIVERSITY PRESS
1980

Oxford University Press, Walton Street, Oxford OX2 6DP

OXFORD LONDON GLASGOW
NEW YORK TORONTO MELBOURNE WELLINGTON
KUALA LUMPUR SINGAPORE HONG KONG TOKYO
DELHI BOMBAY CALCUTTA MADRAS KARACHI
NAIROBI DAR ES SALAAM CAPE TOWN

Published in the United States by
Oxford University Press, New York

British Library Cataloguing in Publication Data
Gold, John R
An introduction to behavioural geography.
1.   Geography
I.   Title
910'.01'9   G116   79–41084

ISBN 0–19–823233–0
ISBN 0–19–823234–9 Pbk

Typeset by Hope Services, Abingdon
Printed in Great Britain
at the University Press, Oxford
by Eric Buckley
Printer to the University

For

MY PARENTS

Preface

The aim of this book is to supply an overview of the emerging field of behavioural geography. In it, I have endeavoured to examine a representative sample of the literature that had come to hand by the beginning of 1978 and to supply an accurate picture of major trends that may be observed to date.

From its inception, this book has been intended as a teaching text. It is a response to the needs I felt at Oxford Polytechnic when teaching an advanced undergraduate module in behavioural geography, in which students had to be guided through the complexities of the research literature without the aid of a basic textbook. I therefore took it as my brief to try to supply a study that could be used in specialized behavioural geography options or in broad man–environment courses in geography or cognate disciplines. Naturally I would hope that the advanced research worker might find this survey worth while, but at the outset I would stress that this book does not contain the exhaustive coverage of bibliographical sources or intensive analysis of research methods that this readership would normally demand. Nor have I attempted to produce an instruction manual for practising environmental planners. Behavioural geography is (rightly) a strongly policy-oriented field of study, but it has been all too common for geographers to make the mistake of claiming too much too early. It is not satisfactory to lecture the planner on his responsibility to adopt geographical concepts and techniques when the material that is being produced contains few usable recommendations. In saying this, I am in no way suggesting that behavioural geographers should turn their backs on the policy implications of their work; rather that if they are to meet their responsibility to contribute to policy debate, they will have to develop the requisite grasp of planning methods and theory. Despite genuine interest and willingness to do so, this understanding is still lacking. Thus, although I shall be pointing to areas where the behavioural geographer could contribute to public policy, I do not seek to put a false gloss on the contribution that has been made so far.

The responsibility for errors and oversights is mine, but I wish to take this opportunity to thank the many people who freely gave me the benefit of their time and expertise while I was preparing this book: namely, Mike Barke, Derek Elsom, Gunter Gad, Brian Goodey, Bob Hall, Heather Jones, Peter Keene, Sue-Ann Lee, David Pepper, Brian Selby, Ifan Shepherd, Janet Spencer, and Ken Westgate. John Coyne and John Mawson loaned me invaluable unpublished materials. Special thanks go to Alan Jenkins for continual assistance and encouragement; to Ian Cook whose whole-hearted generosity supplied me with the stimulus to maintain my research interests during a barren period; David Spencer who helped me to shape the initial ideas; Andrew Schuller of Oxford University Press, whose patience I tested to its limits; and Denis Cosgrove, who wrote Chapter 8 and supplied the initial draft from which Chapter 11 was developed. Thanks as ever to Margaret for putting up with me. While I have not yet worked out a strategy by which I can con her into doing the typing, she did comment critically and constructively upon the text, informed me about the deficiencies of my writing style, and brought to my attention numerous articles of which I was previously unaware. Finally this book is dedicated to my parents, as a token of the gratitude that is genuinely felt but too rarely expressed.

JOHN R. GOLD
'Himalayan View'
October 1978.

Contents

PART ONE

THE UNDERLYING IDEAS

1   Introduction

Hence it is to be regarded as one of the anomalies of our time that those means of thought by means of which we arrive at our most crucial decisions, and through which we seek to diagnose and guide our political and social density, have remained undiagnosed and therefore inaccessible to intellectual control and self-criticism.

(KARL MANNHEIM, *Ideology and Utopia*)

For a short period at the end of the 1960s, it became fashionable to assert that geographical thought was about to experience a 'behavioural revolution' which would transform the subject's traditional standpoints on man-environment relationships. The notion of revolutionary change essentially stemmed from the writings of the philosopher Kuhn (1962) and was an idea that many writers had already applied to describing the impact of quantification and scientific methodology upon geography. Briefly, Kuhn had suggested that important advances in scientific knowledge occur through revolution rather than through evolution. Scientific inquiry takes place within broadly agreed frameworks known as paradigms. Every so often, an established paradigm will be confronted with fundamentally new thinking that it cannot accommodate, a challenge which, if widely accepted, will result in the collapse of the old paradigm and its replacement by a new version. This paradigm then becomes the basic framework for scientific inquiry until it too is eventually overthrown.

This is not the place to discuss whether quantification truly represented a revolution in geographical thought, but experience has shown that any expectations of a 'behavioural revolution' were at best premature. Instead, what has taken place has been the gradual emergence and consolidation of a set of approaches that aim to increase the scope of geographical explanation by seeking a fuller understanding of the processes that underpin real-world behaviour. Their development certainly represents a significant milestone in geographical thought, but hardly constitutes the stuff of which revolutions are made.

This study examines one of the most promising of these approaches—*behavioural geography*. Behavioural geography is the geographical expression of 'behaviouralism', a general movement which has spread into the social sciences in recent years from the behavioural sciences (Berelson, 1968). Behaviouralism itself is a term that defies easy definition, describing an approach and an outlook rather than a specific subject matter (Hurst, 1974). The aim of behaviouralism is to replace the simplistic and mechanistic conceptions that previously characterized much man-environment theory with new versions that explicitly recognize the complexities of behaviour. The behaviouralist views the human subjects of his studies as thinking beings whose actions are mediated by cognitive processes (where cognition is defined as the mental processes by means of which people acquire, organize, and use knowledge). The behaviouralist is therefore interested in the way in which people come to terms with their physical and social milieux and in the factors that influence the interrelationship of thought and action, but, in doing so, he in no way assumes that all decisions are based upon a sequence of reasoned thought with systematic evaluation of all available options. There are times when we respond to environmental stimuli almost slavishly, others when decisions are made with the utmost care and forethought. The full spectrum, from sub-conscious impulse to self-conscious deliberation, is of concern to the behaviouralist.

Seen in this light, 'behavioural geography' may be regarded as the most common name[1] for that part of geography that adopts the behaviouralist approach to man–environment relationships, where explanation of spatial patterns of behaviour is sought primarily in cognitive processes that underpinned that behaviour. The approach typically adopted by the behavioural geographer has four main features.

First, it is argued that the environmental cognitions upon which people act may well differ markedly from the true nature of the real world. Space can be said to have a dual character: as an 'objective environment'—the world of actuality—which may be gauged by some direct means; and as a 'behavioural environment'—the world of the mind—which can be studied only by indirect means. No matter how partial or selective the behavioural environment may be, it is this milieu, as the name would suggest, that is the basis for decision-making and action.

Second, the behavioural geographer asserts that research must recognize the fact that the individual shapes, as well as responds to, his physical and social environments. Over the years, geographical analysis has primarily considered the ways in which the physical environment influences man, but this is clearly only part of the matter. The concept of 'environment' needs to be widened to include the social environment in which an individual lives and, perhaps more significant, it is necessary to recognize that the actions of each and every person can have an impact upon the environment, however slight or inadvertent that impact may be. In turn, these environmental modifications can create circumstances that require further sets of action, either on the part of the initial actor or for other people. In this manner, behaviour is often not just the end-product of a chain of events but also the start of new sequences.

Third, behavioural geography tends to focus upon the individual rather than to approach problems at the level of the social group. The benefits of this strategy for geographical explanation are considerable, but care must always be exercised to avoid 'psychologism'—the fallacy in which social phenomena are explained purely in terms of facts and doctrines about the mental characteristics of individuals (Mills, 1970). Certainly the dangers of psychologistic theory are present in behavioural geography (Ley, 1977), but problems are lessened by an appreciation of the influence that socio-cultural factors exert over cognition and behaviour. Any analysis that neglects such factors is likely to be as partial as one that solely considers group interaction and dynamics and ignores individual cognition and behaviour. Behavioural geography, as we have already noted, is not the only process-oriented approach to man–environment relations to be found in geographical literature and should be taken to complement, rather than compete with, the approaches adopted by, say, social, cultural, or political geographers. It is not a sign of weakness to recognize that behavioural geography has its limitations as well as its advantages and that there will be times when its distinctive viewpoints, concepts, and methods will be more appropriate than at others.

The fourth distinguishing feature of behavioural geography is its multi-disciplinary outlook. As a relative newcomer to behaviouralism, behavioural geography has generally looked to other disciplines to provide initial insight into behavioural processes (even if there are now signs of reciprocal trans-disciplinary flows). By definition, much attention has been devoted to the lessons to be found in the literature of psychology and the behavioural sciences, but important ideas have also been derived from such subjects as sociology, anthropology, planning, architecture, and ethology, all of which have experienced their own movements towards behaviouralism (Gold, 1978). Naturally, this strategy demands a measure of caution. One cannot simply open the textbooks of another discipline, select those parts that appear superficially to be relevant to the problem in hand, and then immediately apply them in geographical contexts. To seize upon ideas in this indiscriminate manner, without due regard for their derivation and the conventions that surround their use is to run the risk of producing spurious research which retards rather than advances knowledge. This is not a new problem for geography, a discipline which has always derived much of its methodological inspiration from other subjects[2], but it is probably more pressing now than ever before as the range of disciplines concerned is so much wider.

For this reason, Part One of this book sets out to provide foundation material upon which the later analysis can be established. Chapter 2 considers the major ways in which psychologists have traditionally viewed behaviour and then charts the emergence of an 'environmental psychology', a branch of psychology with which behavioural geography has strong ties. This chapter also introduces five aspects of human psychology which are of considerable importance in this text: perception, cognition, motivation, emotion, and attitudes. Chapter 3 discusses models of behaviour that have been employed, implicitly and explicitly, by geographers. It surveys environmentalist doctrines, the development of behavioural geography, and the necessary ingredients for a paradigm of individual spatial cognition and behaviour. This paradigm supplies a framework for the text that follows.

Part Two examines the development of spatial cognition. Chapter 4 considers the concept of 'spatial information' and discusses the ways in which the individual extracts such information from his environment. Chapter 5 comments upon the broad influences that shape spatial cognition, with sections upon the role of instinct relative to learning, on the developmental sequence by which the child acquires spatial knowledge, and on the role of socio-cultural factors.

Part Three considers the findings of studies that have examined the nature and characteristics of spatial cognition, with the material divided into four key areas of research activity. Chapter 6 comments upon the concept of territorality and its value as an analogy in the analysis of human cognition of micro-space. Chapter 7 provides a report on the large corpus of literature that deals with urban spatial cognition. Chapter 8 investigates the experience of landscape, a discussion which complements the analysis of cognition of macro-spaces (regional and global) in Chapter 9.

Part Four completes the picture by investigating links between spatial cognition and behaviour. Chapter 10 is devoted to the city as living space. The two ensuing chapters deal with natural environmental topics, 11 with landscape assessment and behaviour and 12 with human response to natural hazards. Chapter 13 is devoted to an area of locational decision-making that has drawn considerable geographical interest, namely, the links between spatial preferences and choice of industrial location. Chapter 14 takes up a theme present in much of the foregoing discussion—the extent to which it is possible to control human behaviour by moulding the environment in the light of particular images. Chapter 15 concludes by summarizing the progress of behavioural geography to date, indicating the achievements but drawing attention to the problems that still exist.

2 Psychological Perspectives

A psychologist may be defined as one who goes to the Folies Bergères in order to look at the audience.

(ANON.)

Given the fact that behavioural geography has drawn heavily upon psychological theory and methods in the course of its early development, a brief review of relevant aspects of psychology is a natural starting-point for this study. The first part of this chapter analyses the views of experimental psychologists from a historical standpoint, identifying some important areas of controversy. The next section discusses the emergence of environmental psychology, a branch of psychology which concentrates upon environmental settings similar to those that interest geographers. The final section introduces five aspects of mental activity that are highly useful in building an understanding of man–environment relationships, namely perception, cognition, motivation, emotion, and attitudes.

THE LABORATORY TRADITION

Whatever superficial unity psychology presents to the outsider, in practice its diverse theoretical, methodological, and empirical content defy easy synthesis. Chaplin and Krawiec (1974) have identified three broad areas of disagreement about the nature of psychological inquiry. First, there is dispute as to whether psychology is rightfully a natural or a social science, with the differences in philosophy and theoretical constructs this entails. Second, there are differences between those who approach psychology from a nomothetic standpoint, seeking to establish the general laws and principles that govern mental processes and behaviour, and those who adopt an idiographic approach, in which the detailed understanding of a specific event or individual subject is stressed. Third, there is still controversy over whether psychology should be concerned primarily with the study of behaviour or whether psychologists should devote more attention to the internal workings of the human mind.

These contrasting viewpoints are not rigid dichotomies, but they do indicate several enduring lines of debate. They also demonstrate the problems inherent in providing an adequate definition of 'psychology'. The one employed here takes a wide view of psychology as the subject that studies the 'relationships between antecedent events and conditions and the behaviour of organisms' (Marx and Hillix, 1973, 44), where 'antecedent events and conditions' are taken to include all aspects of mental life. Psychology is therefore concerned with both mind and behaviour. This said, however, there remains a considerable debate about how mental factors are related to behaviour patterns.

The development of psychology illustrates well the major points of controversy. As Table 1.2 shows, the early years of the subject were dominated by a series of systematic schools of psychological thought[1], which are well worth considering in further detail.

Structuralism. Structuralism, the first of these schools, emerged in the 1870s. Founded by the German psychologist Wundt, structuralism provided the bridge between pre-scientific philosophical inquiry into the nature of human thought and modern psychology. It was concerned with human consciousness—the totality of a person's thoughts and feelings—and employed the age-old philosophical method of introspection in order to investigate the contents of the mind. The major methodological innovation was that introspection was to be carried out by trained observers under laboratory conditions, by which means it was hoped to achieve the controlled conditions of scientific experimentation. On this basis, the structuralist aimed to study the mind by the classic procedure of analysis and synthesis: identifying the 'basic irreducible elements' and then seeking to discover the links between them.

In the event, structuralism was short-lived. Other psychologists disagreed with its objectives, disputed the adequacy of introspection as the methodological basis for a scientific discipline, and argued that psychology should be more concerned with behaviour. Despite this, structuralism was to have a profound impact upon the development of psychology. It established an experimental tradition and perhaps as important, supplied an orthodoxy which stimulated vigorous responses from others.

Functionalism. Functionalism was one such response. Drawing upon the evolutionary theories of Charles Darwin and the pragmatic philosophy of William James[2], this American school of psychology sought to study the mind in terms of its function in the adaptation of an individual to his environment. Functionalists argued that structural analysis failed to indicate the intensely personal qualities of the individual mind. They proposed that mental activity be seen as a 'stream of consciousness', by which the individual continually strove to achieve better adjustment to his environment. In the words of a leading functionalist, the mind was oriented towards the 'acquisition, fixation, retention, organisation, and evaluation of experiences, and their subsequent utilisation in the guidance of conduct' (Carr, 1925, 1). Behaviour was similarly regarded as motivated by the desire to improve environmental adaptation, being conceived as a flow of stimulus and response. This was not the simple relationship of stimulus and response that was to be associated with behaviourism (see below), but a continuing process in which the terms 'stimulus' and 'response' were abstractions which related to the function of an event in a sequence of behaviour. The final state (response) of one chain of behaviour might be the start (stimulus) of another (Neel, 1971).

Table 2.1. *Major figures in the formation and development of five major 'schools' of psychology*

School	1870	1880	1890	1900	1910	1920	1930	1940	1950	1950	1960
STRUCTURALISM		Wundt	Titchener								
FUNCTIONALISM	James			Dewey	Angell	Carr, Woodworth	McGeoch	Melton	Underwood		
BEHAVIOURISM					Meyer, Watson, Weiss	Hunter, Tolman	Skinner, Hull	Miller, Spence			
GESTALT THEORY		Mach	von Ehrenfels		Wertheimer, Koffka	Köhler					
PSYCHOANALYSIS		Breuer, Freud		Adler, Jung, Rank, Ferenczi, Jones		Horney	Sullivan	Fromm			

Source: Adapted from Marx and Hillix (1973, 86). Copyright ©1973 by MacGraw-Hill, Inc., and used with their permission.

Behaviourism. Although behaviourism shared the reductionism of structural psychology and certain of the philosophical underpinnings of functionalism, it is best seen as a reaction to the two previous schools as it rejected any concern with consciousness. Behaviourists viewed psychology as the scientific study of behaviour, with its legitimate concern confined to analysis of what was tangible and measurable, either actually or potentially. Behaviour consisted of stimulus–response (S–R) relationships, in which particular responses could be attributed to given antecedent conditions. Responses were held to become attached to stimuli by reflexes or, in other words, actions that place independently of will. These reflexes may be instinctive but are more often due to learning, in that once a suitable response is learned it would appear whenever the stimulus is presented[3]. It was even believed that the most complex behaviour patterns or finest examples of human creativity could be interpreted in this way. The behaviourist's task was to unravel the chains of S–R relationships and produce an understanding of behaviour on this basis.

Behaviourism represented a radical departure from a psychology preoccupied with mind, dismissing the study of mental life as unscientific and putting forward a view of human beings responding slavishly to given environmental stimuli. Extreme behaviourism may have been, but it was very much in keeping with the spirit of the times. In the late nineteenth and early twentieth centuries, many natural and social sciences had adopted, explicitly and implicitly, highly simplified behavioural models. Behaviourism was contemporaneous with 'environmental determinism' in geography and with the assumptions connected with 'mass society' in sociology and 'economic man' in classical economics. These all conceived of behaviour in terms of the working of causal laws, in which the individual adapted and responded passively to the dictates of forces in his external environment. The exercise of free will and the operation of social and cultural influences, by contrast, received little attention.

Behaviourism therefore accorded with the general trend of scientific thought and had what many would have regarded as the necessary character for a truly scientific discipline, but this was not the only reason for the success it was to enjoy. Behaviourism had a strong intuitive appeal for psychologists in that it removed much of the complexity from psychology, obviating the need to investigate mysterious mental processes, and replacing things by their most tangible manifestation (Miller, 1962). In addition, it laid a firm basis for a coherent programme of research. Yet for a school that was explicitly concerned with human behaviour, it is curious that so little of its experimental data actually stemmed from research on human subjects. The founder of behaviourism, J. B. Watson, worked extensively on animals, as has its most notable recent practitioner, Skinner[4]. The tendency has been to generate data from laboratory experiments on animals and to apply the conclusions directly to human behaviour. Koestler (1975, 17) pointed to the dangers of this strategy, in that behaviourism 'has replaced the anthropomorphic fallacy—ascribing to animals human faculties and sentiments—with the opposite fallacy; denying man faculties not found in lower animals;

it has substituted for the erstwhile anthropomorphic view of the rat, a rato-morphic view of man.' Behaviourists, in effect, were a good example of those who were willing to overlook the whole basis of their own experience of the world in the interest of devising elegant theory. If the spirit of modern psychology has moved away from behaviourism, it is because, first, behaviour-ism drastically oversimplified human behaviour and, second, even if psycho-logical methods do tend to identify S–R relationships, it is far from necessary also to adopt S–R theory. In addition, those concerned about social respon-sibility in psychology have expressed distaste for behaviourism's explicit aim to predict behavioural responses from environmental stimuli, with the threat of deliberate manipulation of behaviour which this brings (Lee, 1976).

Gestalt Psychology. Although also a reaction to structuralism, Gestalt psychology took a very different course. Gestalt psychology was a protest against the oversimplification and reductionist analysis that behaviourism espoused, arguing that it was necessary to face up to the complexity of human psy-chology and to put mind back into the analysis. The central aspect of Gestalt theory was perception, which constituted a variable intervening between stimulus and response. It was believed that perception proceeded according to innate abilities which organized environmental stimuli into coherently organized forms or patterns (*Gestalten*)[5]. Behaviour was mediated by the perceptual process, being caused not by the stimulus properties of the environment but by the way these stimuli were perceived.

The mode of study adopted by Gestaltists derived from the German philo-sophical school of phenomenology, which opposed the reductionism of Western science, maintaining that comprehension of phenomena could be brought about only by the development of a sympathetic understanding based on holistic description[6]. The Gestaltist believed that the whole was greater than the sum of its parts. It was thus pointless to try to divide *Gestalten* into their component elements, because this would never produce an understanding of the operation of the perceptual process as a whole. Instead the Gestaltist proposed a programme of research in which conscious experience was descriptively studied at the holistic (molar) level.

The view that behaviour was rooted in the world as perceived rather than in the world of actuality was an important ingredient in Gestalt theory. The nature of the distinction between these two environments, and their impli-cations for behaviour, was neatly made by Koffka (1935, 36) in an allusion to the medieval Swiss folk tale about a winter traveller:

On a winter evening amidst a driving snow storm a man on horseback arrived at an inn, happy to have reached shelter after hours of riding over the wind-swept plain on which the blanket of snow had covered all paths and landmarks. The landlord who came to the door viewed the stranger with surprise and asked from whence he came. The man pointed in a direction straight away from the inn, whereupon the landlord, in a tone of awe and wonder said: 'Do you know that you have ridden across the Lake of Constance?' At which the rider dropped stone dead at his feet.

(Quoted in Craik, 1970)

One can clearly see the difference between the 'objective environment' of the ice-covered Lake of Constance and the rider's 'behavioural environment' of a wind-swept plain. The rider reacted to the situation by travelling across the lake. as if it were dry land—we may safely surmise that he would have acted otherwise had he but known!

In suggesting the existence of a subjective 'world in the mind', the Gestaltist supplied an observation that is basic to our understanding of environmental behaviour, although it will here be asserted that the behavioural environment is the product of learning rather than of innate perceptual abilities. This also points to a wider conclusion. The lasting significance of Gestalt psychology rests upon its role as a source of humane insights into psychological processes which countered the excesses of behaviourism, rather than as a rigorous form of explanation for cognition and behaviour. While Gestalt psychology retains some limited vitality, both in its orthodox form and as a field theory[7], its explanatory deficiencies led to its decline as a systematic school of psychology.

Psychoanalysis. Strictly speaking, psychoanalysis is a discipline in its own right but its impact upon psychology has been such that most authorities have included it in their discussions of the development of psychological thought. Indeed, Freudian psychoanalytic theory probably exerted as much influence upon the subject as had Darwinism in the formative years of development. Freud enunciated the belief that behaviour was largely decided by drives acquired in early childhood, and thereby stressed the previously neglected role of subconscious motivation. The adult personality was shaped by experiences that occurred in the first years of life, when the child sought to gratify sexual desires. According to Freud, personality rested on the dynamic interaction of three mental elements: the id—the storehouse of subconscious sexual or aggressive impulses; the superego—the conscience; and the ego—the rational self which tries to satisfy the demands of both id and superego. When the id gains the upper hand behaviour will be quite different from when the superego is dominant. The model of 'psychoanalytic man' which stems from this portrays a non-rational decision-maker, whose behaviour reflects the resolution of inner conflicts. In any given situation, the dynamics of personality would be likely to count for more than external environmental conditions.

Psychoanalytic research after Freud developed in various ways, some developing and elaborating the founding theory and others reacting against it. To evaluate psychoanalysis properly, it is necessary to clarify the common misunderstanding over what was meant by 'sexual impulses'. In Freudian theory, it included not only the drives associated with carnal sex but also those associated with the need for food, shelter, and avoidance of pain (Skirnik and George, 1967). Consequently the theory was not as narrow as many have supposed, but even so there is little doubt that it oversimplified personality structure, undervalued the importance of intelligence and learning, and relied upon empirical evidence derived from studies of mentally sick or disturbed subjects. Psychoanalysis therefore, like the other schools of psychology, told only part of the story. It supplied valuable insights into the role of the subconscious and that of sexual drives, but at the same time omitted or did not adequately consider other salient features.

The Legacy of the Schools. The last point is a fitting general comment upon the 'schools'. Although Table 2.1 indicates development into the 1950s, all reached their zenith by 1930, since which time their distinctiveness has faded for two major reasons. First, it was realized that the schools were not irrevocably opposed in all their aspects. Orme (1969), for instance, observed that behaviourism and psychoanalysis could be considered as different sides of the same coin and that adherents of one could easily explain the opposing school's cherished beliefs in their own terms. The axiom common to both was that by and large the child was father to the man. Individuals were driven by the force of present circumstance and the residue of past experience, with both schools denying the importance of purposiveness, the operation of free will, or indeed consciousness at all. Second, modern psychology is marked by problem-orientation. Present-day psychologists generally work on specialized topics, developing narrowly defined bodies of theoretical and empirical research rather than propagating comprehensive schools of psychology.

The schools, however, had a lasting impact. Modern psychology retains the philosophical outlook on human psychology established by the behaviourists, namely, that of positivism. The roots of positivism may be traced back to the great scientific thinkers of the seventeenth century, such as Descartes and Newton, and to the writings of Saint-Simon, Comte, and Laplace in the nineteenth, but it came to full fruition in the twentieth century. The positivist believes that there is a distinction between the subjective properties of the mind, which are largely unknowable, and the external world, which may be comprehended as objective fact. Positivism is characterized by certain basic principles: that there are such things as objective facts; that the scientist should concentrate upon observable phenomena; that it is possible to study the interrelationships between phenomena objectively; and that the proper mode of study is the scientific method of analysis and synthesis. It is, of course, quite possible to take a very different standpoint, as exemplified by Gestalt psychology. The phenomenological approach employed there studied the individual's experience of environmental phenomena, aiming to do so by holistic descriptive means (the whole being greater than the sum of its parts), rejecting the distinction between unknowable subjective and factual objective phenomena. None the less, phenomenology has proved to have few adherents in contemporary psychology.

The implications of this philosophical standpoint for the study of human psychology may be seen in Table 2.2. If one thinks of the various approaches

Table 2.2. *Behaviourist and phenomenological approaches*

Variable	Behaviourist (Positivist)	Phenomenology
Subject matter	Behaviour	Mental Events, Consciousness
Aim of study	Nomothetic	Idiographic
Method of study	Experimental analysis	Phenomenal description
Level of study	Molecular (parts)	Molar (wholes)

as constituting a spectrum, with the positivist (behaviourist) approaches at one end and the phenomenological at the other, the work of most psychologists would be closer to the former than the latter. The typical emphases of such work, as Table 2.2 indicates, are a focus on behaviour, a nomothetic search for causal laws, experimental analysis, and reductionist study of phenomena at the molecular level.

The emphasis on laboratory experimentation is worth considering further, for the classic scientific experiment contains an implicit model of behaviour. The human subject is placed in a carefully constructed and controlled environment, about which he has little or no pre-existing knowledge and over which he has limited influence. In many ways, it is an environment that is more suitable for animal subjects than human. The respondent is placed in the role of the biological organism, coping with stimuli as and when administered, and adapting to conditions as best he may. This effectively reduces the degree of choice about which course of action to follow, greatly undervalues the unique qualities of creative thought and free will that set human beings apart from animals, and removes the subject from the social and cultural context of everyday life. While one should not underestimate the contribution made by laboratory experimentation to the advancement of psychology, research that isolates man in an artificial environment runs the risk of sterility and irrelevance, and the phenomena studied may never occur outside that milieu. Proshansky (1976, 63) summarized this situation admirably:

Since at a very minimum the person's awareness of his being in a given physical setting is a requirement for his behaving and coming to terms with that setting, no laboratory or other artificial setting, no matter how contrived, can serve as a substitute for such a reality. No matter how well a research setting duplicates the real physical world of the individual, his knowledge that it is not the actual setting immediately invalidates the integrity of any person-environment phenomenon being studied in relation to that real-world setting . . .

Recognition of this point has been instrumental in the development of environmental psychology.

THE EMERGENCE OF ENVIRONMENTAL PSYCHOLOGY

The early development of environmental psychology parallels that of behavioural geography (see Chapter 3). Both were products of the intellectual currents of the 1960s and share four characteristics: they deal with the environment defined and ordered through human actions; they include people as an integral part of every problem; they grow out of pressing social problems; and are multi-disciplinary in outlook (Proshansky *et al.*, 1976). The distinguishing feature of environmental psychology perhaps lies in its relationship to its parent discipline. Environmental psychology attempts to broaden the scope of psychology by explicitly studying behavioural processes in real-world settings. This is not to say that it is merely an extension of mainstream psychology. Environmental psychology is more eclectic and outward-looking than experimental psychology, largely because it is faced by sets of problems that are not encountered in the laboratory, and which require fresh approaches. A series of concepts and methods have been developed that are specific to it. Yet environmental psychology has been assimilated into its parent discipline far more easily than has behavioural geography. Whereas environmental psychology is a self-conscious attempt to take psychological research into novel empirical contexts, behavioural geography in part represents a challenge to established modes of explanation, seeking to replace simplistic models by more realistic perspectives. We shall return to this theme later.

There is no generally accepted definition of 'environmental psychology'. Lee (1976) proposed that it was the scientific study of man's relationship to his environment, Leff (forthcoming) that it examined the interrelationships between environmental and psychological variables, and Heimstra and McFarling (1974) that it was concerned with the relations between human behaviour and the physical environment. These are only working definitions, which perhaps suit an embryonic field of study, but they do indicate the main areas of interest.

Disagreement has also been registered with respect to the intellectual origins of environmental psychology. Many observers have attached importance to the subsidiary trend towards environmental or naturalistic research which has always existed in psychology (Williams and Rausch, 1969). To give some examples, Galton was working on genetic and environmental influences upon human abilities in the late nineteenth century (Ross, 1974); Trowbridge (1913) examined the individual's mental representations of specified large-scale environments; and a series of social psychological experiments were carried out at the Hawthorne factory of the Western Electric Company in order to evaluate effects of the working environment on employee behaviour and performance (Roethlisberger and Dickson, 1939).

To do so, however, is to overestimate the influence of isolated projects which had relatively little impact on psychology at the time they were published. Until recently, the role of 'environment' in psychology has almost invariably referred to social or interpersonal influences, with little attention paid to the characteristics and attributes of the physical environment (Wohlwill, 1970). For this reason, it is more realistic to date the development of environmental psychology from the early 1960s, the time at which 'the whole scholarly apparatus of symposia, conferences, newsletters, and abstracts began to appear' (Lee, 1976).

As in many nascent fields of study, the initial wave of research has been followed by extensive efforts to consolidate knowledge. These have taken various forms: edited collections of readings (Proshansky *et al.*, 1970, 1976; Friedmann and Juhasz, 1974; Canter, 1975b, Moore and Golledge, 1976b); papers and proceedings from conferences and symposia (Canter, 1971; Honikman, 1971, 1975; Preiser, 1973; Canter and Lee, 1974; Michelson, 1975; Suedfeld and Russell, 1976), and personal overviews (Craik, 1970; Ittelson *et al.*, 1974; Altman, 1975; Lee, 1976; Stokols, 1978; Leff, forthcoming); as well as countless monographs, articles, and bibliographies on more specific topics. Numerous frameworks have been put forward as a means of integrating available material, based upon either single or multiple dimensions of research.

Two examples of the latter type are worth considering further. The first was put forward by Craik (1968, 1970), who was interested in the way people comprehended the molar physical environment. Craik suggested the term 'environmental display' to describe the entire setting for real-world human behaviour, a concept which could apply with equal facility to buildings, urban scenes, or forest glades. When an environmental psychologist sets out to study the comprehension of any environmental display, he must deal with four issues. The nature of each of these and their inter-relationship embodies a basic paradigm of environmental psychology, as outlined in Table 2.3. The four issues were: whose environmental comprehensions are to be studied (observers)? how should the environmental displays be presented to observers (media of presentation)? what behavioural reactions of the observer are to be elicited and recorded (response formats)? and what are the pertinent characteristics of the environmental displays (environmental dimensions)? The potential *observers* ranged from specialized groups to the general public. The *media of presentation* consisted of direct presentation; using some form of representation (such as a sketch or a model); and imaginal presentation (in which the display is not presented at all except by an identifying name). *Response formats* covered the full extent of formats that had been used in environmental contexts, although those presented in Table 2.3 are far from exhaustive. On the question of *environmental dimensions*, Craik recognized that no coherent system for classification and measurement yet existed, but pointed to some of the rudiments of such a system—a taxonomy of everyday language, techniques for measurement and notation, and basic behavioural attributes.

Table 2.3. *A paradigm for research on the comprehension of environmental displays.*

Observers	Media of Presentation	Response Formats	Environmental Dimensions
Special competence groups	Direct presentation	Descriptive responses	Taxonomy of everyday language
architects	looking at	free	Objective physical and geographic measures
geographers	walking around and through	standardized	Sequential notational systems
planners and designers	driving around and through	ratings	Modal behavioural attributes
real estate appraisers	aerial views	adjective checklists	descriptive assessments
building and 'space' managers	living in	mood and activity checklists	evaluative assessments
interior decorators	Representation	Q-sort decks	predictive assessments
landscape artists and painters	sketches, drawings, maps	Global responses	
natural resources managers	models, replicas	thematic potential analysis	
Special user-client groups	photography	empathic interpretation	
elderly persons	cinema	symbolic and multisensory equivalence	
migrant workers	television	graphic presentation	
college students	Imaginal presentation	Inferential responses	
wilderness area campers		Attitudinal responses	
flood plain dwellers		Preferential responses	
Groups formed on the basis of relevant personality measures			
Everyman, the general public			
(1)	(2)	(3)	(4)

Observers

Environmental Displays ◇ Media of Presentation

Response Formats

Source: Craik (1970, 67).

Craik then went on to identify some of the conceptual and methodological demands of this framework.

A second framework was that devised by Altman (1976), who classified research according to three key dimensions—the spatial units of study, the environmental phenomena that are the subject of the inquiry, and the stages of the design process that the project is intended to assist (see Figure 2.1). The *spatial units* were loosely arranged in order of scale, with clear reference to the contexts that have featured large in the literature, such as residential neighbourhoods and institutional settings, for example prisons and hospitals. The *environmental phenomena* listed by Altman consisted of a somewhat limited range of processes relating to human spatial requirements, but this was intended more for illustration than with any pretence of being an exhaustive selection.[8] The *stages in the design process* covered the full spectrum

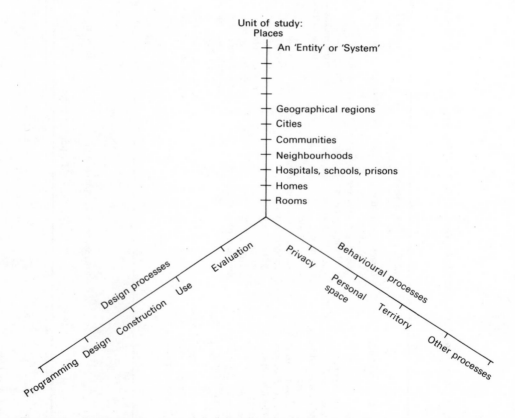

Figure 2.1. Behavioural-scientist and design-practitioner orientations to man–environment phenomena.

Source: Altman (1975, 198). Copyright © 1975 by Wadsworth Inc., reprinted by permission of the publisher, Brooks/Cole Publishing Company.

from the initial identification of design criteria ('programming') to the stage at which the designer assesses the success or otherwise of the project ('evaluation').

Naturally these frameworks are sketches rather than finished portraits, but together they identify some of the most important dimensions of environmental psychology. Altman's framework is useful in that it supplies open-ended dimensions along which to classify data. Furthermore, while the work of environmental psychologists is neither restricted to urban settings nor necessarily concerned with the design process, the framework recognized the significance of urban and design orientations in environmental psychology. Craik's framework, on the other hand, supplies understanding of the research methodology which is missing from that put forward by Altman. Although it would be necessary to up-date this framework to take account of developments since the late 1960s, it clearly indicates the presence of common dimensions in techniques and procedures.

These frameworks indicate the broad areas of agreement on subject matter, research strategies, and methods that can be identified in environmental psychology. While it would be premature and misleading to suggest that these will produce a unified paradigm of man–environment relationships, it is possible to point to certain components of such a paradigm which have manifested themselves in recent research.

The environmental psychologist considers man and environment to be in a state of dynamic interrelationship. The environment is seen as the total milieu in which man lives, an environment with both physical and socio-cultural attributes. There will be circumstances in which the individual has only a limited choice of action and adapts as best he may, but it is more helpful to give full recognition to freedom of will and behaviour, viewing the individual as a goal-directed being who acts upon his environment and is, in turn, influenced by it (Ittelson *et al.*, 1974). The key intervening variables in man–environment transactions are perception and cognition— the internal mental processes by which individuals sense, perceive, interpret, and make decisions about their environment. These processes, plus three concepts that interact with both perception/cognition and behaviour (namely, motivation, emotion, and attitudes), deserve brief review.

PERCEPTION AND COGNITION

'Perception' and 'cognition' are terms used in varying ways, both over the course of history and by different contemporaneous psychologists. Originally they represented separate fields of inquiry in experimental psychology, but their distinctiveness has blurred over time. As Proshansky *et al.* (1976, 102) have pointed out, 'Some writers use one term, some the other, and many use both, but the specific nature of the work done is relatively unrelated to the term chosen to describe it.' In asserting this, the authors were at pains to deny that this policy is due to lack of methodological rigour.

It was argued that the distinction between cognition and perception was derived from the reductionist tradition of experimental psychology which may be less appropriate for the study of environmental psychology. In a passage which has wider relevance than just the study of perception and cognition, Proshansky *et al.* (1976, 103) went on to suggest that:

The question arises of whether any of the traditional distinctions among subtopics within psychology are useful or meaningful when one is thinking in terms of large-scale environmental phenomena. These analytical categories were, after all, developed in a system of thought that for the most part ignored the existence and relevance of the environment. In contrast, thinking on an environmental scale seems almost to force one away from an analytic attitude and toward the study of the total experience of the environment.

Any distinction between perception and cognition should therefore be seen mainly as a heuristic device rather than as a fundamental dichotomy in mental processes. Cognition is regarded as a wider term which, *inter alia*, includes perception. Cognition relates to psychological processes whereby human beings obtain, store, use, and operate upon information. It includes sensing, perceiving, remembering, imagining, judging, deciding, and virtually every other type of mental process, and is intimately related to experience and behaviour. Perception, by comparison, is a more specific term. It is the psychological function that enables the individual to convert sensory stimulation into organized and coherent experience. Perception itself is a cognitive process.

There are two further differences between experimental and environmental psychological approaches to perception and cognition. First, experimental research has been preoccupied with perception of objects rather than with environmental perception—the findings of the former providing the basis for understanding the latter (Ittelson, 1976). Second, whatever the specific topics actually studied, experimental psychology has been essentially concerned with the broad principles that underpin perception and cognition. Environmental psychology, on the other hand, has been concerned with specific content areas, such as urban perception and perception of wilderness, with little attention to the broad underlying principles. Whether this reflects the stage of development of environmental psychology or indicates a lasting trend remains to be seen.

As has already been mentioned, perception and cognition have been treated in various ways by psychologists. Debate has centred on such questions as the types of environmental information upon which perception and cognition are based, the role of hereditary factors as against learning, the development of cognitive processes over time, and the way that individuals attach meaning to environmental phenomena, particularly to large-scale spatial environments. Such questions, however, will be discussed more fully in Part Two and are best postponed until that stage.

MOTIVATION AND EMOTION

Common sense suggests that motivation and emotion play a central role in man–environment relations, for the goals we seek in the everyday world and the way we feel about places and areas are bound to influence both cognition and behaviour. *Motivation* may be defined as the force that leads men to seek certain goals in relation to their needs. 'Needs' can include anything the individual regards as essential for his happiness or well-being, ranging from physiological urges for food and shelter to a desire for recognition by his peers and for self-fulfilment. How motivated a person will be to pursue any course of action will depend on the nature and importance of the needs associated with any particular situation.

Theories about needs may be divided into two categories. On the one hand, there are theories that suggest that man is motivated by the desire to overcome the stresses imposed by his environment and to reduce tension, which appear to be supported by empirical studies carried out in wartime conditions, or when subjects are in pain, or suffering from work-stress, or experiencing some form of deprivation (Evans, 1976). On the other hand, there are theories that suggest that human beings desire novelty, excitement, and stimulation, actually seeking to increase the amount of tension in the environment (Berlyne, 1950; Wohlwill, 1968). Recreational activities supply many appropriate examples of this type of motivation.

These theories are easily brought into line if one recognizes that behaviour is motivated by different types of need. Some needs, such as food and shelter, are 'survival needs', which have to be satisfied for the continuation of normal life. They are of physiological origin and the stresses imposed by their non-fulfilment will cause physical hardship. Other needs are 'social' or 'personal' in character. 'Social needs' would include those connected with the social groups of which the individual is part, such as the need for acceptance and recognition by one's fellows; 'personal needs' are those that drive individuals to fulfil their self-images. Social and personal needs are learned in childhood and vary between social groups and cultures. Their non-achievement would not cause direct physiological hardship, but may well result in mental anguish that has a physical impact.

Certain writers have conceived of needs as a hierarchy, whereby survival needs must be satisfied before seeking 'higher' needs (after Maslow, 1954; see Leff, forthcoming). It is true that one would usually seek to increase environmental stimulation after first coming to terms with the tensions imposed by survival needs, but it would be a mistake to think of this as a rigid hierarchy. Most people, for example, could think of instances when they have stayed out much longer than anticipated and have resisted the pangs of hunger, because they were enjoying the present company or environment. In other words, instances of higher needs being met before basic needs are relatively common, even if this is not the typical situation.

This indicates the essential complexity of motivation. Man is at once a seeker and a neutralizer of stimulation (Wohlwill, 1970). When confronted with the identical set of circumstances, the same individual will be differently motivated at different times, quite apart from interpersonal differences in the goals that would be sought (Argyle, 1973). Furthermore, there will be differences between the way a person would be motivated when by himself compared with when in the company of a group of people. To take the example of people contemplating dangerous sports such as mountaineering and caving, group assessment of the risk to be incurred in pursuing a particular goal differs from the average assessment of its members (Ross, 1974).

One other issue concerning motivation will be significant in this text. Motivation research has seen a long-running debate over the relative importance of instinct as against environment. The question of whether human needs are genetically determined or environmentally acquired by learning will be encountered, for instance, in Chapter 6 when we shall consider the need for territory, examining whether man has innate urges to establish and defend spatial territories, or whether it is a social need which is learned. The argument that will be put forward is that motivation, like other aspects of human psychology, is *primarily* due to learning. No other form of explanation would seem adequate to cope with the rich diversity of human motivation.

Emotion is an area of psychology that traditionally is linked with motivational research. Emotion embraces a vast range of physiological and mental conditions, defined as a state of excitement or perturbation, marked by strong feeling and usually by an impulse towards a definite form of behaviour. Some emotions accompany motivation: for example, when we strongly desire something the accompanying emotional tone increases the strength of our desire to achieve a goal. Other emotions are the result of motivated behaviour, such as the feelings experienced when a course of action succeeds against all the odds.

Although little research has yet been directed at identifying the affective (emotional) attributes of the physical environment and their relationship to behaviour, some exploratory work has been carried out. Rapoport and Kantor (1967), for example, analysed people's affective responses to the built environment and used the results as a basis for suggesting design implications. A more comprehensive approach was put forward by Mehrabian and Russell (1974), who considered man–environment relations in the manner shown in Figure 2.2. Their theory is based on the notion that the information load of different environments coupled with the 'characteristic emotions associated with personality' stimulate primary emotional responses, taking the form of arousal, pleasure, and dominance–submissiveness. These three dimensions of emotion then mediate the behavioural response to the environment, either approach (attraction) or avoidance. This means, for example, that an environment that a person feels is arousing, unpleasant, and one in which he feels submissive will be uncomfortable and to be avoided; whereas one that gives the feeling of low arousal, mild pleasure, and a measure of dominance will be comfortable and attractive. This analysis was applied to environments at various spatial scales and has been further developed by Mehrabian (1976) to spell out the design implications of the theory.

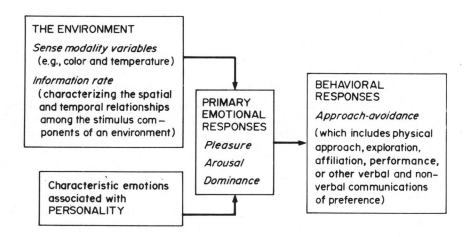

Figure 2.2. The relationship of emotion and behaviour

Source: Mehrabian and Russell (1974, 8). Copyright © 1974 by Massachusetts Institute of Technology. By permission of The MIT Press, Cambridge, Mass.

This approach is a useful means for tackling this neglected aspect of environmental psychology, but it suffers from the familiar problems of theories that consider only a limited range of variables. It is a theory that is suitable only for certain types of environment–behaviour interrelations, with much behaviour left unaccounted (Moore, 1977). As in the case of motivation, much work will be needed before emotion can be incorporated into more comprehensive frameworks of environmental behaviour.

ATTITUDES

The concept of an attitude is invaluable in any behavioural study, for it brings together both internal mental life (including cognition, motivation, and emotion) and overt behavioural responses within one framework. Although there is dispute over definition, most investigators would agree that an attitude can be described as a learned predisposition to respond in a consistently favourable or unfavourable manner with respect to a given object, person, or spatial environment (after Fishbein and Ajzen, 1975). It contains three basic features: the notion that an attitude is learned, that it predisposes to action, and that it is relatively consistent over time.

Perhaps the major feature that distinguishes an attitude from other concepts is that it has an affective component within it. Attitudes may be considered to be enduring cognitive states which are motivational in the sense that, where strongly held, they predispose the individual to react in a certain way—as is so clearly illustrated by racial and religious prejudices (Chaplin and Krawiec, 1974). This point is reinforced by the framework devised by Triandis (1971), who conceived of attitudes as having three main components (Figure 2.3). These were a cognitive element (meaning that the person had some knowledge or opinion about an object, event, or environment), an affective aspect (his feelings towards the stimulus), and a behavioural component (the way he is predisposed to act).

'Attitude' may be taken to be a generic term which includes a host of overlapping concepts, such as belief, bias, doctrine, faith, ideology, judgement, opinion, stereotype, and value. Two of these concepts which will be employed in this text are values and stereotypes and, without wishing to enter the terminological wrangles that beset this field of study, it is worth providing operational definitions at this stage. A 'value' is regarded as an 'enduring belief that a specific mode of conduct or end-state of existence is personally or socially preferable to an opposite or converse mode of conduct or end-state of existence' (Rokeach, 1973, quoted in Reich and Adcock, 1976, 18). A 'stereotype may be defined as a set of beliefs about a particular group of people, or objects, or places, containing no more than a grain of truth, but which forms the basis of opinions about them and 'serves to justify (rationalise) our conduct towards them' (Belcher, 1973). Values and stereotypes, as types of attitude, share the broad characteristics of supplying a rapid, if frequently erroneous, means of coming to terms with environmental complexity. They are ways of arranging information into types in which individual items are all assumed to have the same attributes as the group as a whole. Once a person can identify the category to which an entity belongs, he then has the basis for rapidly assimilating new information and rapidly reaching decisions about behaviour.

The presence of both mental and behavioural elements has ensured

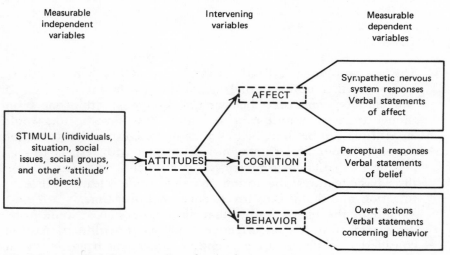

Figure. 2.3. A systematic conception of attitudes

that attitudes are one of the better-researched areas of psychology. Not all this effort stems from a pure academic thirst for knowledge. Large amounts of time and resources have been poured into attitudinal research by the military, government departments, large advertisers, and the mass media. The centre of interest lies in the question of attitude change; in knowing whether attitudes can be altered and, if so, whether this leads to modified patterns of behaviour.

It is doubtful whether they have got value for money. Attitudes are mostly learned in early childhood and, once formed, they are pervasive. Extensive evidence is available from studies of military propaganda and mass communication[9] to show that attitudes can withstand extensive presentation of contrary evidence. In addition, it must be stressed that an attitude is only a predisposition to action. Even if attitudes were in some way changed, there is no necessity for a change in behaviour to follow, for there is frequently a gap between stated attitudes and actual behaviour (Lapiere, 1934; O'Riordan, 1973).

CONCLUSION

Clearly one cannot do full justice to the rich diversity of psychology in one brief chapter, but the material presented here will suffice as the basis for some broad findings. The discussion of the historical development of psychology pointed to what has been termed the *Zeitgeist*, literally the ideas that set the tone or spirit of the times (Boring, 1950). The *Zeitgeist* has been that of psychology as the science of behaviour, with the powerful legacy of the research traditions and philosophy associated with behaviourism (even if not the conceptual frameworks). Experimental psychology was seen to have its limitations when explaining real-world behaviour, for it had sadly neglected study of behaviour in real-world settings. Environmental psychology attempted to fill this gap, but its emergence also reflected a growing multi-disciplinary awareness and orientation towards problems of social relevance. Environmental psychology was seen to be a nascent area of inquiry, lacking a unified conception of man–environment relations, but possessing a number of common research and methodological directions. Some impression of these was obtained by a consideration of frameworks put forward by Altman and Craik, two leading environmental psychologists. The final part of the chapter defined five aspects of mental life that are invaluable in our understanding of man–environment relations. These were perception and cognition, the processes allotted a central role in mediating environmental behaviour, and the three elements that were seen to exert a strong influence over cognitive processes, namely, motivation, emotion, and attitudes. These five mental properties will underpin much of the explanation of environmental behaviour in the pages ahead.

3   Geography and Environmental Behaviour

Paddington liked geography. At least, he liked his sort of geography . . .
                    (MICHAEL BOND, *A Bear Called Paddington*)

The story of geographical endeavour in the study of man and environment is patchy and inconclusive. From being the subject that led scientific thinking in the early part of the twentieth century, geography is now sadly lacking in coherent conceptions of man–environment relations. Indeed, perhaps as the result of past experience, geographers have tended to shy away from specific statements about how the environment influences man and vice versa.

This chapter opens a discussion of environmentalism, a doctrine which is both a feature of geography's past and a persistent theme in its present. The emergence of behavioural geography will be seen against this background, the reasons for its development will be examined and its antecedents traced. We shall then briefly consider its content and organization as a field of study, and present an operational paradigm which will serve as an integrating framework for this book.

ENVIRONMENTALISM

Interest in the relationship of man and his geographical environment (usually conceived of as the physical environment), may be traced back to classical times (Thomas, 1925). As early as the fifth century B.C., the treatise *On Airs, Waters, and Places* by Hippocrates had argued that there was a strong link between bodily diseases and the climatic attributes of places. The emphasis in Hippocrates' work—the impact of the environment upon man—is one that has been echoed down the ages. Ancient Greek ideas on the relationships between climate and human culture became influential in late Medieval Europe, and the connections between climate and human history were explored by French philosophers such as Bodin, de Bos, and Montesquieu in the period between the sixteenth and eighteenth centuries (Glacken, 1967). In the nineteenth century the matter received much greater attention. with views being moulded into the more coherent doctrine that is now termed 'environmentalism'.

Environmentalism[1] may be defined as the view that allotted prime importance to the impact of the physical environment upon man, asserting that the physical milieu set a tightly constrained context for human life. Human behaviour was seen as being primarily adaptive in the face of environmental circumstances, responding to the stimuli imposed by climate, soils, relief, vegetation, and the like. In any given situation, the attributes of the physical environment were to be regarded as forces beyond human control; they constituted the independent variable as against the dependent variable of human behaviour.

Such views were to dominate scientific thinking at the turn of the twentieth century. That they were to do so at a time when Western Europe was witnessing the unprecedented changes brought about by the Industrial Revolution was again proof of the impact of Darwinism and kindred advances in the physical sciences upon the climate of intellectual opinion. The social sciences were to become strongly evolutionary, with facets of human culture being investigated in terms of their origin, development, and survival or disappearance (Goudge, 1967). Yet while the idea of the struggle for survival against a capricious environment was to influence the thinking of many disciplines, with the word 'evolution' appearing in the titles of works by anthropologists, psychologists, sociologists, and historians, few subjects were more swayed by this notion than geography. From the last part of the nineteenth century to the late 1920s, geographical thought centred upon physical (geographical) **determinism**. This branch of environmentalism stipulated that every aspect of human activity could be traced back, by lines of causation, to conditions in the geographical environment, a position usually taken to mean that man was influenced by natural forces beyond his control (Moos, 1976).

There is general agreement that physical determinism was introduced to geography through the work of Friedrich Ratzel. Unlike the majority of his contemporaries in nineteenth-century Germany, Ratzel was interested in human geography rather than in geomorphology. In his two-volume book *Anthropogeographie, or an Introduction to the Application of Geography to History* (1882, 1891; see Wanklyn, 1961), Ratzel expressed the neo-Darwinist view that human communities struggled to survive against their environments in the same manner as do plants and animals. In this struggle for survival, adaptation would take various forms according to the prevailing physical conditions. Spatial variations in activities, social forms, and cultures would be due to differences in physical conditions, particularly in climate, which Ratzel considered to be instrumental in moulding national characteristics. This deterministic relationship therefore held the key to understanding human affairs; if one could discover the physical conditions that shaped social and cultural patterns, then one possessed the key to understanding the historical and geographical development of different peoples.

Like many innovators, Ratzel was aware that his generalizations had flaws, and in both *Anthropogeographie* and later works he was at pains to point out exceptions. In a regional geography of Germany (Ratzel, 1898), for example, he made note of several cases in which cultural differences were more important than variations in the physical character of the land (James, 1973). This element of self-criticism, however, tended to be overlooked by other writers who commented upon and developed his views. This applied especially to a group of American geographers, led by Ratzel's former student Ellen Churchill Semple, who enthusiastically developed the concept of physical determinism. Semple's basic premiss was revealed in the opening paragraph of her book *Influences of Geographic Environment on the Basis of Ratzel's System of Anthropogeography*:

Man is a product of the earth's surface. This means not merely that he is a child of the earth, dust of her dust; but that the earth has mothered him, fed him, set him tasks, directed his thoughts, confronted him with difficulties that have strengthened his body and sharpened his wits, given him problems of navigation or irrigation, and at the same time whispered hints for their solution.   (Semple, 1911, 1)

Her method was to compare the activities and stage of cultural development of people living under similar geographical conditions. If people of different ethnic stocks exhibited similar or related social, economic, or historical development, Semple argued it would be reasonable to infer that such similarities would be due to environment and not race. She provided extensive, but highly sketchy, evidence to support her deterministic thesis, grouping material to exemplify four supposed 'effects' of the physical environment; namely, direct physical effects, psychical effects, economic and social effects, and promoting movements of peoples.

Semple claimed that she supported only a mild determinism, but in practice the effervescence of her literary style and heavy usage of causal verbs gave the book a stronger overtone. Whatever the intention, many of her statements now appear to be crude mechanistic interpretations of complex environmental behaviour, suffering from both inadequate evidence and a one-sided conception of geography as the study of the environment's impact upon man. In this respect, the parallels between geographical determinism and behaviourist psychology are readily apparent. They shared the same mood of scientific inquiry, searching for mechanical laws of cause and effect. Both were heavily influenced by Darwinist theories of evolution and were to become most firmly entrenched in the United States. Perhaps the most important similarity lay in the models of behaviour that geographical determinism and behaviourism espoused. Geographical determinism was based upon a model which was virtually identical to the stimulus–response framework of behaviourism and could even be expressed in similar terms; for example, '. . . any statement is of geographical quality if it contains a reasonable relation between some inorganic element of the earth on which we live acting as a control, and some element of the existence of the earth's organic inhabitants serving as a response' (Davis, 1906[2] quoted in James, 1973). The physical environment therefore presented stimuli to which man was forced to respond, with little or no significance being attached to human cognitive abilities.

Geographical determinism continued to be developed until mid-twentieth century through the writings of such authors as Huntington (1915, 1945) and Taylor (1937, 1940), retained sufficient vigour to generate a lively exchange of articles in the 1950s,[3] and persists in diluted form whenever geographers search for environmental 'influences' upon behaviour (Simons, 1966), but it had reached its zenith by 1925. From this time it came under increasing criticism, with the attack being initially led by the French school of **possibilism**, a countervailing doctrine usually associated with the names of Vidal de la Blache (1926), Brunhes (1920), and Febvre (1925). The possibilists focused attention on certain key flaws in determinist arguments— their use of simple correlations as conclusive evidence for causality, the limited and selective data employed, and overestimation of the direct impact of the environment upon everyday life. The alternative viewpoint which they put forward saw man as the active agent, with the environment as an inert or permissive forum for his activities. To the possibilist, there were 'no necessities, but everywhere possibilities; and that man, as master of the possibilities, is the judge of their use' (Febvre, 1925, 236). This did not mean that man enjoyed complete mastery over nature, but the constraints that nature imposed were invariably generous. Nor did it mean that there were no economic and social limits upon environmental possibilities. Human time and resources are finite; one cannot accomplish everything that is technically feasible, and there is an opportunity cost[4] associated with the projects that do take place (Moos, 1976).

Possibilism and determinism were to serve as the end-points of geographical debate about man and environment until after World War II. Attempts were made to construct bridging viewpoints, the most notable being environmental **probabilism** (Spate, 1953), in which the state of environmental conditions was seen to make some developments probable and others unlikely (see later). Yet determinism and possibilism were not the diametric opposites that most observers have assumed. Harvey (1969, 402) suggested that both schools employed causal reasoning:

To Vidal de la Blache explanation consisted of showing how a particular event stood at the point of intersection of complex causal chains . . . while the geographical determinists such as Semple and Huntington, sought to show how human activity could be related back (often by a complex path) to the ultimate determinant, the environment. The geographical possibilists, on the other hand, seem not so much to have been at war with the causal principle as to have disagreed with the determinists over the identification of the right cause and the right effect.

Moreover determinism and possibilism both regarded the environment as a 'given' factor in any situation, with man's role in shaping that environment being virtually ignored. This in itself proved to be a major reason for the demise of these schools of thought, for exponential advances in technology have progressively reduced the potential influence of natural conditions, an idea which Craik (1970) called the 'recession of the physical environment'. Indeed one might even ask what precisely is a 'natural environment' at the present day.[5] In a world which has been profoundly shaped by modern technology, the 'controls' or even the 'influence' of the natural environment do not offer an adequate basis for understanding human behaviour. Another reason for their decline closely corresponds to the experience of psychology:

that as the discipline developed, researchers no longer felt themselves obliged to work within the bounds of a particular theoretical viewpoint on the environment but free to adopt, on pragmatic grounds, the approach that suited the problem in hand.

This pragmatism, however, was partly attributable to a less positive motive. Once geographical determinism had been shown to be conceptually unsound, it became something of a derogatory term—the 'bogey-man' with which to frighten the sensitive (Eyre and Jones, 1966). For some time it seemed safer to avoid any inquiry that examined links between environmental forces and social consequences (a key area of interest for the behavioural geographer), rather than risk being labelled a 'determinist'. While more mature counsels now prevail, there is no denying the short-term damage this caused.

Environmentalism, as distinct from the specific issue of geographical determinism,[6] none the less persists in geography, most notably as part of the ecological and spatial scientific approaches. **Ecology** still bears the impress of Darwinist ideas of the struggle for survival against the environment, although ecologists have broadened their conception of environment to include human as well as physical factors. Ecological theory contains a holistic view of life-forms striving to adapt successfully to their physical environment and to *one another*, still environmentalist in its orientation but a step away from the crudeness of physical determinism. Perhaps the main problem with ecology has been that

geographers have been so indoctrinated with such homeostatic concerns as characterise the ecosystem approach, with all that this implies, that they are disoriented by the stark possibility that irresistable tendencies already exist which are causing social man to manipulate his resources, including space, in ways which cannot be rationalised solely in terms of short-term equilibrium.   (Chorley, 1973, 161)

In other words, once again a persuasive framework can become a conceptual 'straightjacket' if applied too rigidly to human behaviour. The framework should be tailored to fit the situation, not vice versa.

A rather different neo-environmentalism has been present in the **spatial scientific approach** which swept through human geography in the 1960s, bringing with it model-based theoretical constructs and quantitative methods. This approach was rooted in the work of economists such as Christaller (1933), Lösch (1940), and Isard (1956, 1960), who wished to extend the range of economic analysis by incorporating the spatial dimension. Not surprisingly their writings employed the standard assumptions of microeconomics, which included the conditions that there should be free competition amongst suppliers and consumers for goods and services, a homogeneous physical environment, uniform tastes, and that all decisions made by entrepreneurs and purchasers should be rational on strict economic grounds. The latter assumption is that of 'economic man', an important feature of economic analysis since the time of Adam Smith. Economic man is the omniscient and rational decision-maker who is totally subject to the circumstances of his economic environment. Whenever this presents stimuli in the form of changed market conditions, economic man is assumed to be able to adjust his behaviour in order to find an optimal solution (Knight, 1956).

Later writers have built extensively upon these simplifying assumptions to develop a sophisticated corpus of locational theory. There is, of course, nothing wrong with using simplifying assumptions to develop an initial and partial understanding of the phenomena under scrutiny, but two sets of nagging doubts persist. First, it is often argued that these assumptions are made only in the first instance and are then modified or abandoned as knowledge improves. The experience of economics, however, suggests otherwise, for the deterministic concept of economic man has become the cornerstone of a complex and increasingly abstract body of theory which would seem to have little prospect of internal consistency if its basic assumptions were removed. Indeed there is a strong temptation for researchers to try to improve the applicability of their theories by the opposite means of 'reification', whereby the researcher argues that the real world is in practice like his model rather than trying to make the model more like reality. A good example may be found in the work of the 'social physicists',[8] who have argued that as the principle of optimality is accepted as a normal goal for biological systems, why should it not be so for free-enterprise societies?

Second, economists themselves have increasingly questioned the value of the economic man assumption. Without wishing to enter this heated area of controversy,[9] one can find many economists contending that the notion of the individual decision-maker acting alone and independently in a highly competitive world is unrepresentative of a business environment dominated by large organizations, with complex administrative structures and goals, wielding large measures of monopoly power (Cyert and March, 1963). Even when dealing with a situation in which the individual entrepreneur is the norm, it is doubtful whether his decisions are characterized by optimizing behaviour. As Simon (1952, 1957) has suggested, it is highly unlikely that the entrepreneur would or could achieve more than a satisfactory outcome to an economic problem. Decision-makers have bounded rather than perfect knowledge and operate within conditions of uncertainty; it is inevitable that their rationality will be similarly bounded.

This changing mood in economics has had its parallels in geography. It is significant that one of the earliest works to challenge spatial analytical theory, an article by Wolpert (1964), was itself based upon Simon's 'satisficing' model. Although recognizing that the satisficing model was not easily verifiable, Wolpert used a sample of Middle Swedish farmers to test whether real-world decision-making accorded to satisficing or optimizing principles. Actual farming patterns were compared with those that would have been expected if farmers had used their resources optimally (calculated from sample survey data of land potential). The results showed that crop yields were well below the theoretical optimum—in certain areas as low as 40 per cent of the possible yield. On this basis, Wolpert concluded that the satisficer concept was more descriptively accurate of the behavioural pattern of the sample population than the one that could be inferred from the notion of economic man. The farmers were found to lack perfect knowledge owing to the existence of unpredictable change and lag in the communication and perception of information. The decision behaviour was also found to reflect not only the objective alternatives that are available, but also man's awareness of these alternatives and the consequences of their outcomes, his degree of aversion to risk and uncertainty, and his system of values.

These elements of information availability and varying skills with which to use it were also employed by Pred (1967, 1969) [10] in devising his 'behavioural matrix' of locational decision-making. As shown in Figure 3.1, in any particular situation an entrepreneur can be assigned to a position in the matrix that accords with the amount of knowledge he possesses and his skills at using it. A position near the bottom right would indicate that the entrepreneur will have more chance of making a good locational decision than someone characterized by a position near the top left, yet the emphasis is upon probability. It is always possible for an entrepreneur with little skill and information to reach a better locational solution than one who possesses greater ability and information; it is simply that this eventuality is relatively unlikely.

This attempt to incorporate probability into locational analysis, of which Pred's work is a good example, was an important step towards toning down the neo-environmentalism of spatial-economic models. Probability-based research in this field has taken various forms. Certain writers, for example,

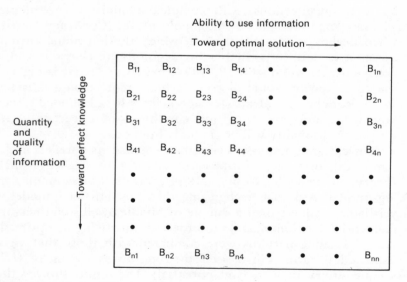

Figure 3.1. The behavioural matrix

Source: Pred (1967, 25).

have employed game theory as a numerical means to simulate the probable strategies of the various participants ('players') against the uncertainties of their environment (Gould, 1963, Chapman, 1974) or against other players in hypothetical environmental contexts (Pred and Kibel, 1970; Wolpert, 1970; R. Cohen *et al.*, 1973). Others have used information theory as a conceptual framework within which to consider the information conditions that surround decision-making (Marchand, 1972; Walsh and Webber, 1977). Game- and information-theory models are but two examples of the common trend towards modifying and extending the behavioural basis of existing spatial theory by introducing probability formulations. Probability offers an opportunity to approximate the idiosyncrasies and inconsistencies of real-world decision-making, and fits easily into the paradigm of quantitative geography. From our point of view, however, there are three reasons why it is unlikely that this strategy would yield models that satisfactorily analyse real-world behaviour.

First, there is no reason why simple inclusion of stochastic (random) elements should transform normative spatial models into adequate statements about the real-world behaviour of groups and individuals. Second, these models are essentially 'mass behavioural': they rely on what Lipsey (1975) termed the 'law of large numbers', or the idea that whereas the actions of individuals may be unpredictable when considered separately, the behaviour of groups will be predictable precisely because the odd things that one individual does will tend to cancel out the odd things that someone else does. While this in itself may seem intuitively reasonable, it is hard to divorce this aspect from the other implications of the mass-behavioural view—for instance, that groups consist of 'atomized' individuals who might be dependent on one another in various ways but who lacked any unifying direction or purpose (Elliott, 1972; Giner, 1976)—concepts inimical to the behaviouralist approach adopted here. Third, this strategy does nothing to alter the fact that the environment is still taken as given. There is no provision for showing how man modifies his environment, nor for investigating the true dynamics of environmental behaviour.

THE EARLY DEVELOPMENT OF BEHAVIOURAL GEOGRAPHY

Without cataloguing the many ways in which the sentiment has been expressed, it may be safely said that disenchantment with existing environmentalist models of man and the desire to find other bases for understanding man–environment relations have been instrumental in the development of behavioural geography. At the same time, two other factors need to be mentioned.

The first is the serious questioning of the progress and conduct of geographical research contained in the so-called 'relevance debate'. The relevance debate has been the name given to the public discussion in the early 1970s[11] of several sets of anxieties and concerns that had been voiced, albeit in a disaggregated manner, throughout the previous decade. In the relevance debate, discussion crystallized around three major issues: that more should be done to study issues of contemporary social concern, such as pollution, poverty, and welfare; that there needs to be more direct input into public planning and policy; and that geographers should be conscious that their work is value-laden and that values influence all stages of inquiry, from choosing the problem for study to the presentation and interpretation of results. Each of these matters has acted as a stimulus for behavioural geography. It is a branch of inquiry that is intimately concerned with environmental and social issues, it is strongly policy-oriented, and recognizes that geographers, as well as the human subjects of their research, are individuals with a distinct outlook on the world rather than detached value-free observers.

The second factor that must be mentioned is the growth of ties between geography and other disciplines. Geographers for many years had sought to create a unique identity for their subject, literally turning their backs on developments taking place in other disciplines (Granö, 1977). The effect of convergence of interests around issues of multi-disciplinary concern has been exactly the same for behavioural geography as for environmental psychology, broadening the outlook of the parent discipline and permitting cross-fertilization of ideas. As was noted previously, there are problems associated with trans-disciplinary flows of concepts and information, but it remains true that many of the works that have had the greatest impact on behavioural geography stem initially from the literature of other disciplines.

This does not mean, of course, that there are no roots of behaviouralism to be found within geography itself; indeed recent researchers have been assiduous in trying to discover them. This can prove to be a somewhat spurious exercise, for writings may in retrospect gain a significance out of all proportion to the impact they had at the time. Richards (1974), for instance, tried to demonstrate that the concept of the 'mental map' was implicit in the work of the eighteenth-century philosopher Immanuel Kant, but this is more an ingenious interpretation than the uncovering of a source that genuinely affected behaviouralist thinking. More likely sources of influence before 1960 are to be found in the writings of three American geographers, Sauer, Wright, and White, and the English geographer Kirk.

Carl Sauer. Sauer was one of the first geographers to express the view that differences in past occupancy of land could be explained in terms of social and cultural differences. Through his publications (see Leighley, 1969) and the work of the school of historical geography that he established at Berkeley (California), attention was focused on the man–land relationship and its implications for landscape. Landscape was investigated in two ways: as the *natural landscape*, comprising the physical qualities (landforms, vegetation, soils, minerals, and other resources) that are of significance to man; and as the *cultural landscape*, which is fashioned by man in the manner shown in Table 3.1. Culture was the agent, the natural environment was the medium, and the cultural landscape the result. Under the influence of a given culture,

Table 3.1. *Diagrammatic representation of the morphology of the cultural Landscape*

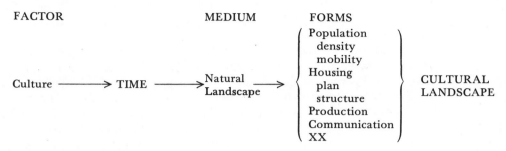

the landscape becomes the repository of that culture's strivings against its environment and the tangible record of man's adaptation to his physical milieu. Such ideas were very much in the ecological tradition, but Sauer's contribution lay in the fact that he fully recognized that man, through the agency of culture, also moulded his environment.

J. K. Wright. Wright was also concerned with the relationship between culture and landscape, although his interests, as expressed by an output of almost 500 publications between 1908 and 1968, covered a wide spectrum of human geography. The essence of his ideas, however, may be gauged from his 1946 Presidential Address to the Association of American Geographers (Wright, 1947), which remained his most influential paper. Wright noted that even if there were no totally unexplored lands remaining, there were still *terrae incognitae* for the geographer to study. These *terrae incognitae* were to be found in the minds of men; private worlds specific to particular individuals, but which would have features shared by others in the same social, cultural, or occupational groups. Like other types of *terrae incognitae*, these would spur endeavour, for 'the unknown stimulates the imagination to conjure up mental images of what to look for within it, and the more there is found, the more the imagination suggests for further search' (Wright, 1947, 4). Wright proposed that a profitable direction for geography would be to study geographical knowledge in all its forms, whether contained in formal geographical inquiries or in the vast range of informal sources, such as travel books, magazines, newspapers, fiction, poetry, and painting. His idea was for a unified branch of study known as 'geosophy', which would examine geographical knowledge 'from any or all points of view'. In retrospect, the concept of geosophy did not gain general acceptance, but the underlying ideas about mental *terrae incognitae* and the role of the imagination were to have a seminal influence (Lowenthal, 1961; Lowenthal and Bowden, 1976).

William Kirk. Kirk (1952, 1963) supplied one of the first behavioural models that would serve as a genuine alternative to environmentalist conceptions of man-land relationships. As a historical geographer, Kirk was interested in the way that societies in different places and times interpreted and responded to their environments. He suggested that people acted according to their environmental perceptions; views of the world that might differ markedly from reality and were heavily influenced by the values of their particular culture.

Kirk's model attempted to introduce Gestalt theory into a geographical context. In keeping with Gestalt psychology, distinction was made between the objective (phenomenal) and behavioural environments. The former was the physical environment coupled with the changes brought about by man; the latter was a 'psycho-physical field in which phenomenal facts are arranged into patterns or structures (*Gestalten*) and acquire values in cultural contexts' (Kirk, 1963, 366). Kirk did not discuss how the behavioural environment evolved, but it was implied that this may be explained by mainstream Gestalt theory. The significant difference between his notion of a behavioural environment and that normally used by Gestaltists was that Kirk regarded the behavioural environment, once formed, as the basis for *rational* human behaviour. In other words, he combined two traditions—the belief in rational decision-making which was common in geography with the perceptual principles of Gestalt psychology.

One way in which Kirk presented the idea of a behavioural environment is depicted in Figure 3.2. The social and physical 'facts' of the objective environment only become part of the behavioural environment when they have penetrated a highly sensitive filter of cultural values. These values vary

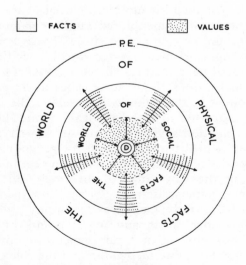

Figure 3.2. The behavioural environment of a decision-maker.

Source: Gold (1977a, 41). By permission of the Editors.

temporally and spatially, so one would expect that the same information would have different meanings for people of different cultures or even for the same society at different times.

The importance of this model was that it introduced the 'behavioural environment' into geographical study, but it contained limitations that derived directly from the two traditions it embodied. First, it retained the belief that decision-making is based on rational appraisal of the total situation. As Hurst (1974) commented, this would sound suspiciously like 'economic man' were it not for the fact that decisions were based on the behavioural rather than the objective environment. Second, it shared the general limitations of Gestalt theory discussed in the previous chapter. Certainly the idea of the behavioural environment was to achieve much greater utility once it shed the overtones of Gestalt theory (e.g. see Lloyd and Dicken, 1972).

Gilbert White. White's work will be considered at length in Chapter 12 and so brief comment will suffice here. White occupies a prominent position in both past and present development of behavioural geography through his leadership and active participation in natural hazards research. Natural hazards research has proceeded on systematic lines, providing a coherence which serves as an exemplar for behavioural geography. Besides this, White firmly established an ethical standpoint in his writings. As Chorley (1976) observed, White was concerned with social involvement with the environment and his work is pervaded by the idea that geography is not a value-free subject. Geographers could not be satisfied with merely describing and analysing the past, they had a moral responsibility to interpret the implications of their work in terms of human improvement. The relationship between these views and the relevance debate will be readily apparent.

THE CURRENT SITUATION[12]

Since the early 1960s behavioural geography has expanded rapidly, although predictions that it would soon 'come to merit a place alongside the quantitative revolution in terms of significant new viewpoints'(Burton, 1963, 159) perhaps implied that the process would have been quicker than it has proved to be. There are two reasons for this situation. First, unlike quantification, behavioural geography did not accord with the *Zeitgeist* of a human geography in which spatial analysis was increasingly emphasized. Second, behavioural geography did not have the advantage of being able to gain a coherent identity by drawing upon an integrated body of theory, as was the case with quantification, but instead depended upon researchers drawing together many diverse strands of thought culled from numerous academic disciplines. Given the diversity of these disciplines, it is hardly surprising that behavioural geography has inherited a 'derived diversity' of conceptual frameworks, methods, and empirical data. A plethora of research directions have been opened up; some highly promising, others contributing little and being allowed to return to a merited obscurity.

None the less, common themes do emerge. Golledge *et al.* (1972) traced major trends that have emerged in behavioural-geographical research over time, Saarinen (1969, 1976) attempted to integrate its content according to the spatial scale of the environments in which perception and behaviour take· place, and Goodey (1971) mapped out common areas of research interest. A rather different approach was adopted by Gold (1977a), who examined the current state of behavioural geography from the standpoint of its content and organization as an undergraduate subject. From a survey of behavioural geography teaching in British institutions of higher education, it was found that behavioural geography appeared in two main guises: almost universally as a component in wider human geography courses and, in a small but growing number of departments, as a specialist subject in its own right. As the latter were found to offer an excellent guide to the character of behavioural geography at the present time, they are worth considering further.

Some impression of these specialist courses is conveyed by Table 3.2. Despite the obvious differences in contact hours, it was found that there were remarkable similarities in both organization of material and topics covered. Dealing first with the organization of material, the main linking theme was a paradigm of man–environment relations of the type shown in Figure 3.3. Man was depicted as a thinking individual whose transactions with the environment are mediated by mental processes and cognitive representations of the external environment. Various concepts were used as a surrogate for these 'cognitive representations', but the one most often employed was the 'image'. In geographical circles, this concept is derived primarily from the work of Boulding (1956) who suggested that over time individuals develop mental impressions of the world (images) through their everyday contacts with the environment and that these images act as the basis for behaviour. The image was therefore conceived as a comprehensive cognitive concept, a quality which, as the next section will show, contains both advantages and drawbacks.

The topics covered by these courses were arranged according to this process paradigm, with their main sections (elements 3–5 in Table 3.2) dealing in turn with the formation and development of images, their structure and character, and their relationship with behaviour. The section on development of images normally involved consideration of relevant aspects

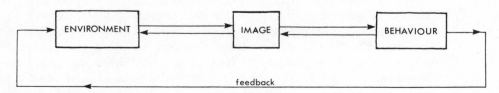

Figure 3.3. A conventional paradigm of man–environment relationships

Table 3.2 *Major topics in teaching syllabuses of specialist behavioural geography courses, 1975–6*

COURSE TOPICS	INDIVIDUAL BEHAVIOURAL GEOGRAPHY COURSES									
1. Contextual										
a. Geographical	X	X	X	N	X	X	X	X	X	X
b. Interdisciplinary	X	X	X		X	X	X	X	X	X
2. Methodology										
a. Philosophy of Method	X	X	X	O	X	X		X	X	X
b. Techniques		X	X			X		X	X	X
3. Psychological Background				D						
a. Sensation and Cognition	X	X	X		X	X	X	X	X	X
b. Developmental	X	X	X		X	X		X		X
c. Structuring Images	X	X	X	A	X	X	X	X	X	X
4. Nature of Environmental Images										
a. Micro-space	X	X	X			X	X	X	X	X
b. Urban	X	X	X	T	X	X	X	X	X	X
c. Landscape	X				X					X
d. Regional	X	X	X		X	X		X	X	X
e. Global	X	X	X		X	X	X	X		X
5. Images and Behaviour				A						
a. Territoriality	X	X	X		X		X	X	X	X
b. Behaviour in Urban Environments	X	X	X				X	X	X	X
c. Landscape Evaluation and Choice					X					X
d. Hazard Perception	X	X	X		X		X	X	X	X
e. Preferences and Relocation	X	X	X		X		X	X	X	X
6. Planning and Design Implications	X	X	X		X		X	X	X	X
7. Project Work		X	X			X		X	X	X
CONTACT TIME (HRS.)	10	24	26	30	23	30	6	30	21	34
COURSE STATUS	*	⟩	*	*	*	*	⟩	*	*	*

For explanation of course topics, see text.

KEY TO SYMBOLS

X –   Topic covered in Course
* –   Optional Course
⟩ –   Compulsory Course

Source: Gold (1977a, 41).

of psychology, examining such questions as the links between sensation and perception, and the development of spatial cognition during childhood. The section on the nature of the image was normally organized around the concept of scale, in which images are considered to be loosely arranged into a hierarchy of bounded spaces ranging from micro-scale environments, such as the room or house, though meso-scale environments, such as the neighbourhood, town, or city, to macro-scale environments of regions and nations.[13] Images were then investigated at various levels, although the dominant trend of inquiry focused upon the urban environment at meso-scale. Discussion of the links between images and behaviour was centred upon discrete areas of research interest, with such issues as response to natural hazards, urban-territorial behaviour, and the role of preferences in intra-urban migration well to the fore.

It is clear from this that the teaching of behavioural geography was research-led. In other words, this is a branch of geography in which the teaching content and orientation have been actively diffused down the academic hierarchy from the work of advanced researchers.[14] As in behavioural geography research, teaching was found to have an exploratory problem- and policy-oriented character, and to be founded upon a common conception of process. Furthermore teaching syllabuses contained the same three sources of bias generally encountered in research. First, behavioural geography courses were primarily neo-positivist in outlook, containing the implicit assumption that elements of mental processes can be isolated and objectively measured. This is not to say that there has not been recognition of the growing literature[15] that advocates usage of phenomenological and related non-positivist philosophical approaches, but to date their writings have scarcely gone beyond the philosophical level. In the absence of practical applications,[16] continued emphasis upon the neo-positivist mainstream of behavioural-geographical research is inevitable, despite genuine interest in the potential insights that other approaches might afford. Second, these courses concentrated upon studies of the urban milieu, a bias which is readily understandable in view of the dominance of urban contexts for research, but which also partly reflected the lack of convincing analytical frameworks for tackling problems associated with the natural environment. Third, these courses were found to have confined their attention to the limited cultural contexts of Europe and North America. This indicated the dominant sources of research material, but to some extent pointed to Western ignorance of non-Western efforts to develop behaviouralist research.

The links between teaching and research were also expressed in another, less positive, manner. Despite the best endeavours of course-organizers, teaching programmes reflected the somewhat disparate state of the research literature, with confused terminology, conflicting aims and objectives, and poorly integrated conceptual and empirical material. Yet as the organization of these courses would suggest, integration is possible if it is based upon explicit recognition and elaboration of the common processes that underpin environmental experience and behaviour. It is to this issue that we now turn.

AN OPERATIONAL PARADIGM

The basic paradigm of man–environment relations is shown in Figure 3.4, which links the simplified version put forward in Figure 3.3 with the discussion of the previous chapter. It aims to clarify the elements that are present and their interrelationships, but is intended to be purely schematic. The 'boxes' identify interrelated rather than mutually exclusive elements, the lines show direction of influence rather than causal relationships, and the paradigm as a whole depicts dynamic processes occurring over varying time-spans. The paradigm also serves as an integrating framework for this book, providing a context for the major questions asked in the next three parts, namely: how does spatial cognition develop? what are the nature and structure of the mental representations of the environment so developed? and how do these mental representations relate to behaviour?

The term 'mental representations', of course, is somewhat vague and thus we shall employ two more specific notions–'images' and 'spatial schemata'. The *image* is used in a manner different from that in common practice in geographical literature, where it has been viewed as a synonym for an individual's organized subjective knowledge of the environment. Here, the image will be defined as the mental picture that may be called to mind when the object, person, place, or area is not part of current sensory information. The image has visual connotations, partly because the term has been utilized extensively by art historians and partly owing to the fact that our stock example of an image is the looking-glass world, a purely visual copy of things opposite the mirror (Langer, 1953). Yet this need not always be the case; an image can equally have elements that have been contributed by other senses besides vision (Gordon, 1972). An image is therefore a perception in the absence of an external stimulus, irrespective of the sensory mode in which this perception occurs.

Schemata, on the other hand, are viewed as the basic frameworks within which past and present environmental experiences are organized. The notion of the schema was derived from the work of cognitive psychologists on object perception (Head, 1920; Bartlett, 1932), being first applied to environmental contexts by Lee (1954). The schema may be defined as the cognitive structure or coding system that allows the individual to respond appropriately to a shifting pattern of environmental stimuli. Schemata themselves are dynamic, changing to incorporate new material, but are selective in what they incorporate (Lee, 1976).

'Spatial schemata', the sub-set of schemata with which we are concerned, may be viewed as the frameworks within which people organize their knowledge of the spatial environment, containing the residue of past experience and accommodating current sensory information. Once established, such schemata may be modified by extension, but they are only rarely radically overhauled. Their content, for convenience, may be divided into two categories: *locational* knowledge, which supplies the basic structure of geographical space and the orientation and relationship of the elements

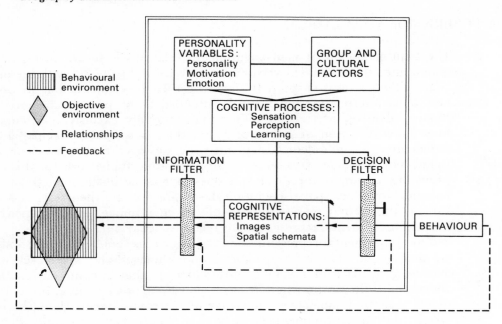

Figure 3.4. A paradigm of individual spatial cognition and behaviour

within it; and *attributive* knowledge, which supplies assessment of the attributes of places and areas, along with information about how various locations compare with one another.

Images and spatial schemata are closely related, but may be distinguished in two ways. First, the image is both etymologically and conceptually associated with imagination. It is thus a particularly useful expression by which to describe conceptions of places that have been seldom or never visited or areas that are too large to conceive of in anything other than broad outline. Schemata, by contrast, are more readily associated with the everyday environment; with the accumulation and organization of spatial knowledge upon which behaviour in that environment is based. Second, there is the question of attention. As Tuan (1975a) has suggested, to see in the mind's eye places we have not visited requires such concentrated attention that the effort immobilizes us or, in other words, makes us temporarily oblivious to the world of current sensory information. By contrast, schemata may be employed almost subconsciously, as in the case of routine travel, where habituation frees the individual's mind to think about other things. Thus although the initial task of orienting oneself in a new environment is undoubtedly difficult, 'once the environment has become familiar and we have established a habitual route it is possible to move in it with only minimal focal attention, and without the conscious recourse to imagery' (Tuan, 1975a, 212). None the less these distinctions between images and spatial schemata are ones of degree rather than type. Any attempt rigidly to demarcate mental activity exclusively into one category or the other would, in the long run, be counter-productive.

Returning to the paradigm shown in Figure 3.4, its application to the everyday environment depicts images and spatial schemata as the basic cognitive elements that mediate behaviour. The individual is simultaneously part of the objective and behavioural environments; receiving locational and attributive information from the behavioural environment, but affecting both environments by his actions. The mental elements and processes discussed earlier are grouped into three convenient categories: the cognitive processes that shape spatial schemata, and the personality variables and socio-cultural factors that are influences upon these processes. Collectively these three categories represent filters which affect the flow of information at two key stages. First, they affect the way that information is extracted from the environment. At any one time, the individual can absorb only a small fraction of the potential information in his environment and, of what is absorbed, most is of a routine nature which simply reinforces schemata or clarifies areas of uncertainty, and produces little need for response. Where the information has a more radical impact, decisions may be necessary, and at this stage there is a second filtering of information. This can produce any one of four outcomes: the individual may give up without reaching a decision; he may decide that he lacks sufficient information and will go back and search for more; he may decide to take no action; or he may reach a decision and undertake a course of action.

This is not the end of the process. In any situation, the individual will seek to monitor the effectiveness of his actions, to assign value to the experience, and to correct future behavioural strategies. These in turn may modify spatial cognition and serve as the stimulus for further behaviour, either for the individual himself or for other people. It cannot be stressed too strongly that man–environment relationships are continuous and dynamic and that the final stage of one sequence is frequently the starting-point for another.

PART TWO

THE DEVELOPMENT OF SPATIAL COGNITION

4　Spatial Information

Beholding (seeing with understanding) is not just a mirror which is always the same, but a living power of apprehension which has its own inward history and has passed through many stages.

(H. WÖLFFLIN, *Principles of Art History*)

Our current understanding of man–environment relationships is clouded by a series of unresolved problems. How do people come to terms with the world around them? How do they develop mental representations of the external environment and what form do these representations take? How does perception relate to sensation? To what extent is perception predetermined by instinct rather than produced by environmental learning? What role do social and cultural groups play in shaping cognitive processes? No simple answers are available, indeed in many cases there are not even the makings of such answers.

The aims of Part Two are necessarily modest, recognizing that the topics covered are ones that have generated much debate and speculation. It sketches out some broad perspectives on information sources and on the development of spatial cognition, seeking to clarify the basic processes and variables involved. This chapter examines the potential sources of spatial information through direct sensory experience and communication from others. Chapter 5 outlines certain factors that influence the way this information is structured into meaningful images and spatial schemata.

SPATIAL INFORMATION AND PERCEPTION

The study of information has been a fertile area of inquiry in the social sciences, with writers regarding information as a potential unifying concept in man–environment relationships. In this view, each sequence of behaviour is related to a particular state of information, which consists of current stimuli plus the residue of past learning. Newell and Simon (1972), for example, supplied a quantitative framework which identified the role of information-processing in human problem-solving. Communications theorists (Sereno and Mortenson, 1970) have identified and measured the passage of information in both animate and mechanical systems, seeing information as being any stimulus in the environment that conveys knowledge about objects, people, or environments. When so defined, however, all that matters is the quantity of information. The nature or quality of that information becomes irrelevant, in just the same way as weight is defined in units which make the nature of the object irrelevant (Brown, 1966).

Clearly this type of definition is inadequate for our purposes, as it ignores four important characteristics of human information-processing. First, it is necessary to distinguish between the stimulus—the external physical entity that presents information to our sense organs and awakens latent percepts in the mind—and the cognitive representations of that stimulus, which are mental entities (Hesselgren, 1975). Contrary to the belief of certain classical philosophers, individuals do not carry around mental pictures which are merely miniaturized replicas of the real world ('eidetic images'), but images and schemata of greater or lesser completeness and accuracy which are organized by the operation of cognitive processes. As Gregory (1966, 69, quoted in Moore and Golledge, 1976a, 9) has pointed out:

We do have 'mental' pictures, but this should not suggest that there are corresponding electrical pictures in the brain. It is possible to represent things in symbols but symbols will generally be very different from the things represented. The notion of brain pictures is conceptually dangerous. It is apt to suggest that these supposed pictures are themselves seen with a kind of inner eye—involving another picture, and another eye. . .

The upshot of this argument is that perception should not be seen as simply a matter of decoding an input of sensory data providing space-time measurement of stimulation. It is an entirely new product created in the brain, partly out of the raw material of the signals sent in by the sense organs and in part modelled by the total incoming and outgoing activity within the central nervous system at the time, together with what has been learned from past experience (Wyburn *et al.*, 1964).

Second, it is necessary to recognize the limited information-handling capacities of the brain, for at any one moment the individual can absorb only a tiny fraction of the potential stimuli in the environment. For the visual sense alone, it has been estimated that the environment supplies 10,000,000 units ('bits') of information every second. In the same period of time, the brain can only absorb around twenty-five units (Held and Richards, 1972). Of necessity, therefore, an extreme selectivity is exercised in the way that information is extracted from the environment.

Most of the rules of this selectivity are derived from the third characteristic of human information-processing, the fact that perception is motivated. The mind, consciously or unconsciously, scans the environment to extract those cues that are useful to the individual in the light of his particular goals. The influence of specific needs will vary, of course, according to the particular situation under consideration. Information search will be quite different at times when basic survival needs are pre-eminent compared with times when the individual is concentrating upon higher needs. The informational stimuli extracted from the environment by a seasoned commuter will differ profoundly from those of a person making the same journey for the first time. The former will have reduced the way-finding decision-making to a matter of mere habituation and will be free to attend to other needs, the latter will have to concentrate much more on the cues that will supply the necessary information for correct navigation. Information should be taken to imply utility; it is knowledge obtained from the environment that is useful in relation to the goal or goals that the individual is or will be pursuing. In everyday life these goals will be linked largely to adaptation, with people seeking information that will allow them to function effectively in their environment (Kaplan, 1976), but it does not follow that only adaptive information is useful. Information that is sought in connection with such goals as personal development or the achievement of an individual's self-image is undoubtedly of utility to a person, although it is not directed toward short- or long-term environmental adaptation.

Fourth, mere availability of information does not place absolute limits upon the operation of cognitive processes. Perception is inferential in that, to borrow a phrase coined by Bruner (1957), it can proceed beyond the information given. Devlin (1976), for instance, demonstrated that when an individual comes to a town for the first time, he will have a series of expectations about the location of various facilities based upon his experience of other such places. Indeed Sutter (1973) recalled a common childhood game whereby members of a group would try, with some success, to guess the layout of small towns in the American Mid-west before they arrived there. Appleyard (1973, 110) described this property of perception in the following way:

As we grow up, we develop a generalizable system of environmental categories, concepts, and relationships which form our coding system for the city—our personal urban model. When we encounter a new city, we match each new experience against our general expectations: events are 'placed', never-before-seen buildings are identified as belonging to a particular class of building, functional and social patterns are inferred.

These findings have a wider relevance than merely applying to perception of the urban environment; they are basic features of all environmental perception.

The concept of 'information' employed here takes account of these four considerations. Information is defined as including anything that plays a part in constructing, reinforcing, expanding, modifying, or changing the schemata around which we organize our environmental experience. 'Spatial information' is regarded as a subset of environmental information, being defined as any stimulus from which the recipient learns something about the structure and organization of space, or that contains the raw material from which that knowledge is extracted. It has both locational and attributive components. The locational component would include all stimuli from which the individual extracts knowledge about the position and areal extent of phenomena in his environment and about the orientational relationships of these phenomena to one another and to himself in terms of distance and direction. Attributive information includes anything from which the individual gains knowledge about the attributes of particular spaces and places against one another.

As Table 4.1 indicates, spatial information comes from two sources. Much is derived from direct sensory experience, which may be designated as 'primary sources' of spatial information, but there is also a considerable amount that is communicated to the individual by other people or by the mass media, information which in qualitative terms is frequently important in the development of spatial cognition. This is because communicated information is a 'secondary' source of information—it consists of the accounts of the direct sensory experience of *other* people and invariably comes complete with their assessments of places and spaces.

SENSORY EXPERIENCE

Although conventional wisdom holds that there are five basic senses, in reality there are more like ten. Besides taste, smell, sight, and hearing, there are the four tactile or skin senses of pressure, pain, cold, and warmth, and the two body senses of balance (the vestibular sense) and kinesthesis (the sense of movement in any part of the body). These senses have their associated receptor organs which respond to some form of energy, for

Table 4.1 *Sources of information and attraction–avoidance in the urban environment*

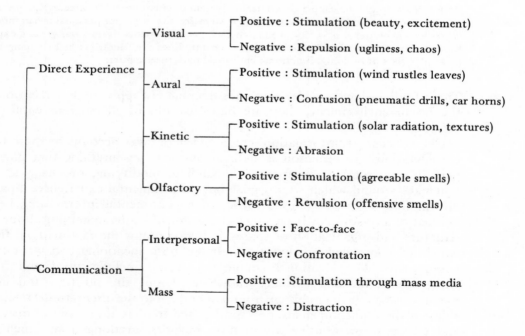

example, the ear to sound waves or the eye to that part of the electromagnetic spectrum known as visible light.[1] This energy is received by sensory receptors and is transformed into neural impulses which are transmitted to the brain by the central nervous system. It is at this stage that the perceptual process begins.

Spatial perception utilizes information that has been produced by the concerted operation of all the senses, with information from one sense being added to, and modified against, that coming from the other senses. This does not, of course, mean that all senses play an equal part in spatial perception. As Figure 4.1 suggests, the detection ranges of the individual senses vary considerably, with only sight, hearing, and smell ('the distance senses') being able to receive stimuli from parts of the spatial environment beyond the tactile zone. Of these, smell has the most limited range, with odours rarely carrying for more than a few hundred metres, whereas the eye is

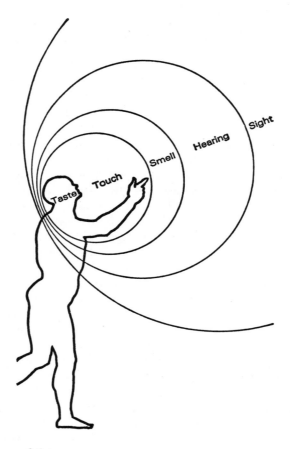

Figure 4.1. The ranges of the senses

Source: Skurnik and George (1967, 14). Copyright © 1964, 1967 by Larry S. Skurnik and Frank George. Reprinted by permission of Penguin Books Ltd.

capable of receiving stimuli from vast distances. Galanter (1962), for example, reported the results of experimental work which showed that on a clear and dark night a single candle flame was visible to the naked eye from a distance of fifty kilometres. The significance of these absolute limits needs to be qualified by the fact that on many occasions smell, hearing, or even tactility could extend the spatial range of the senses far beyond that of the current visual field. This is particularly the case in an urban environment, where the sounds of moving traffic, smells from local factories, or the vibrations experienced from an uneven road surface can provide additional information that, perhaps most significantly, contains a powerful affective component. None the less, it remains true that sight is the most important source of spatial information, with over ninety per cent of human knowledge about the external world being received through our eyes (Dodwell, 1966). Moreover, visual information is recognized to be more precise and detailed than that derived from the other senses, and to be the evidence that people most trust when reaching decisions about the spatial environment. Perception is dominantly visual; seeing is closely linked to believing.

Sight. Human sight represents a near-optimal physiological trade-off between the evolutionary needs for panoramic and stereoscopic vision. Animals that face many predators, such as rabbits or small rodents, rely heavily upon their eyesight to warn them about the approach of their enemies. For example, rabbits have evolved a visual system in which the optic axes of their eyes point laterally, so that their field of vision encompasses wide regions to the back and sides of their bodies. Taken together, the left and right fields of view give a visual angle that comes near to 360°. The advantage of this feature is obvious: the more of the world that is continuously surveyed by the retina, the better will be the warning system. On the other hand, the lack of overlap between the two fields means that the rabbit will not gain the benefits that stem from stereoscopic vision, which allows discrimination of fine differences in depth (Held and Richards, 1972). Stereoscopic vision is thought to have evolved because the complex range of activities of man and the higher primates required accurate estimates to be made of the volume, scale, and relative positions of proximate objects, particularly those that are being manipulated or are about to be manipulated. It operates by virtue of the fact that the eyes of a normal adult are approximately six centimetres apart, which means that each eye has a slightly different view of objects, as illustrated in Figure 4.2. The brain integrates these heavily overlapping images into a three-dimensional view of space. While stereoscopic vision is of limited assistance for objects in the far distance (owing to the relatively small distance between the eyes), it is of great benefit in everyday activities in the proximate environment. Yet it is not an ability that has evolved at the expense of a relatively wide angle of vision. The human visual angle of around 150° still allows the individual to survey a broad field in front of the body.

The human sense of sight provides a wonderfully varied source of sensory

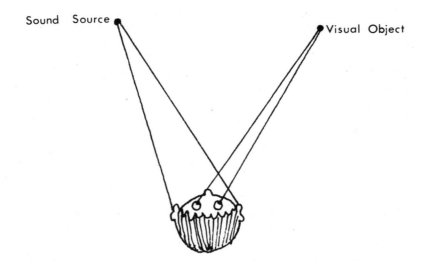

Figure 4.2. Direction-finding in the spatial environment

data about surrounding space, including information about the shape and texture of environmental phenomena, their size and distance from the perceiver, their brightness and colour, and their movement (Schiffman, 1976). Five skills merit particular discussion in this context.

First, human beings have the ability to use visual cues to perceive vertical and horizontal dimensions. Since the external world is fairly stable, people can normally judge the position of an object relative to the horizon or skyline. This supplies a definition of the horizontal; lines perpendicular to this are vertical. Perception of the vertical dimension is also related to the upright position of the body in space, which provides another frame of reference against which the position of objects can be judged.

Second, there is the vital ability to perceive depth and distance. This can be achieved by cues that are apparent to either eye separately (monocular) and by both eyes acting concertedly (the stereoscopic principle discussed above). In many ways, the monocular cues are the more vital, as is shown by the many examples of people who are able to cope perfectly well after losing the sight of one eye, although there may be some loss of efficiency through being deprived of the fine detail that stereoscopic cues provide. Monocular cues will include *inter alia*: interposition, or the rule that where one object blots out another, the latter is presumed to be behind; aerial perspective, where nearer objects are assumed to be less hazy than distant objects; linear perspective, where as distance increases parallel lines appear to converge; light and shade; and the angle of regard, or judging the proximity of an object at ground level by the angle that the individual has to look along to see it.

Third, man has the ability to judge the metric properties of an object accurately regardless of its position in space. If perception were determined solely by the geometry of retinal stimulation, objects would be continually changing in size and shape, yet we see things more or less as they would be if we were touching them. For example, when watching a car drive away, one does not see an object continually diminishing in perspective size as it moves into the distance but as a normal-appearing car. This phenomenon, known as perceptual 'constancy' (Gregory, 1970), is a good example of the difference between what Gibson (1950) termed the 'visual field' and the 'visual world'. In other words, man continuously (and unconsciously) differentiates between the sense impressions that stimulate the retina and what he perceives, which consists of the correction of these data by information derived from other sources.

Fourth, the eyes are able to discern relative movement, which occurs whenever an object moves in relation to some other object. Perception of movement for all creatures has an important biological utility, indeed in many cases it is essential for survival (Schiffman, 1976). The observer is always faced with the problem of deciding which of two objects moved, whether both moved, or whether it was the observer himself who moved. In normal circumstances, the brain can sort this out without difficulty, but as Ross (1974) indicated, illusions can occur, as when one is in novel surroundings or travelling in public transport. For instance, when looking out of the window of a motionless railway carriage standing in a station, it is possible to gain the impression that one's own train is moving when, in point of fact, it is the train on the next line that has started to depart.

Finally, human sight has the property of colour vision. Unlike all animals other than birds and higher primates, man has the ability to perceive and discriminate between lights on the basis of three dimensions: brightness, ranging from white to black; saturation, or the purity of the sensation as opposed to greyness; and hue, which depends on the wavelength composition of the light (McBurney and Collings, 1977). By stimulating colour cells on the retina (whose operations remain a matter for conjecture), information is supplied to the brain about the colour characteristics of external phenomena. The acuteness of human colour vision, with the ability to discern even subtle gradations of colour, lends tone and texture to man's view of the world.

Hearing. The auditory system also provides the means by which the distance and direction of environmental phenomena can be judged. First, an individual can judge distances by the intensity (loudness) of the sounds reaching the ears, which is compared with the intensity one expects, from past experience, the sounds to have. Second, sounds coming from one side of the head reach one ear slightly before the other, owing to the slight difference in distance (see Figure 4.2). This is sufficient information for the brain to locate the direction of a sound source. Most people are able to discriminate the source of sounds to an accuracy of between one to ten degrees of the compass, with an efficiency that varies with the actual direction of the sound, its frequency, and the atmospheric conditions (including competing noises). Auditory localization of an environmental phenomenon, however, is somewhat imprecise and we tend also to rely heavily upon visual cues when judging the exact source of a sound. Perhaps the main informational significance of hearing, therefore, rests in affording elements that vision cannot supply.

First, as we shall see in due course, hearing gives access to information via spoken language, an ability which, as far as is known, is an exclusively human characteristic. Second, hearing brings an affective component to spatial information. As Table 4.1 indicates, sounds can be stimulating, as in the case of the wind rustling piles of leaves, or be confusing and disturbing, as happens when sound becomes classed as 'noise'. From this affective quality flows a mild behavioural element, in that certain sounds bring about attraction to a place and others produce avoidance. In addition, sounds have a mnemonic quality, in that hearing a sound after a long period of time is often sufficient to bring back a series of memories that are somehow attached to this sound. Small wonder then that if this sonic environment is removed, as happens when a person suffers sudden deafness, an essential part of the quality of life disappears (Knapp, 1948).

Despite this, hearing is a relatively neglected aspect of environmental perception. Southworth (1969), for example, showed how evocative sounds could be as part of the sensory experience of cities, but such findings were only produced when subjects were blindfolded to deprive them of vision, the sense that normally would be dominant. Equally, although Banz (1970) suggested that traffic noise would be a source of confusion (see Table 4.1), it is more often the case that, through the process of habituation, such sounds are scarcely noticed.

Smell. Similar conclusions apply to smell, a sense which also has close links with emotion and behaviour. Odours have the power to evoke vivid memories of past scenes and events and act as powerful triggers for avoidance or attraction. Despite this, smell is very much a neglected sense. Hall (1966) speculated that this was a reflection of human evolution. Originally a ground-dwelling animal, man's ancestor was forced by interspecies competition and changes in the environment to desert the ground and take to the trees. Arboreal life called for keen vision, but placed less emphasis on smell, which is crucial for terrestial organisms. In this way, the sense of smell ceased to develop while powers of sight were greatly enhanced. Whatever the truth of this contention, it remains true that smell is neglected by modern man. Society expends considerable time and effort attempting to eliminate odours, with the very word 'smell' coming to connote something unpleasant. Yet as any good gardener or wine-taster knows, the sense of smell can be trained to provide an extremely sensitive source of information. With practice it is possible to discern subtle variations in smell and to attempt detailed classifications of objects or environments.

COMMUNICATION

Interaction with others provides most of our knowledge about the wider world beyond the range of our everyday living and working environments. For places that we have never, or have only seldom, visited, we are dependent upon the information that others provide or that can be gleaned from the mass media. Such information contains both locational and attributive elements, informing the recipient about the contents of space replete with the communicator's views about the attributes of geographical locations and areas.

Before looking at the nature of the information that is being communicated, (known as 'content'), it is as well to know a little more about the communication process. Communication takes two forms: transfer of information through face-to-face groups, termed 'interpersonal communication'; and transmission of information by means of the technological devices of the mass media, (press, radio, films, and so on), known as 'mass communication' (Janowitz, 1968). The key differences between these two types of communication lies in the relationships between the communicator(s) and the audience. The technological agencies of the mass media allow the sender to reach an audience beyond the range of sight and earshot, bringing about contact between individuals and groups separated by space and often by time. In addition, mass communication is generally a one-way movement of information. The return flow of information that takes place so readily in the case of interpersonal communication, in the form of a reply, or facial expression, or gesture, occurs only slowly and ponderously with mass media.

None the less, these forms of communication are not mutually exclusive. This point is illustrated by Figure 4.3, which demonstrates the way that thinking about the mass media has changed over the years. Although mass-communication researchers once believed that the mass media could exert a direct influence upon the attitudes and behaviour of large numbers of people (see Figure 4.3a), this view has been subsequently modified. It was first changed by including the role of interpersonal communication in the form of influential people known as 'opinion leaders', who would absorb media content and then pass on their impressions of it to a wider audience (Lazarsfeld *et al.*, 1944). In turn, while this view (Figure 4.3b) was considered to be an improvement, it was also found to be too rigid. Most researchers would now select some form of multi-step flow model (Figure 4.3c), which is less restrictive than the earlier models and makes fewer assumptions about the way information reaches its ultimate audience. In addition, it permits inclusion of the fact that mass media and interpersonal contacts can perform complementary functions in the flow of spatial information. Available evidence, for example, would certainly suggest that mass media can often be instrumental in spreading awareness of a piece of information, whilst interpersonal channels are the means of which that person is convinced or persuaded that the message conveyed by this piece of information is one worth adopting.

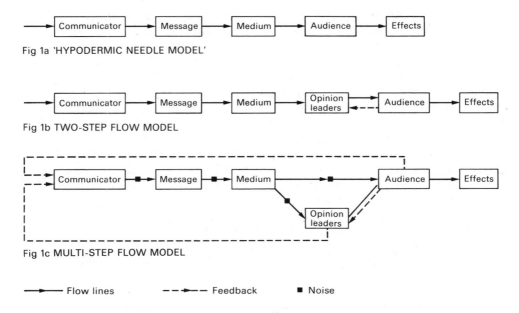

Fig 1a 'HYPODERMIC NEEDLE MODEL'

Fig 1b TWO-STEP FLOW MODEL

Fig 1c MULTI-STEP FLOW MODEL

→ Flow lines　— — ►— — Feedback　■ Noise

Figure 4.3. Models employed in mass communication research

Source: Gold (1974, 10).

It is also possible to subsume mass and interpersonal communication within the same framework by using the well-known paradigm put forward by Lasswell (1966):

> *Who*
> Says *What*
> In *Which Channel*
> To *Whom*
> With *What Effect*

The 'who' are those who communicate (communicators), the 'what' is the message or content, the 'channel' is the medium of communication, the 'whom' is the audience, and the 'effect' is indicated by the impact (if any) on the attitudes or behaviour of the audience. Using this framework, spatial information may be regarded as a specific type of communicated content, which is devised by a communicator or group of communicators and placed in a suitable form for communication. In devising content, the communicator will normally select those bits of information that he deems will best suit his audience and will shape them into a presentable form. In doing so, the communicator will automatically impart his own slant upon the information, deliberately or inadvertently. Whether or not this slant is accepted will depend on a variety of factors. It will be affected by the perceived status and reliability of the communicator, the conditions under which communication takes place, and the nature of the information. With regard to the latter, it is well known that content has greatest effect when it reinforces what the audience already knows or elucidates a topic on which the recipient has little or no knowledge (McQuail, 1972).

In the case of interpersonal communication, content will include all aspects of conversational behaviour that impart information, which will incorporate all purposive uses of languages as well as involuntary exclamations, movements, and gestures. A jerk of the thumb to signify 'over there' can often be as informative as several minutes' speech. Spatial information in interpersonal situations may be directly elicited, as when one is asking directions, but just as often derives from chance or incidental remarks, such as when one adds spatial details to a narrative to give the audience a frame of reference.

Empirical data about the diffusion of spatial information by interpersonal communication are hard to come by, partly reflecting a lack of substantive research in this field and partly reflecting basic weaknesses in interpersonal communication research as a whole (Williams, 1977), but it is possible to discern three relevant areas in which interpersonal communication has a significant role. First, interpersonal communication will be identified as an important informational source in the learning process that occurs whenever an individual searches for a suitable solution to a locational problem. Second, interpersonal communication is instrumental in conveying socially accepted standards about the use of space, a matter which will arise when discussing such issues as human crowding, privacy, and territoriality. Third, interpersonal communication will be seen to be of great significance in the process by which socio-cultural attachments to space are passed from one generation to the next.

In the case of mass communication, there is little doubt that the media now play a greater role in disseminating spatial information than ever before. The exponential growth of media systems over the last fifty years has drastically increased the amount and quality of spatial information. Whether or not one subscribes to McLuhan's ideas about the 'global village',[2] the mass media have unquestionably expanded global awareness. Czechoslovakia, a country which could be considered 'small and faraway' in 1938, somehow seemed much closer in 1968.

The role of mass communication in the diffusion of spatial information has been discussed by the present author extensively elsewhere (Gold, 1974, 1976a); hence a brief summary will suffice here. Besides the usual formal sources of geographical information, such as atlases and wall maps, content may be carried by media as diverse as newspapers, films, postage stamps, road signs, paintings, and romantic novels—in short, the full range of things that Wright (1947) regarded as 'informal sources' of geographical knowledge. In recent years, there has been considerable, if highly disaggregated, research carried out into the nature, properties, and content of such media. For example, with regard to content, one may find studies on such varied topics as signs (Ashley *et al.*, 1971; Venturi *et al.*, 1977), landscape portraits

(Rees, 1975, 1976a, 1976b), regional novels (Gilbert, 1960; Cook, 1974; Shin, 1976), maps (Board, 1967; Gombrich, 1975), town-development promotional literature (Gold, 1974, 1977b; Goodey, 1974a), urban poetry (Paterson, 1976), even the landscape of fictional fantasies (Porteous, 1975). Indeed, the long-running British radio serial *The Archers*, which surely must have coloured images of rural life for many townsfolk, has contained enough (spurious) spatial information over the years for a complete map of the village of Ambridge and its environs to be drawn (Figure 4.4).

The selectivity that is always present in the spatial information propagated by the mass media reflects the motives of the communicator and his assessment of the needs of the audience. Such selectivity will fall into one or more of three categories. First, there is deliberate manipulation of content to produce a specific message. This may be seen in the type of promotional literature that has been used to encourage migrants to new areas, either to try to convey a favourable picture of a particular town or region or to counter popular stereotypes about it (see Chapter 9). Second, there is incidental selectivity in which spatial bias enters as a by-product of other aims. Good examples of this tendency are to be found in the topological maps[3] employed by railway and airline systems throughout the world. These are intended to assist the traveller by simplifying the network and indicating places at which the passenger has to change trains or aircraft, but in doing so may be interpreted (erroneously) as containing information about distance and direction. Third, there are the inadvertent biases that enter communicated content as a result of the limited world-view of the communicator. Any communicator, from the specialist staff-member of a large advertising agency to the humblest reporter on a local newspaper, will have his own outlook on geographical space and will draw upon it to produce content.

The selectivity that is imparted to content by the communicator is matched by that which is present in the way the audience receives and interprets such information. As pointed out earlier, people tend to be most receptive to content that reinforces or elucidates their existing views and outlook, a characteristic that would appear to apply as much to geographical space as to any other topic. Klapper (1960) described three 'self-protective' measures by which individuals defend themselves from 'unsympathetic content'. In the first place, there is 'selective exposure', whereby the individual, consciously or unconsciously, chooses to attend or subscribe only to those media that concentrate upon those areas and places in which he is interested. Secondly, 'selective perception' means that he may fail to perceive content that does not accord to his own spatial knowledge. Thirdly, 'selective retention' means that he will forget unsympathetic content more quickly than that which reinforces his preconceptions of spatial environments.

The main conclusion that may be drawn from these arguments is that the mass media will communicate spatial information most effectively when content supports rather than challenges prior knowledge. The only area where it is likely to be instrumental in moulding spatial schemata will be with regard to what Goodey (1971) termed 'far places', zones that the

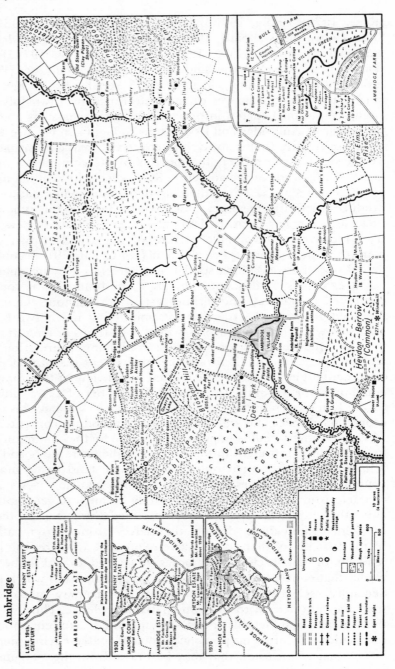

Figure 4.4. Ambridge

Source: Compiled by Turnock for the BBC (1975, 6–7).

individual has never visited and about which his knowledge is either patchy or non-existent. In such circumstances, the mass media can be instrumental in supplying the individual with the information that can form the basis of highly stereotyped images of space. These 'far places' will normally be remote in the sense of geographical distance, but this is not invariably the case. The inhabitants of Latin American shanty towns, for example, often live within a few miles of rich and exclusive suburbs, yet their knowledge of those places is sometimes derived more from 'escapist' television programmes about the trials and tribulations of the urban rich than by personal experience (Wolf and Hansen, 1172). In other words, 'social distance' can have precisely the same effect as geographical distance.

To pursue such themes further, however, it is necessary first to know something about the way that meaning is imparted to space by the recipients of spatial information. It is to this matter that we now turn.

5   The Emergent View: Some Influences upon the Formation of Images and Spatial Schemata

Nor yet do the things themselves enter in; only the images of the things perceived are there in readiness for thought to recall. Which images? how are they formed? who can tell .. ?

(ST. AUGUSTINE, *The Confessions*)

The aim of this chapter is to consider some broad influences upon the process by which meaning is attributed to geographical space. 'Meaning', of course, is a word that is hard to define. In their book *The Meaning of Meaning*, Ogden and Richards (1949) traced at least sixteen different uses of the term in philosophical literature, although even this list was far from exhaustive (Jencks, 1969). In this text, meaning will be defined as the property that, when acquired, 'clothes the perceptual world' (Beck, 1970, 136). It will be argued that it is primarily acquired by learning, both by the child's active exploration of his surroundings and through communication of socio-cultural conventions about the function and use of space. The meaning of space will be regarded as being closely linked to motivation, in that the individual invests the spatial environment with meaning according to his own needs.

The first part of this chapter explains why the role of environmental learning, rather than instinct theory, is emphasized. The next part considers the progress that has been made towards producing an integrated theory of the development of spatial cognition. While no comprehensive theory is as yet available, it will be seen that the basic requirements for such a theory could be found by extending the micro-scale studies of developmental psychologists. The third section considers the influence of social and cultural groups on the individual's view of space.

NATURE OR NURTURE?

The debate about whether hereditary factors or environmental learning may be said to be the more potent force in shaping human cognition is one of the oldest and least conclusive in the history of psychology (Boring, 1942). This 'nature–nurture' controversy has classical origins, but in its present form may be traced back to the early twentieth century. Early psychology was dominated by the view that human and animal behaviour could largely be explained by reference to instincts—innate patterns of activity believed to be universal in a species (Baron *et al.*, 1977). Perhaps the fullest version of this view was to be found in the writings of McDougall (1908), who contended that almost all human behaviour, including complex social interactions, could be explained by the operation of specific instincts. This notion, however, was soon to be challenged by behaviourism, which argued that each child was born equal but became different as the result of environmental experience. Watson (1924), the founder of behaviourism, argued that the child's mind at birth was like a 'tabula rasa', a blank slate upon which would be written the learning that was attributable to S–R relationships.

The development of this particular controversy lies beyond the scope of this book, but we may note that the evidence has strongly supported the empiricist standpoint, which maintains that the differences in the mental or behavioural characteristics of individuals are due to environmental experience. The gist of the argument may be gained by considering the example of the perceptual 'laws' propounded by Gestalt psychologists, a notable area of early research on perception. Gestaltists believed that the brain had innate self-organizing tendencies and tried to explain perception and other cognitive processes in these terms. They believed that the first stage in perception was the ability to distinguish the 'figure' (pattern, *Gestalt*) from the 'ground' (background). From their experimental work, the Gestaltists put forward a series of principles by which such pattern recognition takes place, three of which are illustrated in Figure 5.1. According to the *proximity* principle, demonstrated in Figure 5.1(a), elements that are close together are perceived as a group, and so one sees five columns of dots rather than five rows. *Similarity* is illustrated by Figure 5.1(b), in which a pattern of alternate rows of dots and crosses is seen rather than columns of intermingled dots and crosses. Figure 5.1(c) provides an instance of the principle of *good continuation*, where the figure is usually seen as two intersecting lines of dots rather than two 'V'-shaped figures that share a common base.

These and the other Gestalt principles of perceptual organization were long accepted by psychologists as being innate, but it was an acceptance

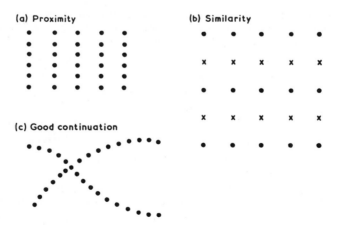

Figure 5.1. Examples of perceptual grouping

Source: Barber and Legge (1976, 27). By permission of Methuen & Co. Ltd.

based on the intuitive plausibility of these principles rather than one based upon extensive testing. When they were analysed in depth, the evidence was unfavourable. *Ceteris paribus*, if these self-organizing tendencies were innate, it might be expected that there would be broad similarities between the perceptual abilities of individuals and that whatever variations do exist owing to environmental learning will cause increasing divergence between individuals as they get older. This has proved not to be the case. Cross-cultural studies have revealed considerable interpersonal differences when comparing adult subjects of similar educational levels (Schwitzgebel, 1962); Vernon (1971) showed that adults within the same culture show differences according to intelligence and education; and Elkind and Scott (1962) that children are less able to differentiate figure from ground than are adults. Indeed in his study, Bower (1965) reported that the supposedly innate principle of proximity did not appear in the perceptual competence of children until the age of one, a finding supported by the extensive research of Brunswik (1956).

It would therefore seem that an alternative explanation is necessary. Rather than being innate, the perceptual abilities studied by the Gestaltists are largely acquired by individuals in early childhood, particularly in the preverbal stage of development. Perceiving objects or shapes as holistic figures against a ground reflects the fact that we learn to allocate them to a specific category of objects or shapes with which we are familiar (Vernon, 1971). The main failing of the Gestaltists was that they focused on the broad similarities to be found in the fundamental perceptual abilities of a limited range of mature adult subjects and ascribed these to genetic factors. In doing so, they indulged in the type of circular logic that was succinctly summarized by Baron *et al.* (1977, 587–8) in the following manner:

First, the widespread occurrence of a given pattern of behaviour was taken as evidence for the existence of a corresponding instinct. Then, in what can only be described as a dazzling display of mental gymnastics, this hypothesised instinct was employed as an explanation for the occurrence of the behaviour in question.

Two qualifications must be made, however, to the view that perception is essentially acquired by learning. First, there should be no attempt to deny that instinct does play a role in perception. Experimental work (see, e.g. Bower *et al.*, 1971; Gibson and Walk, 1960) has suggested that perception of distance and depth—two abilities which appear to have an evolutionary significance—are present in even the youngest children and may well be innate. Second, although nativist arguments are periodically written off, it is important not to underestimate their vitality or potential contribution. The next chapter, for example, will discuss the 'nature–nurture controversy' with respect to territoriality, an area of inquiry initiated by researchers who applied perspectives derived from animal behaviour, considered to be predominantly instinctive, to human contexts. Although their interpretations are questionable, there is no doubt that the debate has been constructive and that the basic ideas are, at least, worth considering. This last point is important, for there has been a tendency in recent years for the nativist viewpoint to fall into disrepute for reasons not wholly connected with psychological theory.[1] It in no way contradicts the idea that human cognition develops primarily by learning to maintain that there is a need to establish a better balance between nativist and empiricist arguments, and not to dismiss the former out of hand for *a priori* theoretical or ideological reasons.

THE DEVELOPMENT OF THE CHILD'S VIEW OF SPACE

Taking as our starting-point the assumption that spatial cognition is derived from learning, the first task is to explain how this learning is accomplished. The research that is currently available contains few real insights. The approach favoured by psychologists has been laboratory analysis of spatial learning, carried out in a 'detailed, precise and fine-grained manner' (Murdock, 1973) and at micro-scale. Much less is known about spatial learning in larger-scale environmental contexts, although two promising lines of inquiry have recently emerged.

First, considerable attention has been devoted to a paper by Tolman (1948) entitled 'Cognitive Maps in Rats and Men' (but which was mainly about rats). This put forward the idea that rats built up over time, by a complex series of psychological processes, 'cognitive maps' which enabled them to steer their way about their environments. Tolman explained the establishment of a 'cognitive map' by means of field theory (see Chapter 2), whereby information would be selectively extracted from the environment by the rat in order to build up a field-like map of that environment. The rat's brain was compared to the central office of a map-making agency:

> The stimuli, which are allowed in, are not connected by just simple one-to-one switches to the outgoing responses. Rather, the incoming impulses are usually worked over and elaborated in the central control room into a tentative, cognitive-like map of the environment. And it is this tentative map, indicating routes and paths and environmental relationships, which finally determines what responses, if any, the animal will finally release.   (Tolman, 1973 edn., 31)

The concept of the 'cognitive map' (otherwise known as the 'mental map') was widely taken up by behavioural geographers and others, but has suffered from two questionable assumptions. In the first place, many have assumed that the analogy of a map that Tolman used meant that people actually do have cartographic representations of the environment in their heads. Downs (1976) suggested that this needed to be countered by laying stress upon the process of mapping rather than the product (the map itself), but it is easy to see that considerable conceptual ambiguity still exists. Secondly, it has been commonly assumed that 'maps in the head' may be externally represented by asking people to draw or respond to cartographic maps. As will be seen later, ability to draw or comment upon map material depends heavily upon education and thus a subject's responses to cognitive mapping exercises may be an imperfect representation of his spatial cognition.

Despite these reservations, useful insights into spatial learning are available from those cognitive mapping studies that have examined the spatial knowledge of children at particular stages in their development. Examples are to be found in the work of Ladd (1970) and Maurer and Baxter (1972) who identified the effect of ethnic group upon the known world of children, of Gould (1973) on the differences encountered when comparing children of different ages, by Saarinen (1973a) on the macro-spatial knowledge of students, and by Spencer and Lloyd (1974) who examined the way that children of mixed age-ranges perceived the same environment (Small Heath, Birmingham). The last study in particular provided a means to investigate the differences in spatial knowledge and ability to represent space that comes with age, a method which would reward replication elsewhere.

The other approach that has shown great promise has been to examine the insights available from existing general theories of cognitive development. Developmental psychology, the branch of psychology directly concerned with the intellectual development of the child, contains a number of theories that provide insight into the way children come to know space, the most notable being those associated with Piaget and Werner (and their respective groups of associates).[2] Their theories share three common characteristics. First, they were based upon the evidence of extensive empirical studies and systematic observations of child behaviour and intellectual growth. Second, both theories stated that as the child grows older, he will have a view of space that is qualitatively different from when he was younger. In other words, spatial learning is not just a question of acquiring more spatial information, it also involves deriving more sophisticated schemata in which to organize this information. Third, these theories were primarily related to micro-space, with little attempt to apply them to larger-scale environments. None the less, there are several writers who consider that these theories may be extended in this manner.

Probably the fullest statement of this view is to be found in the work of Moore. In an early paper, Hart and Moore (1973) had proposed a framework within which the theories of Piaget and Werner, with their varying terminology and initial premises, could be aligned, and suggested that this framework could be applied to macro-spatial contexts. Moore (1976) further refined it in a subsequent paper which is worth considering in greater detail.

From a review of developmental psychological literature, Moore suggested six basic postulates for an environmental theory. First, it was argued that spatial knowledge neither was innate nor consisted simply of passive copying of reality, but was gained by an individual actively constructing his view of reality through his contact with the world. Second, spatial cognition was held to develop from the dynamic interaction between the internal mental characteristics that a person brought to a situation and the demands the situation made upon that individual. Third, Moore emphasized the central role that the child's active exploration of the environment and his transactions with the environment played in the learning process, with cognition arising out of these transactions. Fourth, it was maintained that spatial knowledge was built upon existing cognitive structures, meaning that cognition will be strongly influenced by past experience. Fifth, it was considered that there would be qualitative as well as quantitative changes in a child's spatial cognition over time, with more complex structures replacing the simpler ones of earlier years. Lastly, it was argued that it would only be by comprehending the process by which development came about that we would understand the mature forms of spatial knowledge.

Moore's theory proceeded from this basis. The key to the learning process was the Piagetian concept of adaptation, which included development from lower modes of biological and reflexive functioning, through action-oriented and perceptual functioning, to higher modes of conceptual and symbolic functioning. Although adaptation is intrinsic to all human beings, it is not intelligence itself that is inherited but a mode of intellectual functioning composed of two 'functional invariates'—'assimilation' (the process by which the individual forms schemata of the outside world) and 'accommodation' (the readjustment of schemata to cope with assimilation). This process is summarized in Figure 5.2, in which assimilation and accommodation are the two essential ingredients of successful adaptation. They work continuously to produce changes in the child's conception of the world or his reaction to it. The state of balance between assimilation and accommodation is called equilibrium, which is necessary both to stop the child from being over-whelmed by new experiences and to prevent him from over-reaching himself

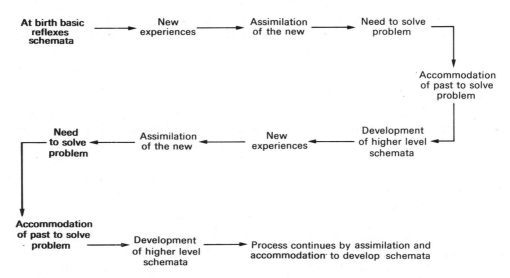

Figure 5.2. Piaget's theory of the development of schemata

Source: Kaluger and Kaluger (1974, 75).

in attempt to accommodate an environment that is changing too rapidly (Pulaski, 1971, quoted in Papalia and Olds, 1975).

The initial framework that Hart and Moore (1973) had devised is summarized in Figure 5.3. This framework relied heavily upon the work of Piaget, who regarded cognitive development as taking place in an invariate sequence of stages which occurred at more or less the same age amongst normal children. There were three such stages, each divided into two or more sub-stages. Broadly, from birth until the age of two, the child goes through the *sensorimotor* period, in which he can visualize things only in terms of actions that are performed upon them. By the end of the sensorimotor period, the child will have formed the basis of schemata for the small and disaggregated spaces in which he lives. He will view space egocentrically and will have a rudimentary concept of distance and direction, but will lack the ability to represent space conceptually. This skill dawns in the *concrete operations* period, with its two sub-stages, the pre-operational stage (lasting from the age of two until seven) and the concrete operations stage (seven until eleven).[3] In this period, the child can conceive of space apart from actions, but his thinking will still be tied to real or represented objects. At first spatial knowledge will consist of intuitive, unco-ordinated images of the world based on memories of previously manipulated or perceived objects, but he will develop representation based upon real or symbolized objects. In the third period of *formal operations*, the child will gain the ability to conceive of space entirely in the abstract without these representations being dependent upon real actions, objects, or spaces.

There is also a developmental sequence in the way that the child learns to construct spatial relations. As Figure 5.3 suggests, the child will progressively learn to construct space according to topological, projective, and Euclidean principles. From the age of two onwards, the child will gradually learn to master topological principles, which are concerned with such qualitative relationships as proximity and separation, order, and whether things are open or closed. Topological principles are later supplemented by projective and Euclidean principles. Projective space introduces perspective and the interrelationships of objects seen from different viewpoints. It develops from the age of three and understanding of it evolves alongside that of topological space, although it is not until the age of eleven or twelve that the child fully learns how to co-ordinate perspectives. Euclidean principles emerge from the age of four onwards and develop over a period of about a decade. The child gradually recognizes the metric properties of space including rectilinear co-ordinates, accuracy of distance, and proportional reduction to scale. By the end of the formal operations period, the child will have attained a co-ordinated reference system which incorporates Euclidean principles alongside topological and projective.

This framework was proposed as the basis for comprehending the way that children came to terms with either micro- or larger-scale spatial environments. Subsequently, with the aid of some exploratory empirical testing, this was extended into a framework that could also be applied to the way

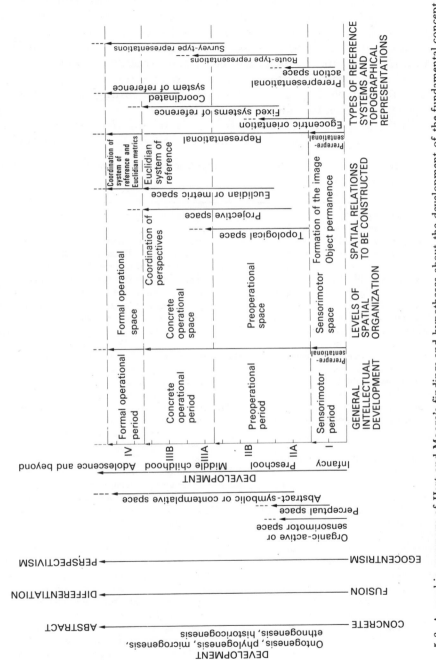

Figure 5.3. A graphic summary of Hart and Moore's findings and hypotheses about the development of the fundamental concept of space and of macro-spatial cognition.

The left side of the chart shows three of the principal dimensions of development along which environmental cognition may be analyzed. The next three columns summarize the findings of Piaget and others on the development of the fundamental concept of space in relation to general cognitive development. The columns on the far right show some of the hypotheses linked to cognition of large-scale environments.

Source: Moore (1976, 149). Copyright © 1976 by Dowden, Hutchinson & Ross, and used with their permission.

that adults learn about new spatial environments (outlined in Table 5.1). There are three stages in the process. In the first, the elements included in the mental representations of the child or the adult were considered to be those of great personal significance. The individual's spatial cognition is egocentric and undifferentiated, in the sense that all information is assimilated according to one viewpoint in which differences and variability in the subject matter are not recognized. Information is viewed in terms of its practical (activity) significance, with positions located mainly through egocentric, sequential, and topological relations.

In the second stage, the environment is organized into groups or clusters of elements, but the groups are not related to one another. The internal

Table 5.1. *General framework for the developmental ordering of cognitive representations*

I. Undifferentiated concrete egocentric
This level includes primitive symbolic representations characterized by:
   a. Lack of differentiation, i.e., all information is assimilated to one undifferentiated viewpoint and differences and variability in the subject matter are not recognized.
   b. Complete egocentrism, i.e., an exclusive conception of all information from one's own egocentric point of view.
   c. Predominance of concrete references, i.e., systematic relations among the elements of the representation are lacking.
   d. Lack of overall organization, i.e., systematic relations among the elements of the representation are lacking.

II. Differentiated and partially coordinated into fixed subgroups
This level includes intermediate symbolic representations characterized by:
   a. Differentiation without integration, i.e., differences and variability are recognized and aspects of the representation are differentiated from each other but are not integrated into an overall structure.
   b. Partial decentering but partially continuing egocentrism, i.e., decentering from own point of view on some but not all aspects and subsequent centering or focusing on some aspects from other points of view.
   c. Concrete and abstract references, i.e., some aspects seen in strictly concrete

terms while others are seen in abstract terms.
   d. Partial coordination into fixed subgroups, i.e., some but not necessarily all information is brought together into partial subgroups, such that the organization of this information within different subgroups is at a higher level than the organization or partial coordination between subgroups.

III. Operationally coordinated and hierarchically integrated
This level includes highly organized representations characterized by:
   a. Differentiation and hierarchic integration, i.e., aspects and points of view are clearly differentiated from each other and are integrated into an overall structure.
   b. Complete decentering and coordination, i.e., decentering from own point of view on most aspects and subsequent coordination of multiple points of view.
   c. Predominance of abstract references, i.e., subject matter information and resultant aspects of the representation are seen in abstract terms.
   d. High degree of overall organization, i.e., most information is brought together into subgroups and the subgroups are hierarchically integrated into an abstractly conceived structure wherein the subgroups are subordinated to the total organization of the representation.

Source: Moore (1976, 154).

organization of the groupings is often based on functional similarity or topological proximities, on the use of projective relations (especially left–right and in front–behind) and occasionally with regard to relative distance. No co-ordinate system is employed to link the clusters.

In the third stage, an overall system of reference is constructed for the co-ordination of viewpoints and of relative distances. This co-ordination is no longer tied to the subject's own actions; he will now be able to describe actions and movements in terms of a systematic abstracted reference system, rather than the reference system being described in terms of concrete actions.

All three of these stages were related to supporting evidence from studies of urban cognition, for both adults and children, and it was also suggested that much the same three-stage development sequence could be applied to other phenomenal domains. These matters, however, lie outside our current concern. With regard to the initial and subsequent extended frameworks put forward by Moore, these mark a bold attempt to integrate work on spatial cognition into the general paradigm of developmental psychology, although there are a variety of criticisms which can be made.

On the one hand, there are the criticisms that have been directed at the developmental theories on which they are based. Piagetian theory, for example, has been criticized *inter alia* for its emphasis on adaptation, for the 'mechanical' nature of the developmental sequence, on its assumptions about the relationship between cognition and reality, about whether Euclidean principles are actually necessary in learning to represent space, and about the fact that little testing and replication has taken place independently of Piaget and his colleagues.[4]

On the other hand, there are the criticisms that stem from Moore's contentions that individuals come to terms with larger-scale environments in the same manner as with micro-space and that adult spatial learning may be subsumed within the same framework as that of children. There are doubts on both scores. With regard to different scales of space, it must be pointed out that there are two important factors that will influence cognition. In the first place, the informational basis of macro-scale schemata, dependent primarily upon communicated information, will be different to that of micro-space, where direct sensory experience dominates. Secondly, the attachment to micro-space is quite different to that of larger-scale environments. Having argued that cognitive processes are motivated, it would seem inevitable that larger-scale environments will be allotted a quite different meaning as compared with micro-space. Similarly, the contention that adult learning would follow the same generalized sequence as that for children must be open to question. Adult cognition has a much greater inferential capability than is found in children, which might well produce qualitative differences in the developmental process.

Perhaps the best policy is to accept Moore's general approach without necessarily adopting his particular developmental scheme (Pick, 1976). Already several writers have adopted developmental theory to examine large-scale spatial environments (Acredolo, 1976; Beck and Wood, 1976; Kates and Katz, 1977) and other work is reported as being in progress (Banerjee and Lynch, 1977). Collectively, these studies point to a highly promising approach to problems of spatial learning. Indeed the force of this conclusion would be little diminished even if it should transpire that there are funda-mental differences between micro–macro or child–adult cognition, for it would be extremely profitable to know where these differences lie.

SOCIO-CULTURAL INFLUENCES

So far the discussion of the child's spatial cognitive development has pro-ceeded without any real mention of the socio-cultural matrix in which the individual grows to maturity, an omission which must now be rectified. Every society has its own rules and conventions about how space is regarded and used by its members. These rules will have been derived over time by the strivings of members of that society to come to terms with their spatial environment and are conditioned by that group's own distinctive way of looking at the world. As such, they cover a multitude of situations that have a spatial dimension, for example, laying down standards for coping with such matters as crowding, privacy, and territoriality (see the following chapter), propagating broad values and aesthetic tastes, and conveying particular attachments to spaces and places.

The preservation of a society, its culture, and its patterns of organization depend upon the young learning and accepting these rules and conventions. These are mainly acquired in early childhood, primarily through the agency of the family but also from elders living in the locality, peer groups (children of similar age and social class), and such institutions as the Church, schools, and the mass media. The process by which this transfer takes place is known as 'socialization'—the name given to the operation of socio-cultural forces that lead a child to think and act in a manner that is acceptable to the social group with which he wishes to identify. In effect socialization performs a dual function, simultaneously preparing the individual for the roles that he will play in society and communicating and perpetuating the culture from one generation to the next (Chinoy, 1967). As might be expected, socializa-tion is an inherently conservative process which discourages excessive deviation or innovation.

The role of socialization in bringing individual spatial cognition into line with the outlook of the wider community was demonstrated by a cross-cultural research programme carried out under the auspices of the United Nations Educational, Scientific and Cultural Organisation (Lynch, 1977). The project supplied comparative analyses of the way that young adoles-cents living in Argentina (Salta), Australia (Melbourne), Poland (Cracow and Warsaw), and Mexico (Ecatepec and Toluca) used and valued their spatial environments. All lived in low-income areas, in homes that were limited in space and often lacked basic amenities. Despite the differences in culture and in the physical character of these residential areas, similar findings emerged. It was clear that the neighbourhood played an important part in adolescent life and that parents, neighbours, and playmates all had their impact upon the development of spatial cognition. Children quickly come to learn the social meaning of space, although their outward degree of acceptance of group attachments to place or taboos will itself reflect the stage of the socialization process the children had reached. All the children studied in this project were in the final stages of socialization prior to being formally admitted into adult society, but breaking into that society is a difficult and frustrating process. When this goal is achieved, it was argued that they will use and value their environment in a manner quite different from when adolescents, for:

adolescent ecology is quite different, and insulated, from that of adults . . . . The lack of opportunities to participate in adult society, or be responsible for shaping and managing the environment, leads to apathy and alienation with place and community. Where such opportunities exist, even minimal ones, place and community both become much more personal to the adolescent.   (Banerjee and Lynch, 1977, 122)

The major form in which society's socializing outlook on space is communicated to the individual adolescent, or to the newcomer to an area, is the symbol. Derived from the Greek word *symbolon* (token), a symbol may be applied to anything that stands for something else. While the term may be applied to a vast range of phenomena (Douglas, 1970), the symbol always has two important properties. First, by definition a symbol always has a latent (hidden) as well as a manifest (surface) meaning. To give an example, a street-corner has a manifest meaning as a physical entity, but may well have a latent meaning as a meeting-point for a gang of youths, or as a point at which individuals make navigational decisions in the course of particular journeys, or as a location that marks the boundary of a particular neighbourhood. Second, the latent meaning of a symbol will generally be specific to a particular group or culture. A good example may be found in the use of metaphor in spoken language, with language itself being a system of communication that relies heavily upon symbols. The architect Jencks (1969), for instance, recalled an occasion when, whilst travelling through France with a native French-speaker, his companion suddenly announced '*jetez un coup d'oeil sur cette flèche*' on spying the distant spire of an ancient cathedral. This phrase, literally translated as 'throw a blow of eye on top of that spire', was part of normal speech for the speaker but had a different meaning for the listener, who was unfamiliar with the metaphor and was left wondering how his eyeball could be detached in the manner suggested!

In terms of spatial psychology, the role of symbols will be considered in two contexts. First, spatial knowledge is influenced, as well as being expressed, by the symbols that are contained within language. This may best be understood by reference to the semiological triangle[5] shown in Figure 5.4, which conveys the relationship between thought, reality, and linguistic symbols. This diagram is in no way intended to indicate causal relationships between elements,[6] but does depict lines of influence, whereby linguistic symbols are influenced by the group's view of the world and vice versa.

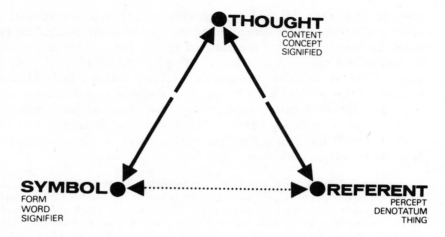

Figure 5.4. The semiological triangle

Source: Adapted from Jencks (1969, 15).

This interrelationship has been repeatedly shown by research carried out by cognitive anthropologists (Tyler, 1969) on the subject of linguistic relativity. Linguistic relativity holds that people living in different environments develop specialized vocabularies in line with their varying experiences and needs (Cole and Scribner, 1974). The Hopi Indians, for example, have a single word that they apply to all flying things other than birds (airplanes, aviators, insects) whereas there are separate words for them in English. By contrast, Eskimo languages contain a number of words that describe conditions covered by the single English word 'snow', although it is noticeable that English-speakers have started to use French Alpine terms such as *piste* and *névé* in order to cope with the linguistic needs associated with winter sports. These examples show the link between environmental experience and vocabulary, and indicate the intimate connection between people and space. The symbols embodied in language are, at the very least, a strong clue to the way a particular people thinks about its spatial environment.

Second, places and spaces themselves serve as symbols for the people of particular cultures. This theme will recur continually in this text. The home, the neighbourhood, a landscape, a city, or a nation-state can all be endowed with a symbolic meaning which transcends their characteristics as physical entities. To take the example of cities serving as symbols, one has many instances of cities serving as places of sanctity in the religious history of a people (Mecca, Jerusalem, Bethlehem), or as expressions of fine arts and culture (Paris, Vienna, Salzburg), or as created centres for countries that previously had only peripheries (Canberra, Brasilia), or as the embodiment of nationalist strivings (the reconstructed Warsaw). In each case, the city stands for a complex set of ideas that encapsulate aspects of the past experience, present outlook, or future aspirations of a people and that may be evoked at the mere mention of a place. Moreover, the concrete reality of the town or city gives a tangible expression to ideas that are deeply felt but difficult to articulate. In this way, spatial symbols may be said to transform a people's 'vague emotions, incoherent impulses and awareness into a commonwealth of feelings, a cohesive common consciousness and collective action' (Barbu, 1971, 98). They are an essential part of the survival of cultures and supply common bonds about which the outsider has little inkling.

CONCLUSION

In Part Two, we have examined the available sources of spatial information and have examined the factors influencing the way that it is fashioned into meaningful spatial knowledge. We have seen that perception is based upon, although not determined by, the information supplied by direct sensory experience and from communication. This raw material is then assimilated and integrated into coherent mental representations of geographical space by the operation of a set of cognitive abilities which are primarily learned. In other words, while it is possible that there are a few basic perceptual skills that are innate, the key to the development of spatial cognition is environmental learning. This learning occurs primarily over the first fifteen years of life, during which time the child acquires, through an orderly sequence of stages, a detailed and co-ordinated view of space. Over time, there will be both quantitative and qualitative changes in spatial knowledge, with the child gradually learning to orient himself in relation to the places and areas in his spatial environment. In part the child's spatial knowledge will be a product of his own active exploration of his environment, but it will also bear the imprint of the social and cultural groups to which he belongs.

The task of Part Three will be to throw light upon the nature and character of the mental representations of geographical space that are so formed.

PART THREE

SPATIAL COGNITION

6 Micro-Space: The Cognitive Significance of Territory

There is a certain etiquette in connection with the retaining of seats which it is considered both rude and unjust to disregard. Thus, the placing of a coat, a book, a newspaper, or any other article, on the seat of a carriage is intended as a token that such a place is engaged. This principle is to be acted on in the retaining of seats, and, whatever the number you require, should have deposited conspicuously upon them anything that comes to hand. This system of occupation by proxy refers, however, more especially to the first-class. With the majority of travellers by second or third class this delicate intimation does not appear to be understood, or, if understood, not recognised.

(ANON., *The Railway Traveller's Handy Book*, 1862)

Micro-spatial schemata are notoriously difficult to study. In the first place, as the physicist Werner Heisenberg (1930) recognized in the very different context of quantum physics, the act of inquiry itself alters the phenomena under scrutiny. Secondly, these schemata are intensely personal, for they relate to the core area with which the individual is most familiar and to which he has the greatest personal attachment. Ask anyone what *his* home, or room, or favourite chair means to him and you invite a long answer. The schemata that are evoked are immensely rich and complex and are filled with symbolic meanings which are hard to express. The poet Laurie Lee (1976), for instance, showed how it was perfectly possible for an eight-year-old child to see, in his mind's eye, the shrubbery of a suburban garden as an African jungle, a strange land which lay adjacent to India and the Antarctic. A schema of micro-space and a world-view, all in one!

One promising approach to such schemata is to be found in the concept of territoriality. Developed from the work of ethologists,[1] territoriality is the name given to the processes and mechanisms by which living organisms lay claim to, mark, and defend their territory against rivals. The underlying ideas were derived from research on non-human subjects, but it has been argued that the same principles are applicable to man. After all, people in many parts of the world have been observed to adopt proprietorial attitudes towards space, in the sense of having 'spatial requirements' or areas claimed as their own into which other people are not permitted without invitation. Does man then regard his immediate surroundings as an animal views its territory or are there important differences which make territoriality little more than an analogy when applied to human contexts?

This chapter considers the available evidence. It discusses the characteristic forms of animal territory, examines the origins and significance of human territoriality, and suggests a broad classification of territories in human spatial experience.[2] Initially two matters need to be clarified. First, while a number of writers (Soja, 1971; Gottmann, 1973) have applied the concept of territoriality to spatial units of the size of the 'region' or 'nation', the term is restricted here to the micro-level. This is because these larger-scale territories are so different in character to micro-space that use of ethological concepts becomes virtually meaningless. To take an example, defence of national territory can often involve actions that take place far beyond the borders of the state and consist of responses to 'threats' that are highly symbolic. Even by analogy, such actions have no equivalent in animal psychology or behaviour.

Second, it is necessary to remove some of the confusion that surrounds the relationship between territoriality and the various other concepts associated with human use of micro-space, such as privacy, personal space, crowding, density, and social dominance. To date, many hypotheses have been put forward about the links between these concepts: Davis (1958) proposing that territoriality and social hierarchy were two poles on a continuum of behaviour that was dependent upon density; Altman (1975) that territoriality and personal space were mechanisms in the achievement of privacy; and Delong (1973) that there was a situationally determined relationship between territoriality and social dominance. Integrating perspectives have been attempted, such as the idea by Hall (1966) for a unified science of proxemics,[3] but these lack effectiveness in the absence of broad agreement on basic definitions.

To clarify matters, *territoriality*, as defined above, is used as a broad term that describes the motivated cognitive and behavioural states that a person displays in relation to a physical environment over which he wishes to exercise proprietorial rights and that he, or he with others, uses more or less exclusively (see Edney, 1976). To prevent any conceptual ambiguity, territoriality will here be taken to include personal space, which is defined as an invisible area surrounding the body through which most other people should not pass (Sommer, 1969). Certain writers (e.g. Altman, 1975) have argued that personal space is conceptually distinct from territoriality on the grounds that personal space is carried everywhere one goes whereas territoriality usually implies a fixed, geographically immobile region. This is true, but stress must be laid on the word 'usually'. Territories can also be transitory and temporary occupations of space. Occupation of a park-bench, for instance, will involve both establishment of territory and personal space, (which will regulate the density of people sitting on that bench). It therefore would seem more satisfactory to see personal space and territoriality as part of the same set of mechanisms that serve particular goals in the spatial environment.

One such goal is *privacy*, defined as selective control of access to the self or to one's group (Altman, 1975). Another goal is *social dominance*, in which the areal extent of territory symbolizes a person's rank or status in the social hierarchy. By contrast, *crowding* and *density* are two aspects of the quality of life that territoriality helps to regulate. Both terms have been used loosely, and sometimes even synonomously, but in practice it is more helpful to regard them as related but distinct. Density is defined as having a purely physical meaning, being a measurement of the number of people per unit area. Crowding, on the other hand, is both a physical and experiential state—crowding exists if one *feels* crowded. Naturally crowding will partly depend on density and, in this sense, territoriality can assist in avoiding crowding by regulating the number of people that will occupy a given area, but motivation will also play its part. It is possible to feel 'crowded' when in the presence of few people, as might occur when a person is seeking solitude, and to feel perfectly at ease when tightly packed in a crowd, as occurs at sports with mass spectator appeal. Much will depend on the particular purpose the individual has in mind.

ANIMAL TERRITORIALITY

Territoriality is a central tenet of ethological theory. It is a phenomenon that has long featured in the writings of natural historians, of which the following extract from the work of the Reverend Gilbert White, the doyen of British naturalists, is a good example:

> during the amorous season, such a jealousy prevails between male birds that they can hardly bear to be together in the same hedge or field. Most of the singing and elation of spirits of that time seem to me to be the effect of rivalry and emulation; and it is to this spirit of jealousy that I chiefly attribute the equal dispersion of birds in the spring over the surface of the country.   (White, 1789; ed. Mabey, 1977, 137)

Systematic observations of territorality, however, date only from the early part of the present century, being concerned first with birdlife (Howard, 1920; Huxley, 1934) but later with a range of other animals (Burt, 1943; Lorenz, 1952; Wynne-Edwards, 1962). These works were later to be consolidated by a series of edited collections and readers (see, e.g. Esser, 1971a; Lorenz and Leyhausen, 1973; Alcock, 1975). Enough is now known to show that while territoriality is not a ubiquitous feature of animal behaviour, it is encountered in the behaviour of a great many species—avian, terrestial, and aquatic, vertebrate and invertebrate, exotic and commonplace.

When such behaviour is subjected to closer scrutiny, numerous common characteristics emerge in both the form of territories and the underlying processes. Starting with the morphology of territory, it has been found that territory takes two main forms: the fixed and spatially delimited territories, permanent and temporary, that are established either by solitary animals or by social groups of animals; and the egocentric 'bubble' of personal space, which moves as the animal itself moves.

Establishment of *fixed territories* is a highly efficient means for animals to come to terms with their natural environment. Although the legacy of Darwinism which pervades ethology has led to an over-dramatization of the 'struggle for survival', there is little doubt that animal behaviour is largely motivated by primary needs. As was noted before, these needs are physiological, the most important being for food, shelter (either from predators or the elements), and reproduction. Each of these needs may be materially assisted by the establishment of fixed territories. Food supply is ensured by the spatial dispersal that is inherent in territoriality. Protection from predators is obtained by having a safe refuge and by the fact that dispersion makes the species harder for predators to find. Possession of territory is a prerequisite for breeding in many species, as Watson and Moss (1971), for example, showed in their study of the territorial behaviour of red grouse.

In non-social species (in other words, those not organized into groups), territories are usually set up by solitary males and will be of a form and size that will be in keeping with the needs of the animal, its mate and offspring. The boundaries will be marked in some manner that is recognized by other members of the same species (Ardrey, 1966), which, for example, can be accomplished by scent (members of the canine family), or marks left on convenient objects (bears), or sound (birds, howler monkeys). The dimensions of the territory should be such as to permit surveillance, although there would be clear differences between the territorial boundaries of song-birds, which are able to survey all their territories from high perching points, and terrestial mammals, for whom lack of surveillance opportunities mean that territories overlap (Leyhausen, 1971). Entry into the territory without invitation is automatically regarded as an intrusion that will call forth resistance from the occupant, which will normally take the form of a ritualized display of aggression—a code that is understood by both parties and avoids the need for actual fighting. The strength of this code has been demonstrated by research on the English robin, a fiercely territorial bird. A robin caged within its territory was observed to drive away intruders by its song and threatening displays, even though it was powerless to take action. When the roles were reversed and the caged robin was moved into its rival's territory, it shrank back and would have fled if that had been possible (Fitter, 1969). None the less while combat may often be unnecessary, symbolic defeat in such a contest can impose its costs upon the losing party, sometimes resulting in inability to breed or even survive.

For animals that maintain group or social territories, much of the above would apply in equal measure, except that establishment, marking, and maintenance becomes a group rather than an individual task. Hediger (1961), however, has suggested that social territories serve three additional functions: they keep animals within communication distance of one another so that food and danger may be signalled; they co-ordinate the activities of the group and keep it together; and supply a framework within which things are done.

Personal space is an essential ingredient in the internal dynamics of group territories. Many animals live together in groups, yet avoid physical contact with one another. In doing so, they observe the basic rules of personal space, which may be likened to an invisible protective 'bubble' which surrounds the animal. Its limits are the distances the animal keeps between itself and its fellows for the sake of personal protection, and these will vary between species and within groups according to a dominance hierarchy.

Personal space is itself an indication of status, with more powerful animals commanding greater respect and larger amounts of personal space than their weaker fellows. Yet while this type of territory is dynamic space which moves with the animal (Hall, 1972), its limits are clear whenever animals interact. It is an essential factor in preserving the internal harmony of social territories.

This last point needs to be emphasized. It is too easy to think of territory as something inherently anti-social, as simply a means of keeping potential combatants apart, but this is only part of the picture. When looked at another way, territoriality may be seen as a major underpinning of social organization in animal species and a major source of stability. Certainly once territories are established, they are rarely challenged in any serious manner. To reiterate an earlier comment, they are the frameworks within which everyday life is enacted.

Two other points also need to be stressed. First, territorial behaviour is not invariate, but changes with the seasonal and daily (circadian) rhythms and activity patterns of the animal in question. Many birds, for example, will hold territory only at certain times of year and even for the rare species that hold territory all year round, there is the problem of competing needs. A starving robin may well not divert itself from searching for food in hard weather even if another robin should stray onto its territory.

Second, most naturalists regard territoriality as an innate part of animal behaviour, with its basis in physiological needs. Current patterns of behaviour have been developed over an evolutionary time-scale and reflect the outcome of satisfactory adaptation to the natural environment. Although the explanation of animal behaviour remains a vexed and complex issue, there is little or no convincing evidence that purposive behaviour plays any real part in determining the shape or structure of territoriality (Fischer, 1975).

THE STRENGTH OF THE ANALOGY

That then is the essence of animal territoriality. What lessons may be drawn with regard to the way human beings regard micro-space? On the surface, there would appear to be marked similarities. Human beings can be observed to maintain both fixed territories and personal space, laying down boundaries to space and reserving the right to decide who may enter and who cannot. This behaviour resembles that of non-contact territorial animals that live in groups for at least part of the time, but it is important to realize that these are purely similarities of form. When looking at the underlying *processes* crucial differences emerge, a point which may be appreciated by a brief consideration of the origins and significance of human territoriality.

The debate about the **origins** of territoriality has followed the lines of the 'nature–nurture' controversy. The nativist standpoint has been expressed by writers whose works have caught the public imagination—Ardrey (1966), Morris (1967), Tiger (1969), and, most notably, Lorenz (1966, 1970).

Lorenz linked territoriality to instinct theory, maintaining that human beings have an instinct for 'aggression' which they share with most other species. Territoriality is an expression of man's aggressive nature, representing both a product of the urge to gain and control a particular portion of territory and a means of reaching a 'steady state' within the organization of the human species. Ardrey took this idea further, arguing for the ubiquity of the territorial principle, with the following quotation perhaps giving the flavour of his contentions:

The continuity of human evolution from the world of the animal to the world of man ensures that a human group will behave according to the universal laws of the territorial principle. What we call patriotism, in other words, is a calculable force which released by a predictable situation, will animate man in a manner no different from other territorial species.   (Ardrey, 1966, 213)

Various explanations have been offered as to the means by which this instinct is transmitted. Esser (1970, 1972) and Greenbie (1975), for example, have suggested that territoriality is derived from sections of the brain that have strong evolutionary roots and are responsible for transmission of the legacy of man's distant past.[4] By contrast, Maier (1975) attempted to explain territoriality by means of Jungian psychoanalysis. Jung (e.g. 1964) had argued that it was possible for drives to be transmitted from one generation to the next by means of a central psychic core. This was held to run through all living matter and to have evolved in exactly the same way as the central nervous system. As may be seen in Figure 6.1, this idea served to link the individual, and the social groups of which he was part, to his human and animal ancestors. Territoriality, as an innate aspect of animal life, could thus be argued to have continuity through into human affairs.

The alternative, empiricist view emphasizes the role of culture and environmental learning. An important early statement of this school of thought was Hall's influential book *The Hidden Dimension* (1966). Hall studied the behaviour of people during everyday encounters and suggested that there were common features to be observed in the disposition and demeanour of interacting individuals. In particular, it seemed that such individuals clearly recognized appropriate distances at which they should stand relative to one another, distances which would vary according to the type of interaction, the position of the participants in social or organizational hierarchies, and with the cultural background of the people concerned. Culture was deemed especially important, for instance, Arabs were shown to accept and expect greater proximity during interaction than do Europeans—a characteristic which could lead to misunderstandings when people of these two cultures come into contact. Hall argued that these differences in proximity and spatial positioning had little to do with hereditary factors; they were derived from contrasting cultural development and were passed from one generation to another by socialization.

Hall dealt primarily with personal space, but his findings have a general

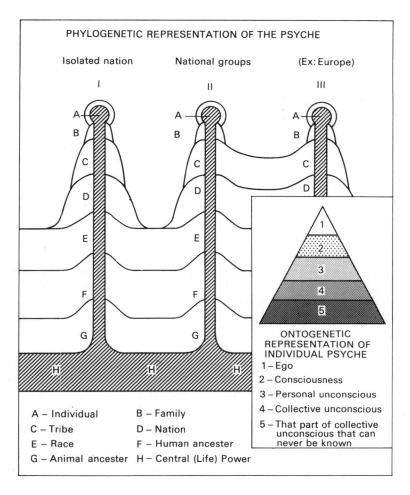

Figure 6.1. The innate roots of territoriality

Source: Maier (1975, 19). By permission of Association of American Geographers.

relevance for territoriality. As Ittelson *et al.* (1974) have pointed out, to assume that human territoriality is rooted in instincts similar to those of animals is simply to ignore the features that set men apart from lower organisms. Human territoriality undoubtedly does serve powerful and deeply rooted needs, but these are far more likely to be derived from culture than genetically transmitted. A ready example can be seen in a situation which, in evolutionary terms, is a very recent development, namely, mass commuting into large cities. The gross invasion of personal space that takes place every rush-hour does not lead to aggression but to simple defence mechanisms that will serve to create some feeling of detachment, such as an 'absent gaze' or preoccupation with a newspaper. In this way, cultural adaptation has supplied man with a means of domesticating himself that is not found in animal society. Besides this, it must also be said that much of the basic research upon which nativist theories are founded has been questioned. For example, serious criticisms have been made of the methodology used in Lorenz's animal experiments and about the applicability of his findings when applied to human beings (Eisenberg, 1972; Nelson, 1974). Furthermore, many nativist theories have placed undue reliance on research that is frankly speculative. How one reacts to Maier's ideas, for instance, depends upon the credence one gives to Jungian psychoanalysis. While this is not the place to offer a critique of Jung's work, there is little convincing evidence for the existence of the 'central psychic core' (Neel, 1971) or for the idea that the symbolic interactions associated with territoriality are innate (Alland, 1972).

In summary, analysis of the origins of territoriality shows marked contrasts between men and animals, a point which is strongly reinforced when one examines the apparent **significance** of territoriality. Whereas animal territories serve basic physiological needs for food, shelter, and reproduction, human territories also serve higher social and personal needs. This is especially true of individual and social fixed territories, which are commonly used as a means to satisfy human needs for status and recognition, and as a medium through which the self-image of the possessor may be communicated to the outside world.

The most obvious case is the 'home', the universally valued environment which lies at the heart of an individual's spatial world. The very richness of the word 'home', as perhaps is indicated by the two-and-a-half pages the *Oxford English Dictionary* devotes to it, makes the term hard to define. Besides being a place in a physical sense, home is very often used as a synonym for a comprehensive experiential entity, a little world which is knowable down to its smallest details (Lenz-Romeiss, 1973). The term always involves feelings of emotional security, of being protected, and of fitting in. The home is often the person's birthplace and the scene of his earliest experiences of the world—in other words, the forum within which he first becomes aware of his environment and is socialized, primarily by his family, into accepting a particular cultural outlook upon space. The link between the individual and his 'home' is a lasting one which is undiminished by physical separation. The feelings of nostalgia that have been experienced by migrants throughout the ages, with its extreme forms in home-sickness, testify to the pervasiveness of attachments to home (Lowenthal, 1975).

In a consideration of the home as the territorial core of a person's spatial world, some progress may be made towards disentangling the various aspects of its true significance by a consideration of the needs that it serves. Porteous (1976, 1977) identified three major needs, primarily social and personal in character, that were to be found in the home and could be satisfied by possession of this form of territory.

First, there was the need for *security*. The basic component of this was physical security, which is ensured by maintaining fixed boundaries which are clearly delimited and by regulating rights of entry. Physical security, individual and collective, has always influenced the design of human habitats, but at the present time would only rarely be the sole need served by the 'home'.[5] Almost as significant is psychic security, the feeling of well-being that stems from possession of this territory and all this entails. Denial of this sense of security, coupled with the distress created by possible non-fulfilment of basic needs, partly explains why homelessness arouses such deep-rooted fears and anxieties.

Second, there was the need for *stimulation*. The previous discussion of the nature of motivation (Chapter 2) showed that individuals will seek at times to increase stimulation and tension in the environment as well as trying to reduce it at others. The issue at stake here is one of control. It may well be that individuals do seek to reduce the complexity of their everyday environment to facilitate the performance of certain activities, for example commuting trips, yet within the controlled environment of the home they may also seek sensory stimulation. The home provides a forum in which this need can be satisfied. Stimulation is achieved by making, modifying, and defending the home and is to be found in the many challenges, great and small, that home-making and maintenance pose for the individual.

Third, the home serves the need for *identity*. Identity is fostered by being surrounded by known and familiar objects, and is particularly important in the child's early development, for his experience is inseparable from its spatial context. Besides being a source of identity, the home and its contents are also a vehicle for communicating that identity to the outside world (Duncan and Duncan, 1976; Becker, 1977). The house has two aspects: an interior which is shown only to those invited in and an exterior which is shown to the outside world (Cooper Marcus, 1974). Although there has been a tendency in the literature to overemphasize the role the home plays in bolstering identity, it would seem that there is truth in the notion that the interior represents intimate space that symbolizes the self as viewed from within, whereas the exterior is the public part of the house, the aspect displayed to other people. Interpretation of the symbols that are presented depends on the culture concerned (Rapoport, 1969). In the English-speaking world, for instance, a premium is placed upon originality, on having a house that somehow stands apart from its neighbours and conveys a sense of personal uniqueness in a world where system house-building has become the rule. None the less, as Cooper Marcus (1974, 132) observed with regard to American society, 'one's house must not be too way-out, for that would label the inhabitant as a non-conformist, and that . . . is a label to be avoided.'

The differences between the significance of territory for animals and humans is further compounded by the fact that the human home is not only a place that is demarcated by accepted social symbols, it is also a territory that is protected by legal ownership. The garden fence of the house or the 'No Trespassers' sign at the edge of a piece of open ground both indicate legal rights. Their owners can ask intruders to leave and can seek redress through the courts for crimes such as wilful damage or invasion of privacy, which is true whether or not the owner is in occupation (as in the case of absentee landlords). There is no evidence that the animal seeks ownership in the same way, and certainly not in the sense of being able to dispose of property to offspring or anyone else the owner chooses.

The contrast between human and animal territoriality is even more apparent when considering the significance of social territories. Social territories are phenomena that can be observed in both third world and developed nations. In the tribal societies of New Guinea, for example, groups will collectively enact displays of aggression from time to time at the boundaries of their territories, simply to probe the strength of their neighbours. If they appear to be in scarce numbers, weak, or just in 'poor condition', the moment is considered right to raid and plunder nearby villages (Attenborough, 1975).

Equally there have been many observations of group territories in the spatial structure of European and North American cities. This was initially indicated by work carried out by the Chicago school of human ecology (Park *et al.*, 1925; Hawley, 1950), which indicated the existence of distinct social territories:

just as there is a plant ecology whereby, in the struggle for existence like geographical regions become associated with like 'communities' of plants, mutually adapted, and adapted to the area, so there is a human ecology whereby, in the competition of the city and according to definable processes, the population of the city is segregated over natural areas into natural groups.   (Zorbaugh, 1926, 192)

Ecological research, however, presented an aggregated and somewhat Darwinist view of social territories. A more useful, if somewhat anecdotal, form of evidence is supplied by a series of participant observation studies on inner-city gang-lands (Whyte, 1943; Suttles, 1968; Patrick, 1973) and on the 'gilded ghettoes' of the wealthy (Firey, 1947). The behavioural aspects of these studies will be discussed in Chapter 10, but in the interim we may note that these studies demonstrated the existence of stable and organized groups, exercising territorial claims over space, and banding together to ward off external threats.

Yet while these studies showed that social territories serve deep-rooted needs, such needs are not wholly, or even largely, rooted in survival. Even in societies at a primitive level of development, such as the warlike tribes of New Guinea mentioned above, territorial defence is primarily a function of tribal prestige. In many cases, the basic needs that were originally embodied in territorial displays may be all but forgotten. A good example is provided by the annual Palio horse-race around the streets of Siena, Italy. This was founded in the seventeenth century to provide an outlet for the territorial hostilities of fifty-two districts (*contrade*) of the city. The present-day race consists of runners from the seventeen reorganized *contrade* of Siena, but although still hotly contested, it is now primarily a matter of *contrada* pride and status.

In summary, it would seem that in human contexts, territoriality is at best an analogy. As with any analogy, it is possible to gain considerable insights when it is used appropriately. Personal space, the home, and the neighbourhood can all be examined in terms of territoriality, with recognition of common features such as boundaries, boundary markers, and defence mechanisms. Territoriality helps to explain some of the deep-rooted attachments that exist for particular places. The problems arise in the extension of ethological processes to situations of human interaction, where failure to recognize the different processes at work can only produce explanation that contains what Rieser (1973) termed the 'territorial illusion'. It is essential to recognize the true complexity of the motivational and cognitive states that are to be found in human territoriality, instead of trying to fit human phenomena into frameworks designed purely for animals. Territoriality is a fresh perspective on the way man regards his immediate spatial surroundings; it is not a mechanical law (or set of laws) that determines spatial cognition and behaviour.

HUMAN TERRITORIES

With this conclusion in mind, how may the various features associated with territoriality best be classifed? A variety of taxonomies are available in the literature, most of which tend to have greater validity when identifying the basic forms of human territories than in distinguishing the underlying cognitive dimensions of that territoriality. Lyman and Scott (1967), for example, supplied a classification based upon the concept of egocentric space, with territories being arranged in ascending order ranging from inner (mental) space, through body territory and free territory (any area where a social gathering occurs), to the largest form of territorial space, public territory. Quite apart from the reservations that might be expressed about the notion of mental territories as part of the analogy of territoriality, such a classification is more useful as a pedagogic device than as a taxonomy that recognizes fundamental dimensions of human experience.

A more useful classification perhaps was that produced by Altman (1975), who distinguished territories on the basis of pervasiveness, personal involvement, centrality to the everyday life of a person or group, and temporal duration. Three categories were recognized—primary, secondary, and public territories.

Primary territories are owned and used exclusively by individuals or groups, are recognized as such by other people, are controlled on a relatively permanent basis, and are central to the day-to-day lives of the occupants. Primary territories are best exemplified by the home, seen, in Western society at least, as an area in which invasion or unpermitted entry by outsiders is a highly serious matter.

Secondary territories are less closely identified with the individual and are less exclusive. They cover a wide range of different spatial environments ranging from institutional settings such as hospitals, prisons, and college halls of residence,[6] to the areas to be found around people's houses. Some secondary territories have a simultaneous blend of public or semi-public availability and control by regular occupants: for instance, an inner-city gang-land might be controlled in the evening when gang-members get home from work or school but be public space during the rest of the day. Other types may have rules that limit access and occupancy, such as premises and ground owned by private clubs, but even within the membership there are often informal territories controlled by particular people. Secondary territories are therefore a bridge between the total and pervasive control allowed to occupants of primary territories and the free availability and access that characterizes public territories. Secondary territories, because of their semi-public quality, often have unclear rules regarding their use and are susceptible to encroachments from a variety of users.

Public territories have a temporary quality and may be used by almost anyone provided that they conform to basic social norms and standards. These territories are not owned by individuals but may be claimed by physical occupancy for a short period of time. Tables in libraries or park benches would be good examples, for tenancy of such spaces is understood to be temporary, even if it may be extended by using some surrogate for physical occupation (such as leaving a bag or a newspaper upon a seat).

This classification has several flaws in that, as argued above, it is advantageous to include personal space as part of territoriality and that at the present time it is better to regard such a classification as a foundation for further conceptualizations rather than a final statement (Edney, 1976). Nevertheless, it does indicate the variety of situations to which the notion of territoriality may be applied, its significance in the spatial experience of individuals and groups, and the way that people are more successful in bringing certain environmental settings under their control than others. In particular, it highlights the problems encountered in secondary territories where the rules as to the establishment and exercise of control are ambiguous. The creation of the physical fabric of such territories through modern building design, and the implications for residents of living in a spatial environment that is unresponsive to their efforts to establish territorial control, is a theme that will figure prominently in Part Four.

7 Urban Schemata

Everyone knows what a city is; except the expert.

(H. MINER, *The City in Modern Africa*)

It was noted earlier that the urban environment[1] has provided the setting for much of the early research in behavioural geography, an emphasis that reflects a growing concern for urban problems and recognizes the fact that cities are now *the* forum for everyday life. This chapter will examine the findings of a representative literature on the nature and structure of urban schemata, but the discussion will be prefaced by a preliminary matter. The city and the life-styles associated with it are a subject that has always aroused controversy. Throughout the ages there have been observers who have believed that city life is inherently beneficial or, at least, contained the conditions for human fulfilment, and those who have been deeply suspicious about the urban environment. For our purposes, such preconceptions are of importance because they influence the way in which researchers have approached urban problems and have affected the findings that they present. Our first task, therefore, is to examine the nature and underlying rationale for such attitudes.

ATTITUDES TOWARDS THE CITY

Assessments of city life have varied over time and between cultures. For the philosophers of ancient Greece, the city state (*polis*) represented the epitome of civilization, a view subsequently adopted in a modified form by the Romans. By contrast, the Bible reveals that Judeo-Christian traditions were dominantly anti-urban. Cain, the first builder of a city, was a fratricide; Nimrod, the founder of great cities, was a descendent of the 'cursed line' of Ham; Sodom and Gomorrah, the cities of the Plain, were destroyed by divine fire and brimstone because of the wickedness of their inhabitants (Genesis 4, 10, 18). The New Testament, as the history of a people who had started to adopt some of the values of Roman culture, was less strongly anti-urban than the Old. None the less while the New Testament culminates in the promise of the sacred city of Revelation 21, it still contains the image of the impenitent and debauched life-style of urban inhabitants (e.g. Matthew 11).

Pro- and anti-urbanism were to coexist throughout the centuries and as late as the eighteenth century concern about the iniquities of urban life was to be found alongside expressions of the civilizing virtues of cities. With industrialization, however, the pendulum was to move sharply in favour of anti-urbanism. London, which was described by Voltaire in the 1730s as the 'rival of Athens', was compared in 1785 with ancient Babylon by the English evangelical poet Cowper. In the same poem (*The Task*), Cowper was to put forward the dictum that has long characterized attitudes towards the city: 'God made the country and man made the town'.

This indicates the basic lines of the debate. Town and country were taken to be the opposites of one another. The town was regarded with suspicion because it subjected man to an *unnatural* existence, from which the effects could only be adverse. One can easily see the reasons for the mistrust. In Britain (excluding Ireland) the population trebled in the nineteenth century, with London growing from 1.1 million in 1801 to 6.6 million in 1901. In one estimate, 21.3 per cent of Englishmen had lived in towns of 20 000 or more inhabitants in 1801, but the figure had reached 61.7 per cent by 1891 (Coleman, 1973). Thus the nineteenth century marked a period of dramatic change in the size and distribution of the British population. Until the advent of industrialization, the vast majority of people lived on the land, on farms, or in villages, or in small country-towns. These were considered to offer the basis for a stable existence rooted in the virtues of family and community life, notwithstanding the appalling picture of rural squalor that emerge from texts such as Cobbett's *Rural Rides* or the Reports of the Poor Law Commission. Rural living was deemed close to Nature and hence God, and was more likely to lead to moral and spiritual well-being. This Arcadian view of the countryside contrasted with the town and city which, with their dark and enclosed spaces, their overcrowding and tension, and noise and dirt, were places to be avoided. Witnessing this unprecedented and largely unplanned 'urban explosion', contemporary commentators were steadfast in their belief that the strains of urban living were sure to tell in the quality of human existence.

Such anti-urbanism was to dominate the thinking of intellectuals in Europe (Schorske, 1963; Colman, 1973; Clayre, 1977) and North America (White and White, 1962; Hadden and Barton, 1973). In Europe it largely stemmed from a reaction to the worst horrors of industrialization, in North America more from an inherent belief in the values and life-styles associated with the self-sufficient rural yeomanry of Middle America, but the net result was much the same. There was a general consensus that the city subverted fundamental values and that it imposed hardships upon urban residents.

At the same time, there was a small but vociferous minority that considered that there were certain factors of the urban environment that were inherently favourable. The novelist Henry James, for example, was deeply disturbed by the human conditions to be found in New York but wrote fulsomely about the historic cities of Europe. In contrast, his brother William James, the philosopher, spent a considerable period living in New York in 1907 and concluded that the city supplied opportunities that were not to be found in the countryside. Perhaps the most notable statement of this pro-urbanism was to be found in the work of the poet Walt Whitman, of which the following extract from *Crossing Brooklyn Ferry* is a representative example:

Thrive cities—bring your freight, bring your shows,
Ample and sufficient rivers,
Expand, being than which none else is perhaps more spiritual,
Keep your places, objects than which none else is more lasting.
We fathom you not—we love you—there is perfection in you also,
You furnish your parts towards eternity,
Great or small, you furnish your parts toward the soul.

(Quoted in Raban, 1974)

Pro-urbanism has taken various forms in modern urban literature. Gans (1962) and Jacobs (1962) both cited the advantages to be found in well-established neighbourhoods in terms of their warmth, cohesiveness, humanity, and cultural richness. Such neighbourhoods were seen as the spontaneous creation of urban society, having an intrinsic value that enriched city life, despite the fact that they were often referred to as 'slums', with all that the word connotes, by those who considered only the run-down state of the physical fabric. Another variant of the pro-urban argument is found in research that denied that the intensified stimulation of the urban environment invariably leads to stress and pathology (for instance, Rapoport and Kantor, 1967; Rapoport and Hawkes, 1970). Drawing upon a theory of motivation that recognized that human beings may seek at times to increase the tension and stimulation to be found in their environment, it was argued that the city environment offered challenge and variety to its inhabitants. An environment that removed all the supposed sources of 'stress' might well be regarded as monotonous or as one that leads to sensory deprivation.

Enough has now been said to show that preconceived attitudes towards the city influence what researchers report and, to a major extent, the problems they study. A researcher who is interested in, say, crime in the inner city is likely to paint a very different picture of city life than one who focuses upon social networks in ethnic neighbourhoods. Moreover, people who write about the urban scene each have their own selective cognitions of that environment, for all the veneer of professional detachment. Whatever their degree of specialist knowledge, no urban writer is omniscient and many bitter controversies in the literature have been based on *a priori* broad-brush generalizations and unrecognized partiality.

ORIENTATION

The starting-point for much of the early research into urban spatial cognition has been the question of orientation. The first-time visitor or the resident of long standing both require to find their way between origins and destinations in a manner that meets their individual needs. The tourist, for example, may seek the route that embraces points of scenic or historic interest, whereas the commuter would demand the route of shortest physical or time-distance, but both will require some means to relate their current position to their specific spatial goals. To be lost is a time-consuming process and not everyone would accept it as philosophically as the traveller in Charles Dicken's *Martin Chuzzlewit*:

> You groped your way for an hour through lanes and bye-ways, and courtyards and passages, and never once emerged upon anything that might reasonably be called a street. A kind of resigned distraction came over the stranger as he trod those devious mazes and giving himself up for lost . . . [he] felt that the means of escape might possibly present themselves in good time, but that to anticipate them was hopeless.

Yet getting lost is a comparatively rare experience and individuals handle the seemingly difficult task of orienting themselves in a complex and dynamic environment with ease.

Orientation involves two related skills, respectively the abilities to perceive direction and distance. Perception of **direction** was first studied in the early years of the present century by Gulliver (1908) and Trowbridge (1913), who demonstrated that orientation was more often achieved by an egocentric reference system than by points of the compass, with Trowbridge recognizing the significance of the home as a fixed point in these reference systems. After these studies, interest in cognitive direction lapsed apart from some limited work on classroom geographical learning (Ridgely, 1922; Howe, 1931; Lord, 1941) and anthropological research on direction-finding in primitive societies (e.g. Hallowell, 1955; Carpenter *et al.*, 1959). What material is available on the urban environment indicates that there are differences according to age, familiarity with the city, and culture (Rapoport, 1977), and that precise compass directions are not a prerequisite for efficient navigation. With regard to this last point, a case-study of eighty-four first-year students showed that sixty-seven were still unable to identify cardinal compass directions after six weeks in Oxford, although they were able to describe appropriate routes for specific journeys and did not report any difficulty in way-finding (Gold, unpublished research). Cognitive direction was seen as a function of the individual's activity patterns, reflecting the relative direction of one goal-related place from another.

Rather more literature is available upon the topic of cognitive **distance**. Research on cognitive distance is frequently based on the assumption that mental representations of space contain information not unlike that contained in maps (a premiss which may be traced back to Tolman (1948) but which remains unproven). If this is so, it follows that these schemata, like maps, will possess a 'scale' by which the physical world is transformed for storage and later retrieval in the memory (Canter, 1977). Various methods have been put forward to investigate cognitive distance. Some studies have asked for direct estimates of physical distance (Lee, 1970), others have sought ratio estimates, where subjects compare two distances and express one as a proportion of the other (Golledge *et al.*, 1969; Briggs, 1973); some have investigated the shortest travel distance (Lee, 1970; Briggs, 1973), whereas others have sought straight-line or 'crow-flight' distances (Lowrey, 1973); and researchers have estimated distances variously in terms of mileage or time.

Each method has its advantages and drawbacks, but it is important to note that they may involve different cognitive abilities. 'Crow-flight' distance, for example, is an abstraction which we might never experience directly (Canter, 1977) and requires sophisticated guesswork, while estimating shortest travel distances may only involve recalling the evidence of the mileage counter on a car's speedometer or the time it takes to walk between two points. Different impressions of cognitive distance may also be obtained depending on whether the researcher uses mileage or time estimates. Time estimation, in particular, is dependent upon the hour of the day, travel mode, and details of the route in question. Even when efforts are made to reduce the effects of these distorting factors, it would appear that time estimates are less accurate than those of physical distance, a finding suggested by Canter (1975a, quoted in Canter, 1977). Canter examined the distance perceptions of travel in the London underground system, a public-transport network with standard routes and where the timings between stations remains relatively consistent. People living along the route of a section of the Underground were interviewed and asked to supply estimates of travel times and direct distances between pairs of stations. The results showed that there were higher correlations between their estimates of direct distance and actual distance than there were between time estimates and the actual travelling times supplied by London Transport. Indeed in some cases, time estimates negatively correlated with the offical figures in that respondents thought that short journeys took the longest and vice versa. Canter concluded that people have a more consistent picture of distances than of time and that the cognitive system of distance transcended any particular experience of time. Owing to the variable factors mentioned above, time is hard to estimate apart from the special circumstances of routes that the respondent uses frequently, whereas distance remains constant. Thus if individuals knew that a distance was great, they would probably assume that travel-time would also be so.

The diversity of method makes it difficult to compare the results produced by different researchers, but broad hypotheses have emerged about the variables that shape cognitive distance. First, it appears that cognition of distance is influenced by the *direction* of the stimulus within the city. From North American research, it was found that people overestimated distances towards the city centre compared with distances away from the downtown area (Golledge *et al.*, 1969; Briggs, 1973). Curiously, West European studies seem to show the opposite. Lee (1962), for example, showed that housewives in Cambridge regarded shops lying towards the city-centre as seeming to be 'nearer' than those situated in the other direction, results which replicated the earlier findings of Brennan (1948) in Wolverhampton.[2] The conclusion that distances towards the city-centre are underestimated was supported by Lee (1970) with regard to students in Dundee, by Heinemeyer (1967) in Amsterdam, and Lamy (1967) in Paris.

A partial explanation for this divergence may be found in the second hypothesis about cognitive distance; that it is influenced by the *attractiveness* of (or preference for) the stimulus. As Rapoport (1976) has noted, there is a broad spread of evidence that supports this hypothesis. If one bears in mind that the central city is often considered somewhere to be avoided in the USA but as a positive attraction in Western Europe, then it may well be the case that cognitive distance may be distorted by the different values attached to the city centre. Support for this idea, however, must be tempered by the various factors that complicate this relationship. For example, Europeans might rely on private cars for trips out into the suburbs but either walk or take public transport to travel into the city centre. As walkers and users of public transport are frequently more distance-conscious than the motorist. it might be expected that people might overestimate distances into the city centre. In turn, this alternative view may be questioned, as to whether potential overestimation is obliterated by the attractions of the centre or even whether researchers have yet conducted sufficiently wide surveys of the population upon which to base their contentions. Indeed, it may be intrinsically easier to make estimates of distances in some cities rather than others, owing perhaps to their regular layout or to the fact that they possess highly distinctive and historic centres (Canter and Tagg, 1975).

Similar reservations may be expressed about the third hypothesis, which holds that accuracy of distance estimation will be related to *familiarity* with the city and, in particular, length of residence. While the idea that people will estimate distance better if they are more familiar with the city has an obvious intuitive appeal, the evidence is strangely inconclusive. Cadwallader (1976), for example, reported that familiarity and length of residence appear to be unrelated to standardized estimation errors but concluded that this might be due to inadequate measurement of the variables or to other variables which had been omitted from the analysis. This reservation about the methodology may well be justified in light of the frequency with which length of residence is cited as a significant factor in the development of urban schemata.

Fourth, it has been hypothesized that cognitive distance varies with the *directness* of the route, in that subjects normally overestimate routes that involve many bends and corners relative to those of the same length that connect two points more directly. Lee (1971), for instance, provided anecdotal and laboratory evidence to show consistent overestimation of route length as a function of the number of corners. By contrast, Briggs (1976) found only limited support for this idea in his study of Columbus (Ohio) although he too pointed to the methodological problems encountered.

The available material, therefore, points to two broad conclusions. First, studies of both directional and distance components of cognitive orientation remain exploratory. While there is evidence of systematic divergence between actual and cognitive orientation, at least part of this divergence might stem from the methods adopted. Second, orientational systems are themselves part of, and dependent upon, urban schemata. It is impossible to orient oneself accurately in urban space unless one can recognize the basic elements of city form and their relationship to one another. This ability depends upon the formation of schemata, in which information about the external environment is processed and organized into a coherent form. It is with the character of these schemata that the next section will be concerned.

THE IMAGE OF THE CITY

The earliest and still the most influential analysis of urban spatial cognition is contained in *The Image of the City* by Lynch (1960). This book marked an important stage in Lynch's own work and yielded empirical results of some interest, but from our point of view its most significant aspect lay in its seminal influence upon later research. More than any other study, *The Image of the City* created the paradigm within which much subsequent research was carried out: It supplied concepts and methods that could be readily adopted by others and provided a point of common interest for the various disciplines that are concerned with the urban milieu.

The contents of *The Image of the City* have been described and evaluated sufficiently elsewhere[3] to make only a brief outline necessary here. Broadly, *The Image of the City* was an exploratory analysis of the visual quality of three American cities, as revealed by an examination of the way the physical features of their cityscapes were perceived by small samples of their residents. The emphasis on the visual aspect of the city largely stemmed from the fact that Lynch was trying to throw light upon problems of urban design, (the visual form of the environment being the element that the designer can most readily manipulate), but this focus influenced the nature of Lynch's findings. Even allowing for the dominance of vision in spatial perception, Lynch could be said to have studied only the visual component of urban schemata. In addition, the main thrust of the analysis was towards identifying the main elements in these schemata and their structural relationship; it did not extend to the functional or symbolic meaning of these elements. Finally, the questions that residents were asked centred on a passive mode of perception, examining the reaction of people to various contrasting environments rather than looking at more active modes of perception, where people *impose* meaning upon their urban environment.

The central concept in *The Image of the City* was the 'legibility' of the cityscape, or the ease with which individuals can organize the various elements of urban form into coherent mental representations (for which Lynch used the term 'images'). Lynch hypothesized that cities varied in the extent to which they evoked a strong image—a quality he termed 'imageability'—but it was most likely that cities that were 'imageable' were places that could be apprehended as patterns of high continuity with interconnected parts. In other words, a city was likely to be 'imageable' if it was also 'legible'.

This hypothesis was tested in three American cities: Boston, Los Angeles, and Jersey City. In each place, a small sample of predominantly middle-class people were interviewed about their perception of the central city,[4] by means of such techniques as sketch maps, verbal lists of distinctive features, directions for making specific trips in the city, and informal questions about orientation.[5] The findings for individual respondents were aggregated and then compared with visual surveys which had been carried out by trained observers. The assessments were made on the basis of a fivefold typology of elements:[6] *paths*, or channels along which people moved through the city, *edges* or boundaries, *districts*, *landmarks*, and *nodes*, strategic places in the city, such as railway stations and road junctions, which may be entered and at which navigational decisions have to be made.

Common themes emerged from the empirical studies. The sample populations conceived of their cities as sets of overlapping schemata, individually unique but collectively found to be arranged around common reference points. Clusters of known points were linked together by clearly defined paths. The path system was found to supply the structural component—the element around which the other elements were arranged. Certain edges emerged as strong boundaries, as in the case of water-fronts, whereas other edges that did not impede movement at ground level, such as overhead-railway lines, did not prove to have a barrier effect. Perception of districts waned as the resident became more familiar with the city, presumably through gaining more detailed knowledge, whereas landmarks assumed greater prominence with familiarity, seemingly because of their role in navigation.

In retrospect, these results were less significant for the development of urban cognitive research than were the basic theory, the concepts of 'legibility' and 'imageability', and the methods of data collection and analysis. The speed with which these aspects of *The Image of the City* were adopted and replicated by other workers indicated that a viable research paradigm had been created. However, *The Image of the City* was not intended to be more than an exploratory study. Those researchers who applied its concepts and methods to their own studies of urban spatial cognition were soon to be found extending and modifying the original version. In doing so, four main deficiencies came to light.

The first concerned methodology, particularly the use of freehand sketch-maps. The validity of this technique depends upon the map being a true representation of a person's cognition of the urban environment. There are reasons to suggest that this assumption may not be correct. Spencer (1973), for instance, found the technique both hard to administer and suspect in its results when studying a working-class community in Birmingham. Spencer concluded that the method might well have worked in Lynch's study because the sample population were familiar with maps and had the requisite skills to draw them. In other words, maps drawn from memory might indicate map-drawing abilities rather than true cognitive representations of the city.

Secondly, several writers have suggested that it is necessary to move away from the emphasis upon vision and explore non-visual components of schemata. After all, sight is not a prerequisite for spatial cognition, as is shown by studies of the blind. Blind people are perfectly capable of forming stable and coherent schemata and have no particular problems in accommodating the results of environmental change. Lynch (1976) has himself moved towards considering the various other forms of sensory information and perception, drawing attention to the important affective properties of the non-visual senses. A similar point was made by Southworth (1969), whose study of the sonic environment provides one of the few environmental analyses of auditory perception. Respondents were divided into three groups—those who could hear and see, a group who were blindfolded, and a group who were deprived of hearing. These people were then taken on a short guided walk around central Boston and asked to record their spontaneous impressions. The findings showed the contrasting environmental experiences derived from different senses and pointed to the close links between hearing and emotion: for example, the Boston water-front was considered monotonous by a person deprived of hearing but thought delightful by one who was blindfolded.

Thirdly, it is argued that more attention be given to the functional and symbolic meaning of urban space. The functional aspect was explored by Steinitz (1968), who re-examined the area of central Boston that had been studied by Lynch. Steinitz considered functional meaning to be fundamental to urban life, quite simply because it is essential to know what is happening and where. From his data Steinitz showed that imageability, as defined by Lynch, depended upon functional meaning, but not necessarily vice versa. In other words, it is possible to have knowledge about activities quite independently of cognitive representations of urban form. He therefore supported a conclusion reached earlier by Gulick (1963), who had suggested that imageability was determined by visual differentiation *combined* with significant social or behavioural associations.

Symbolic meaning is dealt with more fully in the next chapter, but one general observation may be made at this stage. Recognition of symbols, like functions, involves a more active relationship between the individual perceiver and his environment than is implicit in the passive or responsive mode of perception studied by Lynch (Appleyard, 1973). Individuals and groups, in effect, can and do impose their own meaning upon urban space. This point was forcefully made by Johns (1969) in a study of private gardens in cities, where it was shown that their design reflected spatial values imposed upon the environment to obtain human order. Indeed Johns (1969, 48–50) suggested that

'. . . the opposite process to that studied by Lynch, namely the influence *on* the human landscape of a vocabulary of patterns and shapes which all humans possess . . is the most logical way for the geographer to explore "Lynch country".'

Fourthly, the validity of Lynch's typology of five spatial cognitive elements has been questioned. To take some examples, Sarre (1972) employed the five basic elements but felt it necessary to add the additional category of function. Goodey *et al.* (1971) applied more radical changes in the *City-Scene* project. Lynch's five elements were regarded as being conceptually attractive, but were found to be inappropriate for data that had been supplied by people sending in sketch-maps in response to articles in a regional newspaper. Goodey and his associates found, for example, that it was impossible to say with certainty whether a railway station constituted a node or a landmark by simply looking at a submitted sketch-map. With districts not in evidence, they condensed Lynch's typology down to paths, node/landmarks, and edges. There is, of course, nothing wrong in making such modifications, for the original typology has no underlying theoretical justification.[7] Different data-sets may demand other classifications of elements and these can be just as valid as those proposed by Lynch.

For the remainder of this chapter we shall follow one such classification, a modified version of that adopted by Pocock (1975). In his study of Durham, Pocock classified the elements that appeared on sketch-maps into point-features, linear-features, and areas. In essence this is a logical typology and provides the basis for the threefold classification of the elements in urban schemata into buildings, paths, and areas.

BUILDINGS: Monuments and Landmarks

As the basic physical unit of the city, the building is undoubtedly a fundamental part of urban schemata. Quite apart from the functional significance of a building for its users, there are three other important characteristics of buildings for spatial cognition—as territory, as monuments, and as landmarks. The territorial aspect was discussed in the previous chapter, but the monumental and navigational roles of buildings merit further comment.

First, all buildings are *monuments* to the times in which they were built. In this context, one normally thinks of the classic buildings that symbolize the architecture of particular periods, in the manner that Palladio's Villa Rotonda near Vicenza expresses the essence of Renaissance humanism or Le Corbusier's Unité d'Habitation at Marseilles conveys the new spirit of twentieth-century modern architecture, but in many ways these famous buildings only represent the philosophy of an élite class of people who made decisions about building form and style. Of equal relevance is the unselfconscious local or vernacular architecture that still characterizes many towns and cities in Western Europe. Any building, no matter how humble, reflects the attitudes and values that were current in society at the time of its construction. Furthermore, buildings play an important part in everyday life simply because they act as a repository of cultural values. It is noticeable that new European immigrants to North America, for example, built their towns and homesteads in the same styles as those of their areas of origin. While there were undoubtedly practical reasons for doing so, it is also true that such familiar building styles helped to make people feel more at home in their new surroundings (Wagner, 1972). Over the years, these styles were to change and grow apart from those to be found in Europe, but rarely so much as to sever all links with the homeland.

The sense of continuity over time that buildings supply can be an important part of individual well-being. A building can convey a sense of stability and a feeling of belonging (Relph, 1976), perhaps helping to compensate for the fact that 'the world around us, so much of it our own creation, shifts continually and often bewilders us. We reach out to that world and preserve or change it, and so make visible our desire' (Lynch, 1972b, 1). At the same time, it is easy to think that because we live in a period when nostalgia for the past is rife (Lowenthal, 1975), that this has always been the case. This is not so. The architects and master masons of fifteenth- and sixteenth-century Europe ripped cathedrals apart in the name of progress, buildings which were venerable even then. As late as 1962, the superb Doric arch at Euston Station was demolished, a structure which many regarded as London's foremost symbol of the railway age. Yet so rapid has been the reassessment that even Victorian buildings now receive their share of preservation orders, commemorative plaques, and critical acclaim, with their functional role becoming secondary to that of a spectacle and monument (Crosby, 1970; Boulting, 1976).

Second, buildings serve as *landmarks* for orientation and way-finding in the city. While the precise significance of buildings in this context will depend upon the particular form of the city in question (Canter, 1977), it has been suggested that the landmark becomes more important with increased familiarity with the city. An interesting example of this suggestion was seen in the responses of two Oxford Polytechnic students when asked to describe the quickest route to a major bookshop in the city (Gold, unpublished research). The first statement is from a final-year undergraduate student:

The easiest way, I suppose, is to take the bus down to the stop outside the Examination Schools and then turn down Queen's Lane (next to the Coffee House), a narrow street with high stone-walls where traffic isn't allowed. If you follow round past the Church and that old barn, you come to Hertford, (with that superb pseudo-Venetian over-bridge), then you come out onto Catte Street and are faced by the iron-railings of the college opposite. Cross at the lights, avoid the temptation to visit the King's Arms and it is a few doors up on the right.

The other student was new to Oxford, having been in the city for a little over seven weeks: 'If you get off the bus in the High just after the bridge, and then walk up the road opposite called . . . er . . . can't remember . . . anyway it's right opposite and then walk down it, you eventually get to Broad Street. It's on the other side right near the road junction.'

Naturally one cannot claim too much from these statements. They have been deliberately chosen because both students took the same route, whereas there were many different routes in the full sample. Both respondents were non-motorists who relied on public transport to take them into central Oxford and then walked, using a short cut along a street which is closed to through traffic. Despite these qualifications, the difference between the two statements is striking. The latter is purely a brief itinerary using streets, the former contains a wealth of other information (not, alas, entirely accurate), which centres upon landmarks. The nature of these landmarks is also interesting. At first sight, they are an odd collection—a bus-stop, a cafe, an old barn, a foot-overbridge, iron railings, traffic lights, and a public house. Individually these could be landmarks for any one of countless different routes, collectively they form a unique sequence of spatial mnemonics— a code which supplied the guide-lines for one particular journey. A further point is that none of these landmarks, apart perhaps from the overbridge at Hertford College may be said to dominate the scene to any great degree. Rather, all are visually prominent only when the observer is at those strategic points at which navigational decisions are made. This gives tacit support to the idea suggested elsewhere that size of building alone does not make a landmark. The *City-Scene* research team, for instance, were surprised that the sketch-maps supplied by Birmingham residents rarely featured the Post Office Tower, by far the tallest building in Birmingham (Goodey *et al.*, 1971). Similarly Pocock (1975) noted that only a small minority of respondents made use of the Castle and Cathredral, the two visually dominant buildings in central Durham, when orienting themselves.

PATHS

Discussion of paths in cities inevitably focuses upon the road system. Roads and road traffic are an essential part of the character of the modern city and play an important role in urban spatial cognition. It may be recalled, for example, that Lynch (1960) considered that paths of movement (substantially meaning roads), were the structural element of schemata. One can see the justification for this belief, since the ability to move quickly and efficiently from one place to another is a prerequisite of urban life. If one accepts this view, the next problem is to investigate what the individual learns about the spatial structure of the city whilst in transit.

One study that made headway towards answering this question and unravelling the complexity of travel experience was that by Cullen (1961), who examined the way the cityscape was perceived by a moving observer. Even for an observer moving through the city at a uniform speed, the nature of the urban environment was such that the scenery of the town was revealed in a series of jerks or revelations. The observer perceived the cityscape as a sequence which the mind manipulated in order to achieve a dramatic or emotional impact, a phenomenon known as 'serial vision'. It may be argued that this overemphasised the conscious aspect of perception, but the notion of serial vision produced some interesting ideas. The long straight road had little impact because the initial view was soon digested and became monotonous, whereas contrast supplied far more vivid images, coming alive through the 'drama of juxtaposition' (Cullen, 1961, 11). The visual experience of townscape could be divided into two elements, the existing view and the emerging view, with the existing view containing clues from which the mind could draw inferences about the view that was in the process of emerging.

Movement in the city was thus treated as a conscious aesthetic experience, but one that is influenced by the form of movement adopted. Even when motorists and pedestrians follow the same routes, the things they would see would vary according to the different angles and speeds at which stimuli were presented. Moreover, with the advent of urban motorways, pedestrian precincts, and the like, there is an increasing tendency for pedestrian and road-transport systems to be segregated, with different sets of experiences for each group.

An insight into the travel experiences of **motorists** was provided by *The View from the Road* (Appleyard *et al.*, 1964). This study examined the way motorists travelling along freeways into four American cities perceived the urban environment and investigated the aesthetic satisfactions they derived. The project rested upon a similar premiss to that employed by Cullen, in that the city could be regarded as an artistic work in which the viewer was presented with a 'dramatic play of space and motion, light and texture'.

This theatrical analogy must be qualified in three ways. First, the order in which stimuli are presented can be reversed, since the road has two directions. Furthermore, unlike a play, it is by no means necessary to drive from one end to the other, for the motorist is perfectly free to leave or join at any intermediate point. Second, the direction of gaze of the occupants of the car will vary. The driver's vision will normally be confined to a narrow angle in the direction being travelled, whereas the passenger is freer to look at the surrounding cityscape. The latter, however, is not impelled to look out of the windows at all and may even be more concerned with what is going on inside the car. Third, there will be different audiences for the play and what one gets from a trip will depend on the person concerned. The tourist will approach the city with a 'fresh eye', but may be so preoccupied with correct orientation that he takes in relatively little of this new and unfamiliar environment. The commuter, on the other hand, may well be somewhat blasé about a highly familiar journey. While he would be likely to notice any new objects or occurrences, the commuter tends to ignore the larger landscape features in favour of the moving traffic and activities taking place along the road. Indeed, the well-documented cases of 'highway narcosis' show that it is possible to undertake a routine journey in safety with the driver being in a state similar to sleep (Fischer, 1976).

Appleyard *et al.* (1964) considered that the experience of motoring is dominantly visual. The enclosed space of a car removes the perceiver from the sonic and olfactory environments and means that most information is obtained through sight, with a secondary source in touch—the response of the car to the hands and feet of the driver, the vibrations of the road surface through the wheels. Their study thus concentrated upon vision, consisting of two exercises. The authors themselves carried out repeated trips along approach roads to four cities in the north-eastern USA, namely Boston, Hartford (Conn.), New York, and Philadelphia, recording their impressions by means of tape, film, photographs, and field-notebooks. This allowed for pilot-testing of techniques and development of a notation system, itself derived from the work of the architect Thiel (1961). The main interview study was then carried out on a sample of twenty drivers, who were tested over a 7-mile section of the Northeastern Expressway into Boston. The composite view of the road is depicted in Figure 7.1.

Although this was an explanatory study,[8] it illustrated how road travel can shape schemata. The motorist paid attention to the cues necessary to achieve a successful trip and ignored competing and redundant information. Yet as Figure 7.1 demonstrates, he sees and learns far more than just the mundane details of signs, lamp-posts, and other street-furniture. The vista of the distant Boston skyline, the changing impressions of land and water,

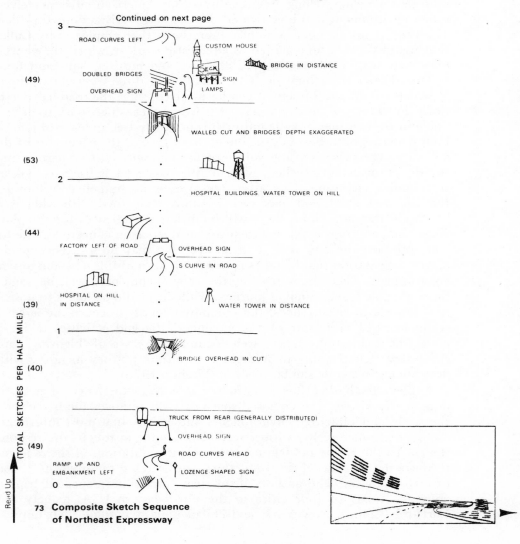

73 **Composite Sketch Sequence of Northeast Expressway**

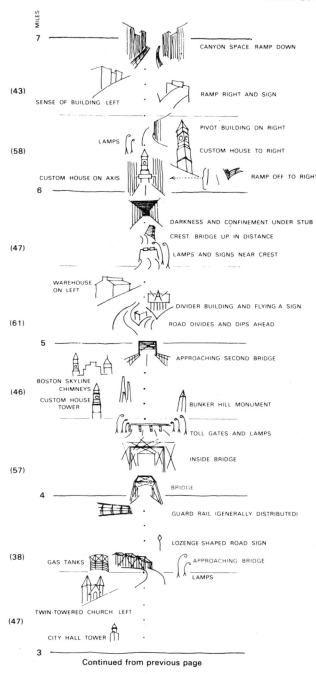

Figure 7.1. A composite sketch sequence of the Northeast Expressway, Boston.

Source: Appleyard, Lynch, and Meyer (1964, 37). Copyright © 1964 by Massachusetts Institute of Technology. By permission of The MIT Press, Cambridge, Mass.

and a series of notable landmarks all serve to give clues about the nature of Boston itself, which the individual can use to make inference.

The experiential qualities of **pedestrian** travel have been analysed by studying responses to given walks or trails through the city. Such trails have long guided the traveller to the major 'sights' of historic cities and occupy a prominent place in environmental education (Goodey, 1974b, 1975), but have only recently been coupled to methods by which environmental experience may be evaluated. Lynch and Rivkin (1959) studied the features that subjects recalled about a walk around a block in central Boston. Lynch (1960) and Southworth (1969) recorded the reactions of people while following sensory walks. Lowenthal and Riel (1972) chose trails that they felt encapsulated the character of four eastern American cities. Respondents were requested to complete the trail and then immediately to record their impressions of that urban environment by means of twenty-five semantic differential scales. These scales consisted of pairs of opposite adjectival words or phrases (constructs), such as ugly–beautiful, old–new, dense–empty, and dark–light. Respondents were able to record the strength of their feelings on a seven-point scale that was attached to each construct, one end of the scale representing the minimum of the attribute, the other end expressing the maximum, and the points between signifying gradations. On this basis, Lowenthal and Riel gained semantic-scale data for a sample of almost 300 respondents, which were then statistically analysed to draw out underlying dimensions of environmental assessment.[9]

This method has attracted widespread attention as an easily administered and incisive means to study the urban environmental experiences of foot-travellers (Wheeler, 1976). One good example is to be found in a paper by Burgess and Hollis (1977), which investigated the responses of students to urban trails in four contrasting areas of London (Tolmers village, Blooms-bury, Soho, and Bond Street) by means of twenty semantic scales. As Figure 7.2. shows, the results varied considerably. Whereas the squares of Bloomsbury were typically viewed as rich, successful, ordered, clean, and relaxed, the rundown area of Tolmers village was characterized as ugly, boring, hostile, and dirty.

Overall, research on the environmental experiences of people when travelling through the city, whether by car or on foot, has not yet reached the stage where broadly applicable findings have emerged, but it is possible to suggest that the path system can play two very different roles in urban spatial cognition. First, paths serve to expand and integrate spatial knowledge. Paths, as we have already seen, are channels along which people move and experience the city. They supply corridors of known territory through otherwise unknown areas, serving as a physical matrix around which other elements are arranged. The extent to which paths act as linking corridors, however, does seem to vary with travel mode. Lee (1971), for instance, showed that children who walked to school possessed schemata that were organized around the twin nodes of their everyday life, their home and the school, with connection supplied by the known route of the road between

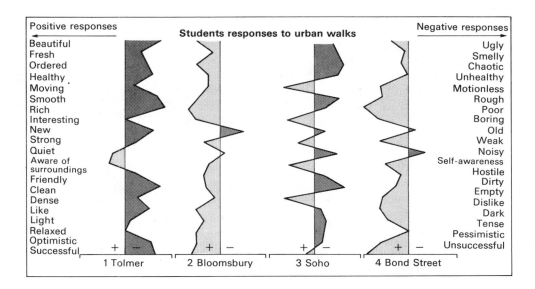

Figure 7.2. Students' responses to urban walks.

Source: Burgess and Hollis (1977, 156).

them. This contrasted with children who came to school by bus, whose schemata of home and school were disconnected primarily because bus travel did not involve the individual child in making navigational decisions.

Second, roads and associated land-uses can also act as a barrier which effectively serves to fragment urban schemata. One way that this has occurred is through roads becoming what Horvath (1974, 168) termed 'machine space' or 'territory devoted to the use of machines . . . [where] machines have taken priority over people.' Mass car ownership has placed enormous demands upon the urban fabric that have not proved easy to accommodate. When carried to its logical conclusion, as many would argue has happened in Los Angeles where 76 per cent of the downtown area is devoted to the car (Figure 7.3), motor transport sets the tone and character of the entire city. This is an extreme example, but similar trends are discernible throughout the Western world. Despite the occasional exhilerating features of road architecture (Halprin, 1966; Banham, 1971), roads and the associated land-uses of garages, parking space, and waste-land have become machine space. As this process has taken place, freedom of mobility for motorist and pedestrian alike has been progressively eroded. Each group needs to be able to move around in safety from the other. The effect that this requirement will have upon urban schemata will depend upon the policies that are adopted.

One solution carried out in the interests of pedestrian safety and/or efficient transit is to create traffic-only areas from which pedestrians are banned, literally placing areas out of bounds for pedestrians. Conversely,

Figure 7.3. Area devoted to road transport in downtown Los Angeles.

Source: Gruen (1965, 80).

rerouting traffic to by-pass town centres or residential areas can have a similar affect upon motorists. In short, this segregation of movement patterns is likely to contribute to a compartmentalizing process where traffic zones are avoided by pedestrians and pedestrian areas are necessarily avoided by motorists. If the individual is not a member of both groups, whole areas will be placed outside his experience. Vertical segregation of pedestrians and vehicles through movement systems on different levels can also have its impact. Both Goodey *et al.* (1971) and Ross (1974) have reported that this 'three-dimensional' arrangement can often be associated with low urban imageability in the minds of both pedestrians and motorists.

When there is no separation of movement systems, on the other hand, the result can be the 'high street battleground' which typifies many English country towns (Sharp, 1968), where there is an area of tension between motorists and pedestrians. The pedestrian has to tolerate noise and fumes and has to cross potentially dangerous roads, the motorist has to cope with limited parking space, people darting out into the road and traffic congestion. The end-product can give little aesthetic satisfaction to either group; it is a zone to avoid.

The whole question of the significance of road transport for urban spatial cognition is one of irony. At a macro-level, the car has expanded personal mobility, yet at a more local scale it can be a divisive force, alienating space from general use, dividing communities and impeding social interaction. These are subjects to which we shall return in Chapter 10.

AREAS

The area, a portion of space that is identifiable by some particular set of characteristics is a fundamental unit of cognitive space. By categorizing space into areas, however vague, one has a ready means of coming to terms with environmental complexity, a process in which the stereotype has a prominent place (see Chapter 9). This chapter has already considered spatial schemata of the central areas of cities. Further insight into the cognitive significance of areas may be gained by examining open spaces and residential neighbourhoods.

Open space serves several important symbolic functions. It is a highly effective medium by which clues are afforded about the structure of the city, in that it provides vistas which allow the observer to discern spatial relationships (Lynch, 1972a). The distant skylines of the central city viewed across the intervening space of a park, river, or vacant land can convey a wealth of information about the city and its site. Next, open space can impart a distinctive character to a city, as do the parks and squares of London and Bath. So distinctive are a few such areal features that they, along with one or two buildings within them, can constitute nationally, or even internationally, known symbols of the city. Examples are provided by the Etoile in Paris (Milgram and Jodelet, 1976), the view of the Palaces of Westminster across the River Thames in London, or Red Square in Moscow. Lastly, many consider that open space symbolizes the 'country' in the city, allowing urban dwellers to escape from the pressures of the urban milieu and to partake in the virtues of a quasi-pastoral environment (Marx, 1968).

Turning to **residential neighbourhoods**, one immediately encounters the problem of the imprecise definitions attached to the term 'neighbourhood'. In social science and planning literature, neighbourhoods are defined in two ways. On the one hand, neighbourhoods are taken to be social units that are identified by the sociability and neighbourliness of their residents; on the other hand, they have been taken to be physical planning units for provision of housing and service facilities—'neighbourhood units'. It may seem that these are quite separate things, but they have become inextricably intertwined by the belief that it is possible to create the necessary preconditions for social neighbourhoods by sensitive physical design of neighbourhood units. Although the deterministic thinking implicit in this has now been widely discredited,[10] it still enjoys sufficient currency to support duality in the meaning of neighbourhood.

Another source of confusion is that 'neighbourhood' has often been used interchangably with the word 'community'. This is understandable for the terms share similar social connotations of homogeneity, real or perceived, of mutual interest and of self-help. The point at which they differ lies in their spatial dimension. It is still possible to talk of 'local communities'. but increasingly the term 'community' has been applied to a wider scale. One can now recognize 'communities of interest' which function effectively over city, regional, national, or even global space. 'Community' has therefore ceased to be a spatial term. Not so for 'neighbourhood', which remains a word applied solely to a localized area. In an urban context, the idea of having neighbours who live miles away is a contradiction in terms.

A neighbourhood, then, is a bounded residential area that is delimited by specific criteria. The problem for the researcher is that it may be hard for an outsider to discern neighbourhood boundaries. While there are cases where boundaries are easily spotted owing to the antipathy of groups living on either side of the divide (Collison, 1963; Boal, 1969, 1976), such instances are the exceptions rather than the rule. Two methods have been commonly employed to delimit urban neighbourhoods. The first seeks a critical level of social interaction to serve as the delimiting criterion. This might be achieved by using the diffusion researcher's concept of the 'neighbourhood effect' (Figure 7.4), but in practice it is hard to operationalize this notion. The other method is to attempt to define neighbourhoods through the eyes of their residents. This sounds a straightforward task, but is beset by conceptual and methodological difficulties. In his thorough review of studies of neighbourhood perception, Spencer (1973) pointed to the factors that had led to inconclusiveness in this research as including the diversity of research aims, lack of standardization of sampling procedures, small sample sizes, problems connected with interview techniques, and conflicting terminology. The nature of these difficulties may perhaps be best illustrated by considering the influential study by Lee (1954, 1968).

Lee had noted the dual meaning of neighbourhood as both a physical and social term and decided that the only way to resolve the confusion was to adopt a phenomenological approach, whereby the concept was viewed through the eyes of the subject. The study was carried out in Cambridge with a sample of 219 housewives, who lived in a predominantly middle-class area. Each respondent was asked to delimit what she considered to be her

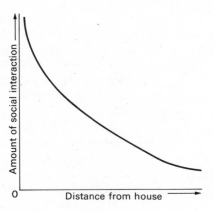

Figure 7.4. The 'Neighbourhood Effect'

neighbourhood or district by placing a line round it on a map and to describe her activities in the locality in terms of shopping, friends, and club membership. In all, 75 per cent of the sample were able to comply with this request.

The findings were extremely varied, with each respondent defining a unique neighbourhood. Each 'neighbourhood schema' was different, even for people living in the same street, but there was a tendency towards 'some norm formation and shared social and spatial experiences', as shown by the fact that neighbourhood schemata could be fitted into three categories. The smallest were 'homogeneous' neighbourhoods, which were mainly found among the lower- and upper-middle class and were delimited on the basis of sentiments like 'our sort' and 'people like us'. The second type was based upon 'social acquaintances', being more extensive than 'homogeneous neighbourhoods' but, curiously, showed no direct relationship with housing density. The third type, 'unit neighbourhoods' were generally larger than the other categories and came closest to the planning concept of a neighbourhood unit, containing a range of shops, facilities, and clubs.

In order to place individual schemata on a standardized scale of measurement, Lee expressed individual schemata as a ratio of a hypothetical locality of half-mile radius from the respondent's house. This was done by means of a scale known as a neighbourhood quotient (Figure 7.5), which took into account the different densities of housing areas as well as shop and amenity provision. This was used to indicate the subject's involvement with her environment. The neighbourhood quotient was then correlated with the social behaviour data, with positive relationships emerging between the

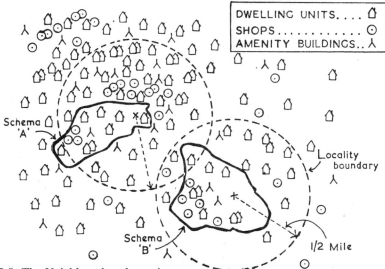

Figure 7.5. The Neighbourhood quotient
Illustrative Calculations: an average Nh.Q. subject from a high-density locality (A) and a high Nh.Q. subject from a low-density locality (B).

Source: Lee (1968, 257).

neighbourhood quotient and social class, age, length of residence, work location, friendship patterns, and active social participation within the locality.

Lee's study provided a plausible and imaginative indication of the nature of neighbourhood. He supplied a comprehensive method for delimiting neighbourhood and formulated a scale by which the neighbourhood schema of a person living in one area may be compared with that of someone living in another area. Yet despite the elegance of the approach, Spencer (1973) showed that there were real problems in its application. Spencer had examined neighbourhood perception in a small physically compact area of working-class terraced housing in Selly Oak, Birmingham. He found that neighbourhood was a difficult concept for many respondents to grasp, and that even when they did understand the subject of the inquiry, their delimited neighbourhoods varied widely. This variance, of course, was also found in Lee's study, but the difference here was that Spencer showed that results would vary markedly depending on what method of neighbourhood delimitation was used. This may be seen by contrasting Figure 7.6, which shows neighbourhoods graphically delimited by Lee's method, with Figure 7.7, which were based on verbal descriptions. Spencer noted that graphic methods have a drawback, in that respondents would draw a boundary round an area, with perhaps a few reference points, but with little real attention to the finished product. To attach the significance to these lines that is necessary to compute neighbourhood quotients would seem to be dangerous. Lee's method contains the implicit assumptions that the houses and shops within a perceived neighbourhood all have significance for the respondent and that the neighbourhood is continuous. The result was that neighbourhoods were delimited that were not an accurate guide to true involvement.

In short, Spencer questioned whether Lee's study was really phenomenological. Rather than seeing things through the eyes of the respondent, the subject was asked to respond by means of a format that was prepared by the researcher. How well the respondent was able to do so would depend upon how far he or she shares the researcher's understanding of the concepts and methods. In his sample of Cambridge middle-class housewives, Lee had respondents who could interpret and respond to maps. By contrast, Spencer found that his working-class sample often did not possess these skills and could only complete the exercise with considerable assistance. It may well be therefore that rather than presenting a true phenomenology of neighbourhood, the graphic delimitations were more fairly a test of map comprehension.

Whatever the problems of technique, however, Spencer did not dispute that neighbourhoods do exist, that they are important in the lives of people, and that they are parochial and individual. Moreover, when asked the right questions, respondents could delimit their neighbourhoods, with the size and form of these perceived neighbourhoods reflecting some behavioural characteristics. The social-class dimension to which Spencer alluded is a significant variable in neighbourhood perception, but it is only one aspect of the complexities involved. In addition, to date we have considered

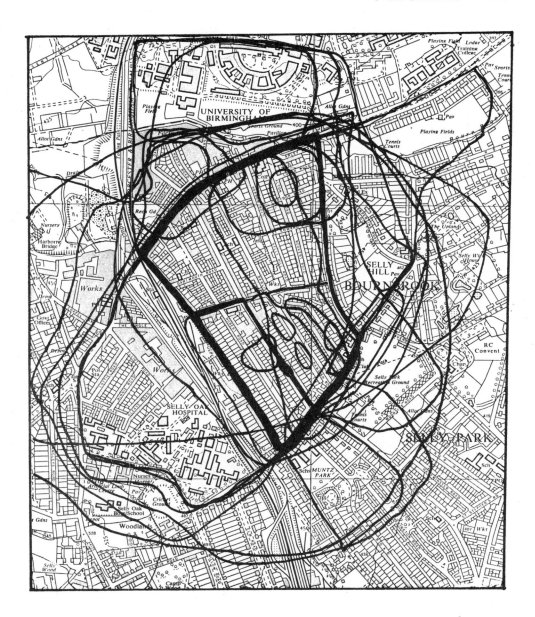

Figure 7.6. Superimposed perceived neighbourhood boundaries, as graphically delimited

Source: Spencer (1973, between pp. 95 and 96).

neighbourhoods purely in terms of home areas; there is also the question of attitudes towards other neighbourhoods and the associated matter of

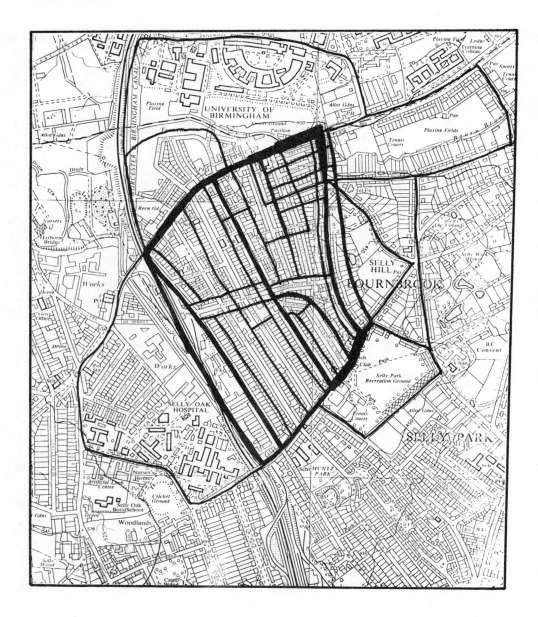

Figure 7.7. Superimposed perceived neighbourhood boundaries, as verbally described

Source: Spencer (1973, between pp. 95 and 96).

neighbourhood preferences. These issues, however, along with their behavioural implications, are best left to Part Four.

8   Images of Landscape

> . . . fair Italy!
> Thou art the garden of the world, the home
> of all Art yields and Nature can decree;
> Even in thy desert what is like to thee?
> Thy very weeds are beautiful, thy waste
> More rich than other climes' fertility . .
>   LORD BYRON, *Childe Harold*

We all possess mental pictures of the landscapes that we find in some way outstanding. They may have the rapturous appeal that Italy held for Byron, and many others of his time and class, or they may be ugly, sordid, and depressing, as many find the pit-heads and spoil-heaps of industrial Britain. Certain landscapes are viewed more in nostalgic than aesthetic terms, as were ivy-covered ruins in the eighteenth century. Such images are at once individual and public, many of their dimensions being held collectively by a nation, a period and a class, but whether personal or collective, such landscapes have a symbolic quality that has been expressed in painting, poetry, and photography.

This chapter examines the nature of such images of landscape and the ways in which they have changed over time. Geographers have taken landscape as a key concept in their study of the earth and man's activities on it, but only a minority have tried to explore the symbolic dimension of landscape and to account for our feelings towards particular landscapes. In an era when man's power to alter, create, and destroy landscapes is perhaps greater than at any time in human history, it has become increasingly necessary to understand what people feel towards the world that they live in.

LANDSCAPE IN GEOGRAPHY

For a period in the early twentieth century, landscape held the role of a central organizing concept in geography (Mikesell, 1968). The German word *Landschaft* was used by writers such as Passarge and Hettner to define a portion of territory that possessed a physical and cultural unity, similar in many ways to the English concept of a 'region', but it is a term that must be interpreted cautiously. There were German geographers who regarded *Landschaft* as having aesthetic and spiritual dimensions, most notably Banse (1928), but the word does not necessarily denote such a meaning. Those English and American geographers who translated *Landschaft* as 'landscape' normally tried to retain an objective scientific meaning. For

*By D. E. Cosgrove

instance, Dickinson (1939) argued that human distributions of a non-material character (social, racial, psychological, and political) were to be excluded from the geographical study of landscape except in so far as they assist in understanding its evolution. Sauer (1925) and Hartshorne (1939) also excluded human attachment and response to landscape from geographical work, although Sauer did acknowledge, almost as an afterthought, that the best geography had never disregarded the aesthetic qualities of landscape (even if this implied subjectivity). As seen in Chapter 3, Sauer suggested that landscape had two aspects, the natural landscape of landforms and vegetation, and the cultural landscape, the evidence of man's activities upon the natural landscape. This approach to landscape study was concerned with morphology and was concerned primarily with explaining observable and measurable traces of human activity, producing an impressive set of studies which ranged from analyses of particular features (such as barns, bridges, and vernacular architecture) to whole associations of forms and their superimposition.[1]

This distinction between natural and human landscapes marked an important step in the early struggle against physical determinism, in that the cultural geographer strove to re-establish a humanistic basis for geography by emphasizing man's ability to modify and reshape the natural landscape. In practice, however, the dichotomy proved to be almost impossible to make. In most parts of the world, man has long since modified landscapes from their (assumed) natural condition to the point at which one can only speak with any confidence about the *degree* of human modification.

For our present purposes, perhaps the most significant criticism of this school of cultural landscape studies lies in the relative disinterest in human attitudes towards landscape and lack of concern for the symbolic properties with which landscape is endowed.[2] The emotional content of landscape is inherent in common usage of the word: for example, since the sixteenth century artists have thought of it as connoting scenic beauty (Jackson, 1964; Gombrich, 1966; Tuan, 1966). Indeed this ambiguity of meaning in the term 'landscape' was to prove attractive to certain English geographers who employed it as an equivalent of *Landschaft*. None the less, the prevailing view in geography was to disregard any such ambiguity in the concept of landscape, with the influential monograph by Hartshorne (1939) rejecting use of the term in favour of 'region'.

How then to deal with the symbolic qualities of landscape? The usual answer was either to argue for its inclusion in the language of an otherwise scientific treatise by means of striking simile or memorable metaphor (Wright, 1947; Johns, 1960) or to establish an 'aesthetic geography' devoted to reproducing in geographical literature the artistic aims of the landscape painter, the poet or the regional novelist (Banse, 1928; Cornish, 1928; Gilbert, 1960). As valuable as some of these works have been, for example Cornish's work had an important impact upon the foundation of National Parks in England and Wales (Goudie, 1972), their substantive results have not been of sufficient standard to prove that geography is a fine art, nor that geographers are artists. Yet even if geographers are not artists, the earth's surface—the subject matter of their studies—may be regarded as an art form. It is precisely this aspect that has led to the ambiguity of meaning encapsulated in the concept of landscape. Landscape is composed of three elements: the tangible and physical features of an area, natural and man-made, such as are included in the cultural geographer's definition of the term; the measurable activities of man; and the meanings or symbols that are imposed by human consciousness (Relph, 1973). It is this third dimension, its symbolic meaning, that gives landscape the character of art in addition to being an artefact. While modifying natural objects to meet human needs, man also re-creates them as 'symbols of sentience' (Langer, 1953), which reflect his intentions, beliefs, values, and opinions. It is this property that defines the nature of art. Such re-creations are the work of not only those who live in the landscape and physically modify it, but also those who experience it as later generations, as visitors, or even at second hand through the media of mass communication. All are involved in the artistic act and all contribute towards making the landscape 'a repository of human striving' (Tuan, 1971).

To analyse symbolic meaning, the geographer has clearly to turn to methods that are quite different from those employed in the scientific analysis of physical features and observable activities, and it will be argued later in this chapter that appropriate methods may be found in the works of the art critic and historian. Before examining this subject, however, it is necessary to say something more about human attitudes to landscape.

ATTITUDES TOWARDS LANDSCAPE

Human beings invest the landscapes they experience with symbolic value. Such symbols yield pleasure, pain, melancholy or nostalgia. To Lorenzo di Medici, for example, paradise meant 'nothing other than a most pleasant garden, abundant with all pleasing and delightful things, of trees, apples, flowers, vivid running waters, songs of birds and in effect all the amenities dreamed of by the heart of man'. Lorenzo here expressed a sentiment embodied in the images of paradise of men of all ages, but his attitude is very typical of the landscape aesthetics of the fifteenth- and sixteenth-century Renaissance. Freed from the bonds of medieval scholastic theology which viewed nature as at best a distraction from man's higher duty of transcendence and at worst an ignoble seductress which had suffered the blemish of man's Fall (Glacken, 1967), nature opened up to reveal luxury and bounty. The concern amongst educated men for classical scholarship had led them to the Virgilian pastoral and the delight in the cultivated and humanized landscape of the *Eclogues*. The pastoral ideal was a dominant landscape image of the Renaissance, celebrated in the works of Bembo, Spenser, and Sidney and in the painting of Giorgione, Titian, and Claude. Marx (1964) and Levin (1969) have shown how this landscape image informed European attitudes to

America, the New-Founde-Land of the Renaissance. Suddenly the European mind, nurtured on the idea of a Golden Age of pastoral idyllic life and landscape which had existed at the time of man's innocence, was confronted with the possibility of recovering that era. The reports of early voyages to America are replete with images of a garden, occupied by a gentle and loving people who lived in a state of innocence and were supplied by the bounty of nature. The confrontation of civilization with this innocence caused tensions, and while the desired brave new world of Miranda in Shakespeare's *Tempest* may not have been realized, the image of America as a garden survived until the nineteenth century. Furthermore, it is an image that still exists in European thought about the South Sea islands (Smith, 1960).

These pleasurable landscape experiences are neatly summarized by Auden's word *topophilia*. It is a term that should not be taken to mean just deep attachments to one's native soil and local patriotism, but has a more embracing meaning of a response of warm, suggestive emotion to particular landscapes, even those that we have never seen or that perhaps cannot even exist. In this sense it has powerful links to the human dream of utopia and heaven. The landscape stands for a degree of perfection for man, it is a preferred location and is thus humanized. Among the specific landscapes which seem to have exerted powerful topophilic effects may be mentioned Italy (see Byron above), California for twentieth-century Americans (Vance, 1972) and British Columbia for Canadians. Of mystical and utopian landscapes, the Virgilian is paralleled by that of the classical Greek city states for eighteenth-century Republican Americans or of an imagined Christian medieval world for nineteenth-century literati like Coleridge, Ruskin, and the Pre-Raphaelite brotherhood.

Topophilia is a personal as well as a shared experience. We may not wish to divulge our personal landscapes of utopia, for as Tuan (1963, 16) noted, 'the specific question is rude because it points—like stabbing with the finger. A specific question is: what particular settings in your own experience, either actual or imaginary, do you associate with a deep sense of satisfaction?' Answering such a question may well touch on our deepest experiences, memories, and hopes for ourselves and our world, and should perhaps remain unveiled.

Landscape may also present images of a less pleasing nature—pain, suffering, fear, or desolation. These *topophobic* images might be less articulated or powerful than topophilia, but show consistency over time. Mountain, forest, and desert have only recently become landscapes of attraction, loved today for the solitude which provides a counterpoint to the pressures of the modern human landscape. In the past adjectives such as 'awful', 'horrible', and 'hideous' were applied to the landscapes of nature upon which human art was unable to act. It is significant that the Old Testament placed the great trial of the Jewish people in the desert of Sinai before they reached the sweet waters and pastures of Jordan, and that the New Testament records the Temptation of Christ in the wilderness. Forests too held dangers and unknown forces, an aspect which is reflected in children's fairy-stories. Mountains have been a particular source of topophobia in past eras (Tuan, 1964). The travellers' descriptions of Alpine regions as the hideous haunts of demons were almost conventional clichés before the sudden reappraisal of such areas by nineteenth-century romantics.

There has been an interesting reversal in topophobic landscapes since industrialization. Having acquired much greater control over nature, the uninhabited and untouched landscapes, which had previously been viewed as awesome and frightful began to be given adjectives such as 'unspoiled', and 'wilderness' shifted from being a word of topophobic content to one of topophilia, to the extent that the search for wilderness has become a search for utopia in the minds of many Americans (Lowenthal, 1964). At the same time the landscapes of man, particularly industrial man, have become topophobic landscapes. As was seen in the previous chapter, the image of the gloomy, polluted industrial landscape is now an established theme in attitudes towards cities, but equally it is the image that has stimulated much of man's current concern with conservation and landscape preservation (invariably taken to imply rural landscapes). None the less, it is interesting that other cultures do not necessarily view the industrial landscape in the same light. Soviet and Chinese art at the present day commonly incorporates industrial scenes, and modern Chinese landscape painting, while emulating the style of earlier periods, can incorporate electricity pylons into the landscape as symbols of progress and improved living.

A major geographical study of attitudes towards landscape was *Traces on the Rhodian Shore* (Glacken, 1967). In this book, Glacken identified three themes that have featured large in European attitudes towards nature. These were the concept of the earth as a purposeful creation, a fitting place for human life and civilization; the idea that the physical environment determines human nature and actions; and the realization that man has altered the earth from its original state, for better or worse. Following the interplay of these ideas from Greek thought to the eighteenth century, Glacken showed how contradictions between accepted theories and theological, scientific, geographical, and economic development have led to changes in environmental attitudes as well as the constant restatement of the three basic themes in different guises. The idea of man's activities as an agent of geographical change, for example, has passed through periods when such change was seen as beneficial (in the sense of taming the wilderness, progress towards an earthly utopia, or fulfilling the creative plan of God), to periods when man's activities has been seen as damaging, a common view today.

Glacken's work is a major source for any study of European topophilia, but he provided an important warning when he noted that we can rarely look at a landscape that has been altered by man and confidently assert that it contains a particular attitude towards nature. Tuan (1968) demonstrated this point in his study of the differing attitudes towards wild nature in Judeo-Christian and Confucian thought; the former seeking to dominate nature, the latter believing in a mere passive co-operative relationship between man and nature. Nevertheless, both cultures produced large-scale transformation of nature, as shown by the wholesale destruction of forests for economic ends, with the attendant problems of erosion. Human action and landscape images might contradict one another and 'a perfect mesh between cosmology[3] and the natural order is seldom realised. Cosmology arises out of the bio-social needs and experiences of man; the natural order is ultra-human reality, indifferent to human aspirations' (Tuan, 1971, 33). Glacken and Tuan were agreed that images of landscape derived from sets of beliefs and interpretations of man, nature, and their ordained relationship. Other writers have taken very different approaches towards interpreting the symbolism of landscape, with perhaps the most innovative in the geographical literature being *The Experience of Landscape* by Appleton (1975b). Rather than exploring aspects of landscape images and tracing their relationships to sets of beliefs and activity patterns, Appleton set out to answer the basic questions of 'What is it that we like about landscape?' and 'Why do we like it?' His answers were derived from two sources, the aesthetic philosophy of John Dewey and the writings of eighteenth-century English philosophers.

Dewey (1929, 1934) contended that beauty lay neither in the particular character of objects nor in the human eye alone. It resulted from 'experience'—the relationship between man and his environment. One of the corollaries of this was that man was held to possess certain biological mechanisms that maintained his relationship with the environment, mechanisms which he shared with other living organisms. For Dewey, all art sprang from this biological relationship between man and nature.

Appleton's second source was the works of English writers on landscape aesthetics. From the writings of Lord Shaftesbury in 1674 to those of John Ruskin in the mid-nineteenth century, landscape was a major focus of philosophical enquiry, and this paralleled a period of development in landscape painting which culminated in the work of Turner and in the evolution of a distinct English school of landscape gardening. From an original emphasis on beauty being inherent in certain shapes and forms (for instance, Hogarth's interest in the serpentine 'line of beauty'), attention shifted to the principle of 'association', whereby it was held that particular scenes evoke specific aesthetic responses because they are associated with inherent human responses (or 'passions' in Burke's terminology). For example, the 'sublime' landscape of barren, craggy mountains was associated with pain, danger, and horror, whereas the 'beautiful' was associated with peace, love, and generation.[4]

Appleton combined the animalist arguments of Dewey with eighteenth-century associationalist thinking to produce 'habitat theory'. Appleton contended that in order to achieve evolutionary survival, man had to learn how to see without being seen. Over time, this experience has been modified into an aesthetic response:

aesthetic satisfaction, experienced in the contemplation of landscape, stems from the spontaneous perception of landscape features which, in their shapes, colours, spatial arrangements and other visible attributes, act as sign stimuli indicative of environmental conditions favourable to survival, whether they *are* favourable or not. This proposition we call *habitat theory*. (Appleton, 1975b, 69).

This theory produced a framework of landscape symbolism which was organized around the central ideas of 'prospect', 'refuge', and 'hazard' (Table 8.1). Since seeing and hiding were crucial and complementary aspects of landscape behaviour for all primitive activities, it was important for a creature to be able to use its environment in a way that allowed it to be warned of an approaching hazard, animate or inanimate, and to gain refuge from it. *Prospects* allow unimpeded opportunities for hiding and are symbolized by darkness, hiding places, buildings, and woods. *Hazards* may be direct environmental threats, the blocking of an escape route, or the lack of materials for human survival. If it were not for the existence of hazards, prospects and refuges would have no meaning; thus hazards articulate the whole theory. Appleton applied habitat theory to a range of landscape experiences, from personal encounters with the real world to the representations of landscape in painting, poetry, and literature.

Despite the elegance of the theory, it presents problems. Appleton emphasized man in his primitive condition as a hunter, an idea that many anthropologists now dispute and which would therefore seem a questionable basis for a universal theory of aesthetic response to landscape. Moreover, there was no explanation for how and when the experiences that were once necessary for survival were transformed into aesthetic reactions. For example, it is known that we undergo numerous physiological reactions if we walk into the path of a car which sounds its horn. Oxygen is cut off from all organs and other parts of the body save those that are necessary for survival, heart-beat and breathing rates increase to provide more energy, and later the adrenal gland provides a chemical for continued energy. Nevertheless, there is no evidence that similar reactions take place when confronted with a landscape painting which depicts an immediate hazard but lacks refuge symbols. Indeed Langer (1953), a prominent philosopher of aesthetics, regarded Dewey's argument that art is experience as being fundamentally mistaken. Langer claimed that it missed the characteristic that made art at once as important as science or religion, yet set it apart as an autonomous creative function of the human mind. She went on to point out that, when applied to works of art, the behaviourist premise has not been verified even on its own scientific terms: 'so far the data furnished by galvanometers and encephalographs have not borne on artistic problems, even to the extent of explaining the simple, obvious difference between a major scale and its parallel minor' (Langer, 1953, 38-9).

Appleton certainly identified recurrent themes in landscape aesthetics. The prospect, the juxtaposition of light and shade, slopes, different types of vegetation and the like, are to be found in all landscapes that are conventionally ascribed a high aesthetic quality. Yet at the same time, his explanation is based upon a theory that is perhaps unverifiable and, even if it could be

Table 8.1 *Framework of Landscape Symbolism*

THE IMAGERY AND SYMBOLISM OF THE PROSPECT

TABLE   A. TYPES OF PROSPECT
1. **Direct Prospects**
   A. *Panoramas*
      (i) Simple panoramas
      (ii) Interrupted panoramas
   B. *Vistas*
      (i) Simple vistas
      (ii) Horizontal vistas   } may occur in multiple form
      (iii) Peepholes
      (Panoramas and vistas may be either 'open' or 'closed' with varying length of 'fetch'.)

2. **Indirect Prospects**
   A. *Secondary panoramas*
   B. *Secondary vistas*
      (i) Deflected vistas
      (ii) Offsets
   C. *Secondary peepholes*

TABLE   B. TYPES OF VANTAGE-POINT
1. **Primary Vantage-points** (commanding direct prospects)

2. **Secondary Vantage-points** (commanding, in the imagination, indirect prospects)
   A. *Natural*   C. *Composite*
   B. *Artificial*
   (*Horizons* comprise a special type of secondary vantage-point).

THE IMAGERY AND SYMBOLISM OF THE REFUGE. BASES OF CLASSIFICATION

---

1. **By Function**
   A. *Hides*
   B. *Shelters*   } C. *Composite*

2. **By origin**
   A. *Natural*
   B. *Artificial*
      (i) Buildings   } C. *Composite*
      (ii) Ships
      (iii) Others

3. **By substance**
   A. *Earth refuges*
      (i) Caves
      (ii) Rocks   } D. *Composite*
      (iii) Hollows   (including most buildings, etc.)
   B. *Vegetation refuges*
      (i) Arboreal
      (ii) Others (reeds, grasses, etc.)
   C. *Nebulous refuges* (mist, smoke, etc.)

4. **By Accessibility** (penetrability of margins etc.)

Table 8.1 (cont.)

THE IMAGERY AND SYMBOLISM OF THE HAZARD

---

1. **Incident Hazards**
   A. *Animate hazards*
      (i) Human hazards
      (ii) Non-human hazards

   B. *Inanimate hazards*
      (i) Meteorological hazards
      (ii) Instability hazards
      (iii) Aquatic hazards
      (iv) Fire hazards
      (v) Locomotion hazards

2. **Impediment Hazards**
   A. *Natural*
   B. *Artificial*

3. **Deficiency Hazards**

Source: Compiled from Appleton (1975b, 88, 96, 102). By permission of John Wiley & Sons Ltd.

verified, would not assist our understanding of variation in landscape images between individuals and groups; images which overlie the supposed common basis.

THE SYMBOLIC LANDSCAPE: Iconography and Iconology

As we have already seen, symbols give landscape its character of art. Appleton has recognized the central role of symbols in human images of landscape, but regarded them as derived from atavistic mechanisms. Others have argued that aesthetic reactions to landscape stem from innate structures that relate to human anatomy or physiology. For example, Tuan (1973) emphasized man's nature as an upright being with a left–right symmetry, a back–front symmetry, and an arrangement of senses in one cardinal direction. Some have argued that the 'mandala', a symbol of the city in many cultures, is derived from such innate qualities (see next section). Symbols, however, are far more likely to be products of the human mind which facilitate the communication of ideas and images, and understanding of such symbols needs to be related to the culture in which they are to be found.

In the study of painting, Panofsky (1970) has claimed that symbolic meaning operates at three levels, which broadly parallel the three elements of landscape (physical features, observable activities, and meanings or symbols) discussed earlier. At a primary level Panofsky identified *factual* meaning, as when the representation of a hat is associated with a real hat, and *expressional* meaning, in which certain psychological states are identified by their representation, for example, a mournful expression in the painting of a face. The secondary level was *conventional* meaning, which is approached through identification of symbols and allegories in the picture. A simple example would be the recognition of a halo as a symbol of holiness. In order to achieve that recognition, we require some knowledge of the traditions of representation in Christian art and of 'iconography'—the study of the meaning of images. The third level was *essential* meaning, a unifying principle that explained the selection of the subject of the painting, its significance and the way that it takes shape. The study of this level of meaning was termed 'iconology', the analysis through art of the deepest beliefs and attitudes of the human group from which essential meaning has derived, whether this group is a nation, a class, or a religious or philosophical sect.

Applying this analysis to landscape, the primary level is equivalent to the geographer identifying the physical features of a landscape. At the secondary level, iconography[5] involves recognizing those aspects of landscape that stand for more than merely the functional satisfaction of human needs. For instance, Scully (1962) demonstrated the importance for Greek temples of location in relation to the topography of mountain, valley, and sea. At the third level, iconology is important in the interpretation of a landscape, because meaning in landscape is founded upon 'a complete conception of man and his relationship with nature and God, and on the possibility of expressing this in particular settings' (Relph, 1973, 153). To comprehend the symbolic landscape, we must necessarily understand the basic values and attitudes of those who produced that landscape and those who hold images of it. Individual images of landscape derive from our personal intentions, desires, beliefs and understanding of ourselves and the world; collective topophilia springs from the culture in which it exists and from the way that culture structures its understanding of man and nature.

CITY SYMBOLS AND THE URBAN LANDSCAPE

In surveys of city forms taken from a wide range of societies and cultures, Stewart (1970) and Rykwert (1976) have demonstrated that the geometrical shapes of the circle, square, and cross have been constantly used in the symbolic representation of the city. The earliest hieroglyphic for the city is the cross contained in a circle (Figure 8.1), or the 'mandala'. In writing about

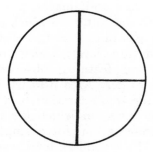

Figure 8.1. The Mandala

the mandala, the psychoanalyst Neumann (quoted in Stewart, 1970, n.p.) stated:

The symbol of the circular *mandala* stands at the beginning as at the end. In the beginning it takes the mythological form of paradise, in the end of Heavenly Jerusalem. The perfect figure of the circle from whose centre radiate the four arms of the cross, in which opposites are at rest is a very early and a very late symbol historically.

The mandala has been regarded by several authors as being derived from internal and innate mental structures (Jung, 1964; Smith, 1975), an argument that leads to the suggestion that such symbolic devices in city layout are used by man to develop images of himself as well as of the cosmos and paradise. Tuan (1972) showed how societies that have achieved urbanism often symbolize the city as the final goal of human progress from original chaos and wilderness, portraying the city itself as the symbol of heaven. Jerusalem and Peking are just two of many such cities that could be cited in this context.

A number of geographical studies have focused upon the relationship between the urban landscape and human beliefs and intentions. In his book *British Townscapes*, Johns (1965) showed how the tendency to shape the townscape according to the *Zeitgeist*, (as expressed by art and literature), gave characteristic form to the present-day British city. In particular, Johns suggested that an understanding of art and literature could assist in comprehending building styles and fashions. The growth of the Romantic movement in arts and letters, for example, helped to explain why city-builders moved away from the eighteenth-century classical architecture of formal lines and severe facades[6] to a self-conscious informality, characterized by eclectic use of supposed medieval architectural forms such as the villa house and the picturesque park. This study, however, was simply iconographic, there is little discussion of how changing literary, artistic, and architectural motifs mirror changing attitudes towards man, society, and nature.

In a similar vein, Price (1964) supplied a valuable iconographic analysis of the central Italian city of Viterbo. *Inter alia*, Price claimed that the urban landscape of Viterbo could be interpreted as an expression of the inner workings and history of the city. Among the elements of the landscape that were discussed were the age and density of the buildings, construction materials, and changes over time. The question of attitudes was raised, for example comparing the differing values of Italians and Americans towards such issues as optimal housing density, open space, and the functional zoning of urban activities, but Price ignored the philosophical, religious, or cultural underpinnings of values. He therefore identified symbols rather than explained them. Price (1964, 274) concluded with the statement that 'Viterbo is a medieval city in the same sense that Rome, even with its much longer historical continuity, is a Baroque city, or that Florence, harder to classify, is possibly a Renaissance city.' If the description of Viterbo as medieval was correct, then one assumes its landscape manifested most clearly those forms which gave fullest expression to that understanding of city symbols that was peculiar to the medieval Italian mind. If not the statement would mean little other than the majority of the buildings were medieval. Price, in fact, was writing about Viterbo as an iconographer, but to achieve an adequate understanding it is necessary to add the iconological dimension. In other words, such an analysis would also require insight into the beliefs and attitudes that were held by both medieval builders and contemporary observers.

Outside the geographical literature, historians of art and architecture have also produced studies of city symbols. The broad perspectives of Saarinen (1943) and Mumford (1963), and the more detailed writings of Summerson (1969) and Wheatley (1969, 1971), have all provided incisive analysis of the city symbol without losing sight of the functional aspects of the city. Summerson (1969), for example, took the two parameters of taste and wealth as key factors in shaping the urban landscape of eighteenth- and nineteenth-century London. None the less, 'taste' in this instance is roughly equivalent to Johns's use of the term 'fashion', a convention that has been adopted in a somewhat arbitrary way by a small group of opinion leaders and has diffused down the social scale. The degree to which taste or fashion spring from more fundamental attitudes, values, and beliefs that are held by particular groups seems a further valuable question.

Architectural studies of townscape have tended to view the city as an art form, often to the exclusion of its activities. Their emphasis has usually been upon appraising the result of the process of landscape creation in achieving pleasing visual spaces, rather than seeking to understand the image that the city presented to the observer. Thus de Wolfe (1963), Nairn (1965), and Sharp (1968) all recognized the need to develop ways of analysing the aesthetics of buildings, surfaces, street furniture, volumes of space, vegetation, and other elements of the urban scene as an interrelated whole, but their approach was in the tradition of 'art for art's sake'. They sought to establish the extent to which the city gave sensory pleasure to the observer who was passing through it rather than to question the meaning of the symbols that it incorporated. Perhaps a more incisive approach was that of Cullen (1961),[7] who took consideration of symbolic meaning much further when he commented that 'vision is not only useful, but it evokes our memories and experiences, those responsive emotions inside us which have the power to disturb the mind when aroused' (Cullen, 1961, 11). This led Cullen to investigate the nature of basic spatial experiences in the urban landscape, attempting to measure the extent to which urban landscapes succeeded in articulating these experiences for people who came into contact with a city. Success was measured in terms of design, and design was seen as more than an autonomous element but as springing from the nature of those who created and chose it, their experiences of themselves and their world.

The city symbol has significance for all groups whose society has experienced urbanism and its particular significance is to be judged iconologically in terms of the deepest beliefs and intentions of these groups. Similarly specific cities have great symbolic importance, as is true of Rome, Jerusalem, New York, Paris, or Peking. These are not necessarily beautiful cities, but they appear to have mediated the city symbol as it emerges both in the minds of their creators and those who experience them. They are among those 'key symbolic landscapes—landscapes that perennially catch the attention of mankind and seem to stand for, reflect or incorporate, the meaning and purpose of life itself' (Lowenthal, 1967, 2).

9 Regional and World Images

STAN: 'But why King's Lynn?'
NICK: 'Because it's further from anywhere than anywhere else I know'
(A. PLATER, *The Trinity Tales*)

The metaphor of the 'shrinking world' has a powerful appeal for contemporary society. Certainly twentieth-century changes in personal mobility and the rapid spread of telecommunications have done much to overcome the constraints of distance, but mere availability of information does not in itself expand the spatial horizons of the individual. Advertising clichés about 'Jet Sets' and 'Getaway People' largely serve to bolster the self-image of modern man, masking the fact that the everyday life of most people still revolves around the twin confines of home and workplace. The world beyond remains unfamiliar, a realm about which knowledge comes from infrequent personal contact or from secondary sources.

This chapter examines images of macro-space—places and areas that are too remote, or large, or both, to be known in detail and about which popular knowledge is heavily stereotyped. The first part indicates the role played by stereotypes in cognition of macro-space and points to the close relationship between stereotyping and motivation. The second section considers the nature of regional images, discussing the role of stereotypes in the historical development of particular areas. The final part deals with the relationship between cosmology and the global images held by members of specific cultural groups.

STEREOTYPES AND MOTIVATION

As noted previously, stereotypes are an essential element in the way that people cope with environmental complexity. Stereotypes form the basis upon which phenomena can be assigned into broad categories, even though the classification is often based on no more than superficial appearance. The word 'stereotype' tends to have unpleasant connotations, primarily because the concept was derived from research into racial prejudice, in which stereotypes are seen to be rooted in fear and anxiety and arise as part of a defence mechanism (Hirsh, 1955). These negative associations need not apply to place or areal stereotypes. Although it is possible to find places that have predominantly negative stereotypes, such as inner city 'slums' or coastal 'swamps', it is equally possible to find places with inherently favourable or romantic stereotypes. California, medieval Italian cities and the islands of the South Seas are three such examples that will be discussed in the course of this chapter.

A further significant feature of stereotypes is their resistance to change, a characteristic that led Belcher (1973, 221) to comment: 'When actual facts do not correspond to stereotyped belief, something has to give and unfortunately it is usually the facts.' This applies to spatial stereotypes just as much as any other form of stereotype. Individual places that fail to conform to a particular stereotype are normally treated as unimportant exceptions to the general rule, and it is unswerving faith in the latter that guides image formation. Nevertheless, it is important not to oversimplify matters. Although, by definition, stereotypes receive broad social acceptance and occupy a prominent place in socialization,[1] individuals can participate in the process by which new stereotypes evolve, are communicated and reinforced. For instance, mass communication researchers have long appreciated that it is possible for the individual, at different times, to be both a communicator and a member of the audience. On receiving a piece of information, he will interpret it according to his own needs and then may pass it on to a secondary audience, who will interpret this message in the light of their own needs. In the process the individual has the opportunity to reinforce stereotypes and perhaps initiate new ones. Whether or not the latter will be accepted will depend largely on whether such stereotypes provide an acceptable description of the phenomenon for other people and meet the spatial informational needs of the wider social group.

For our purposes, the link between stereotyping and motivation is important. Stereotypes are not exogenously created attitudes that are transmitted to an audience of passive recipients, but the end-product of complex interactions between motivated individuals. This point may be substantiated by briefly considering promotional literature of the type that has been used throughout the ages to attract migrants to distance parts.[2] Broadly such literature was disseminated for two reasons, often interlinked. In the first place, the bodies responsible for such developments tried to convey a picture of the undoubted benefits and unlimited opportunities that were to be gained from migration to their particular scheme. The following advertisement from the *Sheffield and Rotherham Independent* (17 Aug. 1875), under the heading of '100,000 ACRES OF THE FINEST FARMING LAND IN AMERICA FOR SALE', is a representative example of this literature:

The land is situated in South Western Minnesota and is open, rolling prairie of unsurpassed fertility and all ready for the plough. The climate is as healthy as any known, so much as to make the state a resort for invalids.

Very unusual opportunities are now presented for profitable farming and investment in this portion of the state. Droughts which are such a frequent cause of loss to farmers in the West have never been known in this region. The country is interspersed with beautiful lakes which abound in fish and wild fowl are plentiful . . .

The art of this form of advertising is to take the requisite 'grains of truth' on which all stereotypes are based and to make these stand for the whole personality of the colony, sometimes to the point at which what was written owed more to what the author would have liked to see than what actually existed.

Secondly, the authors of such literature were often less concerned with initial image creation than attempting to counter unfavourable stereotypes that might already be in vogue. As Jones (1946) noted, one of the principal tasks for promotional literature was to combat the 'flood of slander and malicious gossip' from which most colonial schemes suffered. This was clearly in the mind of the following writer[3] who, in an article entitled 'Immense Arrival of Treasure from Australia', set out to confound those who failed to believe in the unlimited bounty of the sub-continent. *Inter alia*, the author claimed that 'Our problem indeed is not to find where gold is, but to find a place where it certainly is not.'

The same partiality was also to be found in the writings of European travellers and explorers, but for different reasons. Most of this literature represents true reports of the perceptions of explorers (however narrowly based their travels may have been), but like anyone else, explorers had their own needs which were reflected in their writings (Adams, 1962). After devoting much time and resources towards exploring new and potentially dangerous countries, many were somewhat loath to write reports that said that they found little of value or interest. In most cases this led to travellers embroidering upon their findings or at least concentrating on those aspects of their journeys that would appeal most to their readers, but a minority produced reports deliberately falsified to make people believe that the writers had been to places that they had never visited. Jonathan Carver,[4] for example, wrote copiously in the late eighteenth century about the habits of animals that he had never seen, about the vocabularies of North American Indians whom he never met, and about places that he never visited. There were even those such as Daniel Defoe,[5] who amused themselves by writing spurious reports under pseudonyms to see if they could hoodwink people into thinking that these were authentic accounts of journeys.

These reports undoubtedly served the various needs and motives of their authors. None the less, the fact that such writings were accepted as truth and allowed to create stereotypes was primarily because their readers also had needs which this literature served. While there may be a correlation between availability of information and colonial migration (Cameron, 1974), there is little to suggest that this literature alone caused migration. Stereotypes of bounty and opportunity, of riches and adventure struck a resonant chord in the minds of those who migrated through choice (rather than through being driven out of their previous homes), because they *wanted* to believe the claims of the literature. Images of a utopian future were a great comfort to those who were preparing themselves to leave their homes and kinfolk and embark upon journeys that were frequently perilous. In other words, the evidence again indicates that cognition is motivated. People were willing to act upon the good that they heard and to disregard the bad provided that their needs were sufficient to make them feel that it was worth while to do so.

THE REGIONAL IMAGE

The concept of 'the region' is one with which geographers have long been familiar. A region may be defined broadly as a portion of the earth's surface that possesses some characteristic or properties that distinguish it from other such areas. Having said that, one almost exhausts the consensus of agreement about the nature and purpose of regions. While this is not the place to summarize the long debate about the regional concept that has been waged in the geographical literature,[6] two general conclusions may be noted. First, there is no single criterion or set of criteria that will yield regions appropriate for all circumstances. Regions are rarely valid other than for the specific purposes for which they were designed. Second, it must be realized that regions are mental constructs and not objective realities. They are tools in developing an understanding of space, not phenomena with an independent corporeal existence.

These conclusions have considerable relevance for the present discussion. They indicate that geographical attempts at regionalization are frequently no more than a systematic version of the everyday process by which we come to terms with spatial complexity. The regions formulated by the geographer may be no better or more informative than less formal classifications. Indeed some writers have suggested that it would be more useful if geographers used public images of regions as the appropriate framework for analysis rather than designing and imposing their own regional taxonomies. For example, the author of a notable text on the regional geography of North America has commented that if called upon to undertake the same task again, he would attempt to seek regions 'not in rocks and rivers, rainfall and resources, but in the minds of man' (Watson, 1971, 31).

This presupposes that the region is a meaningful concept for the non-geographer, but the evidence suggests that this is a reasonable assumption. Supportive evidence, for example, may be found in the studies carried out in connection with the *Kilbrandon Report* (1973), which contains the findings of a Royal Commission that examined the question of regional devolution in Great Britain. In attempting to investigate attitudes to changes in regional responsibility, it was thought necessary to establish first the extent to which people felt that they belonged to a region, how they identified their region, and the relative strength of regional feeling in different parts of the country. From a sample of 4892 people, it was found that about 75 per cent were

able to think meaningfully in terms of regions. Those who failed to understand the concept were most likely to be those in semi- and unskilled
socio-economic grades, those not interested or involved in political and
community affairs, and the elderly. There were found to be strong spatial
variations in the extent of the perceived regions. Table 9.1 records the
responses of those interviewed when asked a question about what they
considered to be their region (the answers being compared with an 'objective'
map based upon the Economic Planning Regions). While a sizeable proportion of respondents (36 per cent) produced regions that matched the
Economic Planning Regions, figures well above average were recorded in
the South West, Wales, and Scotland, with figures far below the average in
the North (where they took smaller county units. to be their regions) and
the West Midlands (where people considered a larger unit, the Midlands, to
be their region). Notwithstanding these variations, it was recorded that
feelings of regional identity were discernible throughout the country. Their
strength in Scotland and Wales, two regions with a powerful cultural identity
and resurgent nationalism, was almost equalled by the results from the South
West and Yorkshire. Furthermore, around 90 per cent of the British population identified themselves with the region in which they were living, stating
that was where they felt that they belonged.

Individual and group identification with the home region has been consistently shown by the cross-cultural work of Gould and his associates[7] on the
regional preferences of school-leavers and college students. A procedure was
devised in which respondents were presented with a list of administrative
regions, such as the states of the American Union or British counties, and
were asked to rank them in order of residential desirability. These rankings
were then aggregated for the total sample, factor analysed, and presented
graphically as the 'cognitive maps' of the group. While there are reasons
to question the validity of the method,[8] these studies may be said to have
revealed two important findings. First, respondents consistently attached
a high value to their local area. To take the example of the studies carried
out with British school-leavers (Gould and White, 1968), it was found that
there was a 'dome of local desirability' in the cognitive maps produced at
each of the twenty-three study locations. Second, there was an underlying
national consensus on areas of particular desirability, which was revealed by
aggregating the rankings for each study location to produce a 'national'
map. The map depicted in Figure 9.1 reveals a strong preference for the
south coast, the West Country, and the Cambridge area of East Anglia, areas
which would be primarily associated with summer holidays. This point
strongly suggests the role of stereotypes. These areas are generally perceived
as they were during brief and very occasional summer visits, or by listening
to the holiday recollections of others, or by reading travel literature which
invariably presents the 'smiling summer face' of tourist areas. The spoil-heaps
and quarry-faces of Cornish mineral workings, the bleakness of out-of-season
seaside resorts, and the traffic congestion of low-capacity and over-used
roads rarely figure in the image of these regions.

Table 9.1 *Regional Identification*

Question 18(a) "What do you think of as *your* region of the country—what would you call it?"

	Total	Area												
		North	Yorkshire	North West	West Midland	East Midland	East Anglia	South East	Greater London	South	South West	Wales	Scotland
Weighted base: all informants	(4892)	(230)	(496)	(612)	(512)	(224)	(231)	(628)	(753)	(213)	(284)	(244)	(465)
	%	%	%	%	%	%	%	%	%	%	%	%	%
Town and city/Area around city	6	7	6	7	6	7	3	2	5	3	6	4	11
Area small but bigger than town	2	3	2	7	2	1	2	4	0	0	2	1	2
County	12	21	15	18	6	7	18	12	5	12	11	9	12
Sub-region (smaller than map region)	6	52	1	0	5	0	0	2	0	0	3	27	15
Region diff. from area on map	5	0	10	2	13	5	8	8	1	8	2	0	0
Supra-region (larger than map region)	18	0	14	10	42	39	19	16	34	12	5	1	1
Not region person lives in	0	0	0	0	1	0	0	0	0	0	0	1	1
Region correctly defined (as on map)	36	10	40	42	7	25	34	45	32	49	65	48	45
Don't know/Don't understand	11	6	10	14	16	14	11	10	12	15	4	5	10
Great Britain/U.K./England	0	0	0	0	0	0	0	0	0	0	0	3	1
Units smaller than first def. (e.g. village, small London area)	2	2	2	0	2	0	2	1	10	0	1	1	2
Unweighted numbers in each region	(4892)	(159)	(506)	(447)	(508)	(164)	(169)	(461)	(495)	(156)	(209)	(726)	(892)

Source: Kilbrandon Report (1973) Research Paper, 7, 42. By permission of the Controller of Her Majesty's Stationery Office.

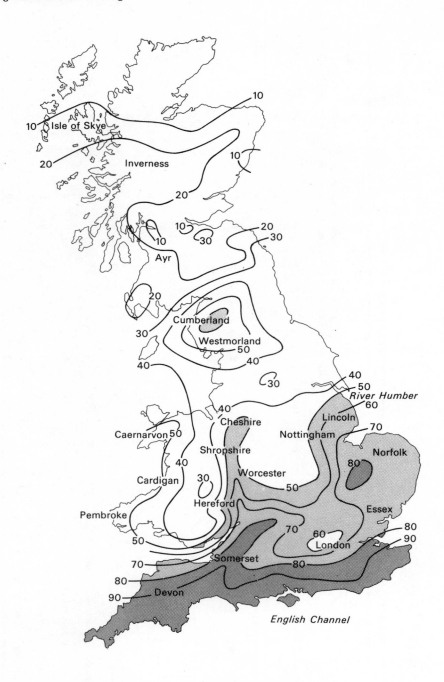

Figure 9.1. The general perception surface for the United Kingdom

Source: Gould and White (1974, 82). Copyright (1968). Reprinted by permission of The Regional
Studies Association.

Regional stereotypes, as suggested previously, show remarkable resilence and consistency over time, a matter that has interested writers on the regional development of such countries as the United States of America or Australia. As countries settled within the span of recorded history, contemporary documentation can be used to discover the motives and attitudes of explorers and pioneers. In doing so, it is clear that specific areas have long been stereotyped in the public imagination as intrinsically attractive or unpleasant, and there is a correlation between such images and the pace of the development process.

California supplies a good example of such a correlation. Before the nineteenth century, California was a poorly explored and scantily settled outpost of New Spain, lying several thousand miles from the nascent states of the American Union, but as time progressed, American interest in the region started to grow. Initial exploration produced standard reports about natural bounty and a land that was uniquely free from known diseases (Cooke, 1973), but the events that really sparked interest were the 'Gold Rush' (1848-53), transfer of sovereignty from Mexico to the USA (1848), and the building of the transcontinental railway linking California to the east (1869). With California now effectively closer to the nation's consciousness, it is apparent that the state soon gained the highly favourable reputation that it has retained until the present day (Vance, 1972). None the less, as Thompson (1969) has pointed out, there were in reality two stereotypes: one that was prominent in attracting migrants to California; the other playing a role in channelling settlement within California.

To understand the nature of these stereotypes, it is necessary to know something about the medical beliefs of the time. Before the late nineteenth century the theory of transmission of disease by germs was unknown. Instead people believed that diseases were caused primarily by physical environmental conditions, particularly the constituents of the climatic environment—'good' and 'bad' air, precipitation, winds, and barometric pressure. Certain aspects of the physical environment were regarded as inherently pathogenic, just as other aspects were thought to be therapeutic.

Viewed in this light, the climate of nineteenth-century California was stereotyped overall as being therapeutic, an image that propagandists were at pains to emphasise. As Thompson (1969) pointed out, of the substantial migrations to California in the late nineteenth century, a remarkably high proportion were invalids, especially sufferers from tuberculosis. Contemporary estimates placed the number of invalids amongst migrants to southern California between 1870 and 1890 at anything between 8 and 75 per cent. Even if the figure were 8 per cent, it could be regarded as high. Yet at the same time that California was generally stereotyped as healthy, there was another equally slenderly based belief which stereotyped large areas as pathogenic. This stereotype was linked to the incidence of malaria and diseases, such as typhoid, which were often confused with it. Medical opinion of the time considered that such diseases were caused by bad air (miasma), and places where such air was to be found would have included marshy areas and zones where there was poor drainage. As indicated in Figure 9.2, the Central Valley of California was generally regarded as miasmatic and an area to be avoided. This stereotype had some truth, although for the wrong reasons. *Some* marshy areas were the breeding-grounds of malarial mosquitoes and the Central Valley did have a higher incidence of the disease than average. Nevertheless, the Central Valley gained a reputation that was quite

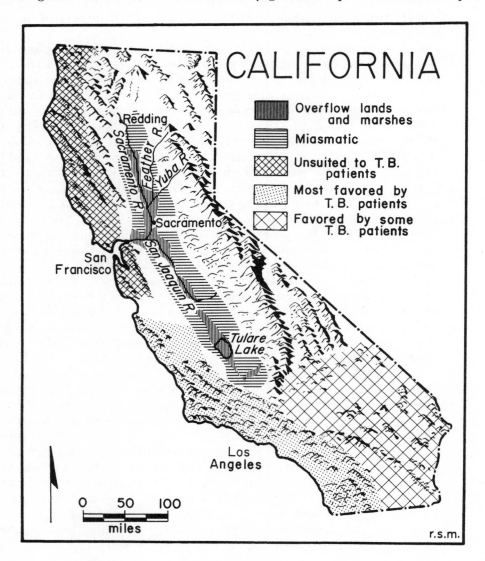

Figure 9.2. Supposed health regions of California in the late nineteenth century

Source: Thompson (1969, 54). By permission of Association of American Geographers.

out of keeping with the facts, an aura that it retained until the lessons of twentieth-century aetiological research on malaria gained full public acceptance.

There are also instances when the same region has been stereotyped in quite contrasting ways, an occurrence seen in the debate over the American purchase of Alaska from Russia in 1867. At the time of the purchase, very little was actually known about Alaska. It was extremely sparsely settled, had only been partially explored, and few areas had been reliably mapped. Despite this lack of knowledge, strong images of Alaska existed in the minds of those who supported or opposed the purchase. As Coyne (1974) has demonstrated in a meticulous study of attitudes towards the purchase, these views could be divided into two groups. On the one hand, those who opposed the purchase drew upon the stereotype of Alaska as a frozen waste or as a region with an unhealthy damp climate. The *New York Tribune* alluded in its editorial comment to 'ice fields' and 'deserts of snow'. A member of the House of Representatives who was opposed to the scheme declared that 'Alaska [is] a barren unproductive region, covered with ice and snow, or shrouded in perpetual fogs and storms, embracing an area nearly one-third of which is within the Arctic circle' (quoted in Coyne, 1974, 28). At the same time, proponents of the purchase were putting forward quite different impressions of Alaska as an area of enormous resource potential or as an area of agricultural opportunity that would make it comparable with New England.

Such polarities of view were possible because so little was actually known about Alaska. Most of the information that was available related to the character of the south coast (which varies considerably), with relatively little firm knowledge about the north coast or the interior. Estimates of resources were based on speculation from limited discoveries or observations. Thus it was possible for supporters or opponents of the purchase to find sources to substantiate the case that they wished to make. For example, opponents drew heavily upon Russian accounts of the area, and, as the party willing to sell, their estimation of Alaska was particularly gloomy. By the same token, supporters drew upon the more optimistic reports of late-eighteenth-century English and French navigators along the south coast of Alaska, upon the exaggerated reports of mineral speculators, and from limited examples of productive agriculture, such as the 'Garden of Alaska' near Cook Inlet. These conflicting reports related to different seasons, periods, and places, but demonstrate clearly how information is open to interpretation by motivated individuals. They could alternatively be used to show Alaska to be a land of timbered slopes and rolling grasslands or a realm of ice and mountains. The fact that the purchase ultimately went ahead reflected that the stereotype of the potential value of natural resources, plus the opportunity to finally remove the Russians from the American continent,[9] outweighed the apparent environmental disadvantages claimed by opponents.

These examples by no means exhaust the available literature, but serve to illustrate the importance of stereotypes and the strong links between beliefs and cognition. People do not necessarily view the world as it is but how they believe it to be, or even as they would like it to be. Once more it should be emphasized that such conceptions of the world are not just the environment's impact upon the individual. It is a true interrelationship in which people also project their feelings and expectations onto the environment. Environmental belief heavily influences spatial cognition.

WORLD IMAGES: Cosmology and Uncharted Realms

Cosmology, it may be recalled, is a theory that explains the universe as a created whole. Since time immemorial, human societies have had a desire to come to terms with the nature of the cosmos. Their motive is more than just curiosity, but reflects a deep-rooted need to have a stable and consistent basis into which to fit information about the known world, to extrapolate what unknown portions of it may be like, and to fit human existence into some form of universal order.

Cosmologies vary considerably from culture to culture and over time. Tuan (1974, 79) recognized that societies at primitive stages of development have cosmologies that are closely linked to the natural environment: 'unless it is derived from an alien culture, [the world view] is necessarily constructed out of the salient elements of a people's social and physical setting. In non-technological societies, the physical setting is the canopy of nature and its myriad contents.' These cosmologies have a diversity which mirrors the contrasting environmental experiences of the cultural group in question. The examples that may be cited from the anthropological literature are legion. The Santa Ana Indians of the New Mexican desert conceive of the earth as a square object, having a stratified structure. The earth itself is regarded as the heart of the cosmos, with the sun, moon, and stars being accessories that make life on earth habitable for mankind. The Yurok Indians of the mountainous north-west of California conceive of their world as a circular disc, which is surrounded by, and floats upon, a universal ocean (Tuan, 1974). The Temne people of the northern rain-forests of Sierra Leone consider the earth to be a flat circular object resting on the head of a giant, and placed there by Kuru (God). Trees and plants are the hair of his head and living creatures, including themselves, are the lice in it (Littlejohn, 1963).

Each of these three cosmologies provides a perfectly workable and manageable framework for everyday life. They may also be taken as representative examples of primitive cosmologies, for although they may seem at first glance to be very different, similarities do abound. In archaic and traditional societies, the known world is conceived as a microcosm. As Eliade (1961, 37–8) has pointed out:

At the limits of this closed world begins the domain of the unknown, of the formless. On this side there is ordered space because it is inhabited and organised, outside this familiar space, there are unknown and dangerous regions of demons, ghosts, the dead and of foreigners—in short a world of chaos, or death and night. This image of an inhabited microcosm, surrounded by desert regions regarded as a chaos, or a kingdom of the dead, has survived even in highly evolved civilisations such as those of China, Mesopotamia, and Egypt.

It is also common for sedentary populations to have a world-view that emphasizes the homeland as the centre of the earth and which stresses the vertical dimension of spatial experience. In other words, with travel being very limited, earth space becomes one component in a stratified cosmos of sky, earth, and underworld (Tuan, 1971).

Similarities are again found in the form of the world that is derived from primitive cosmologies. The symbol of the earth as a floating disc, as a square, as the mandala, or even a sphere are recurrent themes (Eliade, 1961; Brendel, 1977). So too is the idea that the earth is endowed with anthropomorphic properties. Lethbridge (1957), in a masterly if speculative study, traced the ubiquity of earth-god cults in Indo-European cultures, in which the landscape was viewed in terms of the physical attributes of earth deities, with certain places assuming sanctity because of the deity that hills, valleys, or streams represented. Ross (1967), for example, traced the significance of springs, rivers, and wells as divine sanctuaries throughout pagan Celtic Britain. Tuan (1976a) described a sophisticated parallel from ancient Chinese society, whereby the various aspects of the earth were considered as different manifestations of a cosmic being. The mountains were its body, the rocks its bones, water the blood, trees and grasses the hair, and clouds and mists the vapour of its breath. The whole was made more tangible by specific gods who resided in the hills and rivers and needed to be propitiated at suitable sacred places.

Christianity deliberately sought to oppose the view of the world as the abode of earth deities. Churches were deliberately founded at points of sanctity of pagan earth cults. The policy of the early Church was expressed in the instructions that Pope Gregory sent to St. Augustine through his emissary Mellitus:

Do not pull down the fanes. Destroy the idols; purify the temples with holy water; set relics there; and let them become temples of the true God. So the people will have no need to change their places of concourse, and where of old they were wont to sacrifice cattle to demons, let them continue . . . and slay their beasts, no longer as a sacrifice, but for a social meal in honour of Him whom they now worship.

(Quoted in Anderson, 1971, 10)

By this process of accommodation, the Church aimed to retain a measure of the past attachment to place, while removing the pagan symbolic and mystical properties.

Naturally Christianity produced its own cosmology. Dismissing the works of ancient Greek and Roman writers as being pagan, the Bible, particularly the Old Testament, was to provide the established view of the world and its lands. With the Bible being taken as a statement of revealed truth, it was the role of the map-maker to act as cosmographer and translate this into graphic form. This gave rise to the wildly inaccurate 'T-in-O' (*terra in orbis*) maps, where the earth was depicted as a flat circular disc, with Jerusalem at its centre (in keeping with Ezekiel 5). Such maps were to characterize the European world view for more than a millennium, despite the fact that they were patently ususable for navigational purposes. Even Arabic geographers, who maintained at least some Ptolemaic traditions, employed the 'T-in-O' maps. As Barbour (1973) suggested, part of the reason for this was that such maps had the incidental effect of emphasizing the centrality of Muslim holy places as well as those of Christianity.

Yet Christian cosmography should not be completely divorced from the cosmographies of previous eras and cultures. The cosmographical representations of Christian map-makers certainly bear more than a passing similarity to those of other cultures. As Pentland (1975) has noted, map-making is a universal activity. All people, no matter how primitive or advanced their level of technology, feel the need for maps and have established two-dimensional representations of the world. The conventions adopted seem to be cultural universals, with the same artistic styles being found amongst peoples so widely separated in space and time that diffusion seems highly improbable. As Figure 9.3 shows, once the legends and fantastic beasts are stripped off a fifteenth-century *mappa mundi*, it bears a strong resemblance to maps drawn by present-day Cree Indians. Moreover, while the basic form of 'T-in-O' maps were dictated by theological doctrine, they allowed ample scope for the imagination. When faced with the challenge of uncharted regions, the map-maker responded with drawings of mythical and exotic animals or even to sketch in imaginary lands.

This tendency was also carried into more recent times. When gaps existed in knowledge, map-makers were prone to connect up known portions with extrapolated lines of greater or lesser accuracy or to insert mythical lands. A good example of the latter was the 'Terra Incognita Australis', a fictitious continent which, until the time of Captain Cook's voyages, was thought to lie in the southern seas to act as a counterbalance for the landmasses of the northern hemisphere. Occasionally such gratuitous additions were endowed with mystical significance or fabulous wealth. For instance, maps from the tenth to the nineteenth centuries contained pictograms of Golden Kingdoms—the African land of Prester John, the North American seven cities of Cibola, the Latin American realm of El Dorado (Severin, 1973; Honour, 1976). Such addenda were not simply figments of the cartographer's imagination, for more often than not he was responding to ideas then current in society. Even today, when there are no blank spaces left on the map of the world, there remain the exotic lands of the imagination. The recurrent picture of the Earthly Paradise of the South Sea Islands has occupied the European mind for more than 150 years, and has survived all the assaults of geographical or other realities. As Eliade (1961, 11) has noted: 'Geographical "reality" might give the lie to that paradisiac landscape, ugly and corpulent women might confront the travellers' eyes, but these they did not see; each one saw

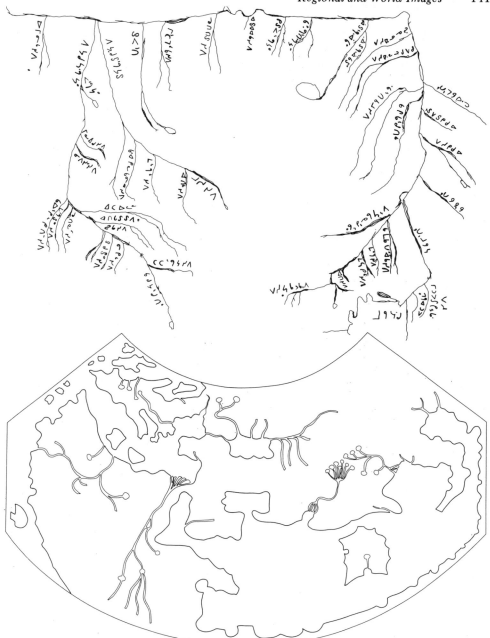

Figure 9.3. Comparison of cartographic styles for different cultures
  (Top) Taken from the Nuremberg Chronicle, 1493, with legends and drawings omitted.
  (Bottom) Part of drawing by James Sack, Sr., 1973, showing Kesagami River and other rivers flowing to James Bay.

Source: Pentland (1975, 150–2)

only the image he had brought with him.' There are other examples that could also be given—frozen Siberian wastes, crude stereotypes of African tribes living in jungle sourroundings—but the basic message remains the same. Despite living in an age dominated by the aura of 'objective' scientific knowledge, the world images of individuals remain partial, ethnocentric, and heavily stereotyped.

PART FOUR

SPATIAL COGNITION AND BEHAVIOUR

10   The City as Living Space

Here also they had the city itself in view, and they thought they heard the bells therein
to ring, and to welcome them thereto. But above all, the warm and joyful thoughts that
they had about their own dwelling there, with such company, and that forever and ever.

(JOHN BUNYAN, *The Pilgrim's Progress*)

Who are the anarchists who have let London become a huge concentration camp of
provincial refugees that hurry to the place and breed and settle down in poverty and
disorganisation?

(ROBERT SINCLAIR, *Metropolitan Man*)

This chapter examines the links between urban spatial cognition and behaviour. Three broad issues will be considered: whether or not there are
inherent properties in the urban environment that lead to given human
behaviours; the role of the locality or 'neighbourhood' in everyday life;
and the relationships between preferences and movement patterns. In considering these issues, particular attention will be paid to two assumptions
that have underpinned many behavioural studies. First, it has been often
asserted that physical distance strongly influences urban spatial interaction,
in that *ceteris paribus* the likelihood and frequency of human intercourse
decreases with increasing distance. Second, many authors have assumed that
the severity of problems found in the city may be directly related to the
quality of the physical environment. A subsidiary aim of this chapter therefore will be to test the validity of such assumptions against the complexities
of real-world behaviour.

THE URBAN AMBIENCE

The origins of present-day theory about the behavioural correlates of urbanism
may be traced back to the writings of nineteenth-century sociologists—the
observers of what Polanyi (1944) termed the 'Great Transformation' in
Western society after the Industrial Revolution. In developing an understanding of societal change, they emphasized the question of scale. Changes in the
technological base of society, coupled with rapid population increase, meant
that the nature of human interaction had changed. Instead of simply being
in contact with a few hundred people as in rural society, an individual living
in a large city would be in touch, directly and indirectly, with thousands
(Fischer, 1976). In such circumstances, writers of very different political
persuasions (e.g. Engels, 1844; Maine, 1861) were united in the belief that
the urban way of life was qualitatively different from that of the rural
and pre-industrial situation.

The fullest analysis was presented by Tönnies (1887). From observations of contemporary German cities, Tönnies claimed to see a new way of life evolving. He argued that rural life took place within the framework of *Gemeinschaft* (community), whereas urban life was characterized by *Gesellschaft* (society). In the city, the warm primary social relationships of the *Gemeinschaft* were replaced by the formalized, contractual, experient, impersonal, and specialized relationships of the *Gesellschaft*. The result was a society that was less cohesive, but one which the newcomer could easily join and be accepted by (Maruyama, 1976).

In the twentieth century, this view of the urban way of life has been supplemented and elaborated by numerous workers, but perhaps the best-known and most influential were those belonging to the Chicago school of urban ecologists. Park (1916), the founder of this school, had proposed that the best method for studying the new way of life was for the social scientist to go out and conduct exploratory studies in his or her own city. On this basis a large volume of research developed, primarily produced at the University of Chicago, which provided a wealth of empirical data with a firm basis in urban ecological theory. Of these studies,[1] the most pertinent here is the essay entitled 'Urbanism as a Way of Life' by Wirth (1938).

In essence, Wirth synthesized elements proposed by previous writers into a coherent theory which contained social structural, cognitive, and behavioural components (see Figure 10.1). This is not the place to discuss Wirth's theory in detail,[2] but it is instructive to explore the way in which he forged links between the cognitive and behavioural levels of the theory. This was based upon a social psychological framework which owed much to the work of Simmel (1903; trans. Wolff, 1950). Simmel had studied rural and urban lifestyles, noting the marked differences in their respective paces of life. The slower tempo of traditional rural society was said to be characterized by unconscious and habitual behaviour patterns. By contrast, the town-dweller was materially affected by the demands placed upon him by his ever-changing environment, particularly by the intensification of nervous stimuli that emanated from such components of urban life as lights, noise, and bustle. These stimuli demand constant and continuous response and, in order to cope, the individual has to adopt a cool and calculating approach to life. He becomes governed by the head rather than the heart, keeping his distance from others and avoiding all but superficial relationships. Simmel suggested that there was a distinct metropolitan personality, characterized by the blasé attitude that inhabitants adopted towards one another.

Wirth followed Simmel's analysis closely.[3] His starting-point was the assumption that the large, crowded, and heterogeneous city environment bombarded the individual with infinitely varied stimuli. The individual had to adapt, but strategies designed to ease the burden inevitably lead to an impersonality that may be discerned in both interpersonal and broader social relationships by 'the substitution of secondary for primary contacts, the weakening of bonds of kinship, the declining social significance of the family, the disappearance of the neighbourhood, and the undermining of the

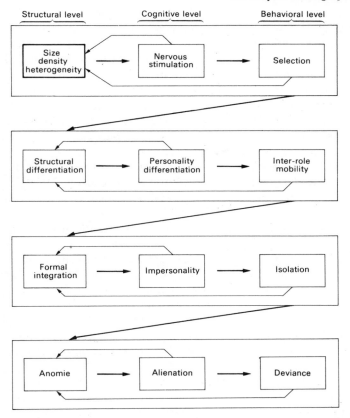

Figure 10.1. Louis Wirth's theory of 'urbanism as a way of life' diagrammed in causal-path form

Source: Berry (1973, 16). By permission of Macmillan, London and Basingstoke.

traditional basis for social solidarity.' The end-products were 'anomie'—a condition in which the normal rules and conventions that regulate social behaviour have atrophied, 'alienation'—the individual's sense of detachment from surrounding society, and 'deviance'.

Wirth's theory supplies a useful starting-point from which to discuss the behavioural implications of urban living. At its roots lies an environmentally deterministic view of behaviour with two key propositions. First, it was argued that the urban environment fosters impersonality, detachment, and avoidance, with the urbanite shunning contact and displaying apathy towards others. Second, it was suggested that the city imposes stresses upon its inhabitants, which could lead progressively to alienation and deviance. As these contentions have underpinned so many studies of behaviour in the urban environment, they merit further consideration.

Apathy or Involvement? It is frequently asserted that urban life is distinguished by the measured indifference city dwellers show towards one another. People jostle in the street, perhaps even ignoring requests for assistance as being none of their concern. Bystander apathy can occasionally take extreme forms. In the summer of 1976, for example, a young Cypriot boy Enrico Sidoli was killed at the Parliament Hill Lido in London, when he was pushed into the water and held underneath until he drowned. Although over a thousand people were at the pool, no one intervened and very few witnesses could be traced. In subsequent inquiries police encountered a 'wall of don't know's' and deliberate obstruction by parents of children they were trying to interview (Knewstub, 1977).

Such incidents are mercifully rare but occur sufficiently often (see, e.g., Milgram and Hollander 1964; Latané and Darley, 1970), to suggest that here is an extreme manifestation of what appears to be a wholly urban phenomenon. Various reasons have been advanced for such behaviour. Milgram (1970) considered that it is partly due to the unwritten law that demands respect for other people's emotional and social privacy, even where lack of space may deprive them of privacy. In situations where the motives of the participants are unclear, it is hard to know whether taking an active role is unwarranted meddling or an appropriate response to a critical situation. Latané and Darley (1970) commented that a failure to respond may be due to two factors—social influence and the diffusion of responsibility. The bystander may be influenced by the reaction of other witnesses. If others present at the scene do not regard the situation as serious, the individual may feel justified in his decision not to intervene. Even if the situation does appear to be an emergency, the presence of others makes it less necessary to take action oneself, with responsibility being diffused over all the bystanders. Stringer (1975a) proposed another view, derived from the ecological psychologist's concept of a behaviour setting.[4] In each behaviour setting, there are a certain number who can be directly involved. If more people than this number are present, the behaviour setting is said to be 'over-manned'. The result of 'over-manning' is that a proportion of those present at a scene are are forced to become onlookers, who are therefore uninvolved and marginal to the situation.

All these are partial but plausible explanations of a disquieting urban phenomenon, but it would be a mistake to believe that the city *per se* generates non-involvement and avoidance behaviour. Nor should one generalize from such events as the Sidoli case without considering the equally valid instances when people have intervened in situations, at great personal risk, to help others. Experimental work (e.g. Piliavin *et al.*, 1969; Milgram, 1970) has indicated that urbanites are not significantly different to others in their willingness to offer assistance, although scale does appear to be an important factor in personal involvement. It might not be possible to identify oneself with the city as a whole but perfectly feasible to be deeply involved in the locality. Numerous studies have drawn attention to the friendliness and mutual concern of inhabitants of urban neighbourhoods (Young and Willmott, 1957; Jacobs, 1962; Lewis, 1968) or in the small town (Mead, 1968). Coupled with this is the fact that people who are part of the locality have greater familiarity with the people and artefacts found there. The familiarity that comes with intimate experience of a small area provides the individual with greater security in dealing with other people in that environment. As Latané and Darley (quoted in Ittelson *et al.*, 1974, 261) suggested, a 'person who is more familiar with his environment is more aware of the way in which the environment works. He is not overloaded with stimuli . . . He may have a greater stake in keeping that environment safe. He is in control. Thus he is more likely to help.' In this way, involvement can be as much a feature of urban behaviour as apathy and avoidance—it is just that they tend to be related to different contexts.

Urban Stress. The second key behavioural proposition centres upon the concept of urban 'stress'. Broadly, it has been argued that man is ill equipped to deal with the intense and infinitely varied stimulation of the city, as evolutionary development makes him much more suited to the slower rhythms of rural life. Man can and does adjust, but in doing so suffers stress, which may be defined as the unpleasant physiological and psychological reactions the individual experiences when faced by the new, demanding, and persistent stimuli that are part of the urban environment. Stress was to be regarded as a personal state, which must be distinguished from the agents that produce stress ('stressors') and the behavioural responses ('stress reactions') that characterize a stressed individual (Selye, 1956; Turan, 1974).

This concept owes much to the writings of Simmel, as discussed earlier, but was elaborated by Plant (1937, 1950), a developmental psychologist who was Director of a juvenile clinic in an overcrowded immigrant area of Newark (New Jersey). Plant considered that the poor living conditions to be found in such areas had a deleterious effect upon the development of the child's personality. The mental strain imposed by living in overcrowded conditions meant that children became touchy and irritable, continually having to hold themselves in check to prevent disputes. Moreover, these children lived in neighbourhoods where crime and delinquency were rife. They might be shocked initially by this type of behaviour, but in the course of time would become hardened and would accept deviance as a normal part of life.

Ideas about urban stress have been welded together into a more comprehensive framework by applying the information theorist's concept of 'overload' (Miller, 1961; Milgram, 1970). Working on the assumption that the city milieu contains intense stimulation, it was hypothesized that all stimuli, pleasant or unpleasant, placed pressure upon the individual. When stimulus presentation exceeded an individual's capacity to scan information, one possible consequence would be 'cognitive overload', in which the individual was too pressurized to behave normally. In such circumstances, the individual has to adopt coping strategies, perhaps withdrawing from social activity or, under more severe stress, displaying pathological reactions.

Physical Stressors. To assess the validity of these contentions, it is necessary to analyse the available evidence upon urban stressors. The first category are known as 'physical stressors' and include such phenomena as noise, mechanical vibration, dirt, dust, and other forms of pollution. These are subjects that have constantly exercised the satirist's pen and appalled the social theorist, yet relatively little firm information is available about their behavioural impact. The reason for this lack of knowledge is partly due to deficiencies in research methodology, but it also reflects the fact that these stressors often occur in conjunction with one another. People living close to industrial plant may experience excessive noise from machinery, smoke and dust from the factory chimneys, and vibrations from traffic moving to and from the factory. Over time, each and any of these may have some effect upon the quality of life and the behaviour of local residents, but quite what may be attributed to any one stressor is difficult to say. Consequently, the lessons of existing research can be quickly summarized.

Noise appears to have its greatest behavioural impact when it is infrequent, intense, and unexpected. Laboratory research has suggested that exposure to unpredictable and uncontrollable noise is associated with poorer performance of tasks (Glass and Singer, 1972), findings which are supported by environmental studies that have traced correlation between the reading abilities of children and traffic noise (Cohen *et al.* 1973; Bronzaft and McCarthy, 1975). Examples may also be found of studies that have found positive correlations between high noise and pathologies as varied as mental illness, psychosomatic complaints and ailments caused by tension, such as duodenal ulcers (McCord *et al.*, 1938; Farr, 1967).

The operative word is 'correlation'. Results from such studies do not indicate causation, no matter how plausible this may seem, but demonstrate associations that may or may not be significant. While it is true that researchers have still to investigate a number of factors that could have an impact upon health, such as long-term loss of sleep due to noise, there is little evidence to support the existence of causal stress relationships, apart from the rare instances of direct damage to hearing caused by very loud and intense noise.

The complexity of noise as a stressor must therefore be recognized. Responses to noise are complicated by adaptation, whereby individuals are able to pay less attention to the stimulus as it becomes more familiar (which happens readily when the noise is frequent and of consistent level). Noise adaptation itself has both personal and cultural dimensions. For the individual, adaptation will depend on personality, familiarity of the noise, the task that person is currently performing, and whether the noise is self-created or produced by someone else. The cultural dimension is added by the fact that there are significant variations in tolerance of noise in different parts of the world. For example, people living in Far Eastern cities have been observed to tolerate noise levels higher than those acceptable to Western society, which Anderson (1972) argued was part of the way this society has come to terms with living at high density. To establish any realistic view of the behavioural impact of noise in urban areas, one certainly needs to know more than just the decibel level.

The same type of complexities are encountered in research about the dangers of *pollution* for the urban population. Available evidence on this topic is bedeveilled by the sheer physical complexity of pollution, by the fact that it is apt to be spatially correlated with other stressors, and occasionally by wilful obstruction of data collection by interested parties (Jones, 1972). There are some limited data that suggest correlation between air pollution and cardiovascular, glandular, and respiratory diseases (Ittelson *et al.*, 1974) and also between water pollution and public health (Condran and Crimmins-Gardner, 1978), but care must be taken in the interpretation of these findings. For example, even in a consideration of cataclysmic pollution events, commonsense conclusions may not be justified. The great 'smogs' of London (1952) and New York (1953) undoubtedly led to an abnormal number of deaths from bronchial and other respiratory diseases, but one cannot conclude from this that atmospheric pollution caused these diseases in the first place. Clearly if a causal relationship did exist, it was mediated by numerous intervening variables.

Several studies have discussed the effects of *traffic density* upon the quality of urban life. Appleyard and Lintell (1972) examined the cognitive and behavioural significance of traffic intensity for three neighbourhoods in San Francisco. These areas were respectively designated as having 'light', 'moderate', and 'heavy' traffic on the basis of the criteria shown in Table 10.1. The authors found that aspects of the perceived livability of cities—absence of stressors, safety, degrees of social interaction, and environmental awareness—correlated inversely with traffic intensity. On the street where traffic intensity was 'heavy', there was little social interaction between neighbours, an absence of peace and quiet, reduced responsibility for external appearance of buildings, and the feeling of living in a restricted environment. Results for the 'light' traffic street contrasted sharply, with residents showing greater interest in the appearance of their street, developing a recognizable community spirit, and having greater pride in their neighbourhood. The main anomalies were for the 'moderate' traffic street, where stronger dissatisfactions were expressed about some aspects of the environment than those recorded in the street with 'heavy' intensity. This puzzling finding was explained in the following manner:

Many respondents on MODERATE STREET had chosen that street for its livable environment. MODERATE STREET, however, was changing from a quiet residential street into a major traffic corridor. Therefore, the residents there were more often dissatisfied than on HEAVY STREET. Their original expectations for the environment were higher and their disappointment was therefore greater.   (Appleyard and Lintell, 1972, 97)

Some qualifications are necessary. Streets with heavy traffic are more likely to suffer physical damage through vibration and air pollution, and this can contribute to an appearance of dilapidation quite independently of residents' pride in the look of their neighbourhood. In addition, as Apple-

Table 10.1 *Street profiles*

Street Characteristics:	HEAVY STREET	MODERATE STREET	LIGHT STREET
Peak hour traffic flow (vehicles/hour)	900	550	200
Average daily traffic flow (vehicles)	15,750	8,700	2,000
Traffic flow direction	one-way	two-way	two-way
Vehicle speed range (mph)	30–50	10–45	10–35
Noise levels (percentage of time above 65 decibels at the sidewalk)	45%	25%	5%
Accidents (per annum over a 4 block length)	17	12	. . .
Land uses	Residential (apartment blocks, apartments)	Residential (apartment blocks, apartments, single family homes), corner store	Residential (apartments, single family homes), corner store, small business
Street width (feet)	69	69	69
Pavement width (feet)	52	41	39
Sidewalk width (feet)	8.5	14	15
Average building height (no. of storeys)	3.5	3.0	2.5

Source: Appleyard and Lintell (1972, 86). Reprinted by permission of Journal of the American Institute of Planners.

yard and Lintell themselves recognized, there is the danger of obtaining defensive answers which say little about real attitudes. Many people have no choice but to go on living where they do at present and are determined to make the best of things. An interviewer who calls to ask people what they *dislike* about their neighbourhood may well find that respondents are reluctant to express critical opinions. After all, the quality of the house and neighbourhood reflects upon individual self-esteem, and respondents may feel uncomfortable about making derogatory remarks to someone who is essentially an 'outsider'. This defensiveness may help to explain why people living on a street with 'heavy' intensity expressed themselves as being less dissatisfied on some counts than their counterparts in the 'moderate' traffic street. Equally, however, habituation may have led to people on the street with 'heavy' intensity being less aware of the traffic than those living on a street where the nuisance from traffic was relatively less severe, but had recently worsened.

Similar conclusions were put forward by Lawson and Walters (1974), who analysed the impact of a new urban motorway upon a high-rise housing estate in Birmingham (England). Starting with the hypothesis that greater noise levels would produce annoyance and reaction from the community, they carried out social surveys and decibel counts prior to, and after, the

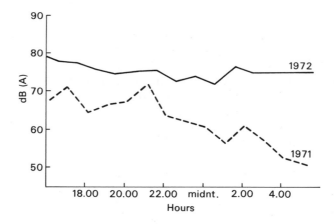

Figure 10.2 Comparison of noise levels measured 1 metre outside window of flat, before and after opening of motorway

Source: Lawson and Walters (1974, 134).

opening of the road. Although noise levels were consistently higher (Figure 10.2), there was little difference in the attitudinal data collected by the two surveys and hence nothing to substantiate the initial hypothesis. Adaptation seemed linked to the fact that residents were resigned to accepting the road. Feeling powerless to remove or even influence the source of stress, they had no choice but to come to terms with it. This mirrors the findings of other studies where communities have been faced with traffic disturbance (Ward and Suedfeld, 1973) or aircraft nuisance (Burrows and Zamarin, 1972).

Crowding and Stress. Another source of stress that has been associated with the city is crowding. It has long been assumed that crowding leads to malaise and misery, a fundamental component of the 'social and moral state' of urban life that depended upon, in the words of Charles Kingsley, 'the physical state of that city; on the food, water, air and lodging of its inhabitants' (quoted in Raban, 1974, 25). The image of the overcrowded, dark, and enclosed inner city slum as the breeding ground for misery and pathology figures large in the work of social improvers and planners and has proved pervasive in social science literature. Indeed, this view has recently been given fresh impetus by the widespread application of analogies from ethological research. In this context, the research most quoted is that by Calhoun (1962, 1966) who, in a celebrated series of experiments, studied the effect of overcrowding on rats. Calhoun found that when there was a rapid population increase in a given area, there came a point at which the internal dominance hierarchy and territorial organization of the species collapsed. This stage, known as the 'behavioural sink', saw overcrowding leading to disorganization and pathology, followed by a rapid decline in the population when behaviour became so deranged that normal reproduction was impossible.

Calhoun's work said nothing about human behaviour and does not command universal acceptance amongst ethologists,[5] but there have been many writers who have not been able to resist the temptation to draw analogies with cities. The real danger here is that those authors who do so are one or two steps removed from direct research on crowding (Gad, 1973), and treat tentative hypotheses for animal society as given facts for humans, ignoring much of the caution that surrounded the original research. By this means, overcrowding became linked to such diverse social problems as disease, pollution, crime, riots, poverty, mental disorders, drug addiction, alcoholism, family disorganization, and aggression (Zlutnick and Altman, 1972).

Besides animal analogies and the statement of 'commonsense' opinions, the evidence on the subject is almost entirely confined to areal correlation. The usual procedure has been to correlate actuarial measures of population *density* with statistical measures of social disorganization. To take correlational studies of urban crime as an example, research would normally begin with the hypothesis that crime rates would become progressively lower as one moved away from the overcrowded inner core of the city towards the suburbs. As such, this hypothesis has been supported by a large number of studies (Schmid, 1960; Zlutnick and Altman, 1972), but these generally have not controlled the sample population for the large number of factors that may also be associated with crime, such as social class, ethnicity, and education. When these are controlled, very few significant correlations have been produced. Only the study by Schmitt (1957) has conclusively correlated gross density and crime figures when such variables as income and education were controlled, whereas most studies (e.g. Winsborough, 1965; Galle *et al.*, 1972; Freedman *et al.*, 1975) fail to show any such relationship. Moreover, Schmitt (1963) himself pointed to the relatively low incidence of crime in Hong Kong, one of the world's most densely populated cities.

This lack of significant findings points to two broad conclusions. First, it demonstrates the limitations of correlation as a means for discerning the links between density and pathology. Correlation serves as a method for discerning patterns in the city, but in no way shows more than association. Whatever the temptations of making 'plausible' generalizations, correlation does not prove causal relationships. Furthermore, where such generalizations are made, it is often possible to suggest other explanations which are equally plausible.

The classic study of the incidence of mental illness in Chicago and Providence (Rhode Island) by Faris and Dunham (1939) provides a good example. Faris and Dunham showed by correlational analysis that the incidence of psychopathology could be associated with particular areas of the city. Schizophrenia, for instance, was strongly associated with the rooming-house areas of the inner city, with decreasing incidence of the disease from the centre outwards (a pattern that has also been shown by a variety of other studies[6]). The problems arose in the way this pattern was interpreted. In keeping with the sociological thought of the time, it was postulated that schizophrenia was caused by the social isolation experienced by inhabitants of the rooming-house areas. The possibility of other viable hypotheses, however, indicate that such conclusions exceeded the limits of correlational data. It is possible that incipient schizophrenics seek living environments that are 'sympathatic' to their pathology. For this purpose, tenements and rooming-house areas, with their shiftless population, are ideal. The individual attracts little personal attention and prospects for self-concealment are legion, truly areas where privacy can be employed as a 'defence mechanism for the protection of anti-social behaviour' (Ardnt, 1949, 70). It may also be that the incidence of schizophrenia in inner areas is linked to the different community attitudes and reactions to abnormal behaviour displayed by people living there (Timms, 1971). What is certain is that statement of definitive theories about the causation of schizophrenia requires a less aggregated approach, employing case-histories to discern the changing relations between the affected individuals and their family, social, cultural, and urban environments (Giggs, 1973).

Second, the lack of significant findings in correlational studies calls into question the use of density measures as a surrogate for crowding. There are various reasons to suggest that density is not an appropriate measure. In the first place, as was discussed previously, density is purely a physical measurement of the number of people per unit area, while crowding is an experiential state. Whether or not one feels crowded in a given situation will depend on the context, duration, intensity, and frequency of that situation and the motivation of the individual concerned. In the second place, toleration of high density varies with culture. If one considers, for example, the evidence of a series of studies on South East Asian cities (Schmitt, 1963; Western *et al.*, 1974; and Mitchell, 1975), the general finding is that the experience of high density is associated with a low level of pathology. Anderson (1972) suggested that cultural adaptation had taken place, in that Chinese society had developed well-articulated mechanisms for using space, which obviated any potentially negative aspects of high density. These 'rules' for adaptation were enshrined in the formalized pattern of family life within the home, the consistent respect for status, meticulously observed courtesies in social interaction, and, as we have seen before, noise was either regarded as desirable or simply ignored. Michelson (1970, 155) commented on the similar situation to be found in Japanese society in the following terms:

The Japanese exemplify successful adjustment to very high densities. Faced with huge urban masses in a country with no room in which to expand, and without the precedents for high rise construction, the Japanese have made their dwellings small, and private open space is minimal. The Japanese have reacted to this pressure by 'turning inward'. They strongly distinguish between what is private and what is public in physical as well as social terms. Interiors of homes are personal, and their lack of size is compensated for by an intensity of detail. Every inch is open for utilisation through physically undifferentiated use of interior space . . . . Perhaps the Japanese garden most exemplifies the intensive use of personal space; it portrays meaning and detail while occupying little space.

Sino-Japanese society had not eliminated potential stressors by these means, but they had developed ways of managing space, time, and people such that even the most extreme crowding did not lead to any particular increase in pathology. This finding is not restricted to Far Eastern cities, as the same culturally derived adaptive rules are to be found elsewhere when coping with conditions of extreme crowding. The individual adapts to daily peak-hour travel on commuter trains or to a crowded lift. Physical contact may be unavoidable, but it is touch without violence or revulsion. The rules are known and followed, it is only on the rare occasions when the social conventions are ignored or misunderstood that problems result.

In summary, there is again little to support the view that pathology is caused directly by conditions in the physical environment of the city. The stressors involved in crowding are far more complex than has been recognized, with weaknesses in both the conceptual and methodological bases of mainstream research on urban crowding. In particular, insufficient attention has been paid to the fact that crowding occurs in conjunction with many other potential stressors and that the most common effect of crowding it to intensify the individual's reactions. In other words, if there were already elements imposing stress, it is likely that the experience of crowding will simply serve to intensify reactions to them. It would only be in the most extreme conditions of long-term crowding that crowding *per se* would be of sufficient stressful magnitude to induce pathology (Freedman, 1975).

The Stresses of High-Rise Living. Arguments about the links between crowding and pathology have been paralleled by a separate, but closely related, debate about the stresses that are thought to be associated with high-rise living. The theme has caught the public imagination on both sides of the Atlantic, with newspaper headlines proclaiming that high-rise estates were hot-beds of vandalism, arson, robbery with violence ('mugging'), rape, and the various other 'crimes of opportunity'. Since the early 1960s, the belief that the physical design of high-rise housing projects encouraged, or even caused, this pathology was increasingly heard, but this idea lacked any theoretical substance until the view of human territoriality spread into the design literature from the social and behavioural sciences.

The leading exponent of the theory that human territoriality influences behavioural patterns in high-rise public housing is the American architect Newman (1969, 1972). Newman considered crime statistics for cities in the United States, noting that there was an areal correlation between high crime rates and high-rise public housing. On the basis of data drawn from the New York City Housing Authority, Newman contended that the abnormally high crime rates were associated with the physical design of the buildings, in that their layout denied people the possibility of establishing claims over the space around their dwellings, a characteristic that had traditionally been present in housing design:

By its very nature, the single-family house is its own statement of territorial claim. It has defined ownership by the very act of its positioning on an integral piece of land buffered from neighbours and public street by intervening grounds. At times the buffer is reinforced by symbolic shrubs or fences, and in other cultures by high walls and gates. The positioning of lights and windows which look out onto the buffering ground also act to reinforce this claim. (Newman, 1972, 51–2)

In the high-rise blocks, by contrast 'most families . . . experience the space outside their apartment unit doors as distinctly public; in effect they relegate responsibility for all activity outside the immediate confines of their apartments to public authority' (Newman, 1972, 52). Thus, large areas of space within, and immediately surrounding, these buildings have become what we have termed 'secondary territories', areas open to all but subject to the control of no specific resident—primarily because these spaces were not overlooked from the dwelling-units. These semi-public spaces—stairs, elevators (lifts), lobbies, roof-spaces, halls, and social areas—became places where crime was rife. Table 10.2, which relates to statistics of felonies, reveals that as building height increased, so did the proportion of crime committed in the interior spaces of the buildings.

Newman's suggestions for alleviating crime reflected his analysis of the

Table 10.2 *The place of occurrence of crimes in buildings of different heights*

	3-storey buildings	6-7-storey buildings	13+-storey buildings
	%	%	%
Apartment Interiors	40.4	35.3	21.3
Halls	3.3	8.9	10.8
Elevators	1.3	9.8	22.6
Lobbies	7.2	11.1	8.1
Stairs	1.3	3.3	5.9
Roofs	1.3	3.9	4.0
Social	2.8	3.2	3.4
Project Grounds	42.4	24.5	23.8
	100.0	100.0	100.0
Proportion of crime in interior public spaces	17.2	40.2	54.2
Mean felony rate (per 1000 population)	9	12	20

Source: Data from New York City Housing Authority Police Report (1969). Adapted from Newman (1972, 33).

cause. Building design and layout needed to be changed to provide residents with opportunities to have 'defensible space', the name given to a residential environment in which latent territoriality and sense of community can be translated into responsibility for ensuring a safe, productive, and well-maintained living space. The potential criminal would perceive such a space as being controlled by its residents, in which he would be quickly spotted as an intruder. Four specific sets of design improvements for high-rise blocks and estates were proposed. First, steps should be taken to create perceived territorial zones around dwelling units, for example, by establishing real and symbolic barriers. Secondly, physical design should be adjusted to allow residents greater opportunity to overlook the semi-public spaces within and outside the buildings. Thirdly, measures should be taken to adjust design to reduce the stigma attached to their status as public housing projects, particularly to reduce the apparent isolation and vulnerability of inhabitants. Lastly, public housing projects should be located in sympathetic areas—places that will provide safe environments for the inhabitants of such housing schemes.

Newman's work has aroused great interest and controversy.[7] Its message was powerful and unequivocal, yet was capable of generating its own mythology. There are problems associated with high-rise living and it seems perfectly plausible that denial of territory does produce stress, but this does not mean that pathology is primarily a product of physical form, with its cure to be found in design improvements. The main thesis of 'defensible space' was produced by generalization from extreme examples. While such instances of pathology are highly useful as a means to focus interest upon a problem, they have the disadvantage in presenting that problem in terms that are too clear-cut. The examples that Newman took from New York, or carefully selected from other American cities,[8] gave credibility to what are essentially architecturally deterministic arguments. Yet middle-class blocks with very similar design in New York do not display such problems, nor do public housing schemes in other parts of the world. Baldwin and Bottoms (1976), for example, found no evidence in their study of Sheffield (England) to support the contention that high-rise buildings have greater crime-rates than low-rise. However plausible the thesis of 'defensible space' may be, it would seem necessary to derive more sophisticated conceptions of man–environment relations before attributing the undoubted problems of high-rise estates exclusively, or even largely, to the stresses connected with denial of territory.

Urban Stress Reconsidered. This last sentiment is one that may be extended to the whole of this discussion of urban stress. Without doubt there are stressful features of city life and there is the possibility that some pathologies may be spatially correlated with stress indices, but the existing evidence demonstrates few direct causal relationships between *individual* stressors and stress reactions. This partly reflects deficiencies in research methods, of which enough has been said, but there are also weaknesses in the basic approaches.

First, it is important to recognize that individual stressors interact to produce stress reactions. It may well be better to adopt multi-stressor approaches in order to broaden the basis of the analysis, perhaps of the type adopted by Clark and Cadwallader (1973) in their study of residential mobility (see Table 10.3).

Table 10.3. *Stressors, stress, and stress reactions*

Stressors	Processes Stress Measurement	Stress Response
Such factors as		
1. Size-facilities of dwelling	Derived from stress model, using individual household attitude scale on stressors. N.B. Subjectively evaluated by households	a. Desire to move
2. Access to work		b. Actual movement
3. Access to friends		c. Modification of dwelling
4. Kind of people in neighborhood		d. Public action, e.g., petition for more services
5. Air pollution (smog)		

Source: Clark and Cadwallader (1973, 35). By permission of the Publisher, Sage Publications, Inc.

Second, it is important not to underestimate the role played by human powers of adaptation. City residents can and do adapt to noise, dirt, pollution, and crowding, all of which might be assumed on *a priori* grounds to have a direct impact upon the quality of life. There may be long-term costs attached to such adaptation, but such suggestions remain speculative in the absence of supporting evidence.

Third, it would appear that there is a heavy anti-urban bias in the literature on urban stress. Early writers concentrated upon the problems of deprived areas of the city, from which generalizations were made about the city as a whole. Even within American research, there has been a preoccupation with cities such as New York and Chicago, with their own specific set of problems. Whatever the merits of the specific studies in question, it would be folly to treat their results as universally applicable.

Fourth, for research to emphasize the stressful and harassing aspects of urbanism is to tell only part of the story. It misses the fact that a city can also be a pleasant and invigorating place in which to live, the source of creativity and inspiration, and the roots of personal identity. Urban residents are far from being the careworn victims of a capricious environment. It is perfectly possible to suggest that their main aim will be to find excitement and novelty or, in other words, to increase the amount of stimulation in an urban environment which many writers (e.g. Relph, 1976) have argued is becoming more predictable and monotonous. By refocusing on ideas of this type, a new range of behavioural hypotheses are available to the researcher. Parr (1964), for example, contended that there could be links between environmental monotony and juvenile delinquency. Cox (1968) hinted that an increasingly homogeneous 'placeless' environment could produce alienation, which in turn could lead to undesirable social consequences. Whether these suggestions actually have any behavioural significance remains to be seen, but they merit investigation just as much as the stresses that are alleged to arise from the city resident's supposed inability to cope with the demands of a complex environment.

Lastly, selection of research problems has been strongly influenced by the passive view of urban behaviour adopted by researchers, explicitly or implicitly. City dwellers were assumed to be people who responded, with little scope for choice, to the stimuli presented by their environment. This conception of man–environment relationships meant that there was no need to consider the cognitive processes and abilities that are intervening variables in urban spatial behaviour. This is a balance that the ensuing discussion seeks to rectify, for the evidence certainly suggests that there are few properties of the urban milieu that automatically evoke given behavioural responses.

URBAN NEIGHBOURHOODS

We have already seen that neighbourhoods are a fundamental part of the social patterning of the city. Chapter 7 demonstrated that, despite methodological difficulties, area residents were able to delimit their home area or neighbourhood as some form of spatial unit. The question of identification *of* neighbourhood, however, is easier to resolve than the related problems of discerning the resident's identification *with* neighbourhood. In other words, it is one thing to show that neighbourhoods exist and quite another to indicate their meaning in terms of that element of social interaction that the very term implies (Herbert, 1972). There are, of course, many studies that show that neighbourhood is, or has been, an important forum for social interaction, with the widespread conclusion that there is an inverse relationship between distance and the frequency and intensity of social interaction.[9] Similarly, self-help, friendliness, and a degree of self-containment are features that have been discerned in studies of working-class (Young and Willmott, 1957; Suttles, 1968; Taylor and Townsend, 1976) and middle-class (Baltzell, 1958; Gans, 1967) neighbourhoods alike.

At the same time, there are those who maintain that the influence of the neighbourhood on patterns of social interaction is inevitably declining, largely due to the changing technological base of society, with rapid improvements in both transport and telecommunications technology (Gold and Barke, 1978). The earliest formal expression of this view may be found in the writings of McClenahan (1929, 1945). Writing from her experience of Los Angeles, McClenahan was impressed by the impact of communications systems upon personal mobility. Although recognizing that communities need to have some common basis, she argued that this did not necessarily imply proximity, for greater mobility made it possible to maintain interaction over increasing distances without in any way impairing these relationships. McClenahan argued that a new social grouping was coming into being, a 'communality', which would be an urban substitute for traditional communities. A communality was to be distinguished from a community by the reduced place attachments of its members.

Similar developments were envisaged by other writers. Janowitz (1952) foresaw the emergence of 'communities of limited liability', where members were likened to investors in a joint-stock company, generally demanding more than they are willing to invest and with less than total commitment, even if they did recognize basic responsibilities. Susser and Watson (1962) and Musgrove (1963) examined the effects of social class on mobility. The famous American architect, Frank Lloyd Wright (1945) incorporated a high degree of mobility into his vision of the future when he asserted that the city of forthcoming years would be 'nowhere and everywhere'. Nevertheless, it is to the work of another California-based writer, Webber, that one looks for the fullest elaboration of the relationship between accessibility and the spatial organization of social activity.

In a series of papers published in the mid-1960s,[10] Webber explored the implications of the set of technological, sociological, and psychological developments that he considered were irrevocably altering the shape of community. From our point of view, this is best illustrated by his essay 'Culture, Territoriality, and the Elastic Mile' (1964a). Webber recognized that people employed in professional or managerial work increasingly needed to be in touch with colleagues many miles distant and apparently could do so as easily as others walked round the block to meet an associate. For such people, favoured by generous expense accounts, high mobility was an integral part of life. Their professional communities might be far-flung spatially, but were close-knit and intimate, held together by shared interests and values. These were communities without propinquity, the so-called 'non-place communities'. Of course, these world-wide or national communities of specialist élites made only partial claims upon their members (Webber, 1964a). The specialist also had many other roles in life that were more place-related, such being a parent, a shopper, a member of local societies, and the like, yet by virtue of the facility with which he could operate in extensive space, it was clear that his overall attachment to a particular locality must be diminished. He and his family were more adaptable, reflecting at least partly their 'inner psychic resources for coping with change'.

This group contrasted markedly with the working class, for whom community organization was territorially coterminous with neighbourhood. The members of these societies rarely left their spatial environs. The paterfamilias might work outside the neighbourhood but he followed a fixed route daily to his destination and returned with little intercourse *en route*. The area beyond a few blocks from the home was foreign territory, which might be held by groups hostile to that which the individual belonged. Physical space became an extension of the ego:

The outer worlds of neighbourhood-based peer groups, neighbourhood-based family, and the physical neighbourhood place itself, seem to become internalised as inseparable aspects of one's inner perceptions of self . . . the physical space and the physical buildings become reified as aspects of the social group. One's conception of himself and of his place in society is thus subtly merged with his conceptions of the spatially limited territory of limited social interaction.   (Webber, 1964a, 63)

Webber realized that the groups so described were little more than stereo-types that represented the poles of a spectrum which, to use Merton's terminology (1957), extended from extreme cosmopolite to extreme localite. The 'typical' member of the real-world professional or working classes might well be assigned to a position some way along the spectrum. If one were to summate the total man-hours spent in participation in each of the various spatial realms for all groups of the population, the result might well be as shown in Figure 10.3. As this graph shows, the local and metropolitan realms would still dominate human activites, but Webber strongly suggested that the

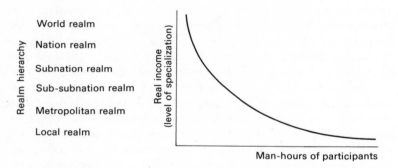

Figure 10.3. The hierarchical continuum of realms

Source: Webber (1964b, 123).

balance would change. Attachment to place typified traditional societies; the way of the future was mobility and reduced place-ties. The non-place community would eventually permeate all segments of society apart from children and adults who, for whatever reasons, had 'not gained access to modern society' (Webber, 1971, 501). The result of this change, presumably, would be that the environmental knowledge of the majority of the population would broaden in scope and deepen in understanding.

Webber's ideas have drawn comment from various quarters. Even those that have tested them in the context of Los Angeles provide only limited agreement. Orleans (1973) found that there was the expected variation in spatial cognition and behaviour between different socio-economic groups, but that upper-income groups by no means showed the city-wide schemata that might be inferred from Webber's research. Indeed all groups lived within their own socio-spatial worlds. Similar results were obtained by Everitt (1976), who suggested that behaviour was less rather than non-propinquitous. Distance and direction were found to be significant variables in analysing spatial cognition and behaviour. Everitt also suggested that the location of workplace played a major role in this relationship, appearing to go some way towards explaining the differences between husbands and wives. Wage-earners frequently are employed at places outside the neighbourhood and this may be expected to exert an influence upon spatial interaction.

Two other factors would also seem to influence strength of place attachment quite independently of social class. First, involvement with locality will vary with stage in the life-cycle. The elderly with their poorer health, limited resources, and narrowly defined social roles experience reduced involvement in the wider community. Young children only gradually gain the freedom to explore the city actively, being restricted to the house and its neighbourhood until adolescence. The spatial horizons of these groups would contrast markedly with the childless newly married couple. Second, the personal significance of the locality is influenced by length of residence. The newcomer often has to come to terms with his or her immediate surroundings before being able to forge real social links with individuals and groups living further afield. Newcomers therefore would attach greatest meaning to the street in which they live and its environs during the period in which they are adjusting to their new environment (Ladd, 1976), which they may not continue to do once they become established.

Quite apart from the elements neglected in Webber's analysis, reservations have also been expressed about his forecast of the effects of social class on place attachments. In the first place, neither working-class nor professional and managerial occupational groups conform entirely to their stereotypes. Lipman and Russell-Lacy (1974), for example, found in their study of Cwmbran New Town (Monmouthshire, South Wales) that individuals living in 'favoured status' areas were actually more likely to engage in social interaction with others in the locality than was the case in areas of 'less-favoured' status. Equally it is possible to find examples of middle or upper-class neighbourhoods that support communities that are as much inward as outward looking (Baltzell, 1958; Greer, 1973).

Secondly, there may be physical factors at work given the fact that, for the present at least, the 'non-place realm' is a correlate of suburbia. Although it could never provide a complete explanation for the increasing spatial span of community, the lower densities of suburbia do imply that greater movement is unavoidable since it is harder to satisfy the same set of needs within a given area (Hall, 1969).

Thirdly, the idea that mobility will progressively spread through all levels of the social scale oversimplifies a series of complex issues. While Webber does isolate a significant trend in contemporary society, and one that is very much in keeping with the 'bias towards mobility' (Lenz-Romeiss,

1973) which has influenced many social scientists, he only takes it to one possible conclusion. There is no reason why extrapolations from the experience of a few, possibly atypical, cities such as Los Angeles should provide a reliable blue-print for the communities of tomorrow. It is noticeable, for instance, that in spite of general increases in physical mobility, large sections of the community have little need or aspiration for high degrees of mobility, particularly with regard to their working lives (Nilles *et al.*, 1976). Indeed there is evidence to suggest that the mobility of the latter is actually *decreasing* in relative terms (Eyles, 1974; Lee, 1975). This matter is further complicated by considerable variation in attitudes towards mobility even when comparing such economically advanced regions as Western Europe and North America, and by the fact that it is by no means inevitable that increased mobility will erode place attachments. It might transpire that greater spatial mobility will create a reciprocal need for a firm home base, thereby *strengthening* place attachment (Norberg-Schulz, 1971). Whatever the validity of these ideas, it is fair to say that Webber underestimated the continuing value of place ties, particularly for the working class. As Harvey (1973) suggested, these may serve as partial compensation for social deprivation. Moreover, the local area can serve as a repository of social traditions which individuals cherish and will want to protect or as a haven in an uncertain environment. This aspect, however, requires discussion in its own right.

DEFENDED SPACE AND SHARED VALUES

Defence has always been an element in urban living. It was part of the founding purpose of many historic cities and remained so until the changing technology of warfare made fortifications and similar measures redundant. Nowadays territorial defence is perhaps more of a live issue at the local level. Observers of contemporary urbanism, particularly in the metropolitan cities of the United States of America, have commented upon the defensive, cellular structure of the city—of separate and unequal groups clustering together in urban space and adopting hostile attitudes towards potential 'intruders' (Gold, 1971; O'Riordan, 1976a). Such groups may be ethnic, socio-economic, or religious in character, but common to all is a belief in certain shared values which they wish to preserve and defend. Defence of these values becomes part of the neighbourhood's *raison d'être* and an essential factor in its internal cohesion.

Probably the foremost statement of this view is that supplied by Suttles (1972, 21), who defined a 'defended neighbourhood' as 'the residential group which seals itself off through the efforts of delinquent gangs, by restrictive covenant, by sharp boundaries, or by a forbidding reputation.' In this way, Suttles identified the defended neighbourhood as being more than just something connected with inner-city working-class areas and extended the concept to cover areas of exclusive housing, the so-called 'gilded ghettoes'

(Kramer and Leventman, 1961) which seek to preserve their exclusive character by legal or quasi-legal means; the process that Clay (1973) termed 'turfing'. This form of defence normally implies negative attitudes, but it can also have positive features. Ethnic groups, for example, might feel impelled to adopt a defensive posture in the face of the perceived hostility of their environment, but they may also wish to protect the way of life of their neighbourhood, with its affiliative ties, local traditions, and its shared knowledge or 'underlife' (Suttles, 1972).

Spatial schemata that contain defended neighbourhoods have a considerable behavioural significance. They tell the individual where his friends and enemies are to be found and how to find them. For the newcomer, the defended neighbourhood might well indicate where it is best to settle in order to achieve a certain way of life, or as Seeley *et al.* (1956) suggested in their study of the Canadian middle-class suburb of 'Crestwood Heights', 'the new resident finds himself in an environment exceedingly well equipped to materialize, feed and cherish his particular version of the common dream.' Above all, the defended neighbourhood simplifies the choices of spatial movement. Choice of location for such activities as shopping and recreation are strongly influenced by the nature and reputation of the areas within which the retail or recreation opportunity is to be found, or the districts that need to be traversed to get there.

The latter point is illustrated by a number of studies of urban activity patterns. For example, Kain (1968) commented on the impact of residential segregation on the journey-to-work patterns of American cities, where people may make considerable detours to avoid inner-city ghetto areas. Similar results have been indicated elsewhere (Horrell, 1965; Berghe, 1972; Gad *et al.*, 1973), but perhaps the most striking and systematic example of activity segregation linked to residential segregation can be seen in the seminal work of Boal on the city of Belfast (Boal 1969, 1970, 1971). This research provided a revealing insight into the anatomy of a province in which religious segregation had been practised for over 300 years. Dealing with the situation that existed before the outbreak of the current troubles in Ulster, Boal described a society polarized into separate residential areas on the basis of religious affiliation and ranked with the Protestants in the ascendency. Figures 10.4–10.7 present a picture of the cleavage between the adjacent and mutually antagonistic Shankill and Clonard districts of west Belfast. Residential segregation (Figure 10.4) is matched by activity segregation, to the extent that the main criterion in movement appeared to be the desire to avoid crossing the territory of the other group rather than to minimize the distance of the trip (Figures 10.5–10.7). In a society in which segregation has been enforced increasingly by violence, it is inevitable that the inhabitants of these defended neighbourhoods will, if anything, display even stronger resistance to sympathetic contacts between their communities.

In the absence of any major change in external circumstances, such neighbourhoods are perpetuated by the process of socialization. Children are

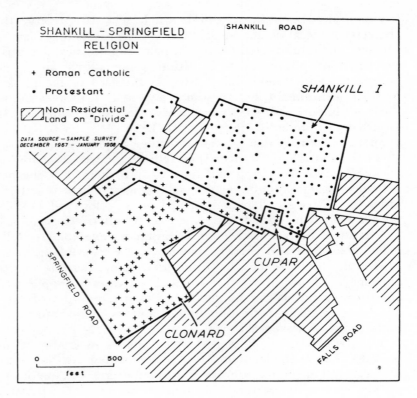

Figure 10.4. Religious segregation between Shankill and Clonard Wards, Belfast

Source: Boal (1969, 37).

taught to fear adjacent territorial groups and avoid such neighbourhoods for fear of dire consequences. Lynch and Banerjee (1976) indicated that the existence of territorial boundaries was important in explaining the behaviour of school-children. Working with small-scale samples of thirteen- to fifteen-year-olds in Argentina, Australia, Mexico, and Poland, the authors reported that while there were some distance-related factors that acted as barriers to spatial movement (such as the cost of public transport), the main factors were personal fear, social barriers, parental controls (especially for girls), and lack of spatial knowledge. The fact that children learn that many parts of the city are dangerous and inaccessible places aids the continued existence of the defended neighbourhood. At the same time, the child will be socialized into the ways of the neighbourhood. He or she will come to know its internal organization and its 'rules' of operation.

The study of the internal order of the defended neighbourhood is one that has posed problems for the urban researcher, in that it is not a structure that is readily apparent. Earlier twentieth-century writers had frequently failed

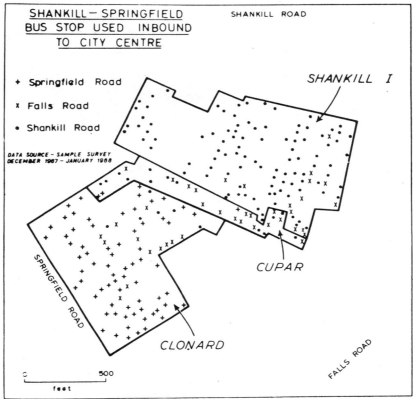

Reproduced from *Irish Geography* by permission of the Editorial Committee

Figure 10.5. Bus-stops used inbound to city centre

Source: Boal (1969, 39).

to appreciate that the inner-city areas with which they were preoccupied could possess an intricate territorial organization based upon defended neighbourhoods. The nature of this misconception may be exemplified by research on gang-lands. Initially the gang was depicted as a symptom of the breakdown of law and order and of the high incidence of deviance in the inner city (Zorbaugh, 1929). It was only more recently that a series of participant observation studies revealed the possibility of territorial order beneath the apparent chaos. One of the first was that by Whyte (1943), who examined the nature and behaviour of corner gangs in the Italian 'ghetto' of an unspecified city of the north-eastern USA. His findings revealed a highly structured youth culture, based upon shared values, commonly recognized rights and duties, and clearly defined territorial units or 'turfs'. Much the same picture has been obtained from later studies in the USA (Suttles, 1968; Hannerz, 1969) and in Britain (Patrick, 1973).

James Patrick's book *A Glasgow Gang Observed* (1973) deserves further

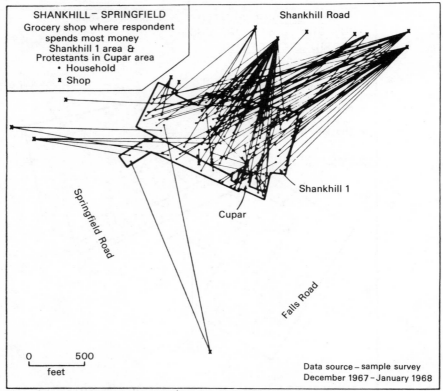

Figure 10.6. Comparison of activity patterns for purchase of groceries: I. Shankhill Ward

Source: Boal (1969, 41).

comment. 'James Patrick' was the pseudonym of an approved school teacher who, through the assistance of one of his pupils, was able to join, and participate in, the activities of a gang in the Maryhill district of Glasgow. The established academic and popular consensus on Glasgow gangs was that they were transitory, arbitrarily violent, and disorganized rabble, led by plotting, charismatic individuals, and were associated with the newer local-authority housing estates of the city. Patrick challenged most of these assertions. He demonstrated that gangs were an endemic part of twentieth-century Glasgow, being more accurately associated with run-down inner-city districts. Indeed contemporary gangs could be found who occupied the same territories as had gangs of identical name forty years previously. In Maryhill as a whole, Patrick found that there were approximately twenty gangs, each of which could be recognized as having its own meeting place ('corner') and territory, the size of which reflected the importance of the gang. Territorial boundaries were not necessarily marked in any rigorous manner, although the use of graffiti provided some indication of possession.[11] Physical combat was rare

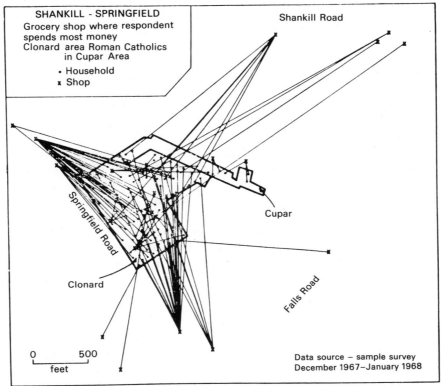

SHANKILL - SPRINGFIELD
Grocery shop where respondent
spends most money
Clonard area Roman Catholics
in Cupar Area
• Household
x Shop

Shankill Road

Springfield Road

Cupar

Clonard

Falls Road

0   500
feet

Data source – sample survey
December 1967–January 1968

Figure 10.7. Comparison of activity patterns for purchase of groceries: II. Clonard Ward

Source: Boal (1969, 42).

but if feuds did break out, they automatically concerned the group as a whole. If for some reason the gang could not cope, it could usually expect support from other gangs in the neighbourhood. Neighbourhood ties were paramount, taking precedence over other loyalties such as religion. Although outsiders might be allowed into Maryhill gangs and be accepted without much comment so long as they were active and loyal members, they would never be completely free from suspicion. As one individual stated when recalling an incident when the gang-leader had deliberately stabbed a member of his own gang, the latter 'wisnae a Maryhill boay [boy], he came fae anither pitch' (Patrick, 1973, 35).

Caution should be exercised, of course, before general conclusions are drawn, for the study of gang-lands is no more representative of defended neighbourhoods as a whole than Glasgow is typical of British cities. These are special circumstances which by their very extremity throw more general patterns and processes into stark relief. Yet the adherence to shared values and their significance in terms of defensive behaviour are phenomena which also may be discerned in far more exclusive urban neighbourhoods.

A good example of this may be found in Firey's research on Boston (1947). Firey noted that certain areas of Boston were devoted to land-uses other than those that might have been expected from classical ecological theory. One area in particular, Beacon Hill, was situated within five minutes' walking time from the city's retail centre and should in theory have been part of the 'zone in transition', but for more than 150 years had retained a reputation as a preferred upper-class residential district. Firey suggested that the reason for this was that there were certain spatially referred values shared by residents of the neighbourhood. These values, articulated in, and symbolized by, Beacon Hill, seemed to be a genuine attractive force to certain old-established families of Boston. Such was the degree of place attachment that Firey could cite many instances of occasions on which residents, both singly and in groups, had successfully defended their area from the encroachments of commercial interests.

The survival of Beacon Hill was thus intimately connected with the fact that people continue to share and act upon the values it symbolized. Tuan (1974) indicated that the same spirit was still thriving in the 1970s, but that Beacon Hill may be an exception rather than the rule. Certainly Tilly (1974) suggested that elsewhere in Boston, areas had lost their significance for particular groups. The old Italian neighbourhood of the West End, for example, was found to have lost its attractions for second-generation Bostonians. Without their support, those who are left fight a losing battle to 'defend' the neighbourhood. If the upper class were to lose its affective attachments to Beacon Hill, it would probably go the same way, with a displacement of existing land-uses by those more in keeping with its location (Firey, 1947).

Naturally defence alone does not supply complete explanation for the continuity of urban neighbourhoods. It is part, but only a part, of the complex matrix of motivation that underpins urban residential behaviour. Even if the character of the neighbourhood remains the same, the people within it change, with individuals moving in and others moving out. Furthermore, to repeat an earlier point, the neighbourhood that possesses such strong qualities that its inhabitants feel duty bound to defend it in the face of external threat is the special case rather than the norm. Neighbourhood character is more often weakly articulated, steadily changing over the years. The need therefore is to consider the wider questions: what are the psychological benefits or dissatisfactions that people derive from their neighbourhoods? what are their preferences for one type of neighbourhood as against another? and how do these satisfactions and preferences relate to residential behaviour?

NEIGHBOURHOOD SATISFACTIONS

'Satisfactions', which in this context may be defined as gratifications or pleasures derived from particular living environments, are seen by many as key variables in urban residential behaviour. The argument is that, subject to certain constraints, residents will remain in their current house and neighbourhood until their dissatisfactions with either house, or neighbourhood, or both, reach such a point that they feel compelled to move. While this approach has its detractors[12] it would seem to have much to commend it. As Boyce (1971) pointed out, 'residential choice appears to be voluntary (i.e. strictly speaking unnecessary) and to be triggered by discontent with the present neighbourhood or house.' At the same time, it is a field of research in which two major problems have to be overcome.

In the first place, satisfactions cannot be directly measured but have to be inferred. To this end, it makes a considerable difference whether 'satisfaction' is operationally defined as an explicit statement that a person likes his or her neighbourhood or 'the absence of complaint when an opportunity for complaint is given' (Schorr, 1964). This latter point again raises the difficulties inherent in social survey methods. It is common for a researcher to select a neighbourhood because he or she believes that it will show generally dissatisfied residents, yet questions designed to give strongly negative responses often yield neutral or defensive answers. This may be because the individual has adapted to potential disadvantages present in that environment or because there are clashes of values between researchers and respondents which mean that the former, as 'outsiders', failed to discern sources of satisfaction in that environment. Interview data on residential satisfactions thus must be treated with some caution.

Secondly, what constitutes a 'satisfactory' residential environment will vary according to the needs and aspirations of particular individuals and groups, which in turn depend on numerous factors. Onibokun (1974) provided some measure of this diversity in his study of residential satisfactions amongst the inhabitants of Canadian public-housing estates. He formulated a list of seventy-four variables to give a comprehensive view of satisfactions, of which twenty-seven related to qualities of the neighbourhood. In a later article, Onibokun (1976) concentrated upon social influences on satisfactions. His broad findings are shown in Table 10.4, with selected variables grouped into five categories—stage in life cycle, socio-economic characteristics, familiarity with neighbourhood, life style, and 'conceived image' (the individual's schema of personal and neighbourhood status). Even in this specific context, 'satisfaction' is clearly a multi-faceted concept. Other studies weight these variables differently or have introduced variables not included by Onibokun, such as ethnic considerations (Kasl and Harburg, 1972) or feelings of insecurity (Carson, 1972). With this in mind, it is worth considering briefly the wide variety of forms that satisfactions can take by examining two poles of the spectrum of urban housing—the working-class slum and the upper-middle-class suburb.

Table 10.4. *Relationships between selected social system characteristics and residential satisfaction.*

Selected Social System Characteristics	Level of Significance	Interpretation
STAGE IN THE LIFE CYCLE		
Size of households	.01	The larger the size of household the lower the RS.
Age of respondent	N.S.	Age had no relation with RS.
Marital status	.01	One-parent families tended to have lower degrees of RS than two-parent families
SOCIO-ECONOMIC CHARACTERISTICS		
Education of head of household	.01	
Occupation of head of household	.01	The higher the socio-economic status the lower
Employment of head of household	.01	the lower the RS.
Income of the household	.01	
Rent	N.S.	
Source of Income	.05	The employed tenants had higher degree of RS than the dependent tenants.
FAMILIARITY WITH NEIGHBORHOOD		
Length of stay in present dwelling	.01	The longer the length of stay in public housing the lower the RS.
Length of stay in city	N.S.	Length of stay in the city had no relation to RS.
Birthplace of respondent	.01	Immigrants from Britain and Europe tended to have lower degree of RS than those born in North America.
LIFE STYLE		
Rural-urban background	N.S.	Rural-urban background had no relation with RS.
Residential status in last previous house	N.S.	Tenants who moved from owner-occupied dwellings to public housing tended to have a lower degree of RS than tenants from rental houses.
Type of last previous house	.01	Tenants who moved from apartment houses to public houses that were either town, semi-detached or single family houses tended to have higher degrees of satisfaction than tenants who moved to public housing from town, semi-detached or single family houses.

Table 10.4. continued.

Selected Social System Characteristics	Level of Significance	Interpretation
CONCEIVED IMAGE		
Social class of area	.01	Tenants who perceived their neighborhoods to be working or middle class neighborhoods tended to have a higher degree of RS than tenants who perceived their neighborhoods to be lower- or upper-class neighborhoods.
Social status of respondent	.01	Tenants who perceived themselves to belong to the working or middle class in social-status tended to convey a higher degree of RS than tenants who perceived themselves as belonging to the lower or upper class in social status.

N.S. indicates that the result was not significant at $p = <.05$.

Source: Onibokun (1976, 326–7). By permission of the Publisher, Sage Publications, Inc.

Satisfactions with Urban Slums. It may seem paradoxical to associated satisfactions with slums. After all the slum has always had the negative connotations mentioned earlier—the strange, dark, overcrowded places of the inner city, with their poor housing, inadequate and overworked services, poor sanitation and health, deviant behaviour, and characteristic attributes of apathy and social isolation. Emphasis on the physical aspect of slums has created a word with strong emotional overtones, so much so that it is commonly replaced by euphemisms. The planner deals with 'redevelopment areas' or 'inner-city zones'. To the resident, the slum rarely exists but is a term used by the media or by other urbanites to prop up their self-esteem. There can be no doubt of the stigma attached to the word 'slum' or of the image of poverty and degradation it conveys.

Nevertheless, there are reasons to suggest that the slum-dweller's regard for his or her home area is not just founded on defensiveness or adaptation. As was seen in the studies by Whyte, Suttles, Patrick, and others, there is more to the slum than the picture of physical decay that immediately occurs to the outsider. The slum can generate its own subculture, a learned 'way of life' which is shared by residents and provides satisfactions which can offset whatever disadvantages are present in the decaying urban fabric.

This is well illustrated by instances in which people have been displaced by slum-clearance schemes. Fried (1963), for example, interviewed families forced to find alternative housing when their neighbourhood in the West End of Boston was redeveloped. He argued that such forced relocation was a highly disruptive and disturbing experience. This working-class community gained satisfaction from its corporate spatial identity and from the warmth of local social relationships. The locality was in effect an extension of the home, an area with which people were personally identified (see also Fried and Gleicher, 1961). When this was destroyed there was a collective feeling of 'grief', which Fried compared to that individuals suffer at the loss of a loved one, leading in some cases to severe depression and psychosomatic illness.

Grief reactions, however, are not necessarily long-lived. Young and Willmott (1957) analysed the social impact caused by movement of people from the inner London borough of Bethnal Green to a London County Council peripheral housing development at Debden (to which they gave the fictitious name of 'Greenleigh'). Bethnal Green was a close-knit inner-city community, heavily dependent on the locality for work, services, and entertainment. Rehousing caused serious dislocation of the existing social network, having a marked effect upon the nature of family life which now tended to focus upon the nuclear rather than the extended family. Shortly after moving, the new residents of Greenleigh expressed dissatisfaction with their environment, but within the space of two years these feelings had largely disappeared. People had settled down, displaying few signs of long-term grief. Stringer (1975a) suggested that this might be because suburbia does offer an alternative, if restricted, social setting, which could eventually supply community life and hence counteract initial dissatisfactions felt by migrants.

These results should be treated with care, for not all slum neighbourhoods possess warm and intricately organized social networks any more than all rehousing projects impoverish life and cause grief for the 'lost home'. None the less, sufficient cross-cultural evidence[13] exists to suggest that such neighbourhoods are not uncommon and that a partial compensatory source of satisfaction can lie in the trade-off between desirable social qualities of slum neighbourhoods and the undesirable state of their housing and amenities.

Satisfaction with Suburban Neighbourhoods. Although the explosive growth of the suburbs is a product of the modern era, both the term and the phenomenon to which it relates are far older. Suburbs were an integral part of the structure of the great cities of the classical era and were also found in smaller provincial centres such as the Roman city of Londinium (Wacher, 1974). The word 'suburb' was certainly in common use by the fourteenth century; Chaucer, for example, referring to 'The suburbs of a toun . . . lurkyne in hernes and lanes blynde'.

The satisfactions supposedly derived from suburban living have also long been extolled, with the firmest advocacy being the promotional material designed for suburban developments. To take the example of suburban development in West London at the turn of the century, the main exponents were the railway companies. The Great Western Railway undertook an intensive campaign in order to encourage businessmen to live in the outer suburbs and in adjacent towns. In a periodical entitled *Homes for All— London's Western Borderland*, details were published of major housing developments together with an outline of the virtues of each district (Wilson, 1970). Other railway companies followed suit in their attempts to generate increased traffic on their local services. This material was reinforced by that of property developers, pressure groups, and suburban settlements themselves. The content of one such brochure, produced by the then small Middlesex town of Ealing ('The Queen of the Suburbs'), is here instructive. Entitled *A Country Town near London*, the pamphlet painted the following picture of the town:

> . . . unusually well blessed with open spaces . . . magnificently wooded with fine old trees . . . an ideal resort for young children and elderly people. .
> . . . has successfully resisted all attempts to make it a dumping ground for London's nuisances. It has no cemeteries except its own, no workhouse within its borders, no Poor Law schools, no lunatic asylum, its police cases go to Brentford to be tried, and free from the manufacturing element . . .
> . . . special transport advantages . . . shortness of journey to and from London, and a fast through service to almost all parts of the Great Western system—the largest in Great Britain.
> . . . famous for its private schools, and certainly no district round London, if anywhere in the country, affords more varied or better educational facilities . . .
> . . . social life is highly developed . .
> . . . one of the best shopping centres out of London . .
> . . . houses built to high standards . . . (to) model building bye-laws . . that are rigorously enforced; the sanitation of the houses is, therefore, of the highest description . . .
> . . . newly developed estates in close touch with the heart of the town, and within as easy reach of its most popular places of resort'   (G. A. C., 1904)

In its final point lies the key to the suburban message. Quite apart from the image of tranquillity, convenience, exclusiveness, and status that this pamphlet tried to convey, the essence of the suburb is that it combines all that is best in the town with the virtues of rural living.

It is a message that appears to have wide acceptance amongst city residents. The characteristics associated with the low-rise suburb are generally found to be valued above those of the high-rise inner city (Lansing and Hendricks, 1967; Ladd, 1970; Hinshaw and Allott, 1970; Cooper Marcus and Hogue, 1976). Michelson (1973) found similar results among a random sample of inhabitants of Toronto. As Table 10.5 demonstrates, there was universal preference for the single-family house as opposed to high-rise schemes regardless of stage in the life cycle.

Despite this, intellectual opinion has been hostile to suburbanization. Several reasons may be advanced for this. First, in terms of areal extent, suburbs are predominantly a product of the present period and of the movement towards system-building. In the absence of contemporary vernacular style, their architects tried hard to lend their buildings the dignity of age by incorporating the external symbols of previous ages (Richards, 1946). While opinion is not unanimous, conventional wisdom has condemned such stylistic devises as being artificial, doing nothing to alleviate the 'placelessness' said to be the concomitant of identical house design and

Table 10.5 *Preferences for the single-family house, sample stratified by stage in life-cycle*

STAGE IN LIFE CYCLE	% Preferring detached, semi-detached or town-house (n)	% Preferring high-rise (n)	Total (n)
Single parents with children at home	55 (6)	45 (5)	11
Single parents with no children at home	61 (28)	39 (18)	46
Married, over 35, no children at home	69 (96)	31 (43)	139
Single under 35	72 (41)	28 (16)	57
Single over 35	83 (10)	17 (2)	12
Married with one child	89 (91)	11 (11)	102
Married, under 35, no children	90 (66)	10 (7)	73
Married, with 2 or more children	96 (125)	4 (5)	130
			570

Source: Michelson, 1973 (quoted in Cooper Marcus and Hogue, 1976, 34).

geometrical estate layouts primarily designed for the private car. Second, there have been numerous criticisms of suburban life-styles, where people are said to engage in escapism, are 'organization men', conformers, and status-seekers.[14] Third, and perhaps most important, the suburb, as the embodiment of the 'town in the countryside', may also be viewed as urban encroachment upon a rural hinterland. There is certainly a long tradition of writers who have looked askance at the sprawl emerging at the city fringe, compared with their cherished ideal of rural life. Equally, modern urban writers, concerned about the loss of agricultural land through urban sprawl, have argued that the 'spreading rash' of suburbia be stopped in favour of higher density redevelopment in the central and inner city (Jensen, 1966).

This is not the place to judge the merits and flaws in these arguments, particularly as values contained in research make it hard to assess the satisfactions undoubtedly derived from suburban living. None the less, some useful insights may be obtained from two exploratory studies, respectively by Zehner (1972) and Herbert (1975). Zehner examined four suburban neighbourhoods in the north-east USA, each located between 15 and 18 miles from major cities, of recent construction, and occupied by upper-middle-class residents. Neighbourhood satisfactions were high, with at least

85 per cent of residents rating their area as 'excellent' or 'good', and only 2–3 per cent rating it as 'poor'. The reasons for their positive evaluation of their community are shown in Table 10.6 and form a concise catalogue of the virtues traditionally attributed to suburbs—good planning, friendly or 'nice' neighbours, safety, good schools, pleasant environment, and so on.

In the second study, Herbert (1975) examined residential satisfactions in two areas of Cardiff; Adamsdown, a run-down area of terraced housing in the central city, and Rhiwbina, one of the most prestigious residential suburbs. The results are shown in Table 10.7. On most counts, Rhiwbina achieved higher ratings than the working-class neighbourhood, with the differences being particularly marked in relation to cleanliness, safety,

Table 10.6 *Reasons for the positive evaluation of the community*

Reason cited	Columbia	Reston	Norbeck	Southfield
Community and neighborhood				
Physical facilities in the area are planned, provided for, accessible; town is planned	22	27	13	10
Schools are good	9	3	24	27
Neighbors are "friendly," "desirable," "nice"	8	12	23	24
Area is safe from crime, traffic	5	10	5	5
Area has general or unspecified appeal	7	5	6	10
Transportation system				
Job, stores, downtown, etc., are accessible	47	28	48	56
Access to freeways is good	5	3	8	20
Environmental quality				
Area has trees, hills, lakes, etc.	13	24	3	3
Area has plenty of space, little or no congestion	12	23	7	7
Property is well kept up	—	1	1	11
Area has general beauty, attractiveness	11	13	5	3
Number of respondents	216	203	99	110

Source: Zehner (1972, 174). Copyright © 1972 by American Psychological Association, and used with their permission.

play facilities, general appearance, open space, and social facilities. Overall, 96 per cent of residents declared themselves satisfied with Rhiwbina as against 67 per cent for Adamsdown.

These two studies are representative of research in this field. Suburbs are generally regarded as being safer (Rossi, 1955; Carson, 1972; Downs, 1973), having better facilities and schools (Clark, 1966; Gans, 1967), offering greater opportunities for privacy and choice of acquaintances (Flaschsbart, 1969), and providing enhanced status for residents. The last point is significant, for suburbia represents 'aspirational space' for many

Table 10.7 *Assessment of neighbourhood qualities*

	Adamsdown			Rhiwbina		
	good	fair	poor	good	fair	poor
Quality	(percentages)			(percentages)		
Cleanliness	16	48	36	74	24	2
Convenient shops	97	3	0	94	4	2
Neighbourly contact	63	26	11	58	32	10
Safety	37	43	20	54	38	8
Privacy	72	20	8	78	20	2
Play facilities	0	16	84	16	52	32
Noise	11	39	50	76	24	0
General appearance	6	47	47	82	18	0
Open space	0	9	91	50	38	12
Social facilities	16	62	22	42	50	8
Accessibility	61	39	0	52	30	18

Source: Herbert (1972, 475). By permission of Longman Group Ltd.

urban residents (Buttimer, 1969)—constituting a goal for people living elsewhere and affording feelings of having 'arrived' for those who are already there. These are essentially private values, deriving from the house and garden, the general appearance of the neighbourhood and its social status. Although suburban residents often express satisfaction with their neighbours, this usually signifies social compatibility, real or perceived. The frequency of neighbourly contact, which served to increase the satisfaction level of the slum neighbourhood, seems to be far less significant.

In conclusion, it is apparent that the contrasts in physical condition between slum and suburb are not matched by polarities in satisfaction levels. Although suburbia represents an ideal for many people, normally urban residents are satisfied with their neighbourhoods and discontent is purely relative. In Herbert's study, for instance, two-thirds of those interviewed in Adamsdown stated that they were satisfied with the area. While this is much less than the 96 per cent recorded at Rhiwbina, it still represents a substantial majority of the sample. Heimstra and McFarling (1974) drew attention to the fact that surveys designed to determine sources of satisfaction may possibly overestimate satisfaction levels because they failed to take sufficient account of disagreeable levels of city life. This is a useful qualification, but satisfaction levels in the above studies were high enough to ensure that even if a sizeable proportion of answers were discounted to avoid possible bias, the result would still be that most people derive satisfaction from their urban neighbourhood. This is further seen in their relocation decisions when faced with the need to move house.

PREFERENCES AND INTRA-URBAN MIGRATION

Movement, as we have seen before, is an endemic part of modern life. In the United States, a country in which it is estimated that the equivalent of one household in five moves annually, it was found that only 47.8 per cent of the population aged five and over occupied the same dwelling in 1960 as they did in 1955. Similar high migration rates have been recorded in many other Western nations (Johnston, 1971b). Much of this migration fits a common pattern. Most is intra-urban, with households often moving within walking distance of their former home. On what grounds is the new residence selected?

Classical urban theorists proposed that residential choice was the outcome of an economically rational process. Alonso (1971, 157), for example, argued that the aim of the resident is to find the optimal location, which will be the point at which satisfactions are maximized: 'A consumer, given his income and pattern of tastes, will seek to balance the costs and bother of commuting against the advantages of cheaper land with increasing distance from the centre of the city and the satisfaction of more space for living.' This suggests a careful and thorough analysis of the merits of all available locations, so as to select the optimum. Although Alonso's model was understandably highly simplified, it suggested a process of locational decision-making that appears to be at variance with reality, where there is little evidence of optimization behaviour.[15] At the same time, one needs to carefully scrutinize the opposite viewpoint that holds that:

> . . . the behaviour of the majority is to buy a house after a very short search which covers only a few houses in a small area. Therefore, the data suggest that search behaviour is not a thorough process. It can be argued that since most people consider buying a home a major decision then their behaviour is not consistent with the obligations of the decision. Clearly home searchers investigate only an incredibly small segment of the vacancy set. It is possible that search behaviour can best be understood as a variation of Zipf's Principle of Least Effort . . .?   (Barrett, 1976, 196)

The criticisms levelled at this statement are in some ways the same as those that apply to optimization models, simply that the researcher does not appreciate the rules under which searching and residential decision-making are carried out. Home-buying is a rare and extremely important event in people's lives. If the process of selection should appear to be haphazard and centred on only a small part of the city, it is probably due to a combination of two factors. On the one hand, searching is a time-consuming and expensive business. If the search is focused on a particular area, the potential migrant has at least a local frame of reference in which to make a decision. On the other hand, the migrant does not approach the city *de nouveau*. For intra-urban migration, the migrant draws upon his urban schemata and acts upon neighbourhood preferences[16] to whittle down the area of search.

This process may be understood in terms of the framework devised by Brown and Moore (1971), depicted in Figure 10.8. The sequence of decisions

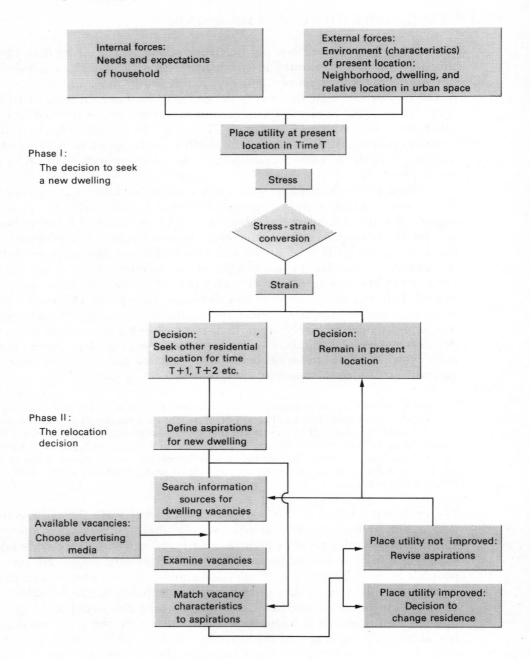

Figure 10.8 A model of the residential location decision process

Source: Brown and Moore (1971, 203).

involved in intra-urban migration is divided into two phases. In Phase 1, it is decided to seek a new residence because the old one is no longer satisfactory, either because it fails to meet the needs and expectations of the household, or because there have been changes in the resident's satisfaction with his or her neighbourhood, or both. Phase 2 indicates the stages by which the final decision is reached. The potential migrant evaluates what type of residence is now required and begins searching. Many people will have little or no knowledge of certain parts of their home city, so that their search will be centred on those that they know and deem to be suitable. After the search process, three outcomes are possible: that an appropriate location has been found that promises a more satisfactory residence than the present abode; that the suggested residence proves not to be suitable and the search process recommences; or that searching is abandoned and the household decide to remain in their current dwelling.

Knowledge about the search process as yet consists of little more than broad principles. The most powerful influence is the home neighbourhood (Simmons, 1968), which acts either as the centre of the search or the standard against which other locations are compared. When searching outside the home neighbourhood the tendency is to concentrate upon adjacent neighbourhoods (Horton and Reynolds, 1969). People are better able to evaluate

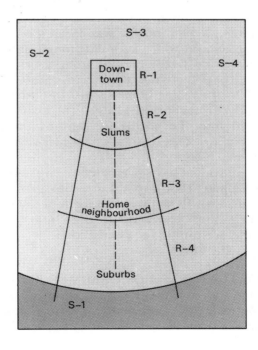

Figure 10.9 The sectoral schema of an urban resident

Source: J. S. Adams (1969, 305).

information relating to such areas and a move there offers the distinct advantage of less disruption to living patterns, for individuals are able to enjoy the benefits of the new house and neighbourhood while still maintaining valued contacts and acquaintances in their former neighbourhood.

J. S. Adams (1969) argued that intra-urban migration took place in accordance with sectoral and directional biases in the urban spatial cognition of migrants. An impression of this, in simplified form, may be gained from Figure 10.9. The resident living at point X will not know all parts of the city, but will have greatest knowledge of a sector containing his or her home area (R–3), the 'downtown' (R–1) and inner-city slum (R–2) zones (built up from repeated journeys to work), and the suburbs on the city fringe (developed by visits to peripheral urban shopping centres). Places in other sectors (S–2, S–3, S–4) are only vaguely known, although they may be strongly positively or negatively stereotyped. Migration will be sectorally biased in that it will look primarily to this sector for a new home. At the same time it is directionally biased. Preference for areas of higher social status means that residents are likely to find outer suburban areas beyond their homes more desirable than the older districts of the inner city (Johnston, 1971b).

Adams couched his model in terms of Burgess's concentric-ring theory of urban structure, but there is no need to do so, for others have found the idea of sectoral and directional bias satisfactory without this element. Johnston (1971a) pointed out that choice of location for affluent citizens of Christchurch, New Zealand, was influenced by a directional factor of availability of land on which to build (found only on the outer edge of the city); and a sectoral factor derived from their desire to remain near their social peers. They therefore tended to construct new residences on the periphery of their existing home sector. In a further study of Christchurch, Donaldson (1973) conducted a survey of people who, over a three-month period, moved into the north-west part of the city. The data indicated support for the idea of a sectoral and wedge-shaped schema, which provides the basis for search behaviour.

While not all studies have given such strong support to Adams's model (e.g. Brown and Holmes, 1970), it still provides a suitable framework for further testing,[17] and serves to show the strength of the relationship between cognition and migration behaviour. It is to other, less permanent, forms of 'migration' that we turn in the next section.

PERCEIVED OPPORTUNITIES AND CONSUMER BEHAVIOUR

There are normally far more places in the city at which goods, entertainments, or services can be obtained than any one individual would ever need. Even in a medium-sized city, the average consumer is unlikely to know about more than a fraction of these potential opportunities. Consumer behaviour is generally aimed at finding places where particular needs may be catered for in a satisfactory manner. Once this has been achieved, possibly with knowledge of one or two other options should the preferred choice not be available, the individual will rarely search further. The same type of behaviour is found in urban travel in which, as was seen earlier, journeys such as commuting or shopping trips quickly become habitual. The 'known area' of the city expands relatively little in the face of such behaviour. If one were to define the city as an 'opportunity surface' which consists of the totality of what a city offers (or allows) its citizens (Stea and Wood, 1974), then the individual will only ever know a small and highly selective portion of that 'surface'.

Quite how the consumer goes about selecting the appropriate locational solution for any particular activity is a question that will occupy social scientists for many years to come. As yet one discerns only the disparate beginnings of research at the cognitive-behavioural level, compared with the considerable effort that has been directed towards the study of activity patterns at the aggregate level. This emphasis is understandable, given the needs of urban planning and the notable complexity of the processes underlying individual consumer behaviour, but there are signs that more study is being devoted to the micro-level. To gain some impression of the nature, scope, and problems of this work, we shall look specifically at the case of intra-urban consumer behaviour.

Consumer Behaviour and the Urban Environment. Despite a long tradition which has recognized the importance of individual preferences in retail consumer behaviour (Brennan, 1948; Stone, 1954; Myers and Reynolds, 1967), most work, particularly by geographers, has been conducted at the aggregate level. Consumer flows were treated as mass-behavioural phenomena, with behaviour patterns that were assumed to be rational and optimizing. Nelson (1958, 185) supplied a typical statement of the implications of such assumptions, in that *ceteris paribus*:

1. shoppers move towards the dominant trading centre
2. shoppers will not go through one trading centre to get to another with equal facilities
3. shoppers will patronise the closest centre with equal facilities
4. shoppers tend to follow traditional circulation patterns

Only the fourth consideration hints at any of the numerous psychological variables that undoubtedly influence consumer behaviour.

The relevant cognitive-behavioural research in this sphere is primarily a product of the last decade, stimulated both by disillusionment with existing modes of explanation and from researchers' increasing interest in the cognitive-behavioural approach. Reviewing early work in this field, Garner (1970) suggested four broad topics that needed investigation—the nature of schemata themselves, the relationship between different schemata and different types of consumer needs, the relationship between the 'known' (behavioural) and objective retailing environments, and the need to understand how schemata change in the light of increasing experience and the provision of new opportunities. If one takes this as a framework within which to review research (Davies, 1976), it is apparent that most work has been concentrated in the first two categories. A considerable amount of research has been carried out on cognition of shopping opportunities. Brennan (1948) pointed to the subjective metrics of schemata of the retailing environment (see also Lee, 1962); Bruce (1971) analysed component elements of preferences for a range of retail stores; Downs (1970) did the same for an entire shopping centre; Heinemeyer (1967), Klein (1967), and Hudson (1974) related residential location to schema development; Parker (1976) commented on the influence of social class; Lentnek *et al.* (1975) recognized the role of household income and the overall level of economic development.

By contrast, the amount of research falling into the third and fourth categories is relatively small and owes much to a paper by Horton and Reynolds (1971). Horton and Reynolds made the distinction between 'action space' and 'activity space' in the spatial behaviour of shoppers. 'Action space' referred to those facilities that a consumer knew about and with which he or she would potentially interact. 'Activity space' on the other hand, was defined as those facilities that an individual visits on a day-to-day basis (Davies, 1976). Horton and Reynolds were primarily interested in the learning processes that underpin the development of spatial schemata. While they pointed out that the nature of this process had not yet been fully investigated, it was suggested that a newcomer would develop such schemata in three stages. In the first, the individual's knowledge would be distance-biased and centred on the immediate home environment and the portion of space known through journey to work. In the next stage, the individual gains knowledge from neighbours and colleagues as part of the socialization process, which expands the range of his or her shopping opportunities. In the final stage, the individual enters a stage of spatial equilibrium where shopping has become a matter of routine and the activity space becomes equivalent to action space.

These ideas were taken up by other writers. Smith (1976c), for example, in his study of Hamilton (Ontario) examined the 'spatial information field' or urban consumers, an idea broadly comparable with 'action space'. The spatial information field was taken to mean the mental information that an individual has about the spatial distribution of a specific set of environmental elements, which in this case was grocery shops within the city. Measurements were made of two properties of the information field—the total number of grocery stores reported by a consumer and the mean distance of store locations from the consumer's place of residence. These were used to test four hypotheses, two of which were related to residential location and drawn direct from Horton and Reynolds, the other two relating to social status. After testing these hypotheses by stepwise multiple regression, Smith concluded that both length of residence and social status were important variables in shaping spatial information fields.

Not all authors, however, have concurred so fully. Hudson (1976) suggested that the learning model advanced by Horton and Reynolds was typical of a number of such conceptualizations, all of which lacked the potential for explicitly investigating the links between spatial cognition and behaviour and which were also frequently of dubious psychological validity. In his paper *Environmental Images, Spatial Choice and Consumer Behaviour*, therefore, Hudson (1976) attempted to remedy this situation. As it is also a paper that thoroughly summarized the current status of cognitive-behavioural research on retail consumers, it is worth examining it in greater detail.

Drawing on his previous research into the structure of schemata of the retailing environment (Hudson, 1974), a conceptual model of the spatial behaviour of individual consumers was proposed and tested. The model, shown in Figure 10.10, was developed initially to apply to food shops, but there would seem to be no reason why it could not be more widely applicable to other situations of spatial choice. It brought out the relationship between what the individual knows about and the type of shop he or she would ideally like, with the former being evaluated against the latter. It had the following elements: a large but finite number of shops that make up the objective retailing environment (A); the individual's total knowledge and basic evaluation of the retailing environment (B) and the sub-set of it that is concerned with the particular retailing activity in question (C); and the actual choice that emerges at the end. The processes by which schema formation comes about and the way that choice emerges are drawn principally from Kelly's work on personal construct theory (Kelly, 1955), the field-theory of Lewin (1951), and Tolman's research on cognitive mapping (Tolman, 1932, 1952), and are outlined synoptically in Figure 10.10. The model was then placed into an operational form by means of multi-dimensional scaling techniques and tested by reference to diary records of individual consumer behaviour over a ten-week period. The main findings were that there was a highly consistent relationship between the favourability of shop images and the frequency of shop choice, but that a large number of anomalies occurred when the distance relationships of patronized shops from the 'preferred' shop were compared with statistics for unpatronized-but-known shops.

Two specific conclusions may be made about this paper. First, as Hudson (1976) himself recognized, the scope of this study is very limited—the empirical evidence is drawn from twenty-six students and is confined to shopping for groceries. Students are a convenient group of respondents to supply social survey data, but they are by no means representative of the population as a whole. Similarly shopping for groceries is an important aspect of retail-consumer behaviour, especially at the intra-urban level, but it tells little about other less frequent types of shopping trips and the processes of spatial choice involved there.

Second, this study represents a welcome departure in that it explicitly utilized a recognized body of psychological theory. Although the theories of Kelly, Tolman, and Lewin all have their detractors, this at least provides

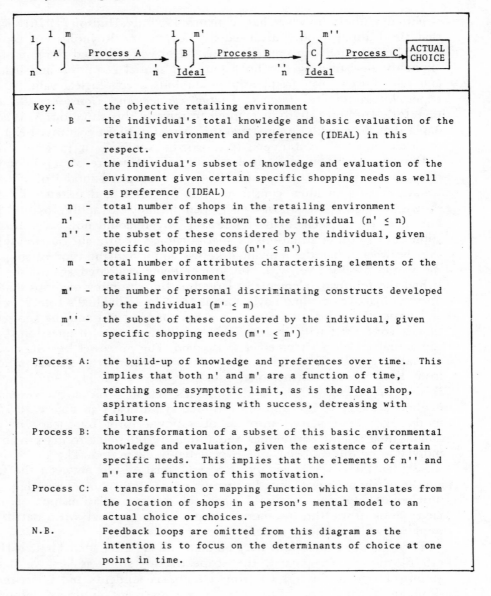

Key: A - the objective retailing environment

B - the individual's total knowledge and basic evaluation of the
retailing environment and preference (IDEAL) in this
respect.

C - the individual's subset of knowledge and evaluation of the
environment given certain specific shopping needs as well
as preference (IDEAL)

n - total number of shops in the retailing environment

n' - the number of these known to the individual (n' $\leq$ n)

n'' - the subset of these considered by the individual, given
specific shopping needs (n'' $\leq$ n')

m - total number of attributes characterising elements of the
retailing environment

m' - the number of personal discriminating constructs developed
by the individual (m' $\leq$ m)

m'' - the subset of these considered by the individual, given
specific shopping needs (m'' $\leq$ m')

Process A: the build-up of knowledge and preferences over time. This
implies that both n' and m' are a function of time,
reaching some asymptotic limit, as is the Ideal shop,
aspirations increasing with success, decreasing with
failure.

Process B: the transformation of a subset of this basic environmental
knowledge and evaluation, given the existence of certain
specific needs. This implies that the elements of n'' and
m'' are a function of this motivation.

Process C: a transformation or mapping function which translates from
the location of shops in a person's mental model to an
actual choice or choices.

N.B. Feedback loops are omitted from this diagram as the
intention is to focus on the determinants of choice at one
point in time.

Figure 10.10 A schematic model of choice at one point in time focusing on the cognitive
aspects of the choice process

Source: Hudson (1976, 3). Reprinted by permission of the author and Editor.

the means by which geographers can contribute to debate on a particular
form of urban behaviour and supply data that can be evaluated by members
of other disciplines.

Two other, more serious, points should be made about behavioural geographical research or shopping patterns. First, it is readily apparent that there are far more conceptual frameworks available than empirical data with which to test them.[18] One of the most familiar concluding paragraphs of articles is that which says that the study was only exploratory and that much more empirical testing would be required. While it is only right and proper that the conceptual frameworks should come first, the testing in many cases never follows.

The second point is one of 'relevance'.[19] To show after dint of considerable effort and quantitative elegance that there is moderate support for the hypothesis that retail-consumer behaviour is influenced by location of shops and the price of goods is a certain way to ensure that such research is not taken seriously. While it cannot be said that the sophisticated pursuit of trivial results is a major feature of this body of research, its presence must not be overlooked any more than it is in other branches of behavioural geography.

CONCLUSION

This chapter has analysed the nature and progress of research in three important areas. First, it looked at whether or not the urban environment contained elements that predisposed behaviour towards specific forms, particularly apathy and pathology. The main findings showed that in spite of the pessimistic expectations of many urbanists, there were few simple, causal environmental influences upon the behaviour of urban inhabitants. This did not mean, of course, that the urban environment has no impact upon city-dwellers, but rather that its influence is less deterministic and more complex than many have supposed. It was therefore suggested that more sophisticated approaches are needed, approaches that explicitly recognize the complexity of environmental variables and processes and the true interrelationship between the environment and the behaviour of thinking human beings. Second, it investigated the role of the locality in the urban experience, demonstrating that the neighbourhood had behavioural as well as cognitive significance. Although it is possible that there are forces that may diminish the role of the neighbourhood in future years, present evidence showed that it remain an important unit for explaining the organization of intra-urban spatial behaviour. Third, this chapter has explored the links between preferences and movement, with emphasis upon intra-urban residential migration and retail-consumer behaviour. In both these areas of study, although research remains at an exploratory stage, the findings were that there were strong links between spatial schemata and behaviour.

11 Behaviour in the Natural Environment: I. Landscape Assessment

. . . Winterbourne did not continue. It seemed as if the knowledge and interests which had formerly moved Grace's mind had quite died away from her. He wondered whether the special attributes of his image in the past had evaporated like these other things.

However that might be, the fact at present was merely this, that where he was seeing John-apples and farm-buildings, she was beholding a much contrasting scene . . .

(THOMAS HARDY, *The Woodlanders*)

Throughout history, the urban and natural[1] environments have enjoyed a symbiotic relationship. The town was the service-centre and workplace for the rural populace, the countryside the source of food and raw materials and the forum for recreation for townsfolk. Yet the values invested in both urban and natural environments meant that the difference between them has been more than just one of 'bricks and mortar'. The anti-urbanism of many writers stemmed, at least in part, from their ideal of the rural way of life, of man's 'proper' habitat. Just as these values were seen to have influenced behavioural research on the city, so too have they for work on behaviour in the natural environment.

In this and the following chapter, we shall consider the natural environment from two standpoints. In this chapter, with the use of land for recreational purposes very much in mind, we consider the natural environment as 'landscape', holding that the image of landscape, however measured, influences behaviour within it. The latter is illustrated by drawing upon the findings of an important body of North American research on recreation in wilderness areas. In the next chapter, the environment is viewed as 'hazard', examining the relationship between the individual's cognition of such environmental hazards as flooding, snow, drought, and hurricanes, on the one hand, and human response to them on the other. In both chapters, particular emphasis will be laid upon the theoretical foundations of research and the methodological problems encountered.

LANDSCAPE ASSESSMENT: THE PLANNING NECESSITY

Two factors have contributed to the growing awareness that landscape, as a finite resource, needs careful control and planning. The first is the continued growth of urban demands upon the countryside. This has two aspects—the loss of land at the urban fringe due to the growth of the city and the general increase in the recreational demands of urban inhabitants, in the sense that general increases in leisure time and personal mobility have placed more pressure upon areas of notable scenic value. Secondly, agriculture itself

*This chapter is co-written with D. E. Cosgrove.

is changing. The development of highly capitalized and mechanized agriculture in Atlantic Europe, for instance, has led to the disappearance of the *bocage* landscape of tiny, hedged, and enclosed fields.

The awareness of the need to cope with problems of resource allocation and conflict of land-use has found concrete expression in the planning legislation of many Western nations. In the United Kingdom, for example, the *Town and Country Planning Act*, 1947 and *National Parks and Access to the Countryside Act*, 1949, made it obligatory for local authorities to evaluate the aesthetic quality of landscapes under their jurisdiction for purposes of protection and improvement. In England and Wales, almost half the total land area now enjoys some form of protected status (Patmore, 1971). This legislation is closely connected with the concept of amenity, in the sense that the landscape of rural England is part of the collective heritage of every Englishman, even though it may often be in private hands (Lowenthal and Prince, 1965). As such it should be accessible to all, and everyone owes a duty to see that it is not altered detrimentally—a duty which is vigorously pursued. This attitude suggests that landscape has inherent value regardless of the quantifiable demands of particular recreational groups.

A similar set of values seems to motivate policy in the USA with regard to wilderness areas. As will be seen, these are landscapes that are substantially unmodified by human action and considered to have a unique spiritual and moral value for human society (Lowenthal, 1964). Legislation to protect the American wilderness, coupled with the enormous popularity of these areas for public recreation, underscores the fact that landscape assessment is an important question for public policy.

To understand the nature of behaviour in the natural environment, and to find ways to plan for it, it is essential to know what attracts the user to certain environments rather than others. It will be argued here that this can only be adequately achieved by considering environmental quality from the standpoint of the user, working on the assumption that preferred landscapes attract greatest usage. This, however, is a task that many writers have argued is impractical or even impossible to accomplish. To resolve this matter, it is necessary to look more closely at the problems encountered in landscape assessment.

LANDSCAPE ASSESSMENT: The Theoretical Problems

The fact that the debate about landscape assessment has been heavily technique-oriented explains, in large measure, why this area of study suffers from a severe theoretical vacuum. In their efforts to meet the practical planning problem of providing techniques for landscape assessment, researchers have succeeded in developing sophisticated methodology, but have failed to provide the corresponding theoretical basis (Appleton, 1975a).[2] The main line of argument has centred on whether landscape assessment should be concerned with the search for an 'objective' definition of landscape quality regardless of an uncertain, and perhaps unknowable, public preference for particular landscapes, or whether planning decisions on landscape quality ought to follow expressed public tastes.

With regard to the first standpoint, Craik (1972) contended that modern aesthetic theory supported a dichotomy between aesthetic evaluation and aesthetic preference. Art commentators are likely to agree with recognized authorities on the *value* of a particular work, even if their personal *preferences* are for works which collective opinion regards as of inferior quality. Thus, Craik maintained that appraised landscape quality might be a poor predictor of landscape preference. Turner (1975) pointed out that landscapes that are currently valued are frequently the product of decisions taken more than a century ago with little regard for popular taste. Turner declared that the prospect of planning landscape on the basis of public preference was fraught with dangers, partly due to the time-scale, whereby the tastes and fashions of one generation would be imposed upon another, but also because 'what makes up a landscape, and why it is enjoyed, is not properly understood' (Turner, 1975, 160). There are strong reasons for supposing that individuals enjoy whatever landscape they grew up with. He too argued that more weight should be given to the consensus of informed opinion than to measured public preference.

The opposing school of thought maintains that planners are ill equipped to make judgements about aesthetic properties of landscapes and that the search for objective evaluation of scenery in the natural environment according to agreed aesthetic standards is fruitless. Planners themselves, despite their professional training, are still individuals with their own tastes in landscape, and these may not be representative of the population at large. By the same token, their estimates of what the public want may not be the same as what the general populace would really choose. Penning-Rowsell (1974), for example, contended that better results could be derived from user-dependent approaches, in which people actually using the landscape are asked to evaluate its quality. It was suggested that this type of landscape evaluation can be considered definitive precisely because, by incorporating the preferences of those who actually used the landscape, it truly constituted the attractiveness of an area to a representative sample of users. Thus, 'if planners want to produce definitive landscape evaluations that truly reflect the landscape attractiveness of their counties, regions or districts, they must approach the problem via the user-dependent or 'participatory' route, and not get misled up the methodological blind alley of so-called objectivity' (Penning-Rowsell, 1974, 934).

The debate between these two viewpoints is perhaps best resolved by treating them as separate, but related, approaches. The first might be termed 'landscape evaluation' in the strict sense, as it measures qualities of the landscape itself, whereas the latter, or 'landscape preference', approach examines the nature of respondents' choice between a given range of options. Some case-studies allow closer examination of each approach and indicate its potential to aid understanding of this form of behaviour.

Landscape Evaluation Studies. Evaluations of landscape quality are founded on the assumption that scenic resources may be objectively assessed. They tend to employ a components approach whereby the separate elements that make up the visible landscape—terrain, water, ground cover, and human artefacts (Crofts, 1975)—are identified and measured. In an early attempt at evaluation, Linton (1968, 223) grouped the physical contents of landscape into 'two truly basic elements in the scenic resources of any area', namely the 'form of the ground', measured in terms of geomorphological landform categories, and the mantle of forest, moorland, farms and factories, natural vegetation and human artefacts. Six morphological categories were used to classify landforms, respectively, relative relief, steepness of slope, abruptness of accidentation, frequency and depth of dissecting valleys in upland regions, and the isolation of hill-masses from their neighbours. Water surfaces were seen as contributing to both basic elements, but were regarded as being sufficiently important to map separately. With the use of his classification system, six 'landform landscapes' were defined—lowland, hill country, bold hills, mountains, plateau uplands, and low uplands. In addition, a ranking system was introduced for features that were superimposed upon the land-form landscapes, such as urban uses (–5 points), continuous forests (–1), treeless farmland (+1), moorland (+3), varied forest and moorland (+4), richly varied farmland (+5), and wild areas (+6).

Linton's system of landscape evaluation ostensibly may seem objective, but in practice both his classification system for landscape and his ranking system were based upon his own preferences. The points scale that he used, for example, is more the expression of the values of a distinguished geo-morphologist who devoted much of his life to the intimate study of the physical landscape than a valid aesthetic standard against which to measure landscape quality. Linton clearly loved the dramatic, highly accidented mountain regions, with little time for the 'tame' lowlands or plateaux. In considering human artefacts, he further displayed his preferences by ranking them negatively, an opinion that those familiar with such cities as Edinburgh, Stirling, or St. Andrews might dispute. Moreover, his map of Scottish scenic resources (Figure 11.1) suffered from substantial over-generalization, since the coarseness of the scoring system, covering large areas with broad categories, easily glosses over many of the subtleties of landscape (Wright, 1974).

A more sophisticated example of this genre of landscape studies is to be found in the work of the Coventry–Solihull–Warwickshire Sub-Regional Planning Group (1971). This research team attempted evaluation of a far smaller area than had Linton, and one consisting of less dramatic scenery. It was decided that the major factors that 'create a landscape, influence people's appreciation of it, or figure in their intuitive assessment of its worth' (1971, 126) were landform (its shape and slope characteristics), land-use (such as residential, water, industrial and rural), and land-features (divided into 'natural' and 'man-made', each with their component aspects). Each factor was measured on the basis of a kilometre grid to provide an inventory for the region.

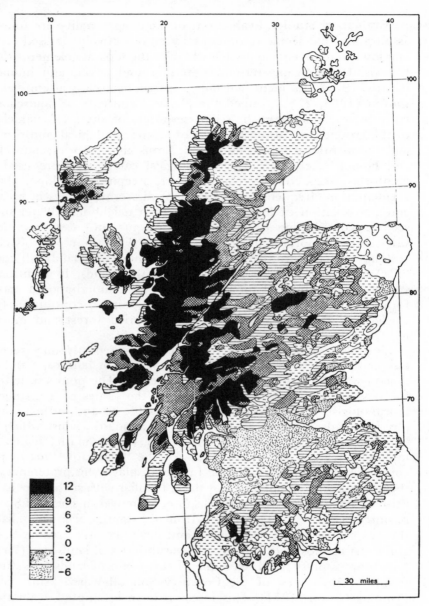

Figure 11.1 Scotland—scenic resources, a composite assessment

Source: Coventry–Solihull–Warwicks Sub-Regional Group (1971, 5, 152). Copyright Warwickshire County Council

Resource ratings

more than 12 points	(black)	0 to +3	(blank)
+9 to +12	(cross-hatched)	0 to –3	(light stipple)
+6 to +9	(solid rule)	–3 to –6	(heavy stipple)
+3 to +6	(broken rule)		

Thereafter two major indices were derived, an index of landscape value, based on the visual quality of the landscape, and an index of intervisibility, calculated so as to include views from outside the kilometre grid-squares into the evaluation. By combining the indices of landscape value and intervisibility, a map of landscape value was obtained which incorporated visibility across the landscape (Figure 11.2).

Greatest value

Least value

Figure 11.2 Map of landscape value and intervisibility

Source: Coventry–Solihull–Warwickshire Sub-Regional Planning Group (1971, 5, 152).

These are by no means the only examples that could have been cited,[3] but they serve to illustrate the general point. These studies sought to produce a measure of objective value without reference to the 'landscape consumer'. Yet from the point of view of understanding the assessments of landscape that underpin behaviour, they have relatively little to tell us. There are two main reasons for this. First, the components approach to landscape quality suffers from the failing described by Duffield and Coppock (1975, 142-3);

> While landscape assessors recognise that the landscape is greater than the sum of its component parts, most procedures of assessment have been based on aggregation, with the assessment of landscape reflecting variations in the mix of resources. The underlying concept of this approach may be sound, but it is clear that the current understanding of the contribution of individual resources to the quality of landscape is severely limited and considerable doubt must surround the synthetic landscapes that assessors have put together.

Second, just as Linton's study was seen to be the work of one individual, albeit a notable geomorphologist, the Coventry–Solihull–Warwickshire study was the work of a small group of professional planning staff. The same small group of people who decided on the main components for analysis also calibrated them against their own subjective assessment of the landscape in the field. Any high level of correlation between selected components and assessments, therefore, must be seen partly in the light of the values of the researchers concerned. These studies are themselves indicative of preferences. At this juncture, it is apposite to consider landscape preference studies in their own right.

Landscape Preference Studies. Although landscape evaluation methods have predominated (Penning-Rowsell, 1975), there is growing interest in landscape preference studies, which rely on the assessments of those who actually use the landscape. The essence of this approach is that the landscape is appraised as a totality rather than the sum of its parts—landforms, land-use, land-features, and the like (Dunn, 1976). Preferences may be elicited by either observational or interview means. The former may be dealt with speedily. It involves making an evaluation of landscape quality according to one of the 'objective' techniques and then relating this to a census of the population actually using different tracts of the landscape, without their conscious knowledge of the event taking place (e.g. Weddle, 1969). Quite apart from the problems associated with the 'objective' techniques, as discussed above, they also suffer from the severe drawback of attempting to infer mental properties from patterns of overt behaviour.

Interview methods, by contrast, build up a picture of the meaning and behavioural significance of landscape from individuals who use or potentially use it, either by on-site evaluations of a series of different landscapes or by employing a surrogate for them, usually photographs (Dunn, 1976).

Penning-Rowsell (1974) exemplified the on-site method in his pilot-study of landscape preference in an Area of Outstanding Natural Beauty in the

Wye Valley. The landscape was divided into tracts of similar topography and land-use, with visitors then being asked to rank the different tracts on the basis of a semantic differential scale, ranging from 'extremely attractive' to 'extremely unattractive'. From this data, maps of individual and group landscape preferences were prepared (see Figure 11.3). This method allowed for account to be taken of the social and demographic characteristics of respondents and permitted subgroups within the population sample to be identified. Against this, it needs to be said that the sample would only be representative of those using the particular landscape in question and not necessarily the population at large.

Turning to the use of surrogates for landscape, the most common approach has been to use photographs (Shafer and Mietz, 1969), which experimental data suggest may be a suitable substitute for landscape experience. Dunn (1974), for instance, concluded that photographs could accurately indicate how people would respond to the actual landscape (Table 11.1) and provide a flexibility which on-site interviews could not match.

An important application of this method is found in a paper by Sonnenfeld (1966). Sonnenfeld employed fifty pairs of photographs to elicit landscape preferences from people living in coastal and inland areas of Arctic Alaska, with respondents divided into natives (Eskimos) and non-natives. The set of photographs were later shown to a group of students in Delaware. The photographs were systematically presented to provide contrasts in the type of vegetation, topography, water features, and apparent temperature depicted.

The study results showed variations between the various components of the sample population, with contrasts between different Alaskan villages, between Alaska and Delaware, and between members of the same groups on the basis of socio-economic and other characteristics. Perhaps the most significant aspect was the dichotomy between the native and non-native. People tended to express preferences for the landscape dimensions that most typified their home area. The significance of the native/non-native distinction, however, became less pronounced in the landscape preferences of those

Table 11.1 *Results obtained from study assessing the equivalence of preferences obtained from on-site and photographic preferences*

	On-site mean	Photo mean	On-site as % of photo mean
Highgate Common	2.95	3.08	95.78
Arley	2.01	2.28	88.16
Kinver Edge	2.22	2.50	88.80
Kingsford	2.05	3.60	56.94
Wyre Forest	2.06	2.14	96.26
Hartlebury Common	3.04	4.12	73.79

(Note: means calculated assuming discrete data set)

Source: Dunn (1974, 936).

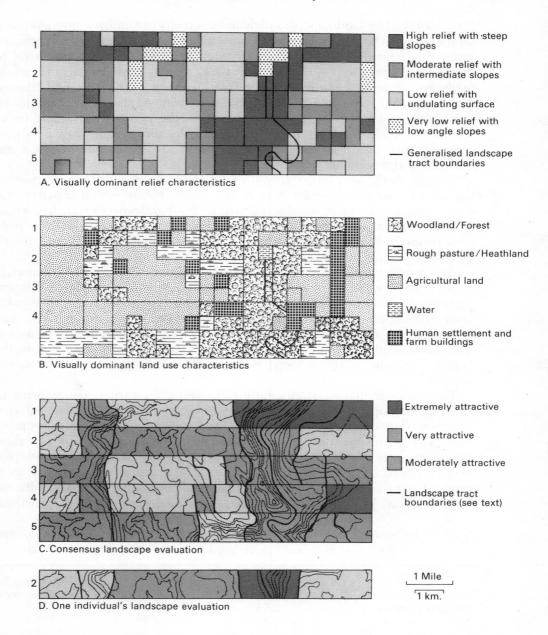

Figure 11.3 Landscape preference: results of a pilot study in the Wye Valley

Source: Penning-Rowsell (1974, 933).

who had been to parts of the world other than the Arctic, than of those who had never left the Arctic.

This diminution in the significance of the native non-native dimension with wider personal environmental experience suggests a point of broader relevance. In analysing tourism or similar recreational pursuits, one is dealing with situations in which almost all respondents would be non-natives (Ittelson *et al.*, 1974), but non-natives with varying amounts of environmental experience. Expressed preferences may thus be influenced not just by how much the landscape resembled the individual's home landscape, but also by the extent of his experience of other landscapes.

Nevertheless, the study by Sonnenfeld (1966) was a valuable starting-point. It revealed an important dichotomy in sample populations, which may be valid independently of culture. Sonnenfeld also went further than most workers in this field by attempting to trace the processes that underpinned landscape preferences and did so by reference to a recognized and testable psychological theory.[4] The fact that consolidatory work has been slow to appear (Stringer, 1975b) does not negate the value of this approach as the basis for further research. At the same time, one has to recognize that photographic stimuli of the type used by Sonnenfeld have certain problems (Rieser, 1972). Photographs relate to visual qualities of the environment, which excludes the fact that other sensory modalities are frequently of significance in the experience of landscape. The photograph also presents a selective view of a landscape, dependent upon the skills and the motives of the photographer, and much will depend upon the order in which photographs are presented. Moreover, photographs cannot take into account the situational factors that may influence the preferences of landscape-users, such as the recreational activity in which the individual is engaged or is about to undertake.

Investigation of preferences by this or any other method involves problems and must perforce rely upon techniques that remain relatively unsophisticated. Despite these qualifications, investigation of preferences would still seem the most profitable way of building up an understanding of behaviour in natural environments and of supplying the basis for management. Even if the theoretical vacuum at the heart of landscape assessment still exists, there is widespread recognition that better theoretical frameworks need to be found; frameworks which many consider would best be produced by closer liaison with established man–environment theory. To evaluate these contentions more fully, it is worth briefly considering the example of research that links preferences for wilderness areas with recreational behaviour.

BEHAVIOUR IN WILDERNESS AREAS

There has been much interest in the role of 'wilderness' areas in recreational behaviour. That most of the research has come from North America should come as no surprise for, compared with Western Europe where very little can be classed as true wilderness, almost 2 per cent of the land area of the contiguous states of the American Union (over 10,000,000 acres) have official status as wilderness areas (Simmons, 1975). The importance attached to wilderness in North American recreation brings with it the heavy pressures that visitors, particularly in summer, impose upon wilderness areas (Hall, 1976), although the demand only stems from a limited section of the com-. munity. Shafer and Mietz (1972) depicted the typical hiker in wilderness areas as professional, middle-class, and of above-average income (characteristics supported by other studies, see ORRRC, 1962).

To understand the basis of this attraction, it is necessary to consider the meaning of 'wilderness' in the American context. 'Wilderness' has traditionally been treated with the same ambiguity that is attached to the term in the Bible (see Chapter 8). On the one hand, the wilderness is treated as a place of evil, of dark and malevolent forces, and as a desolate waste. On the other hand, wilderness emerges as a place for solitude and contemplation, which was free from all temptations and suitable for the cleansing of sins (Tuan, 1974). Both conceptions of wilderness have figured prominently in American culture. In the pioneering days of early colonial settlement, the image of wilderness that dominated was that of the desolate and inhospitable waste. With the passage of time, the maturing of the initial colonies, and the spread of the Romantic movement from Europe, a new mood was generated. The wilderness became something that inspired awe and wonder, symbolizing the 'frontier' and the pioneering spirit. Wilderness areas came to assume the role of a repository of the nation's history, with attachment of moral and even spiritual values (Olson, 1961; Graber, 1976).

It was therefore widely believed that the wilderness offered a variety of psychological benefits for those who sought and used it for recreation.[5] Initial work to interpret the component elements of these 'benefits' was carried out by Bultena and Taves (1961). From data relating to the Quetico Provincial Park (Ontario, Canada) and the adjoining Superior National Park (Minnesota, USA), it was concluded that there were at least five motives for visits to these areas, namely: to partake in sports and recreation, often of types that were not available in their home area; to experience the 'fascination' of wilderness through exploration and discovery; to gain a 'sanctuary' from the everyday world; to see a locality that made tangible the nation's heritage; and to gain various forms of personal gratification—emotional catharsis or the satisfactions gained from having braved the discomfort of the wilderness.

A number of writers have employed attitude scales to supply a more rigorous analysis of preferences for wilderness. Hendee and his associates (1968) produced a 'wildernist' scale to find out how people from different backgrounds viewed the wilderness. This was accomplished by testing a group of respondents about their attitude towards a series of features, activities, and benefits that, in varying degrees, were held to be part of the wilderness experience. The list included both those items that the researchers considered were typical of wilderness, such as absence of people, mountain climbing, solitude, and the pioneering spirit, and those that were felt to be more urban-oriented—for instance, souvenir stands, equipped bathing beaches, and private cottages. People were asked to express their liking or dislike for each item by means of semantic differential scales and the results were factor-analysed to see on what dimensions the 'wildernist' or 'wilderness-purist' tendencies of visitors could be measured (Hendee *et al.*, 1968). The results suggested seven types of preference for wilderness, of which the most significant were 'spartanism', 'anti-artifactualism' (symbolizing the search for contrast with the everyday environment), and 'primevalism'.

In their study of hiking in the White and Adirondack Mountains of the north-east USA, Shafer and Mietz (1972) asked people what they enjoyed most about wilderness recreation. 47.4 per cent of respondents in the sample considered the most important aspect to be the emotional experience of 'new sensations and exploring wild regions—experiences that deal with an *achievement* of some sort'. This was closely followed (36.8 per cent) by the aesthetic experience—'the enjoyment of the beauties and infinite variety of relationships that exist in an unmolested natural environment'. Such goals as physical exercise, educational opportunities, and social experiences were ranked as much less important.

While these are common themes, it is frequently found that there are differences between subgroups of wilderness users. Hendee *et al.* (1968) indicated that the results varied according to the normal place of residence of the respondent (urban–rural) and according to his activity group (for example, campers–non-campers). Lime (1972) and Peterson (1973) both showed that those who use the wilderness for recreation may have different perceptions and preferences from those responsible for its planning and management. Lucas (1970) demonstrated that the significance attached to wilderness qualities in choice of recreational area varied with the group concerned. As Table 11.2 shows, those who valued these qualities most were paddle canoeists, with canoeists as a group valuing wilderness almost twice as highly as other groups.

Interestingly enough, Lucas (1970, 299) did not define what he meant by 'wilderness' and 'respondents did not ask for definitions'. None the less, there were marked differences in the meaning the word had for respondents, as was shown by the widely varying areal extent of what people regarded as 'wilderness'. Lucas recorded that canoeists viewed a much smaller area as wilderness than did campers or individuals using motor-boats. Canoeists were more sensitive to other users and to other developments than were those who had motorized boats: for example, canoeists excluded areas around roads from wilderness. Some impression of these different areal definitions of 'wilderness' is conveyed by Figure 11.4.

This leads back to a more general point. It is virtually impossible to obtain a definition of the term 'wilderness' that is fully comprehensive. It is a complex concept that contains contrasting elements—chaos and calm, danger and tranquillity, peace and excitement—as much 'a state of mind as a description of nature' (Tuan, 1974, 112). Naturally, the realization that wilderness

Table 11.2 *Percentage of parties citing wilderness qualities as a basis for choice of the area*

Type of recreationist	Number of sample groups	Per cent citing wilderness qualities
CANOEISTS:	84	71
Paddlers	63	75
Motorized	21	62
OTHERS:	196	40
Auto campers	86	49
Boat campers	23	35
Resort guests	57	39
Private cabin users	21	10
Day use	9	33

The differences between types were significant at the .005 level tested by chi-square.

Source: Lucas (1970, 299). Copyright © 1970 by Holt, Rinehart and Winston, Inc., and used with their permission.

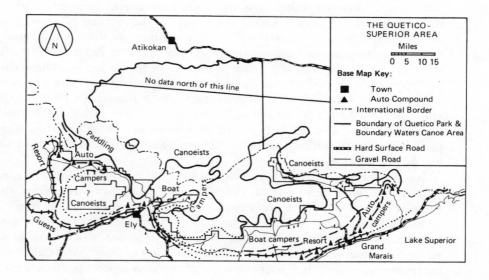

Figure 11.4 The area considered wilderness by at least 50 per cent of the visitors in each of the four major user types

The area in the interior—i.e. away from the roads and generally north of the line for each user type—was rated as 'wilderness' by 50–100 per cent of the visitors of that type reaching the area. The dotted portions of the lines indicate data were lacking, and subjective estimates have been made, based on 1960 data.

Source: Lucas (1970, 299). Copyright © 1970 by Holt, Rinehart and Winston, Inc., and used with their permission.

is valued and that it is under severe pressure from economic developers makes it necessary for planners to find criteria for deciding what is worth preserving and what is not. To some extent, this may seem contradictory. Planning aimed at preserving that which owes its rationale to a relative absence of human intervention may be to create something artificial, like the 'wilderness' to be found in the eighteenth-century formal garden—small areas of carefully planned chaos to contrast with the overriding impression of geometrical precision. Yet the pressures upon wilderness areas mean that there is little choice but to intervene and attempt to manage the demands that the public places upon them, which will require some valid means of landscape assessment.

We thus return to our basic contention, that it is necessary to approach the matter from the point of view of the preferences of users of these environments. The alternative approach of quantitative methods of landscape evaluation, with the concept of an 'objective' environment that it embodies, simply does not offer the basis for understanding what the general public values in landscape. There are still conceptual and methodological problems to be resolved in landscape preference studies and, by its very nature, this research is expensive and time-consuming, but the work is worth pursuing. The aim is more than mere academic interest, for this approach could assist in providing a secure foundation for the business of planning the environment and allocating scarce resources, a task that it would be unreasonable to expect planners alone to undertake. This conclusion has wider relevance than just the specific context of recreational behaviour.

12 Behaviour in the Natural Environment: II. Natural Hazards

And now, for the last two days, the rains on this lower course of the river had been incessant, so that the old men had shaken their heads and talked about sixty years ago, when the same sort of weather, happening about the equinox, brought on the great floods, which swept the bridge away, and reduced the town to great misery. But the younger generation, who had seen several small floods, thought lightly of these sombre recollections and forebodings; and Bob Jakin, naturally prone to take a hopeful view of his own luck, laughed at his mother when she regretted their having taken a house by the river-side; observing that but for that they would have had no boats, which were the most lucky of all possessions in case of flood that obliged them to go to a distance for food.

(GEORGE ELIOT, *The Mill on the Floss*)

As newspaper editors know, natural disasters are 'newsworthy'. In any given year it is certain that some such event, whether severe drought, violent storm, hurricane, earthquake, or even volcanic eruption will steal the head-lines. When it does, it is equally certain that the focus of attention will be the stories of 'human interest' that abound in such circumstances—the havoc and dislocation of everyday life, the destruction of property, possibly the death toll, and word-pictures of the determination of people to remain in the area and re-create their lives there. The latter is a common occurrence, for hazard-prone areas frequently support a heavy density of population and economic activity. At the same time, attention may also be drawn to aspects that may seem surprising. For instance, in the 1976 earthquakes in northern Italy a major earthquake was followed by immediate attempts by victims to rebuild their shattered homes, whereas a subsequent and milder earthquake led to a mass exodus from the region. Similarly, more people were found to have moved into an area of Bangladesh that was devastated by cyclonic storms in November 1970 than were there before the disaster (Burton, 1972).

The problems posed by man's cognition of and response to natural hazards have long been of concern to academics and policy-makers alike. The first part of this chapter considers some broad research findings on this subject. The second part turns the spotlight onto the nature of the research itself. It will be argued that this work contains important pointers for the future development of behavioural geography. Geographical research into natural hazards has evolved steadily over time within a unified paradigm. This has served to give natural hazards research the considerable advantages of a coherence and integration that contrasts markedly with other areas of behavioural geography, although, as we shall see, there are those who would assert that these benefits have been counterbalanced by a somewhat parochial outlook and narrowness of analysis. Discussion of this matter, however, must be postponed until we have examined the nature of hazard events and the range of human responses to them.

NATURAL HAZARDS: COGNITION AND RESPONSE

The Incidence of Natural Hazards. The term 'natural hazard' is remarkably difficult to define. As Burton and Kates (1972) have indicated, natural hazards can include such varied phenomena as blizzards, floods, tornadoes, earthquakes, volcanic eruptions, fungal diseases, infestations, even venomous animal bites. None the less, if one looks through the geographical literature, two things become apparent. In the first place geographers are primarily interested in geophysical (climatological and geological) events as distinct from biological hazards. It is therefore useful to employ the definition put forward by Oliver (1975, 99), who stated that a natural hazard is 'an extreme geophysical event greatly exceeding normal human expectations in terms of magnitude or frequency and causing major human hardship with significant material damage to man and his works and possible loss of life'. Second, as the above definition would imply, natural hazards cannot be considered independently of the individuals and groups that they afflict. As White (1974b, 3) has commented, 'no natural hazard exists apart from human adjustment to it. It always involves human initiative and choice. Floods would not be hazards were not man tempted to occupy floodplains; by his occupance he establishes the damage potential and may well change the flood regimen itself.'

Data about the incidence and impact of natural hazards are produced by many diverse bodies, such as government agencies, research institutions, and various sections of the United Nations Organisation, but aggregated statistics are available. One of the most valuable compilations is that supplied by Sheehan and Hewitt (1969). Table 12.1 shows the global incidence of loss of life from hazard events for a twenty-year period (1947–67). As may be seen, the greatest loss of life was caused by flooding (39.2 per cent), closely followed by typhoons, hurricanes, cyclones, and tidal waves (collectively 35.8 per cent) and earthquakes (12.7 per cent). These figures are valuable as a general guide to hazard losses, but tend to mask significant regional variations in the impact of disasters. Some impression of this point may be obtained from Table 12.2, which considers the spatial distribution of disaster impacts per continent. As this table indicates, there is a marked contrast between the developed world and the third world. For example, 210 disasters were reported in North America as against seventeen for Africa, yet loss of life was far higher in the latter (1216 per disaster) than in the former (thirty-seven). Care must be taken, of course, when interpreting such figures, for they are somewhat gross and unreliable, yet two hypotheses may be offered as to why they follow this pattern. First, news media are far less sensitive to reporting disasters in Africa than they are towards the same events in the USA, with the distinct possibility that only major African disasters come to the attention of the predominantly Western agencies that compile hazard

Table 12.1 *Number of world major natural disasters by causal agent and loss of life by disaster type, 1947–67*

	No. of disasters	No. of lives lost	Percentage of total loss of life
Floods	209	173,170	39.2
Typhoons, Hurricanes, Cyclones, Tidal Waves	153	158,245	35.8
Earthquakes	86	56,100	12.7
Tornadoes	66	3,395	0.8
Gales and Thunderstorms	32	20,940	4.7
Snowstorms	27	3,520	0.8
Heat Waves	16	4,675	1.1
Cold Waves	13	3,370	0.8
Volcanic Eruptions	13	7,220	1.6
Landslips	13	2,880	0.7
Rainstorms	10	1,100	0.2
Avalanches	9	3,680	0.8
Fogs	3	3,550	0.8
Frost	2	0	—
Sand and Dust Storms	2	10	—
Total	654	441,855	100.0

Source: Based on tables from Sheehan and Hewitt (1969).

Table 12.2 *Average loss of life per disaster impact by continents*

Continents	No. of Lives Lost	No. of Disaster Impacts	Average Loss of Life per Disaster Impact
North America	7,965	210	37
Central America and Caribbean	14,820	49	302
South America	15,670	45	348
Africa	18,105	17	1,065
Europe (excl. USSR)	19,575	85	230
Asia (excl. USSR)	361,410	297	1,216
Australasia	4,310	13	332
Totals	441,855	716	618

Source: Sheehan and Hewitt (1969).

statistics. Second, it could be that the developed world has managed to ameliorate many of the disaster tendencies in its environment and thereby reduce the number of casualties per disaster. By contrast, third-world nations are far less able to do so and indeed, because of demographic and economic pressures in hazard zones, may become increasingly vulnerable to disasters. Certainly Table 12.2 demonstrates a correlation between under-development and loss of life (Baird *et al.*, 1975).

Human Responses to Natural Hazards. Compared with information about the physical extent and magnitude of natural hazards, data on human cognition of, and response to, hazards is much harder to come by. Responses to natural hazards involve a highly complex series of individual and socio-cultural variables, so much so that it is possible for the same hazard to be interpreted in diametrically opposite ways. Rowntree (1974), for example, showed that coastal erosion was viewed as a threat to homes and livelihoods by some, but as a positive force symbolizing the triumph of elemental nature over private property by others. Similarly, it has been argued that fires in wilderness areas caused by natural processes should be allowed to burn themselves out, since this represents a normal part of the ecosystem.

None the less, there are general features that recur continually in studies of responses to natural hazards. Complete ignorance of the existence of hazards is rare, but interpretation of the events is normally characterized by 'cognitive dissonance' (Festinger, 1947), which in this case may be taken to mean a situation in which the individual is motivated towards attitudes and behaviour that do not accord with what would be expected from consideration of available information about the objective environment. Ittelson *et al.* (1974, 310) concluded that hazard research has so far put forward four reasons why human reaction varies in this way:

1. In most areas disasters occur with relative infrequency; they are not part of our daily lives. Infrequent perception of hazard conditions leads to distortions in conceptualising the environment. The threat (stimulus) is seen as potential and remote rather than immediate and real.
2. We are dealing with events over which, it is assumed, man has limited control.
3. These events often require major adjustments in our way of life, which people are usually reluctant to make.
4. Information from the hazard environment is frequently ambiguous; it provides us with a paucity of reliable cues. As a result, judgements are less accurate than is normally the case with other environments.

These points themselves hint at the role of a range of underlying factors, four of which—previous experience, personality, attitudes towards nature, and attachment to place—are worth considering further at this stage.

Previous experience of the magnitude and frequency of hazards will influence how people assess the likelihood of possible recurrence, the potential impact on their lives, and the appropriate measures they consider need to be taken. Extreme events tend to act as a fixed point in experience, obliterating memories of earlier occurrences and acting as a standard against which later ones will be compared, although the poignancy of the recollection will fade if the extreme event happens only very rarely. Jackson and Mukerjee (1974), for instance, recorded that very few San Franciscans took the threat of earthquake seriously, despite the fact that there had been six major earthquakes in California between 1872 and 1972 and that the city itself had been devastated within the span of living memory (1906). Furthermore, people tend to be consistently optimistic in their assessment of hazard occurrence. Saarinen (1966), for example, found that farmers in the drought-prone Great Plains of the USA consistently underestimated the frequency of years when drought was experienced and were optimistic about the number of good years and about the size of crops in such years. Successes are recalled more frequently than failures.

This points to the role of *personality* in human responses to natural hazards, but about which disappointingly little is yet known. Much of the evidence on this element remains intuitive, for instance, the hypothesis that people living in hazard zones have personalities similar to gamblers, trading off the odds of losses caused by natural hazards against the prospects of profitable and untroubled living which, in most cases, would be the normal state of affairs. Part of the reason for the speculative nature of such ideas is that they tend to have been derived as by-products of studies that were primarily concerned with methodology (e.g. Barker and Burton, 1969; Golant and Burton, 1970; Saarinen, 1973b), but it also reflects the deficiencies of personality research[1] and the lack of understanding of the complex interaction between individual personality and socio-cultural influences.

Attitudes towards nature strongly show the influence of culture. Kluckhohn (1959) outlined a simple typology of human attitudes towards nature, respectively, man as subject to nature, man existing in harmony with nature, and man dominating nature. The view of man as being subject to nature is one that typifies pre-industrial societies and areas of pioneer settlement. The whims of nature are seen as being beyond the control of society, being often rationalized as indications of divine will. Many theologies depict fire, earthquake, volcanic eruption, lightning, and flood as forces that are used to cleanse evil or as tokens of divine displeasure. Such views coupled with limited technological resources tend to generate resigned acceptance and fatalism. Kluckhohn (1959, 347) herself illustrated this type of attitude by describing the Spanish-American culture of the south-east USA, where, for the typical sheep-rearer 'there is little or nothing which can be done if a storm comes to damage his range lands or destroys his flocks. He simply accepts the inevitable as inevitable' (quoted in Ittelson *et al.*, 1974, 316). The notion of man in harmony with nature typifies ecological thought on the natural environment. Human systems are seen as having their place within the natural order. Individuals may take steps to protect themselves, but essentially have to recognize that the natural environment is unpredictable and that risk cannot be eliminated. Finally, people may see themselves as dominant over nature. It was a fundamental doctrine of Maoist China that man would conquer nature. In a very different ideological context, Ward (1974, 138) suggested that 'Florida horticulturalists often believe that nature is to be manipulated through the application of technological advancement. Many of them reason that as the artificiality of their environment increases, their economic returns should also increase.' The grower regards nature as something that can be manipulated by human ingenuity. Precautions could be taken against frost by means of heating or similar equipment, with the choice about whether or not they are introduced resting solely upon the grower's judgement.

Kluckhohn's typology is useful in that it identified the vital role played by the underlying technological base of the society in question and its relationship to environmental attitudes. There is evidence to suggest that occupants of hazard zones will be influenced in their behaviour by the technological devices that they themselves possess or by those that they believe society has available to deal with the hazard. For example, in a significant observation which will be alluded to again later, White *et al.* (1958) noted that increased spending on flood prevention works in the USA was actually paralleled by greater losses from flood damage, suggesting that people might be led to modify their attitude towards flood-plain occupance by their belief in the available technology. Nevertheless, it is dangerous to think that attitudes towards nature will always fit neatly into one or other of these categories. In the study by Ward (1974) mentioned above, the author found farmers with fatalistic attitudes towards nature existing alongside those who considered that they could master it. Indeed it is possible for an individual to hold attitudes of more than one type, perhaps believing that while control over nature is possible at a minor level, the overall outcomes are predestined.

The question of *attachment to place* has been somewhat neglected in hazard studies. The understandable tendency to concentrate upon the stressful aspects of hazard environments has led certain writers to seem genuinely surprised that anyone should be foolish enough to reside there at all. Yet hazard-prone areas such as the sea-shore and river basins are prime examples of what Tuan (1974, 114) termed 'environments of persistent appeal'. It goes almost without saying that such areas as the Nile, Tigris, Euphrates, Hwang Ho, and Indus valleys, to name but a few, represent major centres of civilization that have a continuous record of settlement that stretches back into pre-history. The flood hazard posed by all these rivers has been formidable, but this pales when compared with the economic advantages of living in adjacent areas or the cultural significance with which such places are endowed. The rivers were tyrants to be mastered; once mastered, they were symbols of that achievement as well as the 'string' that binds the society together. Attachment to place is not only a feature of such illustrious examples, but a strong force which can be witnessed whenever people seek to return to their home areas after the impact of a natural disaster and to reconstruct their lives there.

These factors, individually and collectively, contribute much towards an understanding of response patterns to natural hazards. Hewitt and Burton (1971) suggested six possible response types in their comparative analysis of three different natural hazards (earthquakes, floods, and snow). As Table 12.3 shows, these range from the situation in which the individual simply bears the losses incurred from hazard damage to that in which society seeks to affect the cause of the hazard itself by technological means. The terminology is sufficiently broad to encompass a variety of situations. To give an example, insurance can be taken in its conventional Western meaning or be seen in a wider context, as in the complex arrangements for mutual assistance that often exist in pre-industrial societies in order to cushion individuals against the worst effects of natural disaster (e.g. see Kirkby, 1974).

Kates (1971) summarized these various elements and relationships involved in adjustment to natural hazards in the form of a general systems model (Figure 12.1). The model itself is largely self-explanatory, but, briefly,

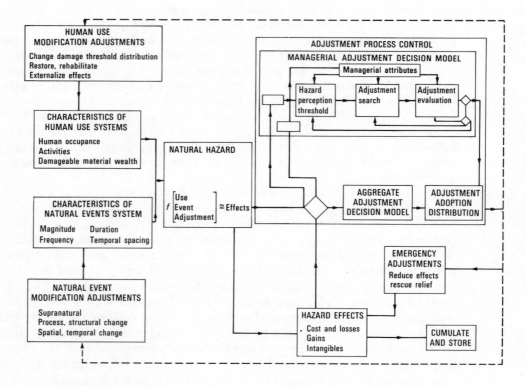

Figure 12.1 Human adjustment to natural hazards: a general systems model

Source: Kates (1971, 444).

Table 12.3 *Theoretical range of adjustments to geophysical events*

Class of Adjustment	EVENT		
	Earthquakes	Floods	Snow
Affect the cause	No known way of altering the earthquake mechanism	Reduce flood flows by: land-use treatment; cloud seeding	Change geographical distribution by: cloud seeding
Modfy the hazard	Stable site selection: soil and slope stabilization; sea wave barriers; fire protection	Control flood flows by: reservoir storage; levees; channel improvement; flood fighting	Reduce impact by: snow fences; snow removal; salting and sanding of highways
Modify loss potential	Warning systems; emergency evacuation and preparation; building design; land-use change; permanent evacuation	Warning systems; emergency evacuation and preparation; building design; land-use change; permanent evacuation	Forecasting; rescheduling; inventory control; building design; seasonal adjustments (snow tyres chains); seasonal migration; designation of snow emergency routes
Adjust to losses:			
Spread the losses	Public relief; subsidized insurance	Public relief; subsidized insurance	Public relief; subsidized insurance
Plan for losses	Insurance and reserve funds	Insurance and reserve funds	Insurance and reserve funds
Bear the losses	Individual loss-bearing	Individual loss-bearing	Individual loss-bearing

Source: Hewitt and Burton (1971, 19).

it depicts the so-called 'human use' and 'natural events' systems as being closely interrelated. The natural hazard is influenced by both systems. Cognition of the hazard and its effects set up a complex response pattern, the results of which 'feed-back' as modifications to either the 'human use' system, or the 'natural events' system, or both. Further attention should be given to 'adjustment process control' subsystem (of which a more detailed version is shown in Figure 12.2). In this, Kates differentiated between societal

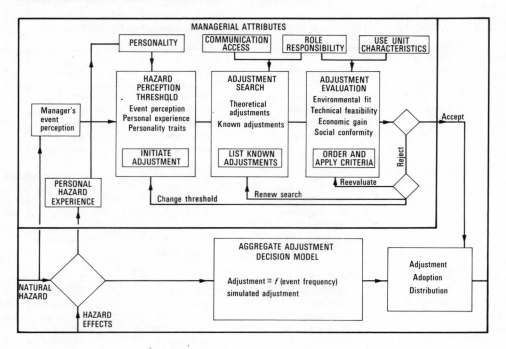

Figure 12.2 Adjustment Process Control

Source: Kates (1971, 447).

and individual managerial levels, the former sketched in crude outline, the latter depicted more fully. For a response to occur at the individual level, the hazard will have to exceed the threshold above which the individual will consider that an adjustment is necessary. That person will examine the range of possible alternatives and select an appropriate one. If none is found, the individual may then re-evaluate the available options, or continue to search for other adjustment strategies, or change his threshold in order to accommodate the situation.

The model has been applied to several contexts. Kates (1971) himself applied it to the East African drought situation, Sarre (1976) showed that it could be used to analyse drought in the Great Plains area of the United States, and Kirkby (1973, quoted in Stringer, 1975b) extended the model to apply to a man-made hazard (pollution from an aluminium smelter). Nevertheless, it remains a conceptual model. Whatever its pedagogic value as a study framework, it would require substantial testing before vindicating Kates's belief that this *could* be an operational model.

THE PROGRESS OF NATURAL HAZARDS RESEARCH

Origins. The main thrust of natural hazards research may be traced back to the work of Gilbert White and his colleagues at the University of Chicago.[2] White's early research was concerned with the physical aspect of flood losses. Writing at a time when most literature on the subject came from engineers and others who essentially looked to technology, particularly dam construction, to alleviate flood loss, White (1939, 1942) began to put forward the unfashionable view that expenditure on flood prevention and similar projects would not have the desired effect of reducing damage. With the aid of official funding, a study group was established in 1956 at the University of Chicago to examine the whole question of human adjustment to floods. The initial report (White *et al.*, 1958) confirmed White's suspicions, for although American expenditure on flood control had risen sharply, the level of flood damages had also risen.

From the work of this group and a number of distinguished graduate students came the development of what has retrospectively been termed the 'Chicago school' of natural hazard studies. Its hall-marks were a concern with policy matters as well as academic matters, and a view of man–environment relations that depicted cognitive processes as central to understanding adjustment strategies.[3] The initial concern was with riverine flooding (Burton, 1962; Kates, 1962, 1965; White, 1964), but soon broadened into other areas of flooding (for example, coastal floods, Burton and Kates, 1964; Kates, 1967) and into studies of other types of natural hazard.

The latter path was initiated by the study carried out by Saarinen (1966) on drought-hazard perception in the Great Plains. While this broke with tradition by focusing on the other end of the spectrum of evapo-transpiration, it retained a continuity of method. Saarinen adapted his basic questionnaire from one devised initially for flood situations, but extended its scope by the addition of projective techniques to explore general attitudes towards nature. This conscious awareness of the need for systematic development of methods and techniques has remained a feature of natural hazards research.

Integrated Research Programmes. From these beginnings, and with the active participation and leadership of the original Chicago group, a range of new research directions have evolved. Of the selected papers cited in Table 12.4, almost all are either by workers connected with the original 'Chicago School' or are those that have participated in one or other of the major research programmes to which this research has led. There is no attempt here to discuss the way these programmes evolved or to summarize their results in detail.[4] Rather the intention here is briefly to survey the major research directions in the continuing North American programme (which has followed the movements of its major workers to Toronto, Colorado, and Clark Universities) and that initiated under the auspices of the Commission of Man and Environment of the International Geographical Union (IGU).

Table 12.4 *Selected papers on natural hazards*

	Authors	Context
1. INDIVIDUAL HAZARDS		
a. Avalanche	Ramsli, 1974	Norway
b. Coastal Hazards	Burton and Kates, 1964	North-east USA
	Kates, 1967	——
	R. L. Adams, 1969	——
	Mitchell, 1974, 1976	——
	Rowntree, 1974	California
c. Drought	Saarinen, 1966	Great Plains, USA
	Heathcote, 1969	South Australia
	Brooks, 1971	North-east Brazil
	Dupree and Roder, 1974	Nigeria
	Kirkby, 1974	Oaxaca, Mexico
d. Earthquake	Kates *et al.*, 1973	Central America
	Jackson and Mukerjee, 1974	California
	Nichols, 1974	Global
e. Flooding	White, 1942, 1964, 1970, 1973	Mainly USA
	White *et al.*, 1958	——
	Ericksen, 1970	New Zealand
	Beyer, 1974	Global
	Harding and Parker, 1974	Shropshire, England
	Ramachandran and Thakur 1974	India
f. Fire	A. D. Hall, 1969	Canada
	Mutch, 1970	USA
	Barrows, 1971	USA
	Edgell, 1975	S. E. Australia
g. Soil Erosion	Parkes and Day, 1975	Ontario, Canada
h. Snow	Rooney, 1967, 1969	USA
	Earney and Knowles, 1974	Michigan
i. Volcano	Murton and Shimabukaro, 1974	Hawaii
j. Wind (i) Hurricane	Baker and Patton, 1974	Gulf Coast, USA
	Baumann and Sims, 1974	——
(ii) Tornado/ Cyclone	Sims and Baumann, 1972	USA
	Islam, 1974	Bangladesh
	Oliver, 1975	Queensland, Australia
2. MULTIPLE HAZARDS		
a. General Surveys	Sheehan and Hewitt, 1969	Global
	Visvader and Burton, 1974	North America
	Nakano, 1974	Japan
	Gerasimov and Zhonkova, 1974	USSR
b. 'All Hazards at a Place'	Arsdol *et al.*, 1964	Los Angeles, California
	Hewitt and Burton, 1971	London, Ontario
	Smith, 1976b, 1976d	Windsor, Ontario

The majority of studies in the last decade have adopted all or part of a paradigm put forward by Burton *et al.* (1968) which sought to:

1) assess the extent of human occupance in hazard zones
2) identify the full range of possible human adjustment to the hazard
3) study how men perceive and estimate the occurrence of the hazard
4) describe the process of adoption of damage reducing adjustments in their social context
5) estimate the optimal set of adjustments in terms of anticipated social consequences.

Within this framework, the main research objectives have been to gain a more complete view of the global extent and range of natural hazards, to attempt comparative analysis of different types of hazard and of the same hazard in different cultural contexts, and to maintain the systematic development of method. All these themes may be exemplified by examining briefly the research linked to the IGU-sponsored programme (White, 1974a, Burton *et al.*, 1978).

This drew upon the work of researchers from fifteen nations and examined nine types of natural hazard. Although this cannot be regarded as complete coverage, it provided the basis upon which to sketch broad themes that were themselves likely to beget further insights. Comparability of data was ensured by using a standardized questionnaire, based upon that employed in the early North American work. In his analysis of the use made of this questionnaire, Saarinen (1974) found that there were many possible sources of error, compounded by limitations of time and money, the need to co-operate with many collaborators who had not previously worked in this field of inquiry and the inevitable problems associated with adapting the questionnaire into other languages. Of the fifty-six questions in the original questionnaire (see White, 1974b), it was found that just over half (thirty) could be applied with little or no difficulty, whereas fourteen caused some difficulty, and fourteen led to considerable difficulty. Saarinen (1974) concluded that there was a spectrum that ranged from simple direct questions which proved easy to adapt, to open-ended, opinion-seeking questions which produced difficulties. The dilemma here was that the 'most interesting questions' created the greatest problems and that the short-answer questions had the disadvantage of depending entirely upon the researcher's ideas, providing no means of tapping the cognitive world of the respondent on his or her own terms.

With this last comment in mind, it is interesting to look at an alternative approach which has been adopted by a number of writers and which is to focus on a particular place or region and to identify the set of conditions within its environment that residents regard as hazardous. A good example of this is found in the study by Smith (1976b, 1976d) on Windsor (Ontario). Necessarily this requires a slightly different definition of 'hazard' from that used previously in this chapter, in this case any 'aspects of the physical environment which urban residents view as a potential threat to their physical or mental health' (Smith, 1976d, 8). Furthermore, the term 'urban environmental hazard' was employed rather than 'natural hazard' as the list of hazards included man-made hazards[5] such as water pollution and road-traffic noise as well as such phenomena as flooding. Equally, Hewitt and Burton's (1971) study of London (Ontario) examined man-made hazards such as fires and industrial dangers as well as the full ambit of natural hazards.

This work remains exploratory, is as yet confined to limited contexts, and has problems over the way to maintain comparability between different types of hazard, yet it represents an interesting new aspect to hazard studies. It offers the prospect of seeing hazards from the resident's rather than from the researcher's point of view. It also may help to close the artificial dichotomy between the so-called man-made hazards (which, for the sake of coherence, were here discussed under their more common name of 'urban stressors' in Chapter 10), and natural hazards. These are both constructive developments.

CONCLUSION

Natural hazards research differs from other areas of behavioural geography in two important respects. First, it is a branch of research that has been dominated by geographers. In this text, it has been usual to find geographers taking up and modifying the work of others, but natural hazards are a topic in which the initial research has been done by geographers themselves. This is due to three main reasons. In the first place, hazard inquiries proceed at the levels with which geographers are most accustomed, ranging from the small region to global space. Next, they involve physical environmental processes, about which geographers can offer an expertise which is unrivalled by the other social sciences. Finally, it is possible that the image of a dominant physical environment imposing forces upon human society fitted in better with traditional conceptions of man–environment relationships in geography than it did in other disciplines.

Second, this branch of research is unusual in that it has been coherent, integrated, policy-oriented, and (recently) has acquired a cross-cultural basis. In part this state of affairs reflects the substantial funding that has been made available for natural hazards research, but more significant is the fact that it has developed from a small number of freely available works, with the original contributors continuing to play a major role. This situation has provided natural hazards research with advantages of continuity and developmental progress that are unique in behavioural geography, but which may also carry certain disadvantages. One effect of the development of research within the essentially geographical paradigm created by White and his associates may have been that researchers have been less responsive to cross-disciplinary influences than in certain other areas of behavioural geography. It is noticeable, for instance, that one virtually never finds reference made in geographical studies of natural hazards to the copious sociological literature (e.g. Young, 1954; Baker and Chapman, 1962; Barton, 1969; Turner, 1976; Davis, 1978). This research, which was focused primarily on social and community adjustment to disasters, has much to offer the geographer interested in natural hazards.

More fundamental criticisms of the paradigm of natural hazards research have been made by a group of radical geographers[6] (Baird *et al.*, 1975; O'Keefe, 1975; Wisner *et al.*, 1976; O'Keefe and Halverston, forthcoming). Their basic objections stem from the belief that research effort should be refocused to give greater attention to third-world nations, which, as we have seen, suffer disproportionately from natural disasters. If this is done, they would contend that the paradigm is an insufficient framework for research, both because it is too parochial (American-oriented) in outlook and because its perspectives on social adjustment to disaster are inadequate for third-world nations. These contentions are worth examining further.

The parochial nature of the research is said to have two main manifestations. First, it is felt that it has led to an American-oriented bias in the goals of researchers. Westgate (1978), for example, argued that the book *Reconstruction after Disaster* (Haas *et al.*, 1977) exemplified this tendency. Haas and his colleagues had examined four case-studies of earthquakes, three of which were from American cities and the other from Managua, the capital of Nicaragua. Yet while the analysis was extended to include a third-world study, the authors' stated aims make it clear that this was done only to see if it 'could provide findings of significance for United States cities in high-risk areas' (Haas *et al.*, 1977, xvii). In other words, the purpose of the cross-cultural comparison was to extract material that could be applied to the American situation. Second, it has been suggested that the standardized questionnaire used in the IGU and earlier research programmes was seriously biased towards the American experience and would need considerable modification before applying satisfactorily to third-world nations (Waddell, 1977).

The question about the treatment of social adjustment to disaster is probably the more serious reservation about the approach of the American hazard researchers. Baird *et al.* (1975) claimed that the tendency has been to view hazards as extraordinary events, whereas they argued that it was more realistic to see disasters as extreme versions of circumstances present in the everyday condition of the population. This led them to ask just how 'natural' were such disasters. The reasoning was as follows: 'As the under-developed population attempts to discover alternative strategies of production on the edges of the imposed system that has controlled the traditional indigenous resource base, it is forced to accept strategies that contain fewer insurance or adoptive mechanisms for survival' (Baird *et al.*, 1975, 29). In this way, the severity of the impact of disasters was seen as being, at least partly, the result of the economic order. The urban and rural poor of the under-developed country have little or no absorptive capacity in the face of extreme phenomena and become, in effect, more vulnerable than previously to the vagaries of the environment (Westgate and O'Keefe, 1976).

These are radical criticisms in more senses than one and, at the time of writing, there has not yet been opportunity for comprehensive comment by any of the established American natural-hazard researchers. Formal assessment of their respective cases would therefore be premature, but a brief note by White (1978) provides some impression of the defence that may be offered. White was responding to a critical review article by Waddell (1977), in which the latter had levelled two charges against the IGU research programme, namely, that its approach to the problem of social adaptation to extreme forces was 'resolutely deterministic' and that the methods used were inappropriate for the problem. To both charges, White's defence was much the same. The basic approach and questionnaire were intended to act as a general guide; no single model of development was assumed, and the suggested questionnaire was to be used, modified, or discarded as the local researcher thought fit. In White's words (1978, 230): 'The purposes of the suggested interview were to develop a common base of observations from which variations could unfold and to encourage comparisons. It was intended to be a springboard rather than a mould.' More general questions about the radical approach itself, however, such as how much may be attributed to economic forces as opposed to the pressures of demographic increase in hazard-prone zones or about the internal logic and consistency of the economic analysis, have yet to be clearly articulated.

One final point needs to be made. In this chapter, we have viewed the natural environment in a quite different way than in the previous chapter. There the emphasis was upon landscape preference and attraction behaviour, here it has been upon stress, adjustment, and avoidance. Chapter 11 concentrated upon the cognition and behaviour of the visitor to an area, the current chapter has focused on the resident. To complete the tale of contrasts, we have witnessed two very different bodies of research material; the one lacking substantive theoretical frameworks and having poorly developed methodology, the other demonstrating the virtues of orderly, self-critical, and logical development. Yet despite appearances, there is an important continuity of material between this and the previous chapter. The desired landscape and the hazard zone are often one and the same thing. The policy-maker has to manage the environment in the light of both perspectives, which may on occasions be in conflict. For example, the desire to provide protective works against hazards may clash with the conservationist's view of how the area should be treated. Each of these needs is important and merits its place in planning priorities. Rationalization and integration of the two viewpoints would be difficult, but the systematic and incremental approach of the hazard researchers surely gives at least a clue as to how it might be achieved.

13 Spatial Cognition and Decision-making Behaviour: The Case of Industrial Location

Where Derwent guide his dusky floods,
Through vaulted mountains and nights of woods,
The nymph 'Gossypia' treads the silver sod,
And warms with rosy smiles the wat'ry God:
His pond'rous oars to slender spindles turns
And pours o'er mossy wheels his foaming urns,
With playful charms her hoary lover wins
And wields his tridents while the monarch spins.

(ERASMUS DARWIN, *Botanic Garden*, commenting on the
site of Arkwright's recently opened mill at Cromford, Derbyshire)

The study of industrial location has provided a point of common interest for economists, geographers, and planners. The *economist* has aimed to extend the range of economic analysis by explicitly considering spatial variables, with the emphasis placed upon formal deductive approaches. The *geographer*, a relative latecomer to location theory, has attempted to explain spatial patterns of industrial activity by arriving at generalization through case-studies which include a largely intuitive content (Mawson, 1975). Their combined efforts have produced a large corpus of research which possesses a substantial theoretical core supported by extensive empirical data. The *planner*, particularly the regional planner, has looked to this literature in the hope of finding insight into the complex process by which industrial locations are selected, with its implications for regional growth and development.

This research has had a considerable value. It has provided models with considerable normative utility, has supplied a point of contact for academic and policy-oriented groups, and for geography it has the added distinction of being the area of study that acted as the precursor of the 'quantitative revolution'. Nevertheless, traditional location theory has been heavily criticized in recent years over the nature of its basic assumptions, its preoccupation with the manufacturing sector as opposed to other types of economic activity, its reliance upon the dominant paradigms of classical micro-economics, its inapplicability to present-day circumstances, and the validity of its methods.[1] This chapter examines the line of criticism that most concerns us here, namely the limitations imposed by the assumptions about decision-making behaviour, and then surveys some research that attempts to view locational decision-making behaviour in a more realistic manner.

BEHAVIOURAL DEFICIENCIES OF CLASSICAL LOCATION THEORY

The model of decision-making behaviour put forward by classical location theorists was outlined earlier (Chapter 3). The entrepreneur was assumed to seek the single goal of profit maximization, which his omniscience and infinite capacity for predicting the future economic circumstances of the firm allowed him to do. The behaviour of the entrepreneur was determined by forces in his economic environment, with him responding to changes in that environment by invariably seeking the location that satisfied the narrow criterion of profit-maximization. The problem was conventionally expressed in terms of transport costs. To take the example of Alfred Weber's (1929) 'least-cost' model, the decision-maker sought the location in which transport costs per unit of production, and hence total costs, were minimized. The only exceptions to this rule were places where the economic benefits of either agglomeration, or labour availability, or both, were sufficient to offset the costs incurred by locating away from the point of least transport costs. Naturally, different industries will have their own optimal locations depending on their individual cost-structures.

Neo-classical theorists themselves criticized Weber for the simplicity of his assumptions about transport costs (Hoover, 1937), for his neglect of market demand (Lösch, 1940), for the need to improve upon indices used in his analysis (Smith, 1955), and for the rigidity of his concept of locational behaviour (Rawstron, 1955), but these criticisms amounted to incremental change rather than fundamental reappraisal. Even in the late 1960s, the essence of location theory was not radically different from that initiated by Weber (Wood, 1969).

At the same time, there were writers who felt that location theorists should pay more attention to real-world decision-making. First, it has been argued that locational models have overemphasized distance costs relative to other factors, creating the impression that they exert a tyranny over location. It is more often the case that distance costs are only one consideration in general investment planning (Hamilton, 1974) and may well be balanced against non-spatial factors (Townroe, 1974). Secondly, there was a general feeling that too much reliance had been placed upon economic analysis. This partly reflected increasing awareness that non-economic variables can and do play a major role in locational decision-making, but was also due to growing recognition of the vigour, stature, and appeal of other social science approaches, particularly in sociology and psychology. Finally, it was felt that the micro-economic emphasis upon the individual entrepreneur, who made decisions for a single-plant firm, was outmoded at a time when the norm had become the multi-plant, multi-functional, and multi-national organization with corporate decision-making.

Collectively, these factors explain why a growing sense of disenchantment with existing directions of research developed, coupled with the belief that new directions were required.

THE DECISION-MAKER AND THE ORGANIZATION[2]

One positive development that emerged from this mood of reappraisal has been interest in organizational theory. By regarding industrial enterprises as diverse types of 'organization', one gains a unifying framework which makes it possible to discern common features which might otherwise have been masked by conflicting terminology or the intricacies of corporate structures. For our purposes, an industrial enterprise may be regarded as a form of organization that has been deliberately 'constructed and reconstructed to seek specific goals' (Etzioni, 1964, 3). These goals will be primarily commercial, but will also include political, social, and personal considerations. Whatever the specific mixture of goals in any particular organization, its goals provide both the key to its character (Perrow, 1971) and the guiding principles for its policy. There is great variation in these goals and in the freedom of operation permitted to individual members of organizations in implementing them. Some organizations formulate policy in detail at head-office and exercise tight control over subsidiary units, others give broad directives and allow their staff greater executive freedom. In the case of branch factories, for example, some have local managements who are tightly constrained by the head office, whereas others are allowed almost complete autonomy within a loose confederal structure. Despite these apparent differences, all such organizations possess the same basic features, namely, a structure of status and responsibility, a network of communication and delegation, and a set of 'rules' and procedures aimed at achieving corporate goals.

A useful analogy is to liken the typical large multi-product firm which operates 'under uncertainty in an imperfect market' to a coalition of mutually dependent, but often conflicting, participants (Cyert and March, 1963). In such a coalition, the whole is greater than the sum of its parts. Decisions may arise that do not represent the choice of any specific individual, but are compromises moulded by internal discussion and consultation. The attitudes and goals of participants are brought into line by bargaining within procedures that have been built up over time by learning. The latter are particularly important, for the existence of precedents and established rules for handling decision-making serve the dual purpose of reducing the possibility of interpersonal conflict within the firm itself and of lessening the uncertainties present in the firm's dealings with the outside world (Mawson, 1975).

In an examination of locational decision-making within such industrial organizations, it should again be stressed that the location decision is only one of an array that businessmen have to make. As Figure 13.1 illustrates, it has to take its place alongside other decisions that have to be made before the firm enters production. The plant exists within three wider environments —industrial, business, and socio-political. Within the internal environment, location is seen as one of four initial 'production decisions' alongside those concerning the product itself, the scale of production, and the technique to be used. Once decisions have been made, they may be relatively fixed in the short term, but in the long term they may be changed in accordance with information that 'feeds back' from either internal or external environments.

The 'entrepreneurial evaluation' box in Figure 13.1 requires further

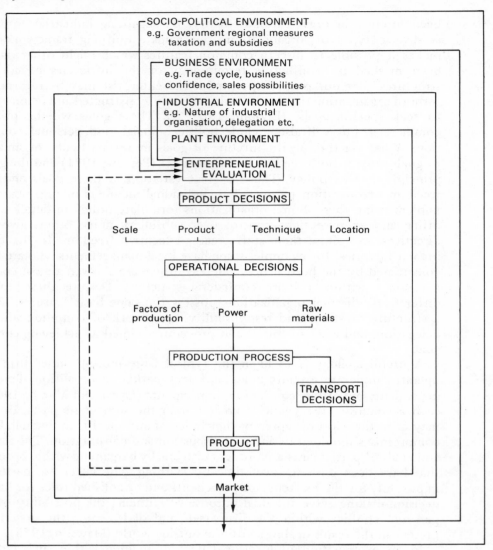

Figure 13.1 Location decisions as part of the investment process

explanation, which is readily available in the form of the framework put forward by Lloyd and Dicken (1972, see Figure 13.2). This framework incorporates the question of the individual's relationships with the external and internal (organizational) environments. As may be seen, decisions made by a firm fundamentally depend upon the information available to it about its performance in a changing environment, but this information will be sought and received selectively, subject to a series of individual and organizational filters. The more intricate the organization, the more complex are these

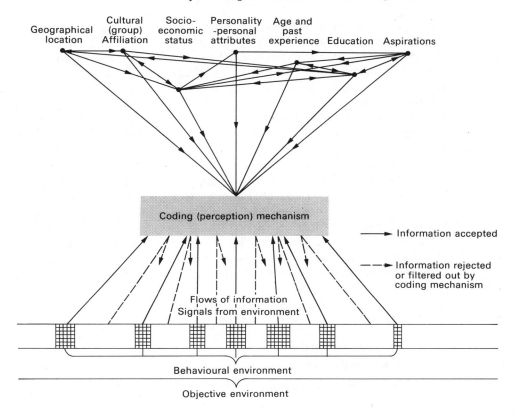

Figure 13.2 The behavioural environment perceived as a component of the total objective environment

Source: Lloyd and Dicken (1972, 139).

filters likely to be. Lloyd and Dicken did not fully develop the nature of the factors that influence individual perception, apart from mentioning some of the factors they regarded as significant, but they indicated that individual perceptions help to create the corporate perceptions of the organization. The latter are more than just the aggretage of the cognition of individual executive members, for they also reflect 'the specific nature of the firm itself and its position within the economic system' (Lloyd and Dicken, 1972, 138).

Naturally, it is difficult to disentangle the individual and collective components of decision-making but, as a first step, it is instructive to examine a study by Taylor and McDermott (1976) of the relative importance of locational and organizational factors upon space preferences. These authors investigated the way managers evaluated the locations at which their firms were currently situated, taking their sample from the Auckland city-region of New Zealand. It was hypothesized that managerial spatial cognition would vary with the personal circumstances of the individual managers, the firm's location, and the type and scale of its organization. Five hundred and forty-eight respondents were interviewed in order to test these ideas, of whom 249 were based in Auckland itself and 279 were located in five adjacent towns (Whangarei, Napier, Wanganui, Nelson, and Timaru). The questionnaires used in the interviews sought attitudinal data about sixteen items thought to be significant in industrial location decisions.

Results were initially compared by constructing attitudinal 'profiles', as shown in Figure 13.3. Differences were recorded in the attitudes of Auckland managers compared with their colleagues in the secondary centres. Auckland manufacturers regarded their city as enjoying marketing and transport advantages, but being less favoured in terms of its land costs and availability of labour. The attitudinal profiles of managers in the smaller towns were markedly different, emphasizing residential attractions and lower

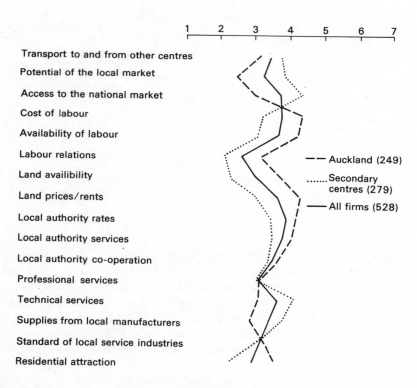

Figure 13.3 Aggregate attitude profiles for managers in primary and secondary centres

Source: Taylor and McDermott (1976, 331).

labour and land costs, but regarding marketing and availability of transport and technical services as distinct disadvantages. The data were further analysed by being divided into organizational categories. While this did not reveal systematic variation, it did suggest that managers discriminated against certain elements in their local environment in accordance with the age, size, and management characteristics of their firms.

While these empirical results are themselves interesting, some broader conclusions are also in order. First, such results must remain tentative in the absence of further testing, particularly as the profiles constitute aggregations that might not truly reflect the environmental outlook of the typical entrepreneur. Second, the researcher who was interested in extending the analysis from attitudes to behaviour might question how far attitudinal data of this type could really be regarded as 'predispositions to action' (see Chapter 2). Attitudes elicited under circumstances in which the firm is actively contemplating a move might well be quite different from answers given to a somewhat hypothetical questionnaire. Furthermore, the evidence obtained from a specific individual may be a poor guide as to the corporate outlook of the organization.

These points illustrate the large number of conceptual and methodological problems that researchers still have to face, but progress is being made—a point that may be demonstrated by briefly examining behavioural research on the process of locational search and selection.

LOCATIONAL SEARCH AND SELECTION

Various conceptual frameworks have been put forward to chart the major stages of industrial location decision-making. Dicken (1971), for example, suggested that there were three broad phases in the process. In the first, the firm starts to feel that the present location is not wholly satisfactory. The organization and its members will be aware, with varying degrees of precision, of their performance in a changing environment. Actual performance is compared with anticipated results, and any shortfall between reality and expectations may be termed 'stress'. Most stresses are ignored or corrected by making minor adjustments to the firm's commercial operations, but if they should prove to exceed a critical threshold level, the decision may be made to look for a new location. This leads on to the second stage of the process, which is known as 'searching'. Searching is aimed at removing locational stress, but is a task that is expensive in terms of time, manpower, and resources. Furthermore, it is rarely delegated below top management (Townroe, 1974). If one accepts that decision-makers recognize the impossibility of achieving optimal solutions, then it is inevitable that searching will be limited in extent and conservative in nature, characterized by procedures that seek to provide a rapid solution in order to avoid delays which might interfere with production and sales. The nature of the search will vary according to the type of firm involved. Established firms can often call upon solutions that have been successfully adopted in the past and learn from their previous errors. For firms where no precedents exist, the main options will either be 'trial-and-error' or to draw upon the experience of other firms. The third stage of the process is 'evaluation', in which available options are considered and one of three possible courses of action adopted: choice of a suitable site, the decision to continue searching, or abandonment of the effort to move.

These ideas were presented in greater detail in Figure 13.4, which elaborated upon the sequence of possible outcomes at each stage of the decision-making process. As logical as this framework may seem, it must be stressed that it and other similar models[3] remain primarily heuristic, with relatively few being generated by empirical research.

Exceptions to this rule, however, are to be found in the study by North (1974). North investigated the growth records of 100 firms in the British plastics industry—an ideal context for this type of project, being an industry which had grown rapidly in the post-war period and one in which it was likely that basic decisions about locational choice would have been made within the recent past. The initial framework adopted by North is shown in Figure 13.5, which depicts the firm's locational decisions as a component part of general investment decision-making.

North's starting-point for his empirical studies was to review the different types of locational decision-making to be found in the firms within the sample. As may be seen in Table 13.1, over 70 per cent of these firms had experienced at least one decision involving selection of a new location, a figure which would have exceeded 90 per cent if extensions, acquisitions, and factory closures had been included. North identified ten types of stress that led to locational decisions: namely, planned growth of existing product lines, development of regional markets for existing products and services, unplanned growth of existing product lines, diversification into new product lines, vertical integration, horizontal integration, externally generated stresses, stresses imposed by the pattern of the market distribution, a decision imposed by the parent company, and rationalization of operations. Particular forms of stress would contribute to some types of locational decision rather than others. For example, relocation decisions were associated with pressures resulting from unplanned production growth and environmental stresses experienced at a particular place, whereas branch decisions usually resulted from pressure exerted on factory capacity by the planned growth of production (in circumstances where expansion *in situ* was impossible) and from the policy of expansion by developing regional markets.

North classified the way in which firms decided their locational response to internally or externally generated stresses by developing a series of decision sequences to cover the various forms of spatial behaviour found in his sample. Lack of space precludes a discussion of all of them, but some idea of their content may be obtained by considering three examples, all of which relate to the search and selection process for branch factories (Figures 13.6–8). The first decision-sequence was generated from the experience of four firms,

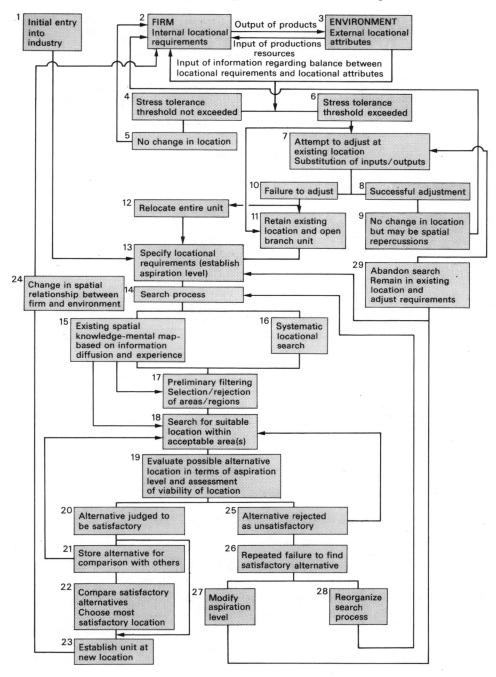

Figure 13.4 A model of the location-decision process

Source: Lloyd and Dicken (1972, 147).

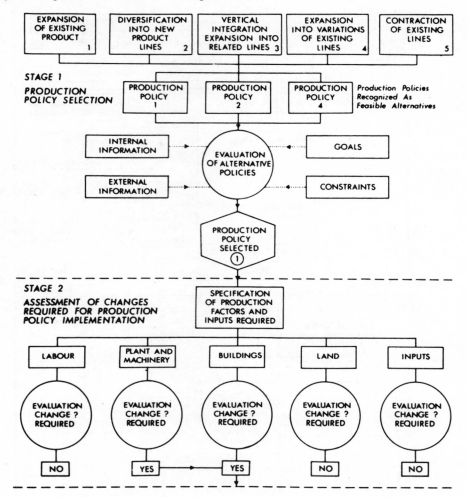

Figure 13.5a Locational change as part of the investment process of the firm

Source: North (1974, 216). Copyright © 1974 by John Wiley & Sons Ltd. Reprinted by permission.

typically representing large publicly owned corporations that were prepared to consider regions other than those in which their activities were currently situated. While these firms employed systematic techniques for locational search and selection, North (1974, 235) recognized that personal factors were still the most significant influence, commenting that 'the reputation of the group in, and the familiarity of senior directors with, a particular region imposed a marked bias upon the search process from the outset.' The second type of decision-sequence (Figure 13.7) involved seven firms which grew by developing regional markets. Here the search process was normally conducted in a predetermined region, attempting to find a site central to the spatial arrangement of the market. Systematic procedures for locational search were

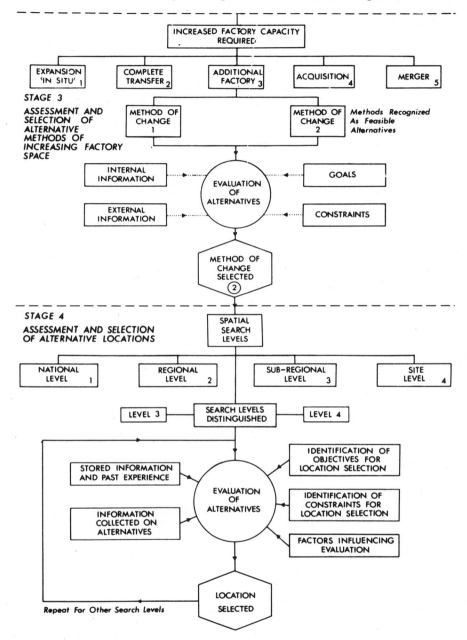

Figure 13.5b Locational change as part of the investment process of the firm

Source: North (1974, 217). Copyright © 1974 by John Wiley & Sons Ltd. Reprinted by permission.

Table 13.1 *The number of firms making each type of location decision at specified numbers of times during the period 1960–71*

No. times decision made:	1		2		3		4		5		
Decision type	No. of firms	% of total	No. of firms	% of total	No. of firms	% of total	No. of firms	% of total	No. of firms	% of total	Total
Complete transfer	26	83.9	5	16.1	—	—	—	—	—	—	31
Branch establishment	19	70.4	7	25.9	—	—	—	—	1	3.7	27
Acquisition	17	63.0	3	11.1	4	14.8	—	—	—	—	24
Extension	20	51.8	10	18.5	7	12.9	3	5.5	6	11.1	54
Closure	3	60.0	2	40.0	—	—	—	—	—	—	5
Initial location decision	24										24
No decision	11										11

Source: North (1974, 221).

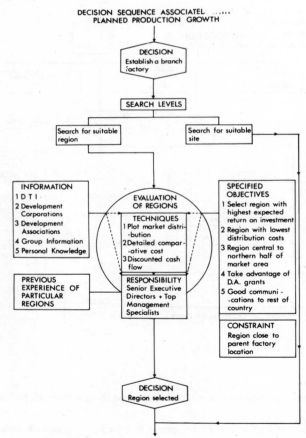

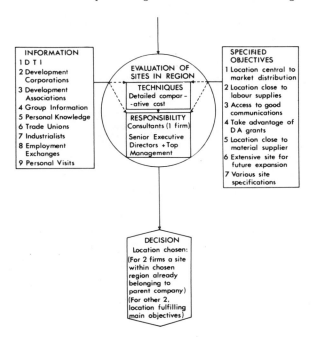

Figure 13.6 The search and selection process at the inter-regional level for a branch-factory decision (four firms)

Source: North (1974, 236–7). Copyright © 1974 by John Wiley & Sons Ltd. Reprinted by permission.

rare, 'rules of thumb' being the order of the day. The third, and most frequent, branch decision (nine firms) was where the new factory was located close to existing plant (Figure 13.8). This involved no formal evaluation procedures as such, firms being unwilling to create a spatially separate branch with the managerial and labour problems that are often associated with such moves and the disruption costs that are frequently encountered.

North's paper, along with several other works in the same vein (e.g. Blackbourn, 1974; Green, 1974; and Walker, 1975) provides useful insights into the nature of locational decision-making but still represent the view of the outsider looking in. In generalizing from *ex post facto* interview data, they clearly indicate the role of individual and organizational factors but tell us tantalizingly little about their dynamics and relative importance. That research which does touch upon the cognitive-behavioural level of study seems to support the basic themes that have been put forward throughout Part Four: that searching begins with the local and familiar, that schemata are highly parochial and partial, and that a quick and satisfactory solution is normally sought for locational problems. The role of preferences has still to be precisely articulated, but the available evidence leaves little doubt as to their importance. To quote an example, a study carried out by Unilever (cited in Mawson, 1975) examined the relocation decisions of firms moving

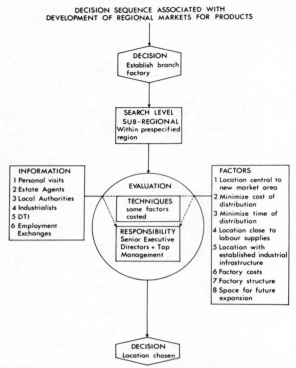

Figure 13.7 The search and selection process within a pre-specified region for a branch-factory decision (seven firms)

Source: North (1974, 238). Copyright © 1974 by John Wiley & Sons Ltd. Reprinted by permission.

their head-offices from Central London. In all but one case it was found that the chosen location was within the Home Counties. When probing the attitudes of sixty senior and middle management towards a move to the north rather than to the Home Counties, it was found that they would overwhelmingly have chosen to find a new job in the Home Counties rather than move to the north. Opposition to the region was not founded on any belief that the business could not be efficiently managed in the north, but rather for a variety of personal reasons, such as the conviction that wives would not be able to find jobs, that the environment would be less stimulating, that the schools were of poorer quality, and that prevalent social attitudes in the area would not be to their liking. There can be no doubt too that policy-makers consider spatial preferences to be of considerable importance, as can be witnessed by the large amounts of resources spent upon industrial and general image creation.[4]

CONCLUSION

The research discussed in this chapter is at an exploratory stage. While

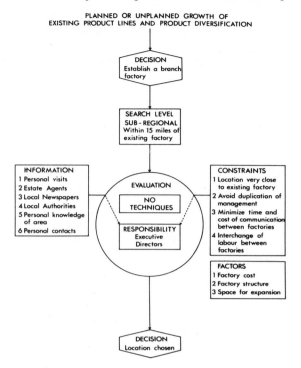

Figure 13.8 The search and selection process at the local level for a branch-factory decision.

Source: North (1974, 239). Copyright © 1974 by John Wiley & Sons Ltd. Reprinted by permission.

industrial location itself is a familiar topic of geographical inquiry, existing theory puts forward a model of behaviour which, by its inherent assumptions, says little about the processes by which real-world locational decisions are reached. Given the increasing prevalence of corporate decision-making in modern industry, it was suggested that locational decisions should be viewed as part of the general investment programme and that the decision-maker should be thought of as a member of an organization. In this way, it was possible both to place locational decisions in true perspective and to gain a framework within which to consider individual and group levels of analysis. If research has so far paid little attention to the role of the individual *within* the organization, it is partly because existing theory overemphasized the individual, solitary decision-maker. The cognitive-behavioural level of analysis, however, remains an essential ingredient in understanding locational decision-making. To date, research has done little more than pose the broad problems, but it provides foundations upon which further studies can be based. Given the extensive interest in this field of study, one suspects that this will be an important proving ground for behavioural geography.

14 The Imposed Image:
Spatial Design and Behaviour

It does not matter into what twisted folly the architecture breaks as long as we can live merrily and affectionately beneath it.

(J. B. PRIESTLEY, *English Journey*)

While spatial environments bear the imprint of the past and present decisions of countless individuals, in developed nations design has become increasingly the preserve of the professional designer.[1] In the face of rapid urbanization, the development of public demands for higher environmental standards, the sophistication of new constructional methods, and the sheer scale and complexity of modern building projects, the traditional connections between the user and the designer have been largely severed. The unself-conscious organic growth of the historic city has been replaced by a self-conscious design process which is handled by trained specialists. It is not possible to consider the role of the professional designer fully, and indeed to do so would go beyond the remit of this text. Instead, we give our attention to an issue which has been mentioned on numerous occasions in this book, namely, the extent to which patterns of behaviour can be influenced by manipulation of spatial design. Before doing so, however, it is necessary to analyse the basic characteristics of the design process.

THE DESIGNER'S ROLE

'Spatial design' may be regarded as the conscious process by which the physical form of the spatial environment is shaped and modified in order to meet certain human needs (after Reekie, 1972). Three key words in this definition supply clues about the nature of spatial design.

First, it is a *conscious* process which involves explicit procedures for sifting available options and reaching solutions to meet the requirements of the situation. Having said that, it would be a mistake to think that the choice of a suitable design can ever be achieved in a value-free and dispassionately rational manner. Despite the claims of architectural writers from Pugin to Pevsner that appropriate designs could be produced by systematic application of rational principles from 'correct' initial premises (Watkin, 1977), the solution that is considered appropriate at one time may be very different from that deemed suitable at another. Moreover, the set of options from which choice is made is far from exhaustive, with individual and socio-cultural filters effectively ensuring that many potential solutions are never part of the equation (Rapoport, 1975b).

Second, the designer is officially the creator and modifier of *physical* forms, but in handling the physical attributes of structure and layout will automatically have an influence upon the aesthetic, symbolic, and social dimensions of the built environment. This is a matter of which designers themselves are perfectly aware and would normally consider a legitimate aspect of their professional activities. As Sanoff (1975, 227) has commented:

It is clear that today's architects are becoming increasingly concerned with social theory. Architects share a sense of social purpose and believe that their work as architects may potentially improve society. Unfortunately, a serious lack of intellectual discipline becomes evident within the profession when the designer confronts social theory. For example, there are expectations among architects that physical design exerts an impact on the patterns of social life among the users and will directly and deterministically affect the way that people behave. As a profession, architects suggest that people are shaped by the environment created for them.

The implications of this style of design philosophy will be discussed later in this chapter.

Third, the aim of the design process is to serve human *needs*. This statement is far less easy to achieve than it sounds, as a series of awkward problems have to be tackled. To begin with, spatial environments serve the full spectrum of human needs, from basic needs for shelter to complex personal needs for recognition and self-esteem. In any specific instance, which needs should be given priority and in what mixture? Next, remembering that human needs change over time, should design be based on current statements of need or on predictions of future needs? How are these needs to be observed and measured? Finally, there is perhaps the key question: whose needs are to be met by the design? As failure to find solutions to this last question provides perhaps the greatest source of dissatisfaction with the designer's work, it merits further consideration.

Designing for Human Needs. At the outset, it is essential to realize that design is not simply a response to the demands of the user. The design process involves the participation of three parties—the designer, the user, and the client who commissions the work. In the past it was common for these roles to overlap, with designers sometimes acting as their own clients or being the intending users. By contrast, the current trend is for them to be mutually exclusive groups, with little basis of shared experience. This tendency has been accentuated in recent years by employment of corporate agencies to undertake design work, bodies which may have little real interest in, or commitment to, the locality in which the project is to be sited. In such circumstances, each group may be expected to have its own set of needs which have to be brought into line in design situations. It is perfectly possible for the needs of either designers or clients to deflect the chosen design away from the one that would be best suited to user requirements.

This is partly a product of the consultative mechanisms found in the design process. The designer, with his training and expertise, is conventionally placed in the role of the interpreter of the needs of others.[2] The designer and client often have much in common, sharing a similar background and outlook (Pawley, 1971). Contact with the client is mainly accomplished by the 'committee method', in which the designer presents simulations of his proposals, in the form of drawings, models, and descriptions, to the client who then comments (Canter, 1977). This gives the client the channels through which he may fully participate; but, lacking mastery of the technical skills, he may well adopt a passive role. This relationship can be exploited. The story is told of a well-known American architect who was always supposed to have prepared two design syntheses to place before a client. One was an outrageous version likely to receive quick rejection; the other, the version that he really wanted to see built, for subsequent presentation in the belief that the client would then be less willing to reject it (Hansen, 1977).

This procedure may seem cynically manipulative, but, ironically, it represents a great deal more consultation than normally applies in the case of designer–user relations, in which there is seldom any obligation or effective mechanism for the designer to consult the user. In most cases, the design team itself has been left to decide the needs of the user population and the appropriate designs required. Introspective methods of this type can produce undesirable results (Sanoff, 1975). From the work of Fried (1963),[3] for instance, there was seen to be a considerable gap between the designer's assessments of user needs and actual user needs. To the designer, the visual appearance of the West End of Boston was sufficient to label it a 'slum' which needed to be cleared in the interests of its inhabitants and the community at large. It seemed to come as a great surprise that there were satisfactions to be derived from living there and that people could grieve over their lost homes.

Failure to appreciate the needs of the user, of course, is not only related to lack of dialogue, but also shows the existence of three factors that affect the designer's behaviour. First, there may well be socio-cultural differences between the designer and user. As we saw above, while designers and clients may have similar backgrounds, it is frequently the case that middle-class designers find themselves producing designs for buildings and environments they will never use themselves. In Fried's Boston study, the designers were predominantly well-educated, middle-class, and non-area residents, compared with the poor, working-class, Italian-American inhabitants of the West End. Not surprisingly, these groups had little in common.

Second, designers have their own needs which may conflict with those of the user. A building or planned environment that wins the admiration and approval of the designer's professional colleagues could well be a great personal triumph, even if the test of time shows that it failed to meet the needs of its users. While the situation has now improved, it remains true that until recently planners and architects worked within closed systems, in which they were responsive primarily to the comments of their peers, both as expressed by the opinion leaders of their profession and by the people with whom they normally worked. The latter point is important, for designers are invariably members of teams. The solution that emerges often represents a compromise between the various members of that team, for it is most unusual for any designer to wield complete power without the collaboration of others (Broadbent, 1973). This further deflects the design solution away from one that might be generated by user needs.

The apparent insularity of the designer is also partly related to the third factor, in that design education and training have not emphasized user needs and expectations. The decisive influence here has come from architecture, in which the main thrust of teaching has traditionally been directed towards the architect/artefact relationship rather than that of user/designed environment. The reasons for this focus of interest mainly lie in two doctrines which have had a lasting impact upon architectural thought. First, there is the still-powerful view that equates architecture with fine art,[4] in which the student is taught to see the development of architecture in the manner in which the art historian identifies the major currents of artistic thought. Attention is centred upon the masterpiece, the great and symbolic building, and upon the testimonies of its creator. The subject thereby gains the image of an art moulded by the will of men of creative genius rather than one that charts the relationship of the built form to its users. Second, at the time when the belief in the artist's right to an unchallengeable creative impulse was subjected to growing scrutiny and scepticism, the new doctrine of the 'environmental engineer' developed (Pawley, 1971).[5] Theories filtered down into architectural education from the writings of the Modern Movement, involving a new conception of the architect as an engineer who moulded his creation to meet objective criteria.[6] A representative statement of this view was expressed by Noble (1963): 'As architects we shape people's future behaviour by the environment we create. At all stages of the design we make assumptions about human behaviour and the success or failure of our work may depend on our ability to predict human behaviour' (quoted in Pawley, 1971, 87). This standpoint again implicitly upholds the freedom of action of the designer as the informed arbiter of the needs of others.

Collectively, these factors have perpetuated a vicious circle of cause and effect. While designers employ traditional 'rules of thumb', they are unlikely to devote much time to explicit analysis of user needs. Yet lacking an adequate theoretical and empirical understanding of user expectations and requirements, it is highly probable that the designer will continue to fall back on these long-recognized assumptions and procedures, notwithstanding the large body of literature (e.g. Perin, 1970; Deasy, 1974; Brolin, 1976) that has indicated the failure of modern design to meet human needs. Nowhere has this been more true than when designers have tried to cater for what *they* regard as social needs.

HOW MUCH CONTROL?

Whatever reappraisals might now be taking place, designers have generally had clear images of, and great confidence in, the environmental forms that they consider will yield socially desirable results. Such images are likely to contain two elements: a topophobic image of what the designer is trying to avoid, which is usually a reaction to what are perceived to be the ills of the current situation, and a topophilic image of the ideal environment. Both elements, for example, may be witnessed in writings on utopian environments, a form of literature which may be traced back to classical times (Lang, 1952; Reiner, 1963; Manuel, 1973). Utopias tend to be coined when writers believe that society is in decline, and represent radical contrasts with the world they see about them. Utopias are environments designed to ensure that all citizens may enjoy the 'good life', although quite what constitutes that happy state of affairs is usually for the designer alone to say. Once established, change would be impossible, for nothing could improve on the best. A pattern of living would be imposed upon the inhabitants; presumably they would see the wisdom contained therein and happily conform.

Few utopian schemes have been enacted and even fewer have survived the trauma of confronting reality.[7] Yet the moving spirit behind them—of devising ideal schemes based on the designer's conception of the world rather than on those of the potential users—has its parallels in more conventional design thought. Social reformers of the late nineteenth century based their schemes on a powerful image of the social ills of low-standard housing in industrial Britain, coupled with the virtues of a better, low-density future (Darley, 1975). Recent town planning in Britain has similarly been guided by *a priori* models of ideal urban forms (Houghton-Evans, 1977).

This point is exemplified by the concept of the 'neighbourhood unit', an issue we previously encountered in Chapter 7. The neighbourhood unit was an idea that had crossed to Britain from North America, stemming initially from the work of two architect-planners, Perry and Stein (Hall, 1974). Perry (1929) had suggested constructing residential areas in new urban developments as complete units that would contain both housing and services. The basic principles are shown in Figure 14.1, which illustrates the design of a neighbourhood unit for around 5000 people. The size was chosen for two reasons: it was large enough to provide a natural catchment area for the community facilities at the centre of the unit, and Perry believed that this was an appropriate size for the unit to gain a distinct sense of identity as a social entity. These ideas were developed by Stein, a close associate of Perry, in his design for a new town at Radburn (New Jersey), adding important physical design elements such as a completely segregated road traffic and pedestrian system.

The neighbourhood unit had spread to Britain before 1939, with the development of an estate on these lines at Wythenshawe (near Manchester), but it was adopted on a much wider scale after the War with the construction of the first fourteen New Towns (1947–50). Neighbourhood units were seen both as pragmatic tools of physical planning and as the means to re-introduce a local element that could offset the perceived alternative of an anonymous urban realm (Pearson, 1972). Designers were given a series of guidelines by official reports as to space standards, ratios of facility provision,

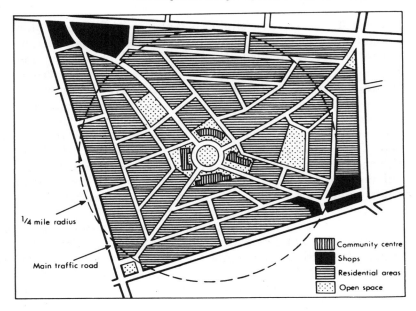

Figure 14.1 The 'neighbourhood unit' principle

Source: Hall (1974, 58). Copyright © 1975 by Peter Hall. Reprinted by permission of Penguin Books Ltd. and A. D. Peters & Co. Ltd.

and the size and layout of neighbourhood units (between 5000 and 10000 people), but were also charged to plan the incipient neighbourhood units to 'allow full growth of community spirit and comprehensible entity' (Dudley Report, 1944).

In the event, these units proved to have little validity as social entities. It would have been surprising if they had. Instead of undertaking studies to determine the likely shape of user needs or even of popular preferences, most consultants proceeded on the basis of a series of social assumptions. They conjured up arbitrary figures about the size of population necessary for community development, assumed that people value convenience (as expressed, say, by easy walking distance to shops and services) rather than lower densities, and that people actually desired to have a physical basis for social interaction. Plausible as these ideas may seem, the patent failure of many such schemes to develop as social units illustrates the complexity of the relationships between users and the physical environment and calls into question the extent to which any physical design can produce a given pattern of behaviour. It is worth considering this matter further.

When looking at the evidence of formal studies that have investigated the links between design and behaviour, one finds that, apart from a limited amount of research that focuses on social behaviour in the interior spaces of buildings (Wells, 1965; Heilweill, 1973), most writers have examined social interaction in the small- to medium-sized housing estate. One of the earliest and best known of these studies is that reported in the book by Leon Festinger and his associates (1950) entitled *Social Pressures in Informal Groups*.

This project examined the formation of friendships and social groups in the newly constructed Westgate and Westgate West residential complexes of the Massachusetts Institute of Technology. The sample was deliberately chosen to provide a homogeneous group of respondents. The students were all young (20–35) ex-servicemen and their families, coming from predominantly upper-middle-class homes. In selecting them, the researchers were able to remove socio-economic factors from the analysis and could concentrate upon the relationship between the physical layout of the buildings and patterns of social interaction. Moreover, these residential units were almost completely isolated from any other residential areas on the campus, so they were likely to be very much self-contained.

Ceteris paribus, the argument was that the development of friendships and associations would be related to the number of times that students met casually (termed 'passive contacts'). This was held to be related to physical distance, in that there was a higher probability of meeting someone living close at hand than further away, but it would also be influenced by functional distance, which took account of the physical design and the relative position of the front-doors of the dwellings. In other words, apartments might adjoin one another, but if they opened out onto a different staircase or courtyard, in effect this would be the same as being located some distance away. From contacts would come friendships, from friendships would develop group associations.

The authors' findings were broadly in line with these hypotheses. Next-door neighbours were most often chosen as friends with less probability of friendship with increasing physical distance. Functional distance was also found to affect the relationship, in that friendships were found to flourish around those dwellings that opened out into interior courtyards rather than those that opened out onto the street. From this the authors concluded:

> In a community of people who are homogeneous with respect to many of the factors which determine the development of friendships, the physical factors arising from the arrangement of houses are major determinants of what friendships will develop and what social groupings will be formed.
>
> (Festinger *et al.*, 1959, 151)

This conclusion has often been quoted, but it must be treated with caution. The operative word is *homogeneous*. The authors were dealing with a population in which the normal social filtering of personal relationships would have less reason to apply. They were dealing with a sample group in their early stages of adjustment to a new environment, a time when, for reasons suggested earlier, the individual is most dependent on the immediate locality. Moreover, the fact that the housing complexes were physically remote from other residential areas would have the effect of throwing the students back onto their own resources. Lastly, the authors were looking at a group of people at a unique time in their lives, being recently demobilized from the Armed Forces after the Second World War. One may question whether similar results would have been obtained if the sample had not been so homogeneous, or if it had been studied over a longer period of time, or even at a more typical time.

Nevertheless, there are some studies that lend support to the findings of Festinger and his associates. Kuper's (1953) study of social relationships in an area of semi-detached housing in Coventry, for example, illustrated further the point about functional distance. In semi-detached housing, each dwelling has a next-door neighbour with whom a common wall is shared and one with whom the dwelling is non-contiguous. When residents were asked to name a familiar neighbour, they invariably cited the next-door neighbour in the non-adjoining house. This was held to be because residents normally used the side-doors for entry, which were situated across the way from those of their non-adjoining neighbour. Further support for the role of proximity in friendship patterns may be gleaned from a variety of other case-studies, for example: Whyte (1956) on Park Forest, Illinois; Willmott (1963) on Dagenham, England; and Rainwater (1966) and Yancey (1972) on the Pruitt-Igoe scheme at St. Louis, Missouri.

Equally, one can find studies that display little evidence of such relationships. Carey and Mapes (1972) undertook a large-scale study of eight new privately built housing estates in Staffordshire, England, with the purpose of studying the way friendship patterns developed amongst a heterogeneous set of housewives. Their findings suggested that variables such as age and stage in the life-cycle explained much of the variance in patterns of visiting and social interaction, but that physical factors had little significance. Similar negative findings may be obtained from Gutman (1966), Gans (1967), and Dennis (1968). Indeed as Gutman (1972) pointed out, it is possible to find similar results from Festinger's own work. In a paper published in 1951, Festinger compared the results obtained from the Westgate project with another scheme at Regent Hill. The latter had a similar layout and size to that of Westgate, and housing within it was also allocated to tenants by a public authority without giving tenants the right to choose the particular unit that they wanted. In other respects Regent Hill was a quite different proposition. It was a project that had been intended for shipyard workers and had been in existence for five years at the time of study (1947). By this time the population had become socially heterogeneous. Only 40 per cent were the original residents who had worked in the shipyards, the remainder having moved in during the period of acute housing shortage. From this study, Festinger (1972 edn., 132) reported: 'We thus have practically the opposite state of affairs from that of Westgate. Instead of a full and satisfying social life there was here a very unsatisfactory state of little social life and great difficulty in achieving group memberships which had the possibility of being satisfactory.' Thus, despite having virtually the same physical layout, the social conditions on the two estates were totally different, and explanation for behaviour had to be sought in other, predominantly social-psychological factors.

All in all, the evidence is inconclusive, yet the debate can raise heated controversy. One side of the argument is expressed in a provocative paper by Broady (1966). Broady, a sociologist, expressed concern about the misuse of social theory by architects and noted their inclination to indulge in a brand of theorizing that he termed 'architectural determinism'. The latter was considered to be akin to the various other forms of determinism that we have encountered in this text. It was a doctrine that maintained that physical forces—in this case manipulation of the built environment—can have a direct impact upon patterns of behaviour. The typical architectural deterministic model of behaviour suggested that design was the independent variable and behaviour the dependent variable. Broady rejected this type of analysis, stressing instead the role of social and cultural influences upon the behaviour of the user. Design therefore did not mould behaviour, nor did it contain any 'magic by which man can be redeemed or society transformed. Its prime social function is to facilitate people's doing what they wish, or are obliged to do' (Broady, 1966, 153).

By way of direct reply, Lee (1971), an environmental psychologist, argued that there were basic misconceptions in Broady's case. While agreeing that modern architecture is not a magical activity, Lee (1971, 255) felt that its ultimate aim ought to be to 'change man a little and not merely to accommodate him'. Lee maintained that environment does have an influence upon behaviour, that architectural determinism is a valid formulation of environmental relationships, and that it provides the best starting-point for developing a theory. None the less, it is clear that Lee had in mind a milder form of determinism than the one that Broady parodied:

To assert that our behaviour is shaped by environment is not to concede that we are helplessly moulded, it is merely to assert the need to generate and maintain, on our own volition, a man–environment interaction that will steer the development of ourselves and our children in the direction of our own choosing . . . . The main misunderstanding arises when critics attribute to architectural determinists the absurd claim that the built environment is the *only* or even the *main* agent in the formation of behaviour.

(Lee, 1971, 255–6)

The impact of the designed environment needs to be placed alongside the other influences that collectively shape behaviour. Failure to do so will be to fall into the opposite trap of 'social determinism'.

To some extent, the polarity between these two papers is less than it might seem at first glance, as both involve an element of ritual huffing and puffing, but there is a real disagreement over the role that physical design *per se* can play in shaping behaviour. The truth would seem to lie between the two, in that design may be able to have an influence over behaviour in certain tightly constrained circumstances (such as the Westgate study), but that these effects are a great deal less than many designers suppose. We must therefore return to a point that by now needs no emphasis—that the processes involved are far more complicated than has often been assumed. The probability of any behaviour taking place needs to be seen as a complex function of the cognitive processes and variables that intervene between man and the spatial environment. Research that does not take this into account is not likely to produce anything much in the way of positive conclusions, and certainly little that can be of practical use to designers. It is still hard to improve on Mumford's dictum that 'to set the stage is not to write the play.'

15 Conclusion

[we cannot] step twice into the same river, for other and yet other waters are ever flowing on.

(HERAKLEITOS)

When any new branch of an academic discipline emerges, its initial development appears to follow a broad pattern. First, there is a period in which those developing the innovative theories and methods are on the fringes of the subject. Next, there is a phase in which their ideas are assessed by the 'establishment', with reactions ranging from the extremes of eulogistic praise to outright rejection. Finally, there comes the time in which the new branch either becomes an established part of the discipline or disappears from view. At present, behavioural geography remains in the second stage. To see how it is likely to fare in the third, it is worth weighing up its characteristics, its actual and potential contribution to geographical knowledge, and the problems it faces.

Behavioural geography is distinguished by a conception of man-environment relationships that is altogether more complex than that traditionally employed by geographers. The behavioural geographer recognizes that man shapes as well as responds to his environment, and that man and environment are dynamically interelated. Man is viewed as a motivated social being, whose decisions and actions are mediated by his cognition of the spatial environment. This said, three qualifications are immediately necessary. First, the behavioural geographer would interpret motivation to include all those needs, goals, and drives, conscious and subconscious, that stimulate behaviour. Second, while the influence of the socio-cultural environment is constantly recognized, the main thrust of research focuses upon the individual perceiver and decision-maker rather than tackling problems at the group level. Third, it is in no way presupposed that cognitive processes will lead to 'rational' decisions and behaviour as suggested by narrow economic or philosophical definitions of the term, or even necessarily by the canons of what other people would regard as being common sense.

On this basis, the behavioural geographer argues that interpretations of behaviour rest upon an understanding of the way spatial cognition develops, the nature of spatial cognition, and the links between cognition and behaviour, and it is these interrelated areas that have been explored by researchers. This research, as this book has revealed, may be described as multi-disciplinary in outlook and broad, but poorly aggregated, in content. These features merit further comment.

Its multi-disciplinary outlook is partly due to recognition that the problems studied transcend the boundaries of academic subjects, but also reflects the pragmatic need for the geographer to seek explanation of behavioural processes in the literature of the social and behavioural sciences. In the early years this was chiefly a one-way flow, but recently a reciprocal exchange of ideas has developed. It is now common to find references to geographical sources in the work of environmental psychologists and sociologists, a trend which is likely to grow.

The broad scope of behavioural geography is perhaps outstanding even by the standards of human geography. There are overall biases in content towards urban topics and towards developed nations, but studies may be found examining human behaviour in numerous different environments, of varying temporal durations, and at all scales from micro- to global space. Methods vary from highly sophisticated quantitative methodologies to equally elegant critical analyses of art, literature, and poetry. While dominantly neo-positivist, it is an area of geography in which researchers have experimented with phenomenology and related non-positivist approaches. Not surprisingly, the breadth of content has been accompanied, at least initially, by a lack of cohesiveness and integration. Apart from areas such as urban spatial cognition or natural hazards, in which extensive programmes of research have been mounted, behavioural geography has been characterized by a lack of synthesis of empirical findings, poor communication, inadvertent duplication, and conflicting terminology.

Nevertheless, the achievements of behavioural geography in a short space of time are real enough. In the first place, it has acted as a leavening influence in human geography at a time when spatial scientific approaches were taking a strong hold. Behavioural geography reasserted the role of the individual in a subject which showed strong signs of wishing to reduce human activities to point patterns and spatial preferences to indifference curves. Moreover, the writings of such authors as Tuan and Lowenthal have reawakened literary standards in geography which had lain dormant since the time of Davis, Semple, and the great regional geographers of the inter-war period. Secondly, it has led to a thorough reappraisal of approaches to man–environment relations, countering environmentalist or neo-environmentalist doctrines by recognizing the true complexities of human behaviour. Thirdly, it has widened the scope and outlook of geography. Behavioural geography has acted as a forum for new philosophies, approaches, and methods as well as reviving interest in older foci, such as landscape and idiographic analysis of place. Furthermore, it has opened up new channels of dialogue and debate with other disciplines, contributing to a valuable cross-fertilization of ideas. Lastly, behavioural geographers have contributed much to the 'relevance debate' in geography; by rejecting the 'myth of value freedom' in asserting that the values of the inquirer affect all aspects of the research process, by promoting interest in problems of social concern, and by supporting greater involvement in public policy issues.

At the same time, many problems have arisen and there are major deficiencies which need to be rectified. Terminology and concepts remain loosely defined and poorly integrated, primarily owing to the lack of a systematically organized theoretical basis. It has been suggested throughout that this situation can be improved by bringing geographical practice more into line with psychology and the behavioural sciences. Naturally, this liaison must be guided by a spirit of discrimination. We have seen in this text a number of occasions on which psychological theories and methods have been abused in geographical studies and several other instances in which geographers have unwittingly selected theories that are, to say the least, controversial. Effort must also be made to build bridges within geography to those approaches in social, cultural, and political geography that analyse behavioural processes at group level. In this context, it is worth repeating a warning given much earlier: namely, that behavioural geography will achieve its full potential only if it complements, rather than competes with, other approaches. Cognitive-behavioural studies cannot provide complete explanation for all behaviours and to believe that they can is to risk psychologism.

Serious problems also exist with regard to methodology. Methodology has been touched on only lightly in this text, but enough has been said to show that some very real questions need to be asked. Generally there has been little replication or comparative evaluation of specific methods. Insufficient attention has been paid to such matters as sample size or bias in sample populations, particularly when it is remembered that the individually collected sample survey is the main source of data in behavioural geography. Perhaps most significant is the fact that certain methods, particularly some commonly accepted forms of cognitive mapping, do not seem to measure what they are supposed to measure. For example, we saw in the case of freehand sketch-maps that the finished product may tell more about cartographic skills than externalize the cognitive representations of space that are in the respondent's mind.

One further deficiency in behavioural geography has been the gap between the claims and achievements of some of its practitioners. This has been most noticeable over the question of public policy. Part of the rationale for behavioural geography is to orient more work towards policy matters, but the behavioural geographer remains the observer rather than the participant. As suggested previously, there is a serious lack of knowledge about planning theories and methods amongst behavioural geographers, which is an impediment to more active involvement. It is a barrier that can be removed only by developing the requisite understanding of the planning process, not one that can be camouflaged by noble sentiments and a moral tone. For instance, it will be only rarely that a small survey carried out upon a sample of students will supply the basis for far-reaching policy recommendations, yet the final paragraph of many such articles contain this seemingly obligatory element. Rather, it is necessary to have research that specifically deals with policy questions, that is well versed in planning theory and methodology, and that communicates the results intelligibly to the interested parties. There are signs that such an approach is developing, but the gap is still wide.

These are significant problems but, by and large, they are shared by cognate branches of man–environment studies. The achievements so far suggest that answers will be forthcoming, but if they are, it will be through the efforts of workers in several different disciplines. This leads to a final and crucial point. Behavioural geography has developed because it offers something both to geographical knowledge and to man–environment studies as a whole. Its eclectic character has been a source of both inspiration and strength. If this were to be sacrificed in an attempt to become 'respectable' in disciplinary terms, then the outlook would be bleak. If, on the other hand, behavioural geography builds its standing within geography while maintaining its multi-disciplinary links, then the future looks highly promising.

Notes

Chapter One

[1] The area here termed 'behavioural geography' is roughly equivalent to that part of geography that others have variously referred to as 'cognitive-behaviouralism' (Sprout and Sprout, 1965, Murton, 1972), 'environmental perception' (Saarinen, 1969), 'psychogeography' (Kates, 1970), 'ethno-geography' (Knight, 1971), 'image geography' (Watson, 1975), and 'perception geography' (Gottmann, 1977).

[2] Geography has always had the character of a 'derivative discipline' (see, e.g., Harvey, 1969; Johnston, 1972).

Chapter Two

[1] For more information about the development of psychology see Herrnstein and Boring (1965), Krantz (1969), Krech *et al.* (1974), Fantino and Reynolds (1975), and Sahakian (1975). On the specific schools, see Skinner (1974) and Rachlin (1976) on behaviourism, Henle (1961) and Wertheimer (1973) on Gestalt psychology, and Wollheim (1971) and Jahoda (1977) on psycho-analysis.

[2] Pragmatism is the doctrine whereby the entire meaning of a conception expresses itself in its practical consequences (Ayer, 1968).

[3] An idea taken from the work of the Russian psychologist Pavlov on the concept of the conditioned reflex (Wright *et al.*, 1970).

[4] e.g. see Skinner (1938, 1971), and comment by Chomsky (1972).

[5] It is not possible here to discuss the large body of literature on Gestaltist research on visual per-ception, which includes some of the best-known work on illusions and similar phenomena. For more information, see Gregory (1970), Barber and Legge (1976), and Prak (1977).

[6] The question of phenomenology vs. positivism (usually in the shape of behaviourism) cannot be discussed fully in this chapter. For information beyond that given here see Wann (1964), Mundle (1971), Misiak and Sexton (1973), and Shotter (1975).

[7] Field theories develop the behavioural implications of an analogy drawn from physics, whereby behaviour was held to be controlled by a field of interacting forces organized into dynamic patterns (see Lewin, 1951; Rummel, 1975).

[8] This emphasis also fits the main thrust of Altman's work, see Altman (1975).

[9] See, e.g., Himmelweit *et al.* (1958), Brown (1972), Tunstall (1970), McQuail (1972).

Chapter Three

[1] 'Environmentalism' in this context should be separated from an alternative meaning, which takes it to mean those doctrines that are linked with the 'environmental movement' (O'Riordan, 1976b).

[2] Although, in fairness to Davis, it must be pointed out that he subsequently retracted the more extreme aspects of these views.

[3] Clark (1951), Martin (1951), Montefiore and Williams (1955), Jones (1956), Tatham (1957), Spate (1958).

[4] Defined as the cost of a project in terms of the next-best use of resources, which, perforce, has been forgone.

[5] See the discussion of the distinction between urban/built and natural environments in Chapter 7.

[6] For further clarification of this distinction see Lewthwaite (1966).

[7] 'Reification' is the name given to the process by which an abstract concept is converted into concrete reality (Berger and Luckmann, 1971).

[8] 'Social physics' was an attempt to apply the laws of physics, for example gravity and thermo-dynamics, to human occupancy of space (Stewart and Warntz, 1958; Warntz, 1973).

[9] See Hollis and Nell (1975) and Leibenstein (1976).

[10] It is perhaps worth noting that both Wolpert and Pred were heavily influenced by the Swedish school of geography, which pioneered much of the work on probability analysis in geography (see Pred, 1973).

[11] The debate has been most strongly developed in British geographical periodicals, see Smith (1971, 1977), Eyles (1971, 1977), Berry (1972), Coppock (1974), and Huckle (1977).

[12] This section is based upon a previous article (Gold, 1977a) which appeared in the *Journal of Geography in Higher Education*. I wish to convey my thanks to the Editors for permission to use it here.

[13] This concept of scale is implicitly employed in Part Three.

[14] An idea developed by Goddard (1976).

[15] See Mercer and Powell (1972), Walmsley (1974), Buttimer (1976), Relph (1976), Tuan (1976), Ley (1977).

[16] Indeed the founder of phenomenology, Husserl, was insistent that phenomenology was not an empirical technique.

Chapter Four

[1] Visible light consists of wavelengths between 0.4 (violet) and 0.7 (red) microns, (a micron being one-millionth of a metre).

[2] The idea that the development of electronic-communications media have so transformed thinking about distance that people all over the world are brought together into a new type of global community which is reminiscent of the close interpersonal contacts found in a village (McLuhan and Fiore, 1967).

[3] Topological space preserves relative positions of objects but ignores compass direction or proportional distance.

Chapter Five

[1] A good illustration of this is to be found in the reaction to the work of educational psychologists such as Jensen (1968) and Eysenck (1971). Both writers have suggested that certain racial groups perform less well than others on measures such as intelligence quotient largely because of genetic factors. Justifiable criticism over the validity of the explanation and the methodology employed, however, tends to have been masked by the more general wave of protest against 'racialist' theories.

[2] See Piaget (1929, 1955, 1963) and Piaget and Inhelder (1956); Werner (1948, 1957), Werner and Kaplan (1963), and Wapner (1973). For further information see Baldwin (1967), Furth (1969), Bee (1975).

[3] Hart and Moore treat these two substages as separate stages.

[4] None the less some work has begun to appear which does so: e.g. the cross-cultural studies in the collection edited by Dasen (1977).

[5] The general science of signs: systems of signification, means of communication by which human beings individually or in groups communicate or attempt to communicate (Seymour-Smith, 1977). For further information see Barthes (1967) and Broadbent (1975).

[6] Various writers, however, have claimed that one particular aspect of the triangle determines the other two. Whorf, for example, argued that language embodied and perpetuated a particular world-view, and that this determined the perception, thought, and action of its users (Carroll, 1956).

Chapter Six

[1] Originally part of zoology, ethology has become distinct as the science that studies the behaviour of animals in their natural habitat.

[2] This chapter will discuss the cognitive significance of territory, with behavioural aspects being examined in Part Four. This format will be followed throughout the ensuing chapters, although the separation of cognitive and behavioural elements is a question of emphasis rather than of rigid dichotomy.

[3] Defined as 'the interrelated observations and theories of human use of space as a specialised elaboration of culture' (Hall, 1966, quoted in Saarinen, 1976, 25).

[4] A theory derived primarily from the work of MacLean (1958; see also 1975) on the 'triune brain'. The brain contains three separate but highly interrelated mechanisms—respectively termed the reptilian, paleomammalian, and neomammalian brains. The paleomammalian and reptilian brains are collectively termed the 'limbic system' and it is the limbic system that transmits the behavioural predispositions of man's evolutionary past. For further discussion and application of these ideas in other contexts, see Esser (1971b), Smith (1974), and Greenbie (1975).

[5] Notwithstanding the security problems that have been engendered by some aspects of twentieth-century housing policy (see Chapter 10).

[6] Work on institutional settings will not be dealt with here. For more information see Altman (1975) and Moos (1976).

Chapter Seven

1   We here sidestep the argument as to what is 'urban' and what is not. Cherry (1974) has suggested three possible definitions based on physical delimiting factors such as land use, administrative boundaries, or the town's service area. In this text, however, we are not so much concerned with delimiting urban areas by their size but by the type of living environment they present—in terms of their compactness, the intensity of their public life, and the small-grained pattern they present in which all types of human life are in close proximity (Gruen, 1965).

2   This matter will be considered again in Chapter 10.

3   See de Jonge (1962), Gulick (1963), Appleyard (1969), Goodey (1971), Francescato and Mebane (1973), Saarinen (1976), and Porteous (1977).

4   In each case, an area of about 3.75 square miles.

5   Thirty people were interviewed in Boston, fifteen each in Los Angeles and Jersey City.

6   There is some dispute as to whether these categories were derived beforehand and then applied or whether they were inductively generated. Lynch does not make this point clear, but it seems likely that it was the former.

7   Although Burnette (1974) suggested that Lynch's elements may be fitted into a theory that related imageability to stages of cognitive development.

8   The reader interested in examining later developments of this work should consult Carr and Schissler (1969).

9   The semantic differential was initially developed as a psychometric technique by linguistic researchers (Osgood *et al.*, 1957). The method has the advantage of being paralleled in its development by a sophisticated body of statistical analysis, with factor analysis being particularly useful as a means of extracting underlying dimensions from semantic data. The semantic differential, however, has certain limitations as a research technique, discussion of which may be found in Cook and Gold (1974) and Whyte (1977).

10 See Chapter 14 for a discussion of this point.

Chapter Eight

1   See, e.g. Broek (1932); Dohrs and Sommers (1967).

2   Although it must be stressed that there is a thin but significant thread of interest in the aesthetic qualities of landscape which can be traced back to Humboldt (1849).

3   'Cosmology' is the name given to a theory that explains the universe as a created whole and identifies the laws that govern its operation.

4   This theory has been criticized for substituting one set of indefinable words for another. In response, Ruskin attempted to determine a relationship between landscape aesthetics and moral qualities.

5   A term introduced into political geography, in a quite separate context—Gottmann (1952). Gottmann used it to identify the symbolic importance of the 'state idea' in the foundation and continued existence of states. While there are interesting connections with landscape, these are best kept as distinct usages.

6   Architecture that blended in well with the eighteenth-century Virgilian landscape of Claude and Poussin.

7   See discussion in Chapter 7.

Chapter Nine

1   See the discussion of socialization in Chapter 5.

2   For instance Beer (1908), Jones (1946), Smith (1957), Lefler (1967), Merrens (1969), Heathcote (1972), Powell (1972), Cameron (1974), Blouet and Lawson (1975).

3   From a report by *The Times* correspondent, reprinted in the *Sheffield Daily Telegraph*, 28 May 1856.

4   In a work entitled *Travels Through the Interior Parts of North America in the Years 1776, 1777 and 1778*.

5   In *A New Voyage round the World*, alleged to report expeditionary findings, but in reality fabricated from reports of other travellers with the addition of spurious material.

6   e.g. Gilbert (1960), Berry (1964), Grigg (1967), Dickinson (1976).

7   Gould (1966, 1969), Gould and Ola (1970), Gould and White (1968, 1974).

8   Ranking techniques may be useful for ranking a few options or selecting the most-favoured choices from a long list, but it is improbable that anyone could objectively rank the former ninety-two British counties in a short space of time. A person may have a clear idea of his first choice or of the area he dislikes most, but can he really distinguish between his thirtieth and thirty-first choices? In addition, if respondents were tested again without their prior knowledge, would their rankings satisfy the criterion of reliability and produce consistent and accurate results?

9 Although this would not have the same implications as it would have today.

Chapter Ten

1 For further information, see Hawley (1950), Quinn (1950), and Burgess and Bogue (1963).
2 See Gans (1968), Morris (1968), and Fischer (1976).
3 Wirth's arguments on the social psychological level were linked to a parallel discussion of social structure, derived primarily from the work of Durkheim (1893).
4 A 'behaviour setting' may be defined as an entity bounded in space and time that has a structure that interrelates physical, social, and cultural properties so that it elicits common or regularized forms of behaviour (Barker, 1968).
5 See reviews by Nelson (1974) and Edney (1977).
6 See Queen (1940) and Timms (1965).
7 See Smith (1973), Cooperman (1977), Mawby (1977).
8 One such example was the Pruitt–Igoe scheme in St. Louis (Missouri), a project initially hailed as a fine design, yet finished in premature demolition by the housing authority due to extreme conditions of lawlessness that prevailed there. However chilling this story may have been, the fact remains that Pruitt–Igoe was very much the exception rather than the rule.
9 Examples are provided by Beshers (1962), Olsson (1965), Ramsøy (1966), Dacey (1971), with discussions in Johnston (1971b) and Forrest (1974).
10 Webber (1963, 1964a, 1964b).
11 See Ley and Cybriwsky (1974) and Gold (1976b) for discussion of this point.
12 On the grounds that it can overemphasize the role of choice relative to the options that may be imposed by the socio-economic constraints present in the housing market.
13 Besides the references given in the previous section, see Mogey (1956), Kerr (1958), Coates and Silburn (1970), and Jackson (1976).
14 Keats (1956), Whyte (1956), Gans (1968), Masotti and Hadden (1973).
15 This also applies to variants of the same argument, which contend that decision-making aims at optimality but is distorted by imperfect information and lack of skills on the part of decision-makers.
16 Used here in the same manner as in the previous chapter. Preferences are estimations of portions of space arranged in some sort of rank order, albeit the criteria used in ranking are frequently vague and loosely organized.
17 e.g. work in progress on Birmingham by R. Ford and G. C. Smith (Smith, 1976a).
18 Although, in fairness, one would also wish to point to a growing number of writers who have supplied considerable amounts of empirical data coupled with rigorous testing procedures (see Parker, 1976; Smith, 1976c).
19 See Chapter 3.

Chapter Eleven

1 Like 'urban environment', the term 'natural environment' presents problems of definition. The definition employed here simply employs the term to apply to the non-urban environment; it in no way implies a landscape that it is totally unaltered by man.
2 Although Appleton (1975b) himself attempted to fill this vacuum by devising habitat theory (see Chapter 8).
3 See Fines (1968), Wright (1974), and Zube *et al.* (1975).
4 Based on the theory of adaptation put forward by Helson (1964).
5 Indeed this is incorporated into official policy in both Canadian and American planning legislation (see respectively Hall, 1976, and Simmons, 1975).

Chapter Twelve

1 See Stokols (1978).
2 White (1973) has himself summarized the history and development of work on hazard cognition and behaviour, with particular reference to flooding.
3 A notable by-product of this research was the stimulus it gave to behavioural geography. For example, the first symposium on the subject given by the Association of American Geographers (Lowenthal, 1967) grew out of an interest in flood hazards.
4 See White (1974a, 1976), Haas *et al.* (1977), Burton *et al.* (1978).
5 This term is used with caution, as man-made hazards are in fact quasi-natural. For example, although air and water pollution are created by man, they are mediated by natural processes.
6 Linked in particular with the work of the Disaster Research Unit of the University of Bradford, England.

Chapter Thirteen

1   See McCrone (1969), Hamilton (1974), Massey (1974).
2   Research on organizations *per se* or use of them as a perspective in locational studies lies outside the scope of this text (for further reading, see Katz and Kahn, 1966; Silverman, 1970).
3   e.g. Townroe (1969) and Walker (1975).
4   See discussion in Chapters 4 and 9.

Chapter Fourteen

1   A collective term used to describe all those individuals—planners, architects, environmental designers, and others—whose professional activities involve them in the business of shaping or modifying spatial environments.
2   A role accentuated by the growth of functionalism in modern architecture, an ideology which held that the purpose of a building, if properly understood, would define its form. As the person with the professional expertise, the designer was cast in the role of the person who supplied the appropriate interpretation (Pawley, 1971).
3   See Chapter 10.
4   e.g. Richardson and Corfiato (1938), Pevsner (1963), and Watkin (1977).
5   Although Lipman (1974) would argue that this self-conception of the architect as a social engineer was equally traditional, albeit relatively latent.
6   See e.g. Gropius (1956), Banham (1963), Alexander and Poyner (1967).
7   e.g. see Lockwood (1973), Hayden (1976), Fishman (1977), and Erasmus (1978).

Further Reading

In the course of the preceding chapters and their respective notes, reference has been made to almost 900 sources. A lengthy guide to alternative literature would be superfluous, and therefore this note simply aims to give the interested reader some directions in which further reading might be pursued. The emphasis is upon substantive treatments of specific topics rather than on short research notes, but the opportunity is also taken to list a variety of useful sources that have appeared too recently to be incorporated into the main body of the text.

Part One

In the last few years, there has been a rapid growth in basic textbooks on *psychology*, most being fairly similar in content and style and aimed at the American undergraduate market. Selection between them is very much a matter of personal taste, but for a highly original and witty presentation see Lefrançois (1974); for a text that depicts environmental psychology alongside mainstream psychology, see Baron *et al.* (1977); and for reviews of various aspects of psychological theory and method, see the *Essential Psychology* series (edited by Peter Herriot, published by Methuen), of which Booth (1975), Shotter (1975), Stacey (1975), Lee (1976), Reich and Adcock (1976), and Serpell (1976) may be recommended. Literature on *environmental psychology* that will supplement the extensive sources listed in the text includes Insel and Moos (1974), Appleyard (1977), Pervin (1978), Stokols (1978), and Leff (forthcoming). For the development and content of *behavioural geography*, useful discussions are to be found in Kasperson and Minghi (1970, 299–318), Hurst (1974), Rees and Newby (1974), Golledge (1977), Downs and Meyer (1978), and Ley and Samuels (1978). The *methodology* of behavioural geography has not been formally discussed in the text, but the reader wishing to pursue this aspect further could profitably consult Saarinen (1973b), Ittelson *et al.* (1974, 208–42), Veal (1974), Golledge and Rushton (1976), and Whyte (1977).

Part Two

Sources worth consulting on topics related to perception and *spatial information* include Neisser (1976), Blakemore (1977), Downs and Stea (1977), Busch (1978), Powell (1978), Tuan (1978a), and Leff (forthcoming). On the *spatial learning* of children, particularly in the urban environment, see Siegel and White (1975), Moore and Golledge (1976b), Lynch (1977), and Ward (1978). Additional sources may be obtained from Boice (1977).

Part Three

Territoriality has continued to form a major focus of empirical and theoretical research. For material beyond that discussed in the text see Watson (1970), Altman (1975), Edney (1976), Esser (1976), Dyson-Hudson and Smith (1978). The growing discussion of sociobiology may soon see a new recasting of the nature–nurture controversy over the origins of territoriality and for an introduction to the contrasting views, see Wilson (1975) and Gould (1978). Additional material on the significance of the home and neighbourhood may be obtained from Raglan (1964), Skaburskis (1974), and Marc (1977). A very large number of studies are now available on *urban schemata*, all with substantial bibliographies. For a cross-section of this material, with its contrasting theoretical standpoints, see Stringer (1975a, 1975c), Lee (1976), Mercer (1976), Rapoport (1976), Saarinen (1976), Bird (1977), Canter (1977), and Porteous (1977). In addition, the continuing *Community Development* series (edited by Richard P. Dober, published by Dowden, Hutchinson, &

Ross) have provided conference readings, edited collections, and monographs which have proved to be of great value. In this context, see particularly Hester (1975), Stearns and Montag (1975), and Pollowy (1977). On the experience of *landscape*, see the two collections of writings by J. B. Jackson (respectively edited by Zube, 1970 and Zube and Zube, 1977). For theoretical discussion of experiential approaches in geography, see Lowenthal and Bowden (1976) and Tuan (1977). Humanistic geography is discussed in Relph (1976) and Ley and Samuels (1978), and criticized in Billinge (1977) and Cosgrove (1978). Additional sources on city symbols are to be found in Bogdanovic (1975) and Rykwert (1976). On *regional and world images*, useful material may be obtained from Wright (1966), Eliade (1968), Nuttgens (1972), Sack (1976), Woollcombe (1976), Lowenthal (1977), and Powell (1978).

Part Four

As suggested in Chapter 10, there is an enormous amount of research available on *cognition and behaviour in urban space*, and only a very small selection of recent literature is presented here. On the urban ambience, see Williams (1975), Collette and Webb (1976), Fischer (1976), Giner (1976), Gillis (1977), Milgram (1977), Gump and Adelberg (1978), and Insel and Lindgren (1978). On the role of neighbourhood in the urban experience, see Gusfield (1977), Boal *et al.* (1978), and Haney and Knowles (1978). Material on residential satisfactions, preferences, and mobility may be found in Buchanan (1975), Adams and Gilder (1976), Francescato *et al.* (1977), Michelson (1977), Newton (1977), and Jones and Zannaras (1978). On consumer behaviour see Meyer (1977) and Potter (1977). On *landscape assessment* and recreation behaviour, see Murphy and Rosenblood (1974), Jacobs (1975), Mercer (1975), Aldskogius (1977), and Palmer *et al.* (1977). Chapter 12 contained a full review of the literature on *natural hazards* and no further reading need be added here, but on *industrial location* decision-making, three further sources that warrant attention are Collins and Walker (1975), Green (1977), and Taylor and McDermott (1977). Literature on *spatial design and behaviour* has been abundant, but some sources that are worth adding at this stage are Sommer (1972, 1974), Canter (1974), Lang *et al.* (1974), Allison (1975), Rapoport (1975a), Lynch (1976), Baum and Valins (1978), and Farbstein and Kantrowitz (1978).

Bibliography

Acredolo, L. P. (1976) 'Frames of Reference used by Children for Orientation in Unfamiliar Spaces', in G. T. Moore and R. G. Golledge, eds., *Environmental Knowing*, Stroudsburg, Pa.: Dowden, Hutchinson, & Ross, 165–72.

Adams, J. S. (1969) 'Directional Bias in Intraurban Migration', *Economic Geography*, 45. 302–23.

—— and Gilder, K. A. (1976) 'Household Location and Intraurban Migration', in D. T. Herbert and R. J. Johnston, eds., *Spatial Processes and Form*, London: Wiley, 159–91.

Adams, P., ed. (1972) *Language in Thinking*, Harmondsworth: Penguin.

Adams, P. G. (1962) *Travellers and Travel Liars, 1660–1800*, Berkeley: University of California Press.

Adams, R. L. (1969) 'Uncertainty in Nature, Cognitive Dissonance and the Perceptual Distortion of Environmental Information: Weather Forecasts and New England Beach Trips', *Economic Geography*, 49. 287–97.

Alcock, A. (1975) *Animal Behaviour: An Evolutionary Approach*, San Francisco: Freeman.

Aldskogius, H. (1977) 'A Conceptual Framework and a Swedish Case Study of Recreational Behaviour and Environmental Cognition', *Economic Geography*, 53. 163–83.

Alexander, C., and Poyner, B. (1967) *The Atoms of Environmental Structure*, London: Ministry of Buildings and Public Works.

Alland, A. (1972) *The Human Imperative*, New York: Columbia University Press.

Allison, L. (1975) *Environmental Planning*, London: Allen & Unwin.

Alonso, W. (1971) 'A Theory of the Urban Land Market', in L. S. Bourne, ed., *Internal Structure of the City*, London: Oxford University Press, 154–9.

Altman, I. (1975) *The Environment and Social Behaviour*, Monterey: Brooks–Cole.

—— (1976) 'Some Perspectives on the Study of Man-Environment Phenomena', in H. M. Proshansky, W. H. Ittelson, and L. G. Rivlin, eds., *Environmental Psychology*, Second Edition, New York: Holt, Rinehart, & Winston, 27–37.

Anderson, E. N. (1972) 'Some Chinese Methods of Dealing with Crowding', *Urban Anthropology*, 1. 141–50.

Anderson, M. D. (1971) *History and Imagery in British Churches*, London: Murray.

Appleton, J. (1975a) 'Landscape Evaluation: The Theoretical Vacuum', *Transactions of the Institute of British Geographers*, 66. 120–3.

—— (1975b) *The Experience of Landscape*, London: Wiley.

Appleyard, D. (1973) 'Notes on Urban Perception and Knowledge', in R. M. Downs and D. Stea, eds., *Image and Environment*, Chicago: Aldine, 109–14.

—— (1977) 'A Planner's Guide to Environmental Psychology', *Journal of the American Institute of Planners*, 43. 184–9.

—— and Lintell, M. (1972) 'Environmental Quality of City Streets: The Residents' Viewpoint', *Journal of the American Institute of Planners*, 38. 84–101.

Appleyard, D., Lynch, K., and Meyer, J. (1964) *The View from the Road*, Cambridge, Mass.: MIT Press.

Ardnt, H. W. (1949) 'The Cult of Privacy', *Australian Quarterly*, 21. 70–1.

Ardrey, R. (1966) *The Territorial Imperative*, New York: Delta.

Argyle, M. (1973) *Social Interaction*, London: Tavistock.

Arsdol, M. D. van, Sabagh, G., and Alexander, F. (1964) 'Reality and the Perception of Environmental Hazards', *Journal of Health and Human Behaviour*, 5. 144–53.

Ashley/Myer/Smith Inc. (1971) *City Signs and Lights*, Boston: Signs/Lights.

Attenborough, D. (1975) *Attenborough round the World*, Radio Broadcast Script, BBC Radio 4, 21 December.

Ayer, A. J. (1968) *The Origins of Pragmatism*, London: Macmillan.

Baird, A., O'Keefe, P., Westgate, K., and Wisner, B. (1975) *Towards an Explanation and Reduction of Disaster Proneness*, Occasional Paper 11, Bradford: Disaster Research Unit, University of Bradford.

Baker, E. J., and Patton, D. J. (1974) 'Attitudes toward Hurricane Hazards on the Gulf Coast', in G. F. White, ed., *Natural Hazards: Local, National, Global*, New York: Oxford University Press, 30–6.

Baker, G. W., and Chapman, D. W., eds. (1962) *Man and Society in Disaster*, New York: Basic Books.

Baldwin, A. L. (1967) *Theories of Child Development*, London: Wiley.

Baldwin, J., and Bottoms, A. E. (1976) *The Urban Criminal*, London; Tavistock.

Baltzell, E. D. (1958) *Philadelphia Gentlemen: The Making of a National Upper Class*, New York: Free Press.

Banerjee, T., and Lynch, K. (1977) 'On People and Places: A Comprehensive Study of the Spatial Environment of Adolescence', *Town Planning Review*, 48, 105–15.

Banham, R. (1963) *Guide to Modern Architecture*, London: Architectural Press.

—— (1971) *Los Angeles: The Architecture of Four Ecologies*, London: Allen Lane.

Banse, E. (1928) *Landschaft und Seele: Neue Wege der Untersuchung und Gestaltung*, Munich.

Banz, G. (1970) *Elements of Urban Form*, New York: McGraw Hill.

Barber, P. J., and Legge, D. (1976) *Perception and Information*, London: Methuen.

Barbour, K. M. (1973) *The Geographical Knowledge of the Medieval Islamic World*, Occasional Paper 22, London: Department of Geography, University College London.

Barbu, Z. (1971) *Society, Culture and Personality*, Oxford: Blackwell.

Barker, M., and Burton, I. (1969) *Differential Response to Stress in Natural and Social Environments: An Application of a Modified Rosensweig Picture-Frustration Test*, Working Paper 5, Toronto: Natural Hazard Research Unit, Department of Geography, University of Toronto.

Barker, R. G. (1968) *Ecological Psychology: Concepts and Methods for Studying the Environment of Behaviour*, Stanford: Stanford University Press.

Baron, R. A., Byrne, D., and Kantowitz, B. H. (1977) *Psychology: Understanding Behaviour*, London: Saunders.

Barrett, F. (1976). 'The Search Process in Residential Relocation', *Environment and Behaviour*, 8. 169–98.

Barrows, J. (1971) 'Forest Fire Research for Environmental Protection', *Journal of Forestry*, 69. 17–20.

Barthes, R. (1967) *Elements of Semiology*, London: Jonathan Cape.

Bartlett, F. C. (1932) *Remembering: A Study in Experimental and Social Psychology*, Cambridge: Cambridge University Press.

Barton, A. H. (1969) *Communities in Disaster: A Sociological Analysis of Collective Stress Situations*, New York: Ward Lock.

Baum, A., and Valins, S. (1978) *Architecture and Social Behaviour: Psychological Studies of Social Density*, London: Wiley.

Baumann, D. D., and Sims, J. H. (1974) 'Human Response to the Hurricane', in G. F. White, ed., *Natural Hazards: Local, National, Global*, New York: Oxford University Press, 25–30.

BBC (British Broadcasting Corporation) (1975) *Twenty-five Years of the Archers*, London: British Broadcasting Corporation.

Beck, R. (1970) 'Spatial Meaning and the Properties of the Environment', in H. M. Proshansky, W. H. Ittelson, and L. G. Rivlin, eds., *Environmental Psychology*, First Edition, New York: Holt, Rinehart, & Winston, 134–41.

Beck, R. and Wood, D. (1976) 'Comparative Developmental Analysis of Individual and Aggregated Cognitive Maps of London', in G. T. Moore and R. G. Golledge, eds., *Environmental Knowing*, Stroudsburg, Pa.: Dowden, Hutchinson, & Ross, 173–84.

Becker, F. D. (1977) *Housing Messages*, London, Wiley.

Bee, H. (1975) *The Developing Child*, London: Harper & Row.

Beer, G. L. (1908) 'The Early English Colonial Movement', *Political Science Quarterly*, 23. 75–94 and 242–58.

Belcher, D. M. (1973) *Giving Psychology Away*, San Francisco: Canfield.

Berelson, B. (1968) 'Behavioral Sciences', in D. L. Sills, ed., *International Encyclopedia of the Social Sciences*, 2, London: Macmillan, 41–5.

Berger, P. L., and Luckmann, T. (1971) *The Social Construction of Reality: A Treatise in the Sociology of Knowledge*, Harmondsworth: Penguin.

Berghe, P. L. van der (1972) 'Distance Mechanisms of Stratification', in A. H. Richmond, ed., *Readings in Race and Ethnic Relations*, London: Oxford University Press, 210–19.

Berlyne, D. E. (1950) 'Novelty and Curiosity as Determinants of Exploratory Behaviour', *British Journal of Psychology*, 41. 68–80.

Berry, B. J. L. (1964) 'Approaches to Regional Analysis: A Synthesis', *Annals of the Association of American Geographers*, 54. 2–11.

—— (1972) 'More on Relevance and Policy Analysis', *Area*, 4. 77–80.

—— (1973) *The Human Consequences of Urbanisation*, London: Macmillan.

Beshers, J. M. (1962) *Urban Social Structure*, New York: Free Press.

Beyer, J. L. (1974) 'Global Summary of Human Response to Natural Hazards: Floods', in G. F. White, ed., *Natural Hazards: Local, National, Global*, New York: Oxford University Press, 265–74.

Billinge, M. (1977) 'In Search of Negativism: Phenomenology and Historical Geography', *Journal of Historical Geography*, 3.55–67.

Bird, J. (1977) *Centrality and Cities*, London: Routledge & Kegan Paul.

Blache, P. V. de la (1926) *Principles of Human Geography* (trans. M. T. Bingham), London: Constable.

Blackbourn, A. (1974) 'The Spatial Behaviour of American Firms in Western Europe', in F. E. I. Hamilton, ed., *Spatial Perspectives on Industrial Organisation and Decision-Making*, London: Wiley, 245–64.

Blakemore, C. (1977) *Mechanics of the Mind*, London: Cambridge University Press.

Blouet, B. N., and Lawson, M. P. (1975) *Images of the Plains*, Lincoln, Neb.: University of Nebraska Press.

Boal, F. W. (1969) 'Territoriality on the Shankhill–Falls Divide, Belfast', *Irish Geography*, 6. 30–50.

—— (1970) 'Social Space in the Belfast Urban Area', in N. Stephens and N. Glasscock, eds., *Irish Geographical Studies*, Belfast: The Queen's University, 373–93.

—— (1971) 'Territoriality and Class: A Study of Two Residential Areas in Belfast', *Irish Geography*, 6. 229–48.

—— (1976) 'Ethnic Residential Segregation', in D. T. Herbert and R. J. Johnston, eds. *Spatial Processes and Form*, London: Wiley, 41–79.

—— Doherty, P., and Pringle, D. (1978) *Social Problems in the Belfast Urban Area: An Exploratory Analysis*, Occasional Paper 12, London: Queen Mary College.

Board, C. (1967) 'Maps as Models', in R. J. Chorley and P. Haggett, eds., *Models in Geography*, London: Methuen, 671–725.

Bogdanovic, B. (1975) 'Symbols in the City and the City as Symbols', *Ekistics*, 39. 140–6.

Boice, L. P. (1977) *Encountering a City: The Spatial Learning Process of Urban Newcomers*, Exchange Bibliography 1264, Monticello, Ill.: Council of Planning Librarians.

Booth, A. (1975) *Growing up in Society*, London: Methuen.

Boring, E. G. (1942) *Sensation and Perception in the History of Experimental Psychology*. New York: Appleton-Century.

—— (1950) *A History of Experimental Psychology*, 2nd edition, New York: Appleton.

Boulding, K. E. (1956) *The Image: Knowledge in Life and Society*, Ann Arbor: University of Michigan Press.

Boulting, N. (1976) 'The Law's Delays: Conservationist Legislation in the British Isles', in J. Fawcett, ed. *The Future of the Past: Attitudes to Conservation*, London: Thames & Hudson, 9–33.

Bower, T. G. R. (1965) 'The Determinants of Perceptual Unity in Infancy', *Psychonomic Science*, 3. 323–4.

—— Broughton, J. M., and Moore, M. K. (1971) 'Infant Responses to Approaching Objects: An Indicator of Response to Distal Variables', *Perception and Psychophysics*, 9. 193–6.

Boyce, R. R. (1971) 'Residential Mobility and its Implications for Urban Spatial Change', in L. S. Bourne, ed., *Internal Structure of the City*, London: Oxford University Press, 338–43.

Brendel, O. J. (1977) *Symbolism of the Sphere*, Leiden: Brill.

Brennan, T. (1948) *Midland City*, London: Dobson.

Briggs, R. (1973) 'On the Relationship between Cognitive and Objective Distance', in W. F. E. Preiser, ed., *Environmental Design Research*, 2, Stroudsburg, Pa.: Dowden, Hutchinson, & Ross, 186–99.

—— (1976) 'Methodologies for the Measurement of Cognitive Distance', in G. T. Moore and R. G. Golledge, eds., *Environmental Knowing*, Stroudsburg, Pa.: Dowden, Hutchinson, & Ross, 325–34.

Broadbent, G. (1973) *Design in Architecture*, London: Wiley.

Broadbent, G. H. (1975) 'Function and Symbolism in Architecture', in B. Honikman, ed. *Responding to Social Change*, Stroudsburg, Pa.: Dowden, Hutchinson, & Ross, 73–95.

Broady, M. (1966) 'Social Theory in Architectural Design', *Arena*, 81. 149–54.

Broek, J. O. M. (1932) *The Santa Clara Valley, California: A Study in Landscape Change*, Utrecht.

Brolin, B. C. (1976) *The Failure of Modern Architecture*, London: Studio Vista.

Bronzaft, A. L., and McCarthy, D. P. (1975) 'The effect of Elevated Train Noise on Reading Ability', *Environment and Behaviour*, 7. 517–27.

Brooks, R. H. (1971) 'Human Resources to Recurrent Drought in Northeastern Brazil', *Professional Geographer*, 23. 42–43.

Brown, J. (1966) 'Information Theory', in B. M. Foss, ed., *New Horizons in Psychology*, Harmondsworth: Penguin, 118–34.

Brown, L. A., and Holmes, J. (1970) *Search Behaviour in an Intraurban Migration Context: A Spatial Perspective*, Research Paper 13, Columbus: Department of Geography, Ohio State University.

Brown, L. A., and Moore, E. G. (1971) 'The Intraurban Migration Process: A Perspective'. *Geografiska Annaler*, Series B, vol. 52B, No. 1, Stockholm, Sweden.

Brown, R. (1962) 'Models of Attitude Change', in *New Directions in Psychology*, 1, New York: Holt, Rinehart & Winston, 1–85.

—— (1973) *A First Language*, Cambridge, Mass: Harvard University Press.

Bruce, A. (1971) 'Housewife Attitudes towards Shops and Shopping Centres', in B. Honikman, ed., *Architectural Psychology '70*, London: RIBA and Kingston Polytechnic, 17–20.

Bruner, J. S. (1957) *On going beyond the Information given*, Cambridge, Mass.: Harvard University Press.

Brunhes, J. (1920) *Human Geography*, Chicago: Rand McNally.

Brunswik, E. (1956) *Perception and the Representative Design of Psychological Experiments*, Berkeley: University of California Press.

Buchanan, M. (1975) 'Attitudes towards the Urban Environment: A Melbourne Study', *Australian Geographer*, 13. 15–22.

Bultena, G.L., and Taves, M. J. (1961) 'Changing Wilderness Images and Forestry Policy', *Journal of Forestry*, 59. 161–71.

Burgess, E. W., and Bogue, D. J., eds. (1963) *Contributions to Urban Sociology*, Chicago: University Press.

Burgess, J. A., and Hollis, G. E. (1977) 'Personal London', *Geographical Magazine*, 50. 155–9.

Burnette, C. (1974) 'The Mental Image and Design', in J. Lang, C. Burnette, C. Moleski, and D. Vachon, eds., *Designing for Human Behaviour: Architecture and the Behavioural Sciences*, Stroudsburg, Pa.: Dowden, Hutchinson, & Ross, 169–82.

Burrows, A. A., and Zamarin, D. M. (1972) 'Aircraft Noise and the Community: Some Recent Survey Findings', *Aerospace Medicine*, 43. 27–33.

Burt, W. H. (1943) 'Territoriality and Home Range as applied to Mammals', *Journal of Mammology*, 24. 346–52.

Burton, I. (1962) *Types of Agricultural Occupance of Flood Plains in the United States*, Research Paper 75, Chicago: Department of Geography, University of Chicago.

—— (1963) 'The Quantitative Revolution and Theoretical Geography', *Canadian Geographer*, 7. 151–62.

—— (1972) 'Cultural and Personality Variables in the Perception of Natural Hazards', in J. F. Wohlwill and D. H. Carson, eds., *Environment and the Social Sciences*, Washington, D. C.: American Psychological Association, 184–95.

—— and Kates, R. W. (1964) 'The Flood Plain and the Seashore: A Comparative Analysis of Hazard Zone Occupance', *Geographical Review*, 54. 366–85.

—— —— (1972) 'The Perception of Natural Hazards in Resource Management', in P. W. English and R. C. Mayfield, eds. *Man, Space and Environment*, New York: Oxford University Press, 282–304.

—— —— and White, G. F. (1968) *The Human Ecology of Extreme Geographical Events*, Working Paper 1, Toronto: Natural Hazard Research Unit, Department of Geography, University of Toronto.

—— —— —— (1978) *The Environment as Hazard*, New York: Oxford University Press.

Busch, L. (1978) 'On Understanding Understanding: Two Views of Communication', *Rural Sociology*, 43. 450–73.

Buttimer, A. (1969) 'Social Space in Interdisciplinary Perspective', *Geographical Review*, 59. 417–26.

—— (1976) 'Grasping the Dynamism of Lifeworld', *Annals of the Association of American Geographers*, 66. 277–92.

Cadwallader, M. T. (1976) 'Cognitive Distance in Intraurban Space', in G. T. Moore and R. G. Golledge, eds. *Environmental Knowing*, Stroudsburg, Pa.: Dowden, Hutchinson, Ross, 316–24.

Calhoun, J. B. (1962) 'Population Density and Social Pathology', *Scientific American*, 206. 139–48.

Calhoun, J. B. (1966) 'The Role of Space in Animal Sociology', *Journal of Social Issues*, 22. 46–58.

Cameron, J. M. R. (1974) 'Information Distortion in Colonial Promotion: The Case of Swan River Colony', *Australian Geographical Studies*, 12. 57–76.

Canter, D. V., ed. (1971) *Architectural Psychology: Proceedings of the Conference held at Dalandhui, University of Strathclyde*, London: RIBA Publications.

—— (1974) *Psychology for Architects*, London: Applied Science Publishers.

—— (1975a) *Distance Estimation in Greater London*, Final Report to the Social Science Research Council, Guildford, Surrey: University of Surrey, mimeo.

—— ed. (1975b) *Environmental Interaction*, London: University of Surrey Press.

—— (1977) *The Psychology of Place*, London: Architectural Press.

—— and Lee, T. R., eds. (1974) *Psychology and the Built Environment*, London: Architectural Press.

—— and Tagg, S. K. (1975) 'Distance Estimation in Cities', *Environment and Behaviour*, 7. 59–80.

Carey, L., and Mapes, R. (1972) *The Sociology of Planning: A Study of Social Activity on New Housing Estates*, London: Batsford.

Carpenter, E., Varley, F., and Flaherty, R. (1959) *Eskimo*, Toronto: University of Toronto Press.

Carr, H. A. (1925) *Psychology: A Study of Mental Activity*, New York: McKay.

Carr, S., and Schissler, D. (1969) 'The City as Trip', *Environment and Behaviour*, 1. 7-35.

Carroll, J. B., ed. (1956) *Language, Thought and Reality: Selected Writings of Benjamin Lee Whorf*, New York: Wiley.

Carson, D. H. (1972) 'Residential Descriptions and Urban Threats', in J. F. Wohlwill and D. H. Carson, eds., *Environment and the Social Sciences*, Washington, D. C.: American Psychological Association, 154-68.

Chaplin, J. P., and Krawiec, T. S. (1974) *Systems and Theories of Psychology*, 3rd edition, New York: Holt, Rinehart, & Winston.

Chapman, G. P. (1974) 'Perception and Regulation: A Case Study of Farmers in Bihar', *Transactions of the Institute of British Geographers*, 62. 71-93.

Cherry, G. E. (1974) *Urban Planning Problems*, London: Leonard Hill.

Chinoy, E. (1967) *Society: An Introduction to Sociology*, New York: Random House.

Chomsky, N. (1972) 'Psychology and Ideology', *Cognition*, 1. 11-46.

Chorley, R. J. (1973) 'Geography as Human Ecology', in R. J. Chorley, ed., *Directions in Geography*, London: Methuen, 155-69.

—— (1976) 'Some Thoughts on the Development of Geography from 1950 to 1975', in D. M. Pepper and A. Jenkins, eds., *Proceedings of the 1975 National Conference on Geography in Higher Education*, Discussion Paper in Geography 3, Headington, Oxford: Oxford Polytechnic Press, 29-35.

Christaller, W. (1933) *Die Zentralen Orte in Suddeutschland* (trans. C. W. Baskin, 1963, as *Central Places in Southern Germany*, Englewood Cliffs, N. J.: Prentice Hall).

Clark, K. G. T. (1951) 'Certain Underpinnings of our Arguments in Human Geography' *Transactions of the Institute of British Geographers*, 16. 15-22.

Clark, S. D. (1966) *The Suburban Society*, Toronto: University of Toronto Press.

Clark, W. A. V., and Cadwallader, M. (1973) 'Locational Stress and Residential Mobility', *Environment and Behaviour*, 5. 29-41.

Clay, G. (1973) *Close-Up: How to Read the American City*, London: Pall Mall.

Clayre, A., ed. (1977) *Nature and Industrialization*, London: Oxford University Press.

Coates, M., and Silburn, R. (1970) *Poverty: The Forgotten Englishmen*, Harmondsworth: Penguin.

Cohen, R., McManus, J., Fox, D., Kasteinik, C. (1973) *Psych City: A Simulated Community*, Oxford: Pergamon.

Cohen, S., Glass, D. C., and Singer, J. E. (1973) 'Apartment Noise, Auditory Discrimination and Reading Ability in Children', *Journal of Experimental Social Psychology*, 9. 407-22.

Cole, M., and Scribner, S. (1974) *Culture and Thought*, New York: Wiley.

Coleman, B. I., ed. (1973) *The Idea of the City in Nineteenth Century Britain*, London: Routledge & Kegan Paul.

Collette, J., and Webb, S. (1976) 'Urban Density, Household Crowding and Stress Reactions', *Australia and New Zealand Journal of Sociology*, 12. 184-91.

Collins, L., and Walker, D. F., eds. (1975) *Locational Dynamics of Manufacturing Activity*, London: Wiley.

Collison, P. (1963) *The Cutteslowe Walls*, London: Faber & Faber.

Condran, G. A., and Crimmins-Gardner, E. (1978) 'Public Health Measures and Mortality in U. S. Cities in the late Nineteenth Century', *Human Ecology*, 6. 27-54.

Conway, D., ed. (1977) *Human Response to Tall Buildings*, London: Wiley.

Cook, I. G. (1974) *The Sense of Place in the Nottingham-Derbyshire Coalfield*, paper presented to Annual Meeting, Institute of British Geographers, University of East Anglia, January.

Cook, I. G. and Gold, J. R. (1974) 'The Allestree Trunk Road: An Analysis of Public Cognition', *Ideas in Geography*, 51, whole issue.

Cooke, A. (1973) *Alistair Cooke's America*, London: British Broadcasting Corporation.

Cooper Marcus, C. (1974) 'The House as Symbol of the Self', in J. Lang, C. Burnette, W. Moleski, and D. Vachon, eds., *Designing for Human Behaviour: Architecture and the Behavioural Sciences*, Stroudsburg, Pa.: Dowden, Hutchinson, & Ross, 130–46.

—— and Hogue, L. (1976) 'Design Guidelines for High-Rise Housing', *Journal of Architectural Research*, 5. 34–49.

Cooperman, D. (1977) 'Social Research on Tall Habitats: A Critique and Proposal for Network Analysis', in D. Conway, ed., *Human Response to Tall Buildings*, Stroudsburg, Pa.: Dowden, Hutchinson & Ross, 29–38.

Coppock, J. T. (1974) 'Geography and Public Policy: Challenges, Opportunities and Implications', *Transactions of the Institute of British Geographers*, 63. 1–16.

Cornish, V. (1928) 'Harmonies of Scenery: An Outline of Aesthetic Geography', *Geography*, 14. 275–83 and 382–94.

Cosgrove, D. E. (1978) 'Place, Landscape and the Dialectics of Cultural Geography', *Canadian Geographer*, 22. 66–72.

Coventry–Solihull–Warwickshire Sub-Regional Planning Study Group (1971) *A Strategy for the Sub-Region*, Supplementary Report 5 'Countryside', Coventry: Study Group.

Cox, H. (1968) 'The Restoration of a Sense of Place', *Ekistics*, 25. 422–4.

Coyne, J. (1974) 'Alaska: Image of a Resource Frontier Region', unpublished Ph.D. thesis, Department of Geography, Birkbeck College, University of London.

Craik, K. H. (1968) 'The Comprehension of the Everyday Physical Environment', *Journal of the American Institute of Planners*, 34. 29–37.

—— (1970) 'Environmental Psychology', *New Directions in Psychology*, 4. New York: Holt, Rinehart, & Winston, 1–121.

—— (1972) 'Psychological Factors in Landscape Appraisal', *Environment and Behaviour*, 4. 255–66.

Crofts, R. S. (1975) 'The Landscape Component Approach to Landscape Evaluation', *Transactions of the Institute of British Geographers*, 66. 124–9.

Cromer, R. F. (1974) 'The Development of Language and Cognition: The Cognition Hypothesis', in B. M. Foss, ed., *New Perspectives in Child Development*, Harmondsworth: Penguin.

Crosby, T. (1970) *The Necessary Monument*, London: Studio Vista.

Cullen, G. (1961) *Townscape*, London: Architectural Press.

Cyert, R. M., and March, J. G. (1963) *A Behavioural Theory of the Firm*, Englewood Cliffs, N. J.: Prentice Hall.

Dacey, M. F. (1971) 'Two-Dimensional Urban Contact Fields', *Geographical Analysis*, 3. 109–20.

Darley, G. (1975) *Villages of Vision*, London: Architectural Press.

Dasen, P. R., ed. (1977) *Piagetian Psychology: Cross-Cultural Contributions*, New York: Halsted.

Davies, R. L. (1976) *Marketing Geography*, Corbridge: Retail and Planning Associates.

Davis, D. E. (1958) 'The Role of Density in Aggressive Behaviour of House Mice', *Animal Behaviour*, 6. 207–10.

Davis, I. R. (1978) *Shelter after Disaster*, Headington, Oxford: Oxford Polytechnic Press.

Davis, W. M. (1906) 'An Inductive Study of the Content of Geography', *Bulletin of the American Geographical Society*, 38. 67–84.

Deasy, C. M. (1974) *Design for Human Affairs*, London: Wiley.

Delong, A. J. (1973) 'Territorial Stability and Hierarchical Formation', *Small Group Behaviour*, 4. 56–63.

Dennis, N. (1968) 'The Popularity of the Neighbourhood Idea', in R. Pahl, ed., *Readings in Urban Sociology*, Oxford: Pergamon, 74–92.

Devlin, A. S. (1976) 'The "Small Town" Cognitive Map: Adjusting to a New Environ-ment', in G. T. Moore and R. G. Golledge, eds., *Environmental Knowing*, Stroudsburg, Pa.: Dowden, Hutchinson, & Ross, 58–66.

Dewey, J. (1929) *Experience and Nature*, London: Allen & Unwin.

—— (1934) *Art as Experience*, New York: Capricorn.

Dicken, P. (1971) 'Some Aspects of the Decision-Making Behaviour of Business Organisa-tions', *Economic Geography*, 47. 426–37.

Dickinson, R. E. (1939) 'Landscape and Society', *Scottish Geographical Magazine*, 55. 1–15.

—— (1976) *The Regional Concept: The Anglo-American Leaders*, London: Routledge & Kegan Paul.

Dodwell, P. C. (1956) 'Studies of the Visual System', in B. M. Foss, ed., *New Horizons in Psychology*, Harmondsworth: Penguin.

Dohrs, F. E., and Sommers, L. M. (1967) *Cultural Geography: Selected Readings*, New York: Crowell.

Donaldson, B. (1973) 'An Empirical Investigation into the Concept of Sectoral Bias in the Mental Maps, Search Spaces and Migration Patterns of Intraurban Migrants', *Geografiska Annaler*, 55B. 13–33.

Douglas, M. (1970) *Natural Symbols*, Harmondsworth: Penguin.

Downs, A. (1973) *Opening up the Suburbs*, New Haven, Conn.: Yale University Press.

Downs, R. M. (1970) 'The Cognitive Structure of an Urban Shopping Centre', *Environ-ment and Behaviour*, 2. 13–39.

—— (1976) 'Cognitive Mapping and Information Processing: A Commentary', in G. T. Moore and R. G. Golledge, eds., *Environmental Knowing*, Stroudsburg, Pa.: Dowden, Hutchinson & Ross, 131–6.

—— and Meyer, J. T. (1978) 'Geography and the Mind: An Exploration of Perceptual Geography', *American Behavioural Scientist*, 22. 59–78.

Downs, R. M. and Stea, D. eds. (1973) *Image and Environment*, Chicago: Aldine.

—— —— (1977) *Maps in Minds*, London: Harper & Row.

Dudley Report, The (1944) *Design of Dwellings*, London: HMSO.

Duffield, B. S., and Coppock, J. T. (1975) 'The Delineation of Recreational Landscapes: The Role of a Computer-based Information System.' *Transactions of the Institute of British Geographers*, 66. 141–8.

Duncan, J. S., and Duncan, N. G. (1976) 'Housing as Presentation of Self and the Struc-ture of Social Networks', in G. T. Moore and R. G. Golledge, eds., *Environmental Knowing*, Stroudsburg, Pa.: Dowden, Hutchinson, & Ross, 247–53.

Dunn, M. C. (1974) 'Landscape Evaluation for Development Plans: A Further Perspec-tive', *Journal of the Royal Planning Institute*, 60. 935–36.

—— (1976) 'Landscape with Photographs: Testing the Preference Approach to Landscape Evaluation', *Journal of Environmental Management*, 4. 15–26.

Dupree, H., and Roder, W. (1974) 'Coping with Drought in a Pre-industrial Pre-literate Farming Society', in G. F. White, ed., *Natural Hazards: Local, National, Global*, New York: Oxford University Press, 115–19.

Durkheim, E. (1893) *The Division of Labour in Society* (trans. G. Simpson, 1933, New York: Free Press).

Dyson-Hudson, R., and Smith, E. A. (1978) 'Human Territoriality: An Ecological Re-assessment', *American Anthropologist*, 80. 21–41.

Earney, F. C. F., and Knowles, B. A. (1974) 'Urban Snow Hazard: Marquette, Michigan', in G. F. White, ed. *Natural Hazards: Local, National, Global*, New York: Oxford University Press, 167–74.

Edgell, M. C. R. (1975) 'The Bushfire Environment of Southeastern Australia', *Journal of Environmental Management*, 3. 329–49.

Edney, J. J. (1976) 'Human Territoriality', in H. M. Proshansky, W. H. Ittelson, and L. G. Rivlin, eds., *Environmental Psychology*, Second Edition, New York: Holt, Rinehart, & Winston, 189-205.

—— (1977) 'Theories of Human Crowding: A Review', *Environment and Planning*, A9. 1211-32.

Eisenberg, L. (1972) 'The *human* nature of human nature', *Science*, 176. 123-8.

Eliade, M. (1961) *Images and Symbols*, London: Harrill.

—— (1968) *Myth and Reality*, New York: Harper & Row.

Elkind, D., and Scott, L. (1962) 'Studies in Perceptual Development I: The Decentering of Perception', *Child Development*, 33. 619.

Elliott, P. (1972) *The Making of a Television Series*, London: Constable.

Engels, F. (1844) *The Condition of the English Working Classes* (trans. W. O. Henderson and W. H. Challoner, 1958, London: Allen & Unwin).

Erasmus, C. J. (1978) *In Search of the Common Good: Utopian Experiments Past and Present*, New York: Free Press.

Ericksen, N. J. (1970) 'Human Adjustment to Floods in New Zealand', *New Zealand Geographer*, 27. 105-29.

Esser, A. H. (1970) 'From Territorial Image to Cultural Environment', *Geloof en Wetenschap*, 68. 89-98.

—— (1971a) *Behaviour and Environment: The Use of Space by Animals and Men*, New York: Plenum Press.

—— (1971b) 'Social Pollution', *Social Education*, 35. 10-18.

—— (1972) 'A Biosocial Perspective on Crowding', in J. F. Wohlwill and D. H. Carson, eds., *Environment and the Social Sciences*, Washington, D. C.: American Psychological Association. 15-28.

—— (1976) 'Theoretical and Empirical Issues with regard to Privacy, Territoriality, Personal Space and Crowding', *Environment and Behaviour*, 8. 117-24.

Etzioni, A. (1964) *Modern Organisations*, Englewood Cliffs, N. J.: Prentice Hall.

Evans, P. (1976) *Motivation*, London: Methuen.

Everitt, J. C. (1976) 'Community and Propinquity in a City', *Annals of the Association of American Geographers*, 66. 104-16.

Eyles, J. (1971) 'Geography and Relevance', *Area*, 3. 158-60.

—— (1974) 'Increased Spatial Mobility: A Minor Social Indicator?', *Area*, 6. 305-8.

—— (1977) 'After the Relevance Debate: The Teaching of Social Geography', *Journal of Geography in Higher Education*, 1 (2). 3-12.

Eyre, S. R., and Jones, G. R. J., eds. (1966) *Geography as Human Ecology: Methodology by Example*, London: Arnold.

Eysenck, H. J. (1953) *The Structure of Human Personality*, London: Wiley.

—— (1971) *Race, Intelligence and Education*, London: Temple Smith.

Fantino, E., and Reynolds, G. S. (1975) *An Introduction to Contemporary Psychology*, San Francisco: Freeman.

Farbstein, J., and Kantrowitz, M. (1978) *People in Places: A Workbook for Knowing, Using and Changing the Built Environment*, Englewood Cliffs, N. J.: Prentice Hall.

Faris, R. E. L., and Dunham, H. W. (1939) *Mental Disorders in Urban Areas*, Chicago: University of Chicago Press.

Farr, L. E. (1967) 'Medical Consequences of Environmental Noises', *Journal of the American Medical Association*, 202. 171-4.

Febvre, L. P. V. (1925) *A Geographical Introduction to History*, New York: Knopf.

Festinger, L. (1947) *A Theory of Cognitive Dissonance*, Evanston: Ross, Peterson.

—— (1951) 'Architecture and Group Membership', *Journal of Social Issues*, 7. 152-63, (also reprinted in R. Gutman, ed., (1972) *People and Buildings*, New York: Basic Books, 120-34).

—— Schachter, S., and Back, K. (1950, 1959) *Social Pressures in Informal Groups: A Study of Human Factors in Housing*, 1st and 2nd editions, London: Tavistock.

Fines, K. D. (1968) 'Landscape Evaluation: A Research Project in East Sussex', *Regional Studies*, 2. 41–55.

Firey, W. (1947) *Land Use in Central Boston*, Cambridge, Mass: Harvard University Press.

Fischer, C. S. (1975) 'The Myth of Territoriality in van der Berghe's "Bringing Beasts Back In" ', *American Sociological Review*, 40. 674–6.

—— (1976) *The Urban Experience*, New York: Harcourt, Brace, & Jovanovitch.

Fishbein, M., and Ajzen, I. (1975) *Belief, Attitude and Behaviour*, Reading, Mass.: Addison-Wesley.

Fishman, R. (1977) *Urban Utopias in the Twentieth Century*, London: Basic Books.

Fitter, R., consulting ed. (1969) *Book of British Birds*, London: Drive Publications.

Flaschbart, P. G. (1969) 'Urban Territorial Behaviour', *Journal of the American Institute of Planners*, 35. 412–16.

Forrest, J. (1974) 'Spatial Aspects of Urban Social Travel', *Urban Studies*, 11. 301–13.

Francescato, D., and Mebane, W. (1973) 'How Citizens view two great Cities: Milan and Rome', in R. M. Downs and D. Stea, eds., *Image and Environment*, Chicago: Aldine, 131–47.

Francescato, G., Weidemann, S., Anderson, J., Chenoweth, R. (1977) 'Predictors of Residents' Satisfaction in High-Rise and Low-Rise Housing', in D. Conway, ed., *Human Response to Tall Buildings*, Stroudsburg, Pa.: Dowden, Hutchinson, & Ross, 160–7.

Freedman, J. L. (1975) *Crowding and Behaviour*, San Francisco: Freeman.

——Heshka, S., and Levy, A. (1975) 'Population Density and Pathology: Is there a Relationship?' *Journal of Experimental Social Psychology*, 11. 539–52.

Fried, M. (1963) 'Grieving for a Lost Home', in L. H. Duhl, ed., *The Urban Condition*, New York: Basic Books, 151–71.

—— and Gleicher, P. (1961) 'Some Sources of Residential Satisfaction in an Urban Slum', *Journal of the American Institute of Planners*, 27. 305–15.

Friedman, S., and Juhasz, J. B. (1974) *Environments: Notes and Selections on Objects, Spaces and Behaviour*, Monterey: Brooks-Cole.

Furth, H. G. (1969) *Piaget and Knowledge*, Englewood Cliffs, N. J.: Prentice Hall.

G. A. C. (1904) *Ealing: A Country Town Near London*, n. p.

Gad, G. H. K. (1973) ' "Crowding" and "Pathologies": Some Critical Remarks', *Canadian Geographer*, 17. 373–90.

—— Peddie, R., and Punter, J. (1973) 'Ethnic Differences in the Residential Search Process', in L. S. Bourne, R. D. MacKinnon, and J. W. Simmons, eds., *The Form of Cities in Canada: Selected Papers*, Toronto: University of Toronto Press, 168–80.

Galanter, E. (1962) 'Contemporary Psychophysics', *New Directions in Psychology*, 1, New York: Holt, 89–156.

Galle, O. R., Gove, W. R., and McPherson, J. M. (1972) 'Population Density and Pathology: What are the Relations for Man?', *Science*, 176. 23–30.

Gans, H. J. (1962) *The Urban Villagers: Group and Class in the Life of Italian-Americans*, New York: Free Press.

—— (1967) *The Levittowners*, New York: Pantheon.

—— (1968) *People and Plans*, New York: Basic Books.

Garner, B. J. (1970) 'Towards a Better Understanding of Shopping Paterns', in R. H. Osborne, F. A. Barnes, and J. C. Doornkamp, eds., *Geographical Essays in Honour of K. C. Edwards*, Nottingham: University of Nottingham Press, 179–86.

Gerasimov, I. P., and Zvonkova, T. G. (1974) 'Natural Hazards in the Territory of the USSR: Study, Control and Warning', in G. F. White, ed., *Natural Hazards: Local, National, Global*, New York: Oxford University Press, 243–51.

Gibson, E. J., and Walk, R. D. (1960) 'The "Visual Cliff" ', *Scientific American*, 202. 64–71.

Gibson, J. J. (1950) *The Perception of the Visual World*, Boston: Houghton-Mifflin.

Giggs, J. A. (1973) 'The Distribution of Schizophrenics in Nottingham', *Transactions of the Institute of Geograpers*, 51. 55–76.

Gilbert, E. W. (1960) 'The Idea of the Region', *Geography*, 45. 157–174.

Gillis, A. R. (1977) 'High-Rise Housing and Psychological Strain', *Journal of Health and Social Behaviour*, 18. 418–32.

Giner, S. (1976) *Mass Society*, London: Martin Robertson.

Glacken, C. J. (1967) *Traces on the Rhodian Shore: Nature and Culture in Western Thought from Ancient Times to the end of the Eighteenth Century*, Berkeley: University of California Press.

Glass, D. C., and Singer, J. E. (1972) *Urban Stress: Experments on Noise and Social Stressors*, New York: Academic Press.

Goddard, J. B. (1976) 'Research and Teaching: Speeding up the Trickling-Down Process', in D. M. Pepper and A. Jenkins, eds., *Proceedings of the 1975 National Conference on Geography in Higher Education*, Discussion Paper in Geography 3, Headington, Oxford: Oxford Polytechnic Press, 38–9.

Golant, S., and Burton, I. (1970) 'A Semantic Differential Experiment in the Interpretation and Grouping of Environmental Hazards', *Geographical Analysis*, 2. 120–34.

Gold, J. R. (1974) *Communicating Images of the Environment: With Case Studies of the Use of the Media by West Midland Overspill Schemes*, Occasional Paper 29, Birmingham, Eng.: Centre for Urban and Regional Studies, University of Birmingham.

—— (1976a) 'Communicating Images of New Urban Developments', paper presented to the Twenty-Third Congress of the International Geographical Union, Moscow, August.

—— (1976b) 'Neighbourhood, Territory and Identity in the City', in J. R. Gold, ed. *Neighbourhood, Planning and Politics*, Discussion Paper in Geography 1, Headington, Oxford: Geography Section, Oxford Polytechnic.

—— (1977a) 'Teaching Behavioural Geography', *Journal of Geography in Higher Education*, 1 (1). 37–46.

—— (1977b) 'Towns get the Marketing Blues', *Urban*, n. v., September–October, 14–16.

—— (1978) 'Some Implications of the Development of Behavioural Geography for Geographical Education', paper presented to the National Conference on Geography in Higher Education, Portsmouth, September.

—— and Barke, M. (1978) *Communications Media and the Future of Cities*, Discussion Paper in Geography 4, Headington, Oxford: Geography Section, Oxford Polytechnic.

Gold, R. (1971) 'Urban Violence and Contemporary Defensive Cities', in W. McQuade, ed., *Cities fit to Live in*, London: Collier-Macmillan, 4–20.

Golledge, R. G. (1977) 'Behavioural Approaches in Geography: Comment and Prospects', in R. Taaffe and J. Odland, eds., *Current Trends in Geography*, Bloomington: Kendall, 87–96.

—— Briggs, R., and Demko, D. (1969) 'The Configuration of Distances in Intraurban Space', *Proceedings of the Association of American Geographers*, 1. 60–5.

—— Brown, L. A., and Williamson, F. (1972) 'Behavioural Approaches in Geography: An Overview', *Australian Geographer*, 12. 59–79.

—— and Rushton, G., eds., (1976) *Spatial Choice and Spatial Behaviour*, Columbus: Ohio State University Press.

Gombrich, E. H. (1966) 'The Renaissance Theory of Art and the Rise of Landscape', in E. H. Gombrich, ed., *Norm and Form: Studies in the Art of the Renaissance*, London: Phaidon, 107–21.

—— (1975) 'Mirror and Map: Theories of Pictorial Presentation', *Philosophical Transactions of the Royal Society of London*, B, 270. 119–49.

Goodey, B. (1971) *Perception of the Environment*, Occasional Paper 17, Birmingham, Eng.: Centre for Urban and Regional Studies, University of Birmingham.

—— (1974a) *Images of Place: Essays on Environmental Perception, Communications, and Education*, Occasional Paper 30, Birmingham, Eng.: Centre for Urban and Regional Studies, University of Birmingham.

Goodey, B. (1974b) *Urban Walks and Town Trails: Origins, Principles and Sources*, Research Memorandum 40, Birmingham, Eng.: Centre for Urban and Regional Studies, University of Birmingham.

—— ed. (1975) *Sensory Walks*, Working Paper 33, Birmingham, Eng.: Centre for Urban and Regional Studies, University of Birmingham.

—— Duffett, A., Gold, J. R., and Spencer, D. (1971) *The City Scene: An Exploration into the Image of Central Birmingham as seen by Area Residents*, Research Memorandum 10, Birmingham, Eng.: Centre for Urban and Regional Studies, University of Birmingham.

Gordon, R. (1972) 'A Very Private World', in P.W. Sheehan, ed., *The Function and Nature of Imagery*, London: Academic Press, 63–80.

Gottmann, J. (1952) 'The Political Partitioning of our World: An Attempt at Analysis', *World Politics*, 4. 512–19.

—— (1973) *The Significance of Territory*, Charlottesville: University Press of Virginia.

—— (1977) 'Geography', in A. Bullock and O. Stallybrass, eds., *The Fontana Dictionary of Modern Thought*, London: Fontana, 260–1.

Goudge, T. A. (1967) 'Evolutionism', *Dictionary of the History of Ideas*, 1, New York: Scribner, 174–89.

Goudie, A. S. (1972) 'Vaughan Cornish: Geographer, with a Bibliography of his Published Works', *Transactions of the Institute of British Geographers*, 55. 1–16.

Gould, P. R. (1963) 'Man against his Environment: A Game Theoretic Framework', *Annals of the Association of American Geographers*, 53, 290–7.

—— (1966) *On Mental Maps*, Discussion Paper 9, Michigan Inter-University Community of Mathematical Geographers, Ann Arbor: Department of Geography, University of Michigan Press.

—— (1969) 'Problems of Space Preferences, Measures and Relationships', *Geographical Analysis*, 1. 34–44.

—— (1973) 'The Black Boxes of Jönköping: Spatial Information and Preference', in R. M. Downs and D. Stea, eds., *Image and Environment*, Chicago: Aldine, 235–45.

—— and Ola, D. (1970) 'The Perception of Residential Desirability in the Western Region of Nigeria', *Environment and Planning*, 2. 73–88.

—— and White, R. R. (1968) 'The Mental Maps of British School Leavers', *Regional Studies*, 2. 161–82.

—— —— (1974) *Mental Maps*, Harmondsworth: Penguin.

Gould, S. J. (1978) 'Sociobiology: The Art of Storytelling', *New Scientist*, 80. 530–3.

Graber, L. H. (1976) *Wilderness as Sacred Space*, Monograph 8, Washington, D. C.: Association of American Geographers.

Granö, O. (1977) 'Maantiede ja tieteen kehityksen Ongelma', *Terra*, 89. 1–9.

Green, D. H. (1974) 'Information, Perception and Decision-Making in the Industrial Relocation Decision', unpublished Ph. D. thesis, University of Reading.

—— (1977) 'Industrialists' Information Levels of Regional Incentives', *Regional Studies*, 11. 7–18.

Greenbie, B. B. (1975) *Design for Diversity*, Amsterdam: Elsevier.

Greer, S. (1973) 'The Family in Suburbia', in L. H. Masotti and J. K. Hadden, eds., *The Urbanisation of the Suburbs*, Beverley Hills: Sage, 149–70.

Gregory, R. L. (1966) *Eye and Brain*, London: World University Library.

—— (1970) *The Intelligent Eye*, New York: McGraw Hill.

Grigg, D. (1967) 'Regions, Models and Classes', in R. J. Chorley and P. Haggett, eds., *Models in Geography*, London: Methuen, 461–501.

Gropius, W. (1956) *The Scope of Modern Architecture*, London: Allen & Unwin.

Gruen, V. (1965) *The Heart of our Cities*, London: Thames & Hudson.

Gulick, J. (1963) 'Images of an Arab City', *Journal of the American Institute of Planners*, 29. 179–97.

Gulliver, F. P. (1908) 'Orientation of Maps', *Journal of Geography*, 7. 55–8.

Gump, P., and Adelberg, B. (1978) 'Urbanism from the Perspective of Ecological Psychologists', *Environment and Behaviour*, 10. 171-92.

Gusfield, J. R. (1977) *Community: A Critical Response*, Oxford: Blackwell.

Gutman, R. (1966) 'Site Planning and Social Behaviour', *Journal of Social Issues*, 22. 103-15.

—— ed. (1972) *People and Buildings*, New York: Basic Books.

Haas, J. E., Kates, R. W., and Bowden, M. J. (1977) *Reconstruction following Disaster*, Cambridge, Mass.: MIT Press.

Hadden, J. K., and Barton, J. J. (1973) 'An Image that will not die: Thoughts on the History of anti-urban Ideology', in L. H. Masotti and J. K. Hadden, eds., *The Urbanisation of the Suburbs*, Beverley Hills: Sage, 79-116.

Hall, A. D. (1969) 'Forest fire Prevention in Canada: An Assessment', *Pulp and Paper Magazine of Canada*, 70. 125-7.

Hall, E. T. (1966) *The Hidden Dimension*, New York: Doubleday.

—— (1972) 'Art, Space and the Human Experience', in G. Kepes, ed., *Arts of the Environment*, London: Aidan Ellis. 52-9.

Hall, P. (1969) 'The Urban Culture and the Suburban Culture', in R. Eells and C. Walton, eds., *Man in the City of the Future*, London: Collier-Macmillan, 99-146.

—— (1974) *Urban and Regional Planning*, Harmondsworth: Penguin.

Hall, R. K. (1976) *Outdoor Recreation Provision in Canada*, Discussion Paper in Geography 2, Headington, Oxford: Geography Section, Oxford Polytechnic.

Hallowell, A. I. (1955) *Culture and Experience*, Philadelphia: University of Pennsylvania Press.

Halprin, L. (1966) *Freeways*, New York: Reinhold.

Hamilton, F. E. I., ed. (1974) *Spatial Perspectives on Industrial Organisation and Decision-Making*, London: Wiley.

Haney, W. G., and Knowles, E. S. (1978) 'Perception of Neighbourhoods by City and Suburban Residents', *Human Ecology*, 6. 201-14.

Hannerz, U. (1969) *Soulside: Inquiries into Ghetto Culture and Community*, New York: Columbia University Press.

Hansen, J. (1977) Personal Communication.

Harding, D. M., and Parker, D. J. (1974) 'Flood Hazard at Shrewsbury, United Kingdom', in G. F. White, ed., *Natural Hazards: Local, National, Global*, New York: Oxford University Press, 43-52.

Hart, R. A., and Moore, G. T. (1973) 'The Development of Spatial Cognition: A Review', in R. M. Downs and D. Stea, eds., *Image and Environment*, Chicago: Aldine, 246-88.

Hartshorne, R. (1939) *The Nature of Geography*, Washington, D. C.: Association of American Geographers.

Harvey, D. W. (1969) *Explanation in Geography*, London: Arnold.

—— (1973) *Social Justice and the City*, London: Arnold.

Hawley, A. (1950) *Human Ecology*, New York: Ronald Press.

Hayden, D. (1976) *Seven American Utopias: The Architecture of Communitarian Socialism, 1770-1975*, Cambridge, Mass.: MIT Press.

Head, H. (1920) *Studies in Neurology*, London: Oxford University Press.

Heathcote, R. L. (1969) 'Drought in Australia: A Problem of Perception', *Geographical Review*, 59. 175-94.

—— (1972) 'The Visions of Australia, 1770-1970', in A. Rapoport, ed., *Australia as Human Setting*, Sydney: Angus & Robertson, 77-99.

Hediger, H. (1961) 'The Evolution of Territorial Behaviour', in S. L. Washburn, ed., *The Social Life of Early Man*, New York: Wenner-Gren Foundation for Anthropological Research, 34-57.

Heilweill, M. (1973) 'Influence of Dormitory Architecture on Resident Behaviour', *Environment and Behaviour*, 5. 377-412.

Heimstra, N. W., and McFarling, L. H. (1974) *Environmental Psychology*, Monterey: Brooks–Cole.

Heinemeyer, W. F. (1967) 'The Urban Core as a Centre of Attraction', in *Urban Core and Inner City*, Leiden: Brill, 82–99.

Heisenberg, W. (1930) *The Physical Principles of Quantum Physics* (trans. C. Eckart and F. C. Hoyt), Chicago: University of Chicago Press.

Held, R., and Richards, W., eds. (1972) *Perception: Mechanisms and Models*, San Francisco: Freeman.

Helson, H. (1964) *Adaptation Level Theory: An Experimental and Systematic Approach to Behaviour*, London: Harper & Row.

Hendee, J. C., Catton, W. R., Marlow, L. D., and Brockmar, C. F. (1968) *Wilderness Users in the Pacific Northwest: Their Characteristics, Values and Management Preferences*, Research Paper PNW 61, Portland, Oreg.: Forest Service, United States Department of Agriculture.

Henle, M., ed. (1961) *Documents of Gestalt Psychology*, Berkeley: University of California Press.

Herbert, D. T. (1972) *Urban Geography: A Social Perspective*, Newton Abbot: David & Charles.

—— (1975) 'Urban Neighbourhoods and Social Geographical Research', in A. D. M. Phillips and B. J. Turton, eds., *Environment, Man and Economic Change*, London: Longman, 459–78.

Herrnstein, R. J., and Boring, E. G. (1965) *A Sourcebook in the History of Psychology*, Cambridge, Mass.: Harvard University Press.

Hesselgren, S. (1975) *Man's Perception of Man-Made Environment*, Stroudsburg, Pa.: Dowden, Hutchinson, & Ross.

Hester, R. T. (1975) *Neighbourhood Space*, Stroudsburg, Pa.: Dowden, Hutchinson, & Ross.

Hewitt, K. and Burton, I. (1971) *The Hazardousness of a Place: A Regional Ecology of Damaging Events*, Working Paper 6, Toronto: Natural Hazard Research Unit, Department of Geography, University of Toronto.

Himmelweit, H. T., Oppenheim, A. N., and Vince, P. (1958) *Television and the Child*, London: Oxford University Press.

Hinshaw, M., and Allott, K. (1972) 'Environmental Preferences of Future Housing Consumers', *Journal of the American Institute of Planners*, 38. 102–7.

Hirsh, S. (1955) *The Fears Men Live By*, New York: Harper.

Hollis, M., and Nell, E. J. (1975) *Rational Economic Man: A Philosophical Critique of Neo-Classical Economics*, London: Cambridge University Press.

Honikman, B., ed. (1971) *Architectural Psychology '70*, London: RIBA and Kingston Polytechnic.

—— (1975) *Responding to Social Change*, Stroudsburg, Pa: Dowden, Hutchinson & Ross.

Honour, H. (1976) *The New Golden Land: European Images of America from the Discoveries to the Present Time*, Harmondsworth: Allen Lane.

Hoover, E. M. (1937) *Location Theory and the Shoe and Leather Industries*, Cambridge, Mass: Harvard University Press.

Horrell, M., ed. (1965) *A Survey of Race Relations in South Africa*, annual, Johannesburg: South African Institute of Race Relations.

Horton, F., and Reynolds, D. R. (1969) 'An Investigation of Individual Action Spaces: A Progress Report, *Proceedings of the Association of American Geographers*, 1. 70–5.

—— —— (1971) 'Effects of Urban Spatial Structure on Individual Behaviour', *Economic Geography*, 47. 36–48.

Horvath, R. J. (1974) 'Machine Space', *Geographical Review*, 64. 167–88.

Houghton-Evans, W. (1977) 'Schemata in British New Town Planning', paper presented to the First International Conference on History of Planning, Bedford College, University of London.

Howard, H. E. (1920) *Territory in Bird Life*, London: Murray.

Howe, G. F. (1931) 'A Study of Children's Knowledge of Directions', *Journal of Geography*, 31. 207-10.

Huckle, J. (1977) 'Geography and Values in Higher Education, Part 1', *Journal of Geography in Higher Education*, 1 (2). 13-19.

Hudson, R. (1974) 'Images of the Retailing Environment: An Example of the Use of Repertory Grid Methodology', *Environment and Behaviour*, 6. 470-94.

—— (1976) *Environmental Images, Spatial Choice and Consumer Behaviour*, Occasional Publication (New Series) 9, Durham: Department of Geography, University of Durham.

Humboldt, A. von (1849) *Cosmos: A Sketch of a Physical Description of the Universe*, (trans. E. C. Otte), London: Bohn.

Huntington, E. (1915) *Civilisation and Climate*, New Haven: Yale University Press.

—— (1945) *Mainsprings of Civilisation*, New York: Wiley.

Hurst, M. E. E. (1974) *A Geography of Economic Behaviour*, London: Prentice Hall International.

Huxley, J. (1934) 'A Natural Experiment on the Territorial Instinct', *British Birds*, 27. 270-7.

Insel, P., and Lindgren, H. (1978) *Too Close for Comfort: The Psychology of Crowding Behaviour*, Englewood Cliffs, N. J.: Prentice Hall.

Insel, P., and Moos, R. H. (1974) 'Psychological Experiments: Expanding the Scope of Human Ecology', *American Psychologist*, 29. 179-88.

Isard, W. (1956) *Location and Space Economy*, Cambridge, Mass: MIT Press.

—— (1960) *Methods of Regional Analysis*, Cambridge, Mass.: MIT Press.

Islam, M. A. (1974) 'Tropical Cyclones: Coastal Bangladesh', in G. F. White, ed., *Natural Hazards: Local, National, Global*, New York: Oxford University Press, 19-25.

Ittelson, W. H. (1976) 'Environment Perception and Contemporary Perceptual Theory', in H. M. Proshansky, W. H. Ittelson, and L. G. Rivlin, eds., *Environmental Psychology*, Second Edition, New York: Holt, Rinehart, & Winston, 141-54.

—— Proshansky, H. M., Rivlin, L. G., and Winkel, G. H. (1974) *An Introduction to Environmental Psychology*, New York: Holt, Rinehart, & Winston.

Jackson, A. (1976) *A Place called Home: A History of Low-Cost Housing in Manhattan*, Cambridge, Mass.: MIT Press.

Jackson, E. L., and Mukerjee, T. (1974) 'Human Adjustment to the Earthquake Hazard of San Francisco, California', in G. F. White, ed., *Natural Hazards: Local, National, Global*, New York: Oxford University Press, 160-6.

Jackson, J. B. (1964) 'The Meanings of Landscape', *Kulturgeografie*, 88. 47-51.

Jacobs, J. (1962) *The Death and Life of Great American Cities*, New York: Random House.

Jacobs, P. (1975) 'The Landscape Image: Current Approaches to the Visual Analysis of the Landscape', *Town Planning Review*, 46. 127-50.

Jahoda, M. (1977) *Freud and the Dilemmas of Psychology*, London: Hogarth.

James, P. E. (1973) *All Possible Worlds*, Indianapolis: Bobbs-Merrill.

Janowitz, M. (1952) *The Community Press in an Urban Setting*, Chicago: University of Chicago Press.

—— (1968) 'Communications, Mass', in D. L. Sills, ed., *International Encyclopedia of the Social Sciences*, 3, London: Macmillan, 41-53.

Jeans, D. N. (1974) 'Changing Formulations of the Man–Environment Relationship in Anglo-American Geography', *Journal of Geography*, 73 (3). 36-40.

Jencks, C. (1969) 'Semiology and Architecture', in C. Jencks and G. Baird, eds., *Meaning in Architecture*, London: Barrie & Rockliff, 11-26.

Jensen, A. R. (1968) 'Social Class, Race and Genetics: Implications for Education', *American Educational Research Journal*, 5. 1-42.

Jensen, R. A. (1966) *High Density Living*, London: Leonard Hill.

Johns, E. (1960) 'Langstone Rock: An Experiment in the Art of Landscape Description', *Geography*, 45. 176–82.

—— (1965) *British Townscapes*, London: Arnold.

—— (1969) 'Symmetry and Asymmetry in the Urban Scene', *Area*, 2. 48–57.

Johnston, R. J. (1971a) 'Mental Maps of the City: Suburban Preferences', *Environment and Planning*, 3. 63–71.

—— (1971b) *Urban Residential Patterns*, London: Bell.

—— (1972) 'Continually changing Human Geography: A Review of some recent Literature', *New Zealand Geographer*, 28. 78–96.

Jones, E. (1956) 'Cause and Effect in Human Geography', *Annals of the Association of American Geographers*, 46. 369–77.

Jones, H. M. (1946) 'The Colonial Impulse: An Analysis of the Promotion Literature of Colonisation', *Proceedings of the American Philosophical Society*, 90. 131–61.

Jones, M. H. (1972) 'Pain Thresholds for Smog Components', in J. F. Wohlwill and D. H. Carson, eds., *Environment and the Social Sciences*, Washington, D. C.: American Psychological Association, 61–5.

Jones, R. C., and Zannaras, G. (1978) 'The Role of Awareness of Space in Urban Residential Preferences: A Case Study of Venezuelan Youth', *Annals of Regional Science*, 12. 36–52.

Jonge, D. de (1962) 'Images of Urban Areas: Their Structure and Psychological Foundations', *Journal of the American Institute of Planners*, 28. 266–76.

Jung, C. G., ed. (1964) *Man and his Symbols*, London: Aldous.

Kain, J. F. (1968) 'Urban Travel Behaviour', in L. F. Schnore, ed., *Social Science and the City*, New York: Praeger, 161–92.

Kaluger, G., and Kaluger, M. F. (1974) *Human Development: The Span of Life* 2nd edn., St. Louis, Mo.: C. V. Mosby Company.

Kaplan, S. (1976) 'Adaptation, Structure and Knowledge', in G. T. Moore and R. G. Golledge, eds., *Environmental Knowing*, Stroudsburg, Pa.: Dowden, Hutchinson, & Ross, 32–45.

Kasl, S. V., and Harburg, E. (1972) 'Perceptions of the Neighbourhood and the Desire to Move Out', *Journal of the American Institute of Planners*, 38. 318–24.

Kasperson, R. E., and Minghi, J. V., eds. (1970) *The Structure of Political Geography*, London: University of London Press.

Kates, R. W. (1962) *Hazard and Choice Perception in Flood Plain Management*, Research Paper 78, Chicago: Department of Geography, University of Chicago.

—— (1965) *Industrial Flood Losses: Damage Estimation in the Lehigh Valley*, Research Paper 98, Chicago: Department of Geography, University of Chicago.

—— (1967) 'The Perception of Storm Hazard on the Shores of Megalopolis', in D. Lowenthal, ed., *Environmental Perception and Behaviour*, Research Paper 109, Chicago: Department of Geography, University of Chicago.

—— (1970) 'Human Perception of the Environment', *International Social Science Journal*, 22. 648–60.

—— (1971) 'Natural Hazard in Human Ecological Perspectives: Hypotheses and Models', *Economic Geography*, 47. 438–51.

—— (1975) *Natural Disasters and Development*, paper presented at the Wingspread Conference, Racine, Wis., October.

—— Haas, J. E., Amaral, O. J., Olson, R. A., Ramos, R., and Olson, R. (1973) 'Human Impact of the Managua Earthquake', *Science*, 182. 981–90.

—— and Katz, C. (1977) 'The Hydrological Cycle and the Wisdom of the Child', *Geographical Review*, 67. 51–62.

Katz, D., and Kahn, R. L. (1966) *The Social Psychology of Organisations*, New York: Wiley.

Keats, J. (1956) *The Crack in the Picture Window*, Boston, Mass.

Kelly, G. A. (1955) *The Psychology of Personal Constructs*, New York: Norton.

Kerr, M. (1958) *The People of Ship Street*, New York: Humanities Press.

Kilbrandon Report, The (1973) *Devolution and other Aspects of Government: An Attitudes Survey*, presented as Research Paper 7, the Report of the Commission on the Constitution, London: HMSO.

Kirk, W. (1952) 'Historical Geography and the Concept of the Behavioural Environment', *Indian Geographical Journal*, Jubilee Edition, 152–60.

—— (1963) 'Problems of Geography', *Geography*, 48. 357–71.

Kirkby, A. V. (1973) *Some Perspectives on Environmental Hazard Research*, Bristol: Department of Psychology, University of Bristol.

—— (1974) 'Individual and Community Response to Rainfall Variability in Oaxaca, Mexico', in G. F. White, ed., *Natural Hazards: Local, National, Global*, New York: Oxford University Press, 119–28.

Klapper, J. T. (1960) *The Effects of Mass Communication*, Glencoe, Ill.: Free Press.

Klein, H. J. (1967) 'The Delimitation of the Town Centre in the Image of its Citizens: A Report of Methods and Preliminary Results of a Town-Sociological Study', in *Urban Core and Inner City*, Leiden: Brill 286–306.

Kluckhohn, F. R. (1959) 'Dominant and Variant Value Orientations', in C. Kluckhohn, H. A. Murray, and D. M. Schneider, eds., *Personality in Nature, Culture and Society*, New York: Knopf, 342–57.

Knapp, P. H. (1948) 'Emotional Aspects of Hearing Loss', *Psychosomatic Medicine*, 10. 203–22.

Knewstub, N. (1977) 'Teenager told Police he drowned Boy', *Guardian*, 28 January, 4.

Knight, C. G. (1971) 'Ethnogeography and Change', *Journal of Geography*, 70. 47–51.

Knight, F. H. (1956) *On the History and Method of Economics*, Chicago: University of Chicago Press.

Koestler, A. (1975) *The Ghost in the Machine*, London: Picador.

Koffka, K. (1935) *Principles of Gestalt Psychology*, New York: Harcourt, Brace.

Kramer, J., and Leventman, S. (1961) *Children of the Gilded Ghetto*, New Haven: Yale University Press.

Krantz, D. L. (1969) *Schools of Psychology: A Symposium*, New York: Meredith.

Krech, D., Crutchfield, R. S., and Livson, N. (1974) *Elements of Psychology*, 3rd Edition, New York: Knopf.

Kuhn, T. S. (1962) *The Structure of Scientific Revolutions*, Chicago: University of Chicago Press.

Kuper, L., ed. (1953) *Living in Towns*, London: Cresset Press.

Ladd, F. L. (1970) 'Black Youths view their Environment', *Environment and Behaviour*, 2. 74–99.

—— (1976) 'Black Perspectives on American Cities', in J. W. Watson and T. O'Riordan, eds., *The American Environment*, London: Wiley, 132–43.

Lamy, B. (1967) 'The Use of the Inner City of Paris and Social Stratification', in *Urban Core and Inner City*, Leiden: Brill, 356–67.

Lang, J., Burnette, C., Moleski, W., and Vachon, D., eds.(1974) *Designing for Human Behaviour: Architecture and the Behavioural Sciences*, Stroudsburg, Pa.: Dowden, Hutchinson, & Ross.

Lang, S. (1952) 'The Ideal City from Plato to Howard', *Architectural Review*, 112. 91–101.

Langer, S. K. (1953) *Feeling and Form*, London: Routledge & Kegan Paul.

Lansing, J. B., and Hendricks, G. (1967) *Living Patterns and Attitudes in the Detroit Region*, Detroit: Southeast Michigan Council of Governments.

Lapiere, R. T. (1934) 'Attitudes vs. Actions', *Social Forces*, 13. 230–37.

Lasswell, H. (1966) 'The Structure and Function of Communication', in B. Berelson and M. Janowitz, eds., *Reader in Public Opinion and Communication*, New York: Free Press, 178–90.

Latané, B., and Darley, J. (1970) *The Unresponsive Bystander*, New York: Appleton, Century, Croft.

Lawson, B. R., and Walters, D. (1974) 'The Effects of a New Motorway on an Established Residential Area', in D. V. Canter and T. R. Lee, eds., *Psychology and the Built Environment*, London: Architectural Press, 132–8.

Lazarsfeld, P. F., Berelson, B., and Gaudet, H. (1944) *The People's Choice: How the Voter makes up his Mind in a Presidential Campaign*, New York: Duell, Sloan, & Pearce.

Lee, L. (1976) 'A Voyage of Imagination', Radio Broadcast Script, BBC Radio 4, 1 January.

Lee, S. A. (1975) 'The Local Area in the Urban Context', paper presented to the Architectural Psychology Conference, University of Sheffield, July.

Lee, T. R. (1954) 'A Study of Urban Neighbourhood', unpublished Ph.D. thesis, University of Cambridge.

—— (1962) ' "Brennan's Law" of Shopping Behaviour', *Psychological Reports*, 11, 662.

—— (1968) 'Urban Neighbourhood as a Socio-spatial Schema', *Human Relations*, 21. 241–68.

—— (1970) 'Perceived Distance as a Function of Direction in the City', *Environment and Behaviour*, 2. 40–51.

—— (1971) 'Psychology and Architectural Determinism' (essay in three parts), *Architects' Journal*, 154. 253–61, 475–83, and 651–9.

—— (1976) *Psychology and the Environment*, London: Methuen.

Leff, H. L. (forthcoming) *Experience, Environment and Human Potentials*, London: Oxford University Press.

Lefler, H. T. (1967) 'Promotional Literature of the Southern Colonies', *Jounal of Southern History*, 33. 3–25.

Lefrançois, G. R. (1974) *Of Humans: Introductory Psychology by Kongor*, Monterey: Brooks–Cole.

Leibenstein, H. (1976) *Beyond Economic Man*, Cambridge, Mass.: Harvard University Press.

Leighley, J., ed. (1969) *Land and Life: A Selection from the Writings of Carl Ortwin Sauer*, Berkeley: University of California Press.

Lentnek, B., Lieber, S. R., and Sheskin, I. (1975) 'Consumer Behaviour in Different Areas', *Annals of the Association of American Geographers*, 65. 538–45.

Lenz-Romeiss, F. (1973) *The City: Home Town or New Town?*, London: Pall Mall.

Lethbridge, T. C. (1957) *Gogmagog*, London: Routledge & Kegan Paul.

Levin, H. (1969) *The Myth of the Golden Age in the Renaissance*, London: Faber & Faber.

Lewin, K. (1951) *Field Theory in Social Science*, New York: Harper & Row.

Lewis, O. (1968) *La Vida*, New York: Vintage Books.

Lewthwaite, G. R. (1966) 'Environmentalism and Determinism: A Search for Clarification', *Annals of the Association of American Geographers*, 56. 1–23.

Ley, D. (1977) 'Social Geography and the Taken-for-Granted World', *Transactions of the Institute of British Geographers (New Series)*, 2. 498–512.

—— and Cybriwsky, R. (1974) 'Urban Graffiti as Territorial Markers', *Annals of the Association of American Geographers*, 64. 491–505.

Ley, D., and Samuels, M. S., eds. (1978) *Humanistic Geography*, London: Croom Helm.

Leyhausen, P. (1971) 'Dominance and Territoriality as Complemented in Mammalian Social Structure', in A. H. Esser, ed., *Behaviour and Environment: The Use of Space by Animals and Men*, London: Plenum, 22–33.

Lime, D. W. (1972) 'Behavioural Research in Outdoor Recreation Management: An Example of how Visitors select Campgrounds', in J. H. Wohlwill and D. H. Carson, eds., *Environment and the Social Sciences*, Washington, D. C.: American Psychological Association, 198–206.

Linton, D. L. (1968) 'The Assessment of Scenery as a Natural Resource', *Scottish Geographical Magazine*, 84. 219–38.

Lipman, A. (1974) 'The Architectural Belief System and Social Behaviour', in J. Lang, C. Burnette, W. Moleski, and D. Vachon, eds., *Designing for Human Behaviour: Architecture and the Behavioural Sciences*, Stroudsburg, Pa: Dowden, Hutchinson, & Ross, 23–30.

—— and Russell-Lacy, S. (1974) 'Some Social Psychological Correlates of New Town Residential Location', in D. V. Canter and T. R. Lee, eds., *Psychology and the Built Environment*, London: Architectural Press, 139–47.

Lipsey, R. G. (1975) *An Introduction to Positive Economics*, 4th edition, London: Weidenfeld & Nicolson.

Littlejohn, J. (1963) 'Temne Space', *Anthropology Quarterly*, 36. 1–17.

Lloyd, P. E., and Dicken, P. (1972) *Location in Space*, London: Harper & Row.

Lockwood, M. (1973) 'The Experimental Utopia in America', in F. E. Manuel, ed., *Utopias and Utopian Thought*, London: Souvenir Press, 183–200.

Lord, F. E. (1941) 'A Study of Spatial Orientation in Children', *Journal of Educational Research*, 34. 481–505.

Lorenz, K. (1952) *King Solomon's Ring*, London: Methuen.

—— (1966) *On Aggression*, New York: Harcourt.

—— (1970) *Studies in Animal and Human Behaviour*, 1 (trans. R. Martin), Cambridge, Mass: Harvard University Press.

—— and Leyhausen, P. (1973) *Motivation of Human and Animal Behaviour*, New York: Van Nostrand Reinhold.

Lösch, A. (1940) *Die räumliche Ordung der Wirtschaft* (trans. W. H. Woglom, 1954, as *The Economics of Location*, New Haven: Yale University Press).

Lowenthal, D. (1961) 'Geography, Experience and Imagination: Towards a Geographical Epistemology', *Annals of the Association of American Geographers*, 51. 241–60.

—— (1964) 'The American Scene', *Geographical Review*, 58. 61–88.

—— ed. (1967) *Environmental Perception and Behaviour*, Research Paper 109, Chicago: Department of Geography, University of Chicago.

—— (1975) 'Past time, Present place: Landscape and Memory', *Geographical Review*, 65. 1–36.

—— (1977) 'The Bicentennial Landscape: A Mirror held up to the Past', *Geographical Review*, 67. 253–67.

—— and Bowden, M. J., eds. (1976) *Geographies of the Mind*, London: Oxford University Press.

—— and Prince, H. C. (1965) 'English Landscape Tastes', *Geographical Review*, 55. 186–222.

—— and Riel, M. (1972) *Milieu and Observer Differences in Environmental Associations*, Publications on Environmental Perception 7, New York: American Geographical Society.

Lowrey, R. A. (1973) 'A Method for Analysing Distance Concepts of Urban Residents', in R. M. Downs and D. Stea, eds., *Image and Environment*, Chicago: Aldine, 338–60.

Lucas, R. C. (1970) 'User Concepts of Wilderness and their Implications for Resource Management', in H. M. Proshansky, W. H. Ittelson, and L. G. Rivlin, eds., *Environmental Psychology*, First Edition, New York: Holt, Rinehart, & Winston, 297–303.

Lyman, S. M., and Scott, M. B. (1967) 'Territoriality: A Neglected Sociological Dimension', *Social Problems*, 15. 236–49.

Lynch, K. (1960) *The Image of the City*, Cambridge, Mass.: MIT Press.

—— (1972a) 'The Openness of Open Space', in G. Kepes, ed., *Arts of the Environment*, London: Aidan Ellis, 108–24.

—— (1972b) *What Time is this Place?*, Cambridge, Mass.: MIT Press.

—— (1976) *Managing the Sense of a Region*, Cambridge, Mass.: MIT Press.

—— ed. (1977) *Growing up in Cities*, Cambridge, Mass.: MIT Press.

—— and Banerjee, T. (1976) 'Growing up in Cities', *New Society*, 37. 281–4.

—— and Rivkin, M. (1959) 'A Walk around the Block', *Landscape*, 8. 24–34.

McBurney, D. H., and Collings, V. B. (1977) *An Introduction to Sensation/Perception*, Englewood Cliffs, N. J.: Prentice Hall.

McClenahan, B. (1929) *The Changing Urban Neighbourhood*, Los Angeles: University of Southern California.

—— (1946) 'The Communality: The Urban Substitute for the Traditional Community', *Sociology and Social Research*, 30. 264–74.

McCord, C. P., Teal, E. E., and Witheridge, W. N. (1938) 'Noise and its Effect on Human Beings: Noise Control as a By-product of Air Conditioning', *Journal of the American Medical Association*, 110, 1553–60.

McCrone, G. (1969) *Regional Policy in Britain*, London: Allen & Unwin.

McDougall, W. (1908) *An Introduction to Social Psychology*, London: Methuen.

MacLean, P. D. (1958) 'Contrasting Functions of Limbic and Neocortical Systems of the Brain and their Relevance to Psychophysiological Aspects of Medicine', *American Journal of Medicine*, 25, 611–26.

—— (1975) 'On the Evolution of three Mentalities', *Man–Environment Systems*, 5. 213–24.

McLuhan, H. M., and Fiore, Q. (1967) *The Medium is the Massage*, London: Allen Lane.

McQuail, D., ed. (1972) *Sociology of Mass Communications*, Harmondsworth: Penguin.

Maier, E. (1975) 'Torah as Moveable Territory', *Annals of the Association of American Geographers*, 65. 18–23.

Maine, H. (1861) *Ancient Law*, London: Murray.

Mannheim, K. (1960) *Ideology and Utopia*, London: Routledge & Kegan Paul.

Manuel, F. E. (1973) 'Toward a Psychological History of Utopias', in F. E. Manuel, ed. *Utopias and Utopian Thought*, London: Souvenir Press, 69–98.

Marc, O. (1977) *Psychology of the House*, London: Thames & Hudson.

Marchand, B. (1972) 'Information Theory and Geography', *Geographical Analysis*, 4. 234–58.

Martin, A. F. (1951) 'The Necessity for Determinism: A Metaphysical Problem confronting Geographers', *Transactions of the Institute of British Geographers*, 17. 1–11.

Maruyama, M. (1976) 'Design Principles for Extra-Terrestial Communities', *Futures*, 8. 104–21.

Marx, L. (1964) *The Machine in the Garden: Technology and the Pastoral Ideal in America*, London: Oxford University Press.

—— (1968) 'Pastoral Ideals and City Troubles', in *The Quality of Man's Environment: Voice of America Forum Lectures*, New York: Smithsonian Institute, 119–44.

Marx, M. H., and Hillix, W. A. (1973) *Systems and Theories in Psychology*, Second Edition, New York: McGraw Hill.

Maslow, A. H. (1954) *Motivation and Personality*, New York: Harper.

Masotti, L. H., and Hadden, J. K., eds. (1973) *The Urbanisation of the Suburbs*, Beverley Hills: Sage.

Massey, D. (1974) *Towards a Critique of Industrial Location Theory*, Research Paper 5, London: Centre for Environmental Studies.

Maurer, R., and Baxter, J. C. (1972) 'Images of the Neighbourhood and City among Black-, Anglo- and Mexican-American Children', *Environment and Behaviour*, 4. 351–88.

Mawby, R. I. (1977) 'Defensible Space: A Theoretical and Empirical Appraisal', *Urban Studies*, 14. 169–79.

Mawson, J. (1975) 'Organisation Theory, Location Theory and British Regional Policy', unpublished M. Phil. thesis, Department of Town Planning, University College London.

Mead, M. (1968) 'The Crucial Role of the Small City in meeting the Urban Crisis', in R. Eells and C. Walton, eds., *Man in the City of the Future*, London: Collier-Macmillan, 29–57.

Medici, L. de (1939) *Opere*, A Simioni, ed., Bari: Larenza.

Mehrabian, A. (1976) *Public Places and Private Spaces*, New York: Basic Books.

—— and Russell, J. A. (1974) *An Approach to Environmental Psychology*,

Cambridge, Mass.: MIT Press.

Mercer, D. C. (1975) 'Perception in Outdoor Recreation', in P. Lavery, ed., *Recreational Geography*, Newton Abbot, Devon: David & Charles, 50–69.

—— and Powell, J. M. (1972) *Phenomenology and Related Non-Positivistic Viewpoints in the Social Sciences*, Monash Publications in Geography 1, Melbourne: University of Monash.

Mercer, J. C. (1976) *Living in Cities*, Harmondsworth: Penguin.

Merrens, H. R. (1969) 'The Physical Environment in Early America: Images and Image Makers in Colonial South Carolina', *Geographical Review*, 59. 530–56.

Merton, R. K. (1957) *Social Theory and Social Structure*, New York: Free Press.

Meyer, G. (1977) 'Distance Perception of Consumers in Shopping Streets', *Tijdschrift voor Economische en Sociale Geografie*, 68. 355–61.

Michelson, W. (1970) *Man and his Urban Environment: A Sociological Approach*, Reading, Mass.: Addison–Wesley.

—— (1973) *Residential Mobility as a Deficit Compensating Process*, paper presented to meeting of the Canadian Sociology and Anthropology Association, Kingston, Ontario, May.

—— ed. (1975) *Behavioural Research Methods in Environmental Design*, Stroudsburg, Pa.: Dowden, Hutchinson & Ross.

—— (1977) *Environmental Choice, Human Behaviour and Residential Satisfactions*, New York: Oxford University Press.

Mikesell, M. W. (1968) 'Landscape', in D. R. Sills, ed., *International Encyclopedia of the Social Sciences*, 8, London: Macmillan, 575–80.

Milgram, S. (1970) 'The Experience of Living in Cities', *Science*, 167. 1461–8.

—— (1977) *The Individual in a Social World*, London: Addison–Wesley.

—— and Hollander, P. (1964) 'Paralysed Witnesses: The Murder they heard', *Nation*, 602–4.

Milgram, S., and Jodelet, D. (1976) 'Psychological Maps of Paris', in H. M. Proshansky, W. H. Ittelson, and L. G. Rivlin, eds., *Environmental Psychology*, 2nd edition, New York: Holt, Rinehart, & Winston, 104–24.

Miller, G. A. (1962) *Psychology: The Science of Mental Life*, Harmondsworth: Penguin.

Miller, J. M. (1961) 'Residential Density: Relating People to Space rather than to Ground Area', *Journal of the American Institute of Planners*, 27. 77–8.

Mills, C. W. (1970) *The Sociological Imagination*, Harmondsworth,: Penguin.

Misiak, H., and Sexton, V. S. (1973) *Phenomenological, Existential and Humanistic Psychologies*, New York: Grune & Stratton.

Mitchell, J. K. (1974) *Community Response to Coastal Erosion: Individual and Collective Adjustments to Hazard on the Atlantic Shore*, Research Paper 156, Chicago: University of Chicago Press.

—— (1976) 'Adjustment to new Physical Environments beyond the Metropolitan Fringe, *Geographical Review*, 66. 59–72.

Mitchell, R. E. (1975) 'Ethnographic and Historical Perspectives on Relationships between Physical and Socio-spatial Environments', *Sociological Symposium*, 14. 25–42.

Mogey, J. M. (1956) *Family and Neighbourhood*, London: Oxford University Press.

Montefiore, A. C., and Williams, W. W. (1955) 'Determinism and Possibilism', *Geographical Studies*, 2. 1–11.

Moore, G. T. (1976) 'Theory and Research on the Development of Environmental Knowing', in G. T. Moore and R. G. Golledge, eds., *Environmental Knowing*, Stroudsburg, Pa.: Dowden, Hutchinson, & Ross, 138–64.

—— (1977) 'Review', *Journal of the American Institute of Planners*, 43. 192–94.

—— and Golledge, R. G. (1976a) 'Environmental Knowing: Concepts and Theories', in G. T. Moore and R. G. Golledge, eds., *Environmental Knowing*, Stroudsburg, Pa.: Dowden, Hutchinson, & Ross, 3-30.

—— eds. (1976b) *Environmental Knowing*, Stroudsburg, Pa. Dowden, Hutchinson, & Ross.

Moos, R. H. (1976) *The Human Context*, London: Wiley.

Morris, D. (1967) *The Naked Ape*, London: Jonathan Cape.

Morris, R. N. (1968) *Urban Sociology*, London: Allen & Unwin.

Mumford, L. (1963) *The City as History*, Harmondsworth: Penguin.

Mundle, C. W. K. (1971) *Perception: Facts and Theories*, London: Oxford University Press.

Murdock, B. B. (1973) 'Learning and Memory', in P. Mussen and M. R. Rosenzweig, eds., *Psychology*, Lexington: Heath, 447-532.

Murphy, P. E., and Rosenblood, L. (1974) 'Tourism: An Exercise in Spatial Search', *Canadian Geographer*, 18. 201-10.

Murton, B. J. (1972) 'Some Aspects of a Cognitive-Behavioural Approach to Environment: A Review', *New Zealand Journal of Geography*, 53. 1-8.

—— and Shimabukuro, S. (1974) 'Human Adjustment to Volcanic Hazard in Puna District, Hawaii', in G. F. White, ed., *Natural Hazards: Local, National, Global*, New York: Oxford University Press, 151-9.

Musgrove, F. (1963) *The Migratory Elite*, London: Heinemann.

Mutch, R. N. (1970) 'Wildland Fires and Ecosystems: A Hypothesis', *Ecology*, 51. 1046-51.

Myers, J. H., and Reynolds, W. H. (1967) *Consumer Behaviour and Marketing Management*, Boston: Houghton Mifflin.

Nairn, I. (1965) *The American Landscape*, New York: Random House.

Nakano, T. (1974) 'Natural Hazards: Report from Japan', in G. F. White, ed., *Natural Hazards: Local, National, Global*, London: Oxford University Press, 231-43.

Neel, A. F. (1971) *Theories of Psychology*, London: University of London Press.

Neisser, U. (1976) *Cognition and Reality*, San Francisco: Freeman.

Nelson, R. L. (1958) *The Selection of Retail Locations*, New York: Dodge.

Nelson, S. D. (1974) 'Nature–Nurture Revisited I: A Review of the Biological Bases of Conflict', *Journal of Conflict Resolution*, 18. 285-335.

Newell, A., and Simon, H. A. (1972) *Human Problem Solving*, Englewood Cliffs, N. J.: Prentice Hall.

Newman, O. (1969) *Physical Parameters of Defensible Space: Past Experiences and Hypotheses*, New York: Columbia University Press.

—— (1972) *Defensible Space*, New York: Macmillan and the Architectural Press Ltd.

Newton, P. W. (1977) 'Choice of Residential Location in an Urban Environment', *Australian Geographical Studies*, 15. 3-21.

Nichols, T. C. (1974) 'Global Summary of Human Response to Natural Hazards: Earthquakes', in G. F. White, ed., *Natural Hazards: Local, National, Global*, New York: Oxford University Press, 274-84.

Nilles, J. M., Carlson, F. R., Gray, P., and Hanneman, G. J. (1976) *The Telecommunications-Transportation Tradeoff*, New York: Wiley.

Noble, J. (1963) 'The How and Why of Behaviour: Social Psychology for the Architect', *Architects' Journal*, 137. 531-46.

Norberg-Schulz, C. (1971) *Existence, Space and Architecture*, London: Studio Vista.

North, D. J. (1974) 'The Process of Locational Change in different Manufacturing Organisations', in F. E. I. Hamilton, ed., *Spatial Perspectives on Industrial Organisation and Decision-Making*, London: Wiley, 213-44.

Nuttgens, P. (1972) *The Landscape of Ideas*, London: Faber & Faber.

Ogden, C. K. and Richards, I. (1949) *The Meaning of Meaning*, London: Routledge.

O'Keefe, P. (1975) *African Drought: A Review*, Occasional Paper 8, Bradford, York.: Disaster Research Unit, University of Bradford.

O'Keefe, P., and Halverston, B. (forthcoming) 'The MacNamara Medicine Show: The Use of Theatre in the Classroom', *Journal of Geography in Higher Education*, 3(1), 29-37.

Oliver, J. (1975) 'The Significance of Natural Hazards in a Developing Area: A Case Study from North Queensland', *Geography*, 60. 99-110.

Olson, S. (1961) 'The Spiritual Aspects of Wilderness', in D. Brower, ed., *Wilderness: America's Living Heritage*, San Francisco: Freeman, 16–25.

Olsson, G. (1965) *Distance and Human Interaction*, Bibliography Series 2, Philadelphia: Regional Science Research Institute.

Onibokun, A. G. (1974) 'Evaluating Consumers' Satisfaction with Housing', *Journal of the American Institute of Planners*, 40. 189–200.

—— (1976) 'Social System Correlates of Residential Satisfaction', *Environment and Behaviour*, 8. 323–44.

O'Riordan, T. (1973) 'Some Reflections on Environmental Attitudes and Environmental Behaviour', *Area*, 5. 17–19.

—— (1976a) 'Black Culture, Violence and the American City', in J. W. Watson and T. O'Riordan, eds. *The American Environment*, London: Wiley, 109–13.

—— (1976b) *Environmentalism*, London: Pion.

Orleans, P. (1973) 'Differential Cognition of Urban Residents: Effects of Social Scale on Mapping', in R. M. Downs and D. Stea, eds., *Image and Environment*, Chicago: Aldine, 115–30.

Orme, J. E. (1969) *Time, Experience and Behaviour*, London: Iliffe.

ORRRC (Outdoor Recreation Resources Review Commission) (1962) *Outdoor Recreation for America*, Washington, D. C.: United States Government Printing Office.

Osgood, C. E., Suci, G. J., and Tannenbaum, P. H. (1957) *The Measurement of Meaning*, Urbana: University of Illinois Press.

Palmer, C., Robinson, M., and Thomas, R. (1977) 'The Countryside Image: An Investigation of Structure and Meaning', *Environment and Planning*, A9. 739–49.

Panofsky, E. (1970) *Meaning in the Visual Arts*, Harmondsworth: Penguin.

Papalia, D. E., and Olds, S. W. (1975) *A Child's World: Infancy through Adolescence*, New York: McGraw Hill.

Park, R. E. (1916) 'The City: Suggestions for the Investigation of Human Behaviour in the Urban Environment', *American Journal of Sociology*, 20. 577–612.

—— Burgess, E. W., and Mackenzie, R. D. (1925) *The City*, Chicago: University of Chicago Press.

Parker, A. J. (1976) *Consumer Behaviour, Motivation and Perception: A Study of Dublin*, Research Report, Dublin, Eire: Department of Geography, University College, Dublin.

Parkes, J. G. M., and Day, J. C. (1975) 'The Hazard of Sensitive Clays: A Case Study of the Ottawa Hull Area', *Geographical Review*, 65. 198–213.

Parr, A. E. (1964) 'Environmental Design and Psychology', *Landscape*, 14. 15–18.

Paterson, J. (1976) 'The Poet and the Metropolis', in J. W. Watson and T. O'Riordan, eds. *The American Environment*, London: Wiley, 93–108.

Patmore, J. A. (1971) *Land and Leisure*, Harmondsworth: Penguin.

Patrick, J. (1973) *A Glasgow Gang Observed*, London: Eyre Methuen.

Pawley, M. (1971) *Architecture versus Housing*, London: Studio Vista.

Pearson, N. (1972) 'Planning a Social Unit', in G. Bell and J. Tyrwhitt, eds., *Human Identity in the Urban Environment*, Harmondsworth: Penguin, 252–61.

Penning-Rowsell, E. C. (1974) 'Landscape Evaluation for Development Plans', *Journal of the Royal Town Planning Institute*, 60. 930–4.

—— (1975) 'Constraints on the Application of Landscape Evaluation', *Transactions of the Institute of British Geographers*, 66. 149–55.

Pentland, D. H. (1975) 'Cartographic Concepts of the Northern Algonquians', *Canadian Cartographer*, 12. 149–60.

Perin, C. (1970) *With Man in Mind*, Cambridge, Mass.: MIT Press.

Perrow, C. (1971) *Organisational Analysis*, London: Tavistock.

Perry, C. (1929) 'The Neighbourhood Unit Formula', in W. C. L. Wheaton, G. Milgram, and M. E. Meyson, eds., *Urban Housing*, New York: Free Press.

Pervin, L. A. (1978) 'Definitions, Measurements and Classifications of Stimuli, Situations and Environments', *Human Ecology*, 6. 71–105.

Peterson, G. L. (1973) 'Psychology and Environmental Management for Outdoor Recrea-
    tion', in W. F. E. Preiser, ed., *Environmental Design Research*, 1, Stroudsburg, Pa.:
    Dowden, Hutchinson, & Ross, 161–74.

Pevsner, N. (1963) *An Outline of European Architecture*, 7th edition, London: Allen Lane.

Piaget, J. (1929) *The Child's Conception of the World*, London: Routledge & Kegan Paul.

—— (1955) 'Perceptual and Cognitive (or Operational) Structures in the Development of
    the Concept of Space in the Child', *Acta Psychologica*, 11. 41–6.

—— (1963) *The Psychology of Intelligence*, Totowa, N. J.: Littlefield, Adams.

—— and Inhelder, B. (1956) *The Child's Conception of Space*, New York: Norton.

Pick, H. L. (1976) 'Transactional-Constructivist Approach to Environmental Knowing:
    A Commentary', in G. T. Moore and R. G. Golledge, eds., *Environmental Knowing*,
    Stroudsburg, Pa.: Dowden, Hutchinson, & Ross, 185–88.

Piliavin, J., Rodin, J., and Piliavin, J. A. (1969) 'Good Samaritanism: An Underground
    Phenomenon?', *Journal of Personality and Social Psychology*, 13. 289–330.

Plant, J. S. (1937) *Personality and the Cultural Pattern*, New York: New Commonwealth
    Fund.

—— (1950) *The Envelope: A Study of the Impact of the World upon the Child*, New
    York: New Commonwealth Fund.

Pocock, D. C. D. (1975) *Durham: Images of a Cathedral City*, Occasional Publication
    (New Series) 6, Durham: Department of Geography, University of Durham.

Polanyi, K. (1944) *The Great Transformation*, Boston: Beacon.

Pollowy, A. M. (1977) *The Urban Nest*, Stroudsburg, Pa.: Dowden, Hutchinson, &Ross.

Porteous, J. D. (1975) 'A Preliminary Landscape Analysis of Middle Earth during its
    Third Age, *Landscape*, 19. 33–8.

—— (1976) 'Home: The Territorial Core', *Geographical Review*, 66. 383–90.

—— (1977)*Environment and Behaviour*, London: Houghton Mifflin.

Potter, R. B. (1977) 'Spatial Patterns of Consumer Behaviour and Perception in relation
    to the Social Class Variable', *Area*, 9. 153–6.

Powell, J. M . (1972) *Images of Australia, 1788–1914*, Monash Publications in Geography
    3, Melbourne: University of Monash.

—— (1978) *Mirrors of the New World: Images and Image-Makers in the Settlement
    Process*, Folkestone: Dawson.

Prak, N. L. (1977) *The Visual Perception of the Built Environment*, Delft: Delft Univer-
    sity Press.

Pred, A. R. (1967, 1969) *Behaviour and Location: Foundations for a Geographic and
    Dynamic Location Theory*, Parts 1 and 2, Lund Studies in Geography, B, 27 and 28,
    Lund: Gleerup.

—— (1973) 'Urbanisation, Domestic Planning Problems and Swedish Geographic Research',
    in C. Board, R. J. Chorley, P. Haggett, and D. Stoddart, eds., *Progress in Geography*, 5.
    London: Arnold, 1–76.

—— and Kibel, B. M. (1970) 'An Application of Gaming Simulation to a General Model of
    Economic Locational Processes', *Economic Geography*, 46. 136–56.

Preiser, W. F. E. (1973) *Environmental Design Research*, 2 volumes, Stroudsburg, Pa.:
    Dowden, Hutchinson, & Ross.

Price, E. T. (1964) 'Viterbo: Landscape of an Italian City', *Annals of the Association
    of American Geographers*, 54. 242–75.

Proshansky, H. M. (1976) 'Environmental Psychology: A Methodological Orientation', in
    H. M. Proshansky, W. H. Ittelson and L. G. Rivlin, eds., *Environmental Psychology*,
    Second Edition, New York: Holt, Rinehart, & Winston, 59–68.

—— Ittelson, W. H., and Rivlin, L. G., eds. (1970, 1976) *Environmental Psychology*, 1st
    and 2nd editions, New York: Holt, Rinehart, & Winston.

Pryce, R. (1977) 'Approaches to the Study of Man and Environment', Unit 2, in *Man and
    Environment*, Milton Keynes: Open University, 45–90.

Queen, S. A. (1940) 'Ecological Study of Mental Disorders', *American Sociological Review*, 5. 201-9.

Quinn, J. A. (1950) *Human Ecology*, Englewood Cliffs, N. J.: Prentice Hall.

Raban, J. (1974) *Soft City*, London: Hamish Hamilton.

Rachlin, H. (1976) *An Introduction to Modern Behaviourism*, 2nd edition, San Francisco: Freeman.

Raglan, Lord (1964) *The Temple and the House*, London: Routledge & Kegan Paul.

Rainwater, L. (1966 'Fear and the House-as-Haven in the Lower Class', *Journal of the American Institute of Planners*, 32. 23-31.

Ramachandran, R., and Thakur, S. C. (1974) 'India and the Ganga Floodplains', in G. F. White, ed., *Natural Hazards: Local, National, Global*, New York: Oxford University Press, 36-43.

Ramsli, G. (1974) 'Avalanche Problems in Norway', in G. F. White, ed., *Natural Hazards: Local, National, Global*, New York: Oxford University Press, 175-80.

Ramsøy, N. R. (1966) 'Assortative Mating and the Structure of Cities', *American Sociological Review*, 31. 773-86.

Rapoport, A. (1969) *House Form and Culture*, Englewood Cliffs, N. J.: Prentice Hall.

—— (1975a) 'An "Anthropological" Approach to Environmental Design Research', in B. Honikman, ed. *Responding to Social Change*, Stroudsburg, Pa.: Dowden, Hutchinson, & Ross, 145-51.

—— (1975b) 'Images, Symbols and Popular Design', *Ekistics*, 232. 165-68.

—— (1976) 'Environmental Cognition in Cross-Cultural Perspective', in G. T. Moore and R. G. Golledge, eds., *Environmental Knowing*, Stroudsburg, Pa.: Dowden, Hutchinson, & Ross, 220-34.

—— (1977) *Human Aspects of Urban Form*, Oxford: Pergamon.

—— and Hawkes, R. (1970) 'The Perception of Urban Complexity', *Journal of the American Institute of Planners*, 36. 106-11.

—— and Kantor, R. E. (1967) 'Complexity and Ambiguity in Environmental Design', *Journal of the American Institute of Planners*, 33. 210-21.

Ratzel, F. (1882, 1891) *Anthropogeographie*, 2 volumes, Stuttgart: Engelhorn.

—— (1898) *Deutschland*, Leipzig: Grunow.

Rawstron, E. M. (1955) 'Three Principles of Industrial Location', *Transactions of the Institute of British Geographers*, 23. 132-42.

Reekie, R. F. (1972) *Design in the Built Environment*, London: Arnold.

Rees, J., and Newby, P., eds. (1974) *Behavioural Perspectives in Geography*, Monograph in Geography 1, Hendon: Middlesex Polytechnic.

Rees, R. (1975) 'The Scenery Cult: Changing Landscape Tastes over three Centuries', *Landscape*, 19. 39-47.

—— (1976a) 'Images of the Prairie: Landscape Painting and Perception in the Western Interior of Canada', *Canadian Geographer*, 20. 259-78.

—— (1976b) 'John Constable and the Art of Geography', *Geographical Review*, 66. 59-72.

Reich, B., and Adcock, C. (1976) *Values, Attitudes and Behaviour Change*, London: Methuen.

Reiner, T. A. (1963) *The Place of the Ideal Community in Urban Planning*, Philadelphia: University of Pennsylvania Press.

Relph, E. C. (1973) 'The Phenomenon of Place: An Investigation of the Experience and Identity of Places', unpublished Ph. D. thesis, Department of Geography, University of Toronto.

—— (1976) *Place and Placelessness*, London: Pion.

Revelle, R. (1970) 'Pollution and Cities', in J. Q. Wilson, ed., *The Metropolitan Enigma*, New York: Doubleday Anchor, 96-143.

Richards, J. M. (1946) *The Castles on the Ground: The Anatomy of Suburbia*, London: Architectural Press.

Richards, P. (1974) 'Kant's Geography and Mental Maps', *Transactions of the Institute of British Geographers*, 61. 1–16.

Richardson, A. E., and Corfiato, H. O. (1938) *The Art of Architecture*, London: English Universities Press.

Ridgely, D. (1922) 'The Teaching of Directions in Space and on Maps', *Journal of Geography*, 21. 66–72.

Rieser, R. (1972) *Urban Spatial Images: An Appraisal of the Choice of Respondents and Measurement Situation*, Discussion Paper 42, London: Graduate School of Geography, London School of Economics.

—— (1973) 'The Territorial Illusion and Behavioural Sink: Critical Notes on Behavioural Geography', *Antipode*, 5. 52–7.

Roethlisberger, R. J., and Dickson, W. J. (1939) *Management and the Worker*, Cambridge, Mass.: Harvard University Press.

Rogers, E. M., and Shoemaker, F. F. (1971) *Communication of Innovations*, New York: Free Press.

Rokeach, M. (1973) *The Open and Closed Mind*, New York: Basic Books.

Rooney, J. F. (1967) 'The Urban Snow Hazard in the United States', *Geographical Review*, 57. 538–59.

—— (1969) 'The Economic and Social Implications of Snow and Ice', in R. J. Chorley, ed., *Water, Earth and Man*, London: Methuen, 389–401.

Ross, A. (1967) *Pagan Celtic Britain: Studies in Iconography and Tradition*, London: Routledge & Kegan Paul.

Ross, H. E. (1974) *Behaviour and Perception in Strange Environments*, London: Allen & Unwin.

Rossi, P. H. (1955) *Why Families Move: A Study in the Social Psychology of Urban Residential Mobility*, New York: Free Press.

Rowntree, R. R. (1974) 'Coastal Erosion: The Meaning of a Natural Hazard in the Cultural and Ecological Context', in G. F. White, ed., *Natural Hazards: Local, National, Global*, New York: Oxford University Press, 71–9.

Rummel, R. J. (1975) *Understanding Conflict and War*, 1, New York: Halsted.

Rykwert, J. (1976) *The Idea of a Town: The Anthropology of Urban Form in Rome, Italy and the Ancient World*, London: Faber & Faber.

Saarinen, L. (1943) *The City: Its Growth, its Decay, its Future*, New York: Rheinhold.

Saarinen, T. F. (1966) *Perception of Drought Hazard on the Great Plains*, Research Paper 106, Chicago: Department of Geography, University of Chicago.

—— (1969) *Perception of the Environment*, Commission on College Geography Resource Paper 5, Washington, D. C.: Association of American Geographers.

—— (1973a) 'Student Views of the World', in R. M. Downs and D. Stea, eds., *Image and Environment*, Chicago: Aldine, 148–61.

—— (1973b) 'The Use of Projective Techniques in Geographic Research', in W. H. Ittelson, ed., *Environment and Cognition*, New York: Seminar Press, 29–52.

—— (1974) 'Problems in the use of a Standardised Questionnaire for Cross-Cultural Research on Perception of Natural Hazards', in G. F. White, ed., *Natural Hazards: Local, National, Global*, New York: Oxford University Press, 180–84.

—— (1976) *Environmental Planning: Perception and Behaviour*, Boston: Houghton Mifflin.

Sack, R. D. (1976) 'Magic and Space', *Annals of the Association of American Geographers*, 66. 309–22.

Sahakian, W. S. (1975) *History and Systems of Psychology*, New York: Halsted.

Sanoff, H. (1975) 'Son of Rationality', in B. Honikman, ed., *Responding to Social Change*, Stroudsburg, Pa.: Dowden, Hutchinson, & Ross, 225–34.

Sarre, P. V. (1972) 'Perception', Unit 16, in *New Trends in Geography*, Milton Keynes: Open University, 10–43.

Sarre, P. V. (1976) 'Understanding Environments', Unit 1, in *Man and Environment*, Milton Keynes: Open University, 5–44.

Sauer, C. O. (1925) 'The Morphology of Landscape', in J. Leighley, ed. (1969), *Land and Life: A Selection from the Writings of Carl Ortwin Sauer*, Berkeley: University of California Press, 315–50.

Schiffman, H. R. (1976) *Sensation and Perception: An Integrated Approach*, London: Wiley.

Schmid, C. (1960) 'Urban Crime Areas', *American Sociological Review*, 25, 655–78.

Schmitt, R. C. (1957) 'Density, Delinquency and Crime in Honolulu', *Sociology and Social Research*, 41. 274–6.

—— (1963) 'Implications of Density in Hong Kong', *Journal of the American Institute of Planners*, 29. 210–17.

Schorr, A. L. (1964) *Slums and Social Insecurity*, London: Nelson.

Schorske, C. E. (1963) 'The Idea of the City in European Thought: Voltaire to Spengler', in O. Handlin and J. Burchard, eds., *The Historian and the City*, Cambridge, Mass.: Harvard University Press, 95–115.

Schwitzgebel, R. (1962) 'The Performance of Dutch and Zulu Adults on Selected Perceptual Tasks', *Journal of Social Psychology*, 57. 73.

Scully, V. (1962) *The Earth, the Temple and the Gods: Greek Sacred Architecture*, New Haven, Conn.: Yale University Press.

Seeley, R., Sim, A., and Loosley, E. W. (1956) *Crestwood Heights*, New York: Basic Books.

Selye, H. (1956) *The Stress of Life*, New York: McGraw Hill.

Semple, E. C. (1911) *Influences of Geographical Environment, on the Basis of Ratzel's System of Anthropo-Geography*, New York: Holt.

Sereno, K. K., and Mortensen, C. D., eds. (1970) *Foundations of Communication Theory*, London: Harper & Row.

Serpell, R. (1976) *Culture's Influence on Behaviour*, London: Methuen.

Severin, T. (1973) *African Adventure*, London: Hamish Hamilton.

Seymour-Smith, M. (1977) 'Semiology', in A. Bullock and O. Stallybrass, eds., *Fontana Dictionary of Modern Thought*, London: Fontana, 566–7.

Shafer, E. L., Hamilton, J. E., and Schmidt, E. A. (1969) 'Natural Landscape Preferences: A Predictive Model', *Journal of Leisure Research*, 1. 1–20.

Shafer, E. L., and Mietz, J. (1972) 'Aesthetic and Emotional Experiences rate highly with Northeast Wilderness Hikers', in J. F. Wohlwill and D. H. Carson, eds., *Environment and the Social Sciences*, Washington, D. C.: American Psychological Association, 207–16.

Sharp, T. (1968) *Town and Townscape*, London: Murray.

Sheehan, L., and Hewitt, K. (1969) *A Pilot Study of Global Natural Disasters of the past Twenty Years*, Working Paper 1, Toronto: Natural Hazard Research Unit, Department of Geography, University of Toronto.

Shin, M. (1976) 'Geographical Knowledge in three Southwestern Novels', in G. T. Moore and R. G. Golledge, eds., *Environmental Knowing*, Stroudsburg, Pa.: Dowden, Hutchinson & Ross, 273–8.

Shotter, J. (1975) *Images of Man in Psychological Research*, London: Methuen.

Siegel, A. W., and White, S. H. (1975) 'The Development of Spatial Representations of Large–Scale Environments', in H. W. Reese, ed., *Advances in Child Development and Behaviour*, 10, New York: Academic Press, 9–55.

Silverman, D. (1970) *The Theory of Organisations*, London: Heinemann.

Simmel, G. (1950) *The Sociology of Georg Simmel* (trans. K. H. Wolff), New York: Free Press.

Simmons, I. G. (1975) *Rural Recreation in the Industrial World*, London: Arnold.

Simmons, J. W. (1968) 'Changing Residence in the City: A Review of Intraurban Mobility', *Geographical Review*, 58. 622–51.

Simon, H. A. (1952) 'A Behavioural Model of Rational Choice', *Quarterly Journal of Economics*, 69. 99–118.

—— (1957) *Models of Man*, New York: Wiley.

Simons, M. (1966) 'What is a Geographical Factor?', *Geography*, 51. 210–17.

Sims, J. H., and Baumann, D. D. (1972) 'The Tornado Threat: Coping Styles of the North and South', *Science*, 176. 1386–92.

Skaburskis, J. W. (1974) 'Territoriality and its relevance to Neighbourhood Design: A Review', *Journal of Architectural Research*, 3. 39–44.

Skinner, B. F. (1938) *The Behaviour of Organisms*, New York: Appleton.

—— (1971) *Beyond Freedom and Dignity*, New York: Knopf.

—— (1974) *About Behaviourism*, London: Jonathan Cape.

Skurnik, L. S., and George, F. (1967) *Psychology for Everyman* (Pelican Original, 2nd edn.), Harmondsworth: Penguin.

Smith, B. (1960) *European Vision and the South Pacific, 1768–1850*, London: Oxford University Press.

Smith, D. M. (1971) 'Radical Geography: The Next Revolution', *Area*, 3. 153–7.

—— (1977) *Human Geography: A Welfare Approach*, London: Arnold.

Smith, G. C. (1976a) Personal Communication.

—— (1976b) 'Responses of Residents and Policy-Makers to Urban Environmental Hazards', *Area*, 8. 279–83.

—— (1976c) 'The Spatial Information Fields of Urban Consumers', *Transactions of the Institute of British Geographers (New Series)*, 1. 175–89.

—— (1976d) *Urban Environmental Hazard Cognition and Concern*, Occasional Paper 3, Birmingham, Eng.: Department of Geography, University of Birmingham.

Smith, H. N. (1957) *Virgin Land: The American West as Symbol and Myth*, New York: Vintage Books.

Smith, P. F. (1974) *The Dynamics of Urbanism*, London: Hutchinson.

—— (1975) 'Symbolic Meaning in Contemporary Cities', *Ekistics*, 39. 159–64.

Smith, R. W. (1973) 'Territoriality and Space Planning: Some Limitations and Prospects', *Urban and Social Change Review*, 6. 50–8.

Smith, W. (1955) 'The Location of Industry', *Transactions of the Institute of British Geographers*, 21. 1–18.

Soja, E. W. (1971) *The Political Organisation of Space*, Commission on College Geography Resource Paper 8, Washington, D. C.: Association of American Geographers.

Sommer, R. (1969) *Personal Space*, Englewood Cliffs, N. J.: Prentice Hall.

—— (1972) *Design Awareness*, San Francisco: Rinehart.

—— (1974) *Tight Spaces: Hard Architecture and how to Humanise it*, Englewood Cliffs, N. J.: Prentice Hall.

Sonnenfeld, J. (1966) 'Variable Values in Space and Landscape: An Inquiry into the nature of Environmental Necessity', *Journal of Social Issues*, 22. 71–82.

Southworth, M. (1969) 'The Sonic Environment of Cities', *Environment and Behaviour*, 1. 49–70.

Spate, O. H. K. (1953) *The Compass of Geography*, Canberra.

—— (1958) 'The End of an Old Song? The Determinism–Possibilism Problem', *Geographical Review*, 48. 280–2.

Spencer, D. (1973) *An Evaluation of Cognitive Mapping in Neighbourhood Perception*, Research Memorandum 23, Birmingham, Eng.: Centre for Urban and Regional Studies, University of Birmingham.

—— and Lloyd, J. (1974) *The Small Heath Schools Session: Mental Maps of Routes from Home to School*, Working Paper 24, Birmingham, Eng.: Centre for Urban and Regional Studies, University of Birmingham.

Sprout, H., and Sprout, M. (1965) *The Ecological Perspective on Human Affairs with special reference to International Politics*, Princeton, N. J.: Princeton University Press.

Stacey, B. (1975) *Psychology and Social Structure*, London: Methuen.

Stea, D., and Wood, D. (1974) *A Cognitive Atlas: The Psychological Geography of four Mexican Cities*, Mexico: Instituto Nacional de Bellas Artes, Cuadernos de Arquitectura.

Stearns, F. W., and Montag, T. (1975) *The Urban Ecosystem*, Stroudsburg, Pa.: Dowden, Hutchinson, & Ross.

Steinitz, C. (1968) 'Meaning and the Congruence of Urban Form and Activity', *Journal of the American Institute of Planners*, 34. 233–48.

Stewart, J. Q., and Warntz, W. (1958) *Physics of Population*, Philadelphia: Regional Science Institute.

Stewart, T. C. (1970) *The City as an Image of Man*, London: Latimer Press.

Stokols, D. (1978) 'Environmental Psychology', in M. R. Rosenzweig and L. W. Porter, eds., *Annual Review of Psychology*, 29. 253–96.

Stone, G. P. (1954) 'City Shoppers and Urban Identification: Observations on the Social Psychology of City Life', *American Journal of Sociology*, 60. 36–45.

Stringer, P. (1975a) 'Living in the City', in D. V. Canter, ed., *Environmental Interaction*, London: Surrey University Press, 253–80.

—— (1975b) 'The Natural Environment', in D. V. Canter, ed., *Environmental Interaction*, London: Surrey University Press, 281–320.

—— (1975c) 'Understanding the City', in D. V. Canter, ed., *Environmental Interaction*, London: Surrey University Press, 215–52.

Suedfeld, P., and Russell, J., eds. (1976) *The Behavioural Basis of Design*, Stroudsburg, Pa.: Dowden, Hutchinson, & Ross.

Summerston, J. (1969) *Georgian London*, Harmondsworth: Penguin.

Susser, M., and Watson, A. (1962) *Sociology in Medicine*, London: Oxford University Press.

Sutter, R. (1973) *The Next Place you come to: A Historical Introduction to Communities in North America*, Englewood Cliffs, N. J.: Prentice Hall.

Suttles, G. D. (1968) *The Social Order of the Slum*, Chicago: University of Chicago Press.

—— (1972) *The Social Construction of Communities*, Chicago: University of Chicago Press.

Tatham, G. (1957) 'Environmentalism and Possibilism', in G. Taylor, ed., *Geography in the Twentieth Century*, New York: Philosophical Library, 128–62.

Taylor, C. C., and Townsend, A. R. (1976) 'The Local "Sense of Place" as evidenced in North-east England', *Urban Studies*, 13. 133–46.

Taylor, G. (1937) *Environment, Race and Migration*, Toronto: University of Toronto Press.

—— (1940) *Australia*, London: Methuen.

Taylor, M. J., and McDermott, P. J. (1976) 'Attitudes, Images and Location: The Subjective Context of Decision-Making in New Zealand Manufacturing', *Economic Geography*, 52. 325–46.

—— —— (1977) 'Perception of Location and Industrial Decision-Making: The Example of New Zealand Manufacturing', *New Zealand Geographer*, 33. 26–33.

Thiel, P. (1961) 'A Sequence-Experience Notation for Architectural and Urban Space', *Town Planning Review* 32. 33–52.

Thomas, F. (1925) *The Environmental Basis of Society*, New York: Century.

Thompson, K. (1969) 'Insalubrious California: Perception and Reality', *Annals of the Association of American Geographers*, 59. 50–64.

Tiger, L. (1969) *Men in Groups*, New York: Random House.

Tilly, C. (1974) 'Metropolitan Boston's Social Structure', in C. Tilly, ed., *An Urban World*, Boston: Little, Brown, 250–73.

Timms, D. W. G. (1965) 'The Spatial Distribution of Social Deviants in Luton, England', *Australia and New Zealand Journal of Sociology*, 1. 38–52.

—— (1971) *The Urban Mosaic*, Cambridge: Cambridge University Press.

Tolman, E. C. (1932) *Purposive Behaviour in Animals and Men*, New York: Century, Crofts.

—— (1948) 'Cognitive Maps in Rats and Men', *Psychological Review*, 55. 189–208, (also reprinted in R. M. Downs and D. Stea, eds. (1973) *Image and Environment*, Chicago: Aldine, 27–50).

—— (1952) 'A Cognition-Motivation Model', *Psychological Review*, 59. 389–408.

Tönnies, F. (1887) *Gemeinschaft und Gesellschaft* (trans. C. P. Loomis, 1955, as *Community and Association*, London: Routledge & Kegan Paul).

Torrance, J. R. (1977) 'Phenomenology', in A. Bullock and O. Stallybrass, eds., *Fontana Dictionary of Modern Thought*, London: Fontana, 469.

Townroe, P. M. (1969) 'Locational Choice and the Individual Firm', *Regional Studies*, 3. 15–24.

—— (1974) 'Post-move Stability and the Location Decision', in F. E. I. Hamilton, ed., *Spatial Perspectives on Industrial Organisation and Decision-Making*, London: Wiley, 287–307.

Triandis, H. C. (1971) *Attitude and Attitude Change*, New York: Wiley.

Trowbridge, C. C. (1913) 'On Fundamental Methods of Orientation and Imaginary Maps', *Science*, 38. 888–97.

Tuan, Y. F. (1963) 'Architecture and Human Nature: Can there be an Existential Architecture?', *Landscape*, 13. 16–19.

—— (1964) 'Mountains, Ruins and the Sentiment of Melancholy', *Landscape*, 14. 27–30.

—— (1966) 'Man and Nature: an Eclectic Reading', *Landscape*, 16. 30–6.

—— (1968) 'Discrepancies between Environmental Attitude and Behaviour: Examples from Europe and China', *Canadian Geographer*, 12. 176–91.

—— (1971) 'Geography, Phenomenology and the Study of Human Nature', *Canadian Geographer*, 15. 181–92.

—— (1972) 'Structuralism, Existentialism and Environmental Perception', *Environment and Behaviour*, 4. 319–31.

—— (1973) 'Ambiguity in Attitudes towards Environment', *Annals of the Association of American Geographers*, 63. 411–23.

—— (1974) *Topophilia: A Study of Environmental Perception, Attitudes and Values*, Englewood Cliffs, N. J.: Prentice Hall.

—— (1975a) 'Images and Mental Maps', *Annals of the Association of American Geographers*, 65. 205–14.

—— (1975b) 'Place: An Experiential Perspective', *Geographical Review*, 65. 151–65.

—— (1976a) 'Geopiety: A Theme in Man's Attachment to Nature and to Place', in D. Lowenthal and M. J. Bowden, eds., *Geographies of the Mind*, New York: Oxford University Press, 11–39.

—— (1976b) 'Humanistic Geography', *Annals of the Association of American Geographers*, 66. 266–76.

—— (1977) *Space and Place*, London: Arnold.

—— (1978a) 'Sign and Metaphor', *Annals of the Association of American Geographers*, 68. 363–72.

—— (1978b) 'The City: Its Distance from Nature', *Geographical Review*, 68. 1–12.

Tunstall, J. (1970) *Media Sociology*, London: Constable.

Turan, M. H. (1974) 'Environmental Stress: An Ecological Approach, with special reference to Housing', unpublished Ph. D. thesis, Department of Architecture, Columbia University.

Turner, B. (1976) 'Development of Disasters: A Sequence Model for the Analysis of the Origins of Disaster', *Sociological Review*, 24. 753–74.

Turner, J. R. (1975) 'Applications of Landscape Evaluation: A Planner's View', *Transactions of the Institute of British Geographers*, 66. 156–61.

Tyler, S. A., ed. (1969) *Cognitive Anthropology*, New York: Holt, Rinehart, & Winston.

Vance, J. E. (1972) 'California and the Search for the Ideal', *Annals of the Association of American Geographers*, 62. 185–210.

Veal, A. J. (1974) *Environmental Perception and Recreation: A Review and Annotated Bibliography*, Research Memorandum 39, Birmingham, Eng.: Centre for Urban and Regional Studies, University of Birmingham.

Venturi, R., Brown, D. S., and Izenour, S. (1977) *Learning from Las Vegas*, 2nd edition, Cambridge, Mass.: MIT Press.

Vernon, M. D. (1971) *Perception through Experience*, London: Methuen.

Visvader, H., and Burton, I. (1974) 'Natural Hazards and Hazard Policy in Canada and the United States', in G. F. White, ed., *Natural Hazards: Local, National, Global*, New York: Oxford University Press, 219–30.

Wacher, J. D. (1974) *The Towns of Roman Britain*, London: Book Club Associates.

Waddell, E. (1977) 'The Hazards of Scientism: A Review Article', *Human Ecology*, 5. 69–76.

Wagner, P. L. (1972) *Environments and People*, Englewood Cliffs, N. J.: Prentice Hall.

Walker, D. F. (1975) 'A Behavioural Approach to Industrial Location', in L. Collins and D. F. Walker, eds., *Locational Dynamics of Manufacturing Activity*, London: Wiley, 135–58.

Walmsley, D. J. (1974) 'Positivism and Phenomenology in Human Geography', *Canadian Geographer*, 18. 95–107.

Walsh, J. A., and Webber, M. J. (1977) 'Information Theory: Some Concepts and Measures', *Environment and Planning*, A9. 395–417.

Wanklyn, H. (1961) *Friedrich Ratzel: A Bibliographical Memoir and Bibliography*, Cambridge: Cambridge University Press.

Wann, T. W. (1964) *Behaviourism and Phenomenology*, Chicago: William Marsh Rice University.

Wapner, S. (1973) 'An Organismic-Developmental Perspective for understanding Transactions of Men and Environments', *Environment and Behaviour*, 5. 255–89.

Ward, C. (1978) *The Child in the City*, London: Architectural Press.

Ward, L. M., and Suedfeld, P. (1973) 'Human Responses to Highway Noise', *Environmental Research*, 6. 306–26.

Ward, R. M. (1974) 'Decisions by Florida Citrus Growers and Adjustments to Freeze Hazards', in G. F. White, ed. *Natural Hazards: Local, National, Global*, New York: Oxford University Press, 137–45.

Warntz, W. (1973) 'New Geography as General Spatial Systems Theory.—Old Social Physics writ large?', in R. J. Chorley, ed. *Directions in Geography*, London: Methuen, 89–126.

Watkin, D. (1977) *Morality and Architecture*, London: Oxford University Press.

Watson, A., and Moss, R. (1971) 'Spacing as affected by Territorial Behaviour, Habitat and Nutrition in Red Grouse (Lagopus I. Scotius)', in A. H. Esser, ed., *Behaviour and Environment*, New York: Plenum, 92–111.

Watson, J. B. (1913) 'Psychology as the Behaviourist views it', *Psychological Review*, 20. 158–77.

—— (1924) *Behaviourism*, New York: Norton.

Watson, J. W. (1971) 'Geography and Image Regions', *Geographica Helvetica*, 1 (26), 31–3.

—— (1975) 'Perception and Place', *Geographical Journal*, 141. 271–4.

Watson, M. O. (1970) *Proxemic Behaviour: A Cross-Cultural Study*, The Hague: Mouton.

Webber, M. M. (1963) 'Order in Diversity: Community without Propinquity', in L. Wingo, ed., *Cities and Space*, Baltimore: John Hopkins Press, for Resources for the Future Inc., 23–56.

—— (1964a) 'Culture, Territoriality and the Elastic Mile', *Papers and Proceedings of the Regional Science Association*, 13. 59–70.

—— (1964b) 'The Urban Place and the Nonplace Urban Realm', in M. M. Webber, J. W. Dyckham, D. L. Foley, A. Z. Guttenberg, W. L. C. Wheaton, and C. B. Wurster *Explorations into Urban Structure*, Philadelphia, University of Pennsylvania Press. 79–153.

Webber, M. M. (1971) 'The Post-City Age', in L. S. Bourne, ed., *Internal Structure of the City*, London: Oxford University Press, 496–501.

Weber, A. (1929) *Theory of the Location of Industries* (trans. C. J. Friedrich), Chicago: University of Chicago Press.

Weddle, A. E. (1969) 'Techniques in Landscape Planning: Landscape Evaluation', *Journal of the Royal Town Planning Institute*, 55. 387–81.

Wells, B. W. P. (1965) 'The Psycho-Social Influence of Building Environment: Socio-metric Findings in large and small Office Spaces', *Building Science*, 1. 153–65.

Werner, H. (1948) *Comparative Psychology of Mental Development*, New York: International Universities Press.

—— (1957) 'The Concept of Development from a Comparative and Organismic Point of View', in D. B. Harris, ed., *The Concept of Development*, Minneapolis: University of Minnesota Press, 125–48.

—— and Kaplan, B. (1963) *Symbol Formation: An Organismic-Developmental Approach to Language and the Expression of Thought*, New York: Wiley.

Wertheimer, M. (1973) 'The Psychology of Perception', in P. Mussen and M. R. Rosenzweig, eds., *Psychology: An Introduction*, Lexington: Heath, 523–628.

Western, J. S. Weldon, P. D., and Huang, T. T. (1974) 'Housing and Satisfaction with Environment in Singapore', *Journal of the American Institute of Planners*, 39. 201–8.

Westgate, K. (1978) 'A Necessary Bandwagon', *Futures*, 10. 163–6.

—— and O'Keefe, P. (1976) *Some Definitions of Disaster*, Occasional Paper 4, Bradford, York.: Disaster Research Unit, University of Bradford.

Wheatley, P. (1969) *The City as Symbol*, London: Lewis.

—— (1971) *The Pivot of the Four Quarters*, Edinburgh: University of Edinburgh Press.

Wheeler, K., ed. (1976) 'Experiencing Townscape', *Bulletin of Environmental Education*, 68 (December), 1–28.

White, G. (1789) *The Natural History of Selbourne* (R. Mabey, ed., 1977, Harmondsworth,: Penguin).

White, G. F. (1939) 'Economic Aspects of Flood Forecasting', *Transactions of the American Geophysical Union*, 20. 218–33.

—— (1942) *Human Adjustment to Floods: A Geographical Approach to the Flood Problem in the United States*, Research Paper 29, Chicago: Department of Geography, University of Chicago.

—— (1964) *Choice of Adjustment to Floods*, Research Paper 93, Chicago: Department of Geography, University of Chicago.

—— (1970) 'Recent Developments in Flood Plain Research', *Geographical Review*, 60. 440–3.

—— (1973) 'Natural Hazards Research', in R. J. Chorley, ed., *Directions in Geography*, London: Methuen, 193–216.

—— (1974a) *Natural Hazards: Local, National, Global*, New York: Oxford University Press.

—— (1974b) 'Natural Hazards Research: Concepts, Methods and Policy Implications', in G. F. White, ed., *Natural Hazards: Local, National, Global*, New York: Oxford University Press, 3–16.

—— (1976) 'Commission on Man and Environment', in I. P. Gerasimov, ed., *International Geography '76*, 11, Moscow, USSR: International Geographical Union, 11–13.

—— (1978) 'Natural Hazards and the Third World: A Reply', *Human Ecology*, 6. 229–31.

—— Calef, W. C., Hudson, J. W., Mayer, H. M., Sheaffer, J. R., and Volk, D. J. (1958) *Changes in Urban Occupance of Flood Plains in the United States*, Research Paper 57, Chicago: Department of Geography, University of Chicago.

White, M., and White, L. (1962) *The Intellectual versus the City*, Cambridge, Mass.: MIT Press.

Whyte, A. V. T. (1977) *Guidelines for Field Studies in Environmental Perception*, Paris: UNESCO.

Whyte, W. F. (1943) *Street Corner Society: The Social Structure of an Italian Slum*, Chicago: University of Chicago Press.

—— (1956) *The Organisation Man*, New York: Simon & Shuster.

Williams, E. (1977) 'Experimental Comparisons of Face-to-Face and Mediated Communication', *Psychological Bulletin*, 84. 963–76.

Williams, E. P., and Rausch, H. L. (1969) *Naturalistic Viewpoints in Psychological Research*, New York: Holt, Rinehart, & Winston.

Williams, R. (1975) *The Country and the City*, London: Paladin.

Willmott, P. (1963) *The Evolution of a Community*, London: Routledge.

Wilson, E. O. (1975) *Sociobiology: The New Synthesis*, Cambridge, Mass.: Harvard University Press.

Wilson, R. B. (1970) *Go Great Western: A History of GWR Publicity*, Newton Abbot: David & Charles.

Winsborough, H. (1965) 'The Social Consequences of high Population Density', *Law and Contemporary Problems*, 30. 120–6.

Wirth, L. (1938) 'Urbanism as a Way of Life', *American Journal of Sociology*, 44. 1–24.

Wisner, B., Westgate, K., and O'Keefe, P. (1976) 'Poverty and Disaster', *New Society*, 37. 546–8.

Wohlwill, J. F. (1968) 'Amount of Stimulus Exploration and Preference as differential Functions of Stimulus Complexity', *Perception and Psychophysics*, 4. 307–12.

—— (1970) 'The Emerging Discipline of Environmental Psychology', *American Psychologist*, 25. 303–12.

Wolf, E. R., and Hansen, E. C. (1972) *The Human Condition in Latin America*, London: Oxford University Press.

Wolfe, I. de (1963) *The Italian Townscape*, London: Architectural Press.

Wollheim, R. (1971) *Freud*, London: Fontana.

Wolpert, J. (1964) 'The Decision Process in Spatial Perspective', *Annals of the Association of American Geographers*, 54. 537–58.

—— (1970) 'Departures from the usual Environment in Locational Analysis', *Annals of the Association of American Geographers*, 60. 220–9.

Wood, P. (1969) 'Industrial Location and Linkage', *Area*, 2. 32–9.

Woollcombe, K. (1976) 'The Beginning and the End', *Oxford Diocesan Magazine*, 9 (11). 6–7.

Wright, D. S., Taylor, A., Davies, D. R., Sluckin, W., Lee, S. G. M., and Reason, J. T. (1970) *Introducing Psychology: An Experimental Approach*, Harmondsworth: Penguin.

Wright, F. L. (1945) *When Democracy Builds*, Chicago: University of Chicago Press.

Wright, G. (1974) 'Appraisal of Visual Landscape Qualities in a Region selected for accelerated Growth', *Landscape Planning*, 1. 307–27.

Wright, J. K. (1947) 'Terrae Incognitae: The Place of the Imagination in Geography', *Annals of the Association of American Geographers*, 37. 1–15.

—— (1966) *Human Nature in Geography*, Cambridge, Mass.: Harvard University Press.

Wyburn, G. M., Pickford, R. W., and Hurst, R. J. (1964) *Human Senses and Perception*, Edinburgh: Oliver & Boyd.

Wynne-Edwards, V. C. (1962) *Animal Dispersal in relation to Social Behaviour*, Edinburgh: Oliver & Boyd.

Yancey, W. L. (1972) 'Architecture, Interaction and Social Control: The Case of a large-scale Housing Project', in J. F. Wohlwill and D. H. Carson, eds., *Environment and the Social Sciences*, Washington, D. C.: American Psychological Association, 126–36.

Young, M. (1954) 'The Role of the Extended Family in a Disaster', *Human Relations*, 7. 383–91.

—— and Willmott, P. (1957) *Family and Kinship in East London*, Harmondsworth: Penguin.

Zehner, R. B. (1972) 'Neighbourhood and Community Satisfaction: A Report on New Towns and less-planned Suburbs', in J. H. Wohlwill and D. H. Carson, eds., *Environment and the Social Sciences*, Washington, D. C.: American Psychological Association, 169-83.

Zlutnick, S., and Altman, I. (1972) 'Crowding and Human Behaviour', in J. F. Wohlwill and D. H. Carson, eds., *Environment and the Social Sciences*, Washington, D. C.: American Psychological Association, 44-58.

Zorbaugh, H. W. (1926) 'The Natural Areas of the City', *Publications of the American Sociological Society*, 20. 188-97.

—— (1929) *The Gold Coast and the Slum: A Sociological Study of Chicago's Near North Side*, Chicago: University of Chicago Press.

Zube, E. H., ed. (1970) *Landscapes: Selected Writings of J. B. Jackson*, Amherst: University of Massachusetts Press.

—— Brush, R. O., and Fabos, G. Y. (1975) *Landscape Assessment: Values, Perceptions and Resources*, Stroudsburg, Pa.: Dowden, Hutchinson, & Ross.

Zube, E. H., and Zube, M. (1977) *Changing Rural Landscapes*, Amherst: University of Massachusetts Press.

Index